The American School
1642–1985

The American School 1642–1985

Varieties of Historical Interpretation of the Foundations and Development of American Education

Joel Spring
University of Cincinnati

105402

Longman
New York & London

Executive Editor: Raymond T. O'Connell
Developmental Editor: Naomi Silverman
Production Editor: Halley Gatenby
Text Design: Laura Ierardi
Cover Design: Steven August Krastin
Production Supervisor: Judith Stern
Compositor: TC Systems

The American School 1642–1985

Longman Inc.
95 Church Street
White Plains, N.Y. 10601

Associated companies:
Longman Group Ltd., London
Longman Cheshire Pty., Melbourne
Longman Paul Pty., Auckland
Copp Clark Pitman, Toronto
Pitman Publishing Inc., Boston

Library of Congress Cataloging-in-Publication Data

Spring, Joel H.
  The American school, 1642–1985.

  1. Education—United States—History. 2. Education—
Social aspects—United States—History. 3. United
States—Social conditions. I. Title.
LA205.S64 1986   370′.973   85-19749
ISBN 0-582-28571-2

86 87 88 89   9 8 7 6 5 4 3 2 1

Contents

Preface

Varieties of Historical Interpretation

A variety of interpretations exists for each period of American educational history, providing unique windows through which to view the unfolding of events. For each historical period, the major interpretations, and in some cases, my own interpretation of events, are described in this book. Often, interpretations of historical events reflect the social and political concerns of the historian. For instance, in the early twentieth century, historian Ellwood Cubberley was concerned with defending and expanding the role of the public school in American society. Consequently, he portrayed the history of education as a struggle between advocates of public schooling and those who resisted its development. Within his historical picture, the forces of good were on the side of the public school while the forces of evil worked on the side of the public school's detractors. Michael Katz, writing during the turbulent period of racial strife and social conflict of the 1960s, portrayed the expansion of public schooling as in the interest of elite groups that wanted to maintain social-class and racial differences in society. Within Katz's interpretative framework, the public school was primarily an instrument for social control.

Historical interpretations shape our image of the past and have an impact on future actions. Individuals often make decisions based on what they believe to be the historical purposes and goals of an institution. Given the variety and number of events that occur on any particular day, a historian can be selective about which events and combination of social activities he or she wishes to emphasize. Thus two different historians can give differing interpretations to historical events yet remain accurate to historical fact.

The history of American education is primarily the story of the expanding political, economic, and social role of the school in American society. Seventeenth-century North American colonists would have been surprised to learn that by the twentieth century the school would become an important public institution. Historical events propelled the school into a central place in the hopes of America's peoples. In the nineteenth century, individuals tried to use the school to produce good citizens, eliminate crime, cure social problems, and create an American community. In addition, people began to place their faith in the school as a means of achieving upward mobility and increased personal income. In the twentieth century, the school has been viewed as an institution for increasing the nation's economic productivity through the proper education of future workers, and it has also been called on to solve problems of national defense, to end unemployment, and to maintain America's position in international trade.

The story of the evolution of the modern school is important because it contains so much of the social history of the American people. To understand the history of the school is to understand the hopes and aspirations of the American people and the uses of power in American society. The role of the school in American history can be understood from a variety of perspectives. On one hand, for many generations, immigrants, the poor, and minority groups have looked to the school to help them attain integration in the economic and social system of the United States. On the other hand, many people have attempted to use the school to restrict the advancement of certain social groups and as a means of control. The history of education has often been a struggle between people seeking to use the school for the purpose of domination and perpetuation of power and those seeking to use it to expand freedom and improve social conditions.

The varieties of interpretation presented in this book provide the reader with an opportunity to judge past events. Like historians who weave together the drama of the past, consumers of history have their own political and social opinions. Ideally, the reading of history should stimulate an intellectual dialogue between the reader and the text. In particular, intellectual discourse about the history of education should clarify opinions about the process of education and the relationship of education to other institutions and to social events.

The American School
1642–1985

1

Religion and Authority in Colonial Education

In the North American colonies in the seventeenth century, the primary purpose of education was to maintain Protestant religious beliefs and ensure social stability. Some historians have emphasized the Protestant nature of colonial education and the effect of that legacy on the development of public schools in the nineteenth century. Most historians who offer this interpretation of education in seventeenth-century New England emphasize the colonists' growing faith in education as a panacea for social problems.[1] Other historians have stressed the authoritarian nature of colonial education as an example of schooling being used to maintain the power of established leadership.[2]

Ellwood Cubberley, who has portrayed the rise of the public school as a struggle between the forces of good and evil, argued that since their origins in colonial times, schools in America gradually have been transformed from instruments of religion into instruments of the state.[3] "The first schools in America were clearly the fruits of the Protestant Revolts in Europe." And of all the Protestant groups that settled in colonial America, according to Cubberley, "the Puritans who settled New England contributed most that was valuable for our future educational development."[4]

The view that the roots of American public schools lie primarily in the Protestant church and in New England has had a profound impact on the history of education. Historian Carl Kaestle has recently argued that the public school movement in the nineteenth century was essentially a result of a desire to protect a Protestant orthodoxy.[5] Catholic groups in the nineteenth century rebelled against the Protestant quality of public schools and established their own school system, and in the nineteenth and twentieth centuries, Catholics referred to public schools as Protestant schools. Even in this century, after Bible reading and school prayer were banned by the United States Supreme Court, many religious groups protested the loss of what they believed to be the traditional

1

Christian morality of the public schools. From the viewpoint of a historian like Cubberley, the secularization of public schooling did represent a break with tradition.

Not all historians agree with the idea of a continuity of development in schools from colonial times to the emergence of public schools in the nineteenth century. Rush Welter argued that the public school movement of the nineteenth century resulted from a consensus about the need for educated citizens in a democratic society. Welter found little in colonial education that contributed to a democratic theory of education, and he viewed colonial education as a "false start from which it was necessary to turn away before education could become a key principle of democratic faith."[6] According to Welter, colonial education was oriented toward teaching respect for authority and maintaining existing social and religious order. This orientation was contrary, in his opinion, to later educational emphasis on preparing citizens for independent democratic behavior.

These differences in interpretation can be best understood by considering the development of colonial education. Education in Puritan New England, with its emphasis on individual conduct, bore the seeds for the nineteenth-century view of education as a panacea for society. This view can be traced to the Protestant Reformation, one result of which was an emphasis on individual instruction for the development of piety with the goal of creating "the good society."

Many of these themes can be found in colonial education in seventeenth-century Puritan New England. When the Puritans settled in the Massachusetts Bay Colony in the 1630s, they considered themselves to be creating a model religious commonwealth in the wilderness. The early Puritan leader John Winthrop told his fellow colonists in 1630, "We must consider that we shall be as a city upon a hill, the eyes of all people are upon us."[7] Their goal was to create the good society, which meant a well-ordered religious society that would win God's approval and be used as a model by the rest of the world.

Within the context of creating a model religious commonwealth, education was considered essential to maintaining religious piety and social stability. The purpose in teaching reading and writing was to ensure not only that individuals read the Bible and religious tracts but also that they became good workers and obeyed the laws of the community. These educational goals are explicitly given in the earliest colonial law regarding education, the Massachusetts Law of 1642. This law opens with a general complaint about the neglect of parents and masters in the training of children in learning and labor and calls for the appointment of individuals to investigate the ability of children "to read and understand the principles of religion and the capital laws of this country."[8]

The religious theme received even greater emphasis five years later in the famous "Old Deluder Satan Law," enacted in 1647 in Massachusetts. This law has become famous because it required communities to establish and support schools. Specifically, the law required any community having at least 50 households to appoint a teacher to provide instruction in reading and writing and any community of 100 or more households to establish a grammar school. The law opens with the famous words, "It being the chief project of old deluder, Satan, to keep men from the knowledge of the Scriptures. . . . It is therefore ordered. . . ."[9]

Several important points about these two laws should be noted. The first is the reference to masters and parents. In both the colonies and England, some children were apprenticed to a master for seven years. During the apprenticeship, the master had the responsibility for assuring that the apprentice learned to read and write. The shortage of labor in the colonies often led to a shortening of the apprenticeship period and to the neglect by masters and parents of their obligation to provide instruction. Both these laws were intended to correct this neglect. Second, both laws made a distinction between instruction in reading and writing schools and in grammar schools. Unlike reading and writing schools, grammar schools primarily provided instruction that prepared their students for college and for leadership positions.

When historians argue that colonial schools perpetuated an existing social order, what they have in mind are the implications of the distinctions among apprenticeship, reading and writing schools, and grammar schools. This argument is made most forcefully by Merle Curti in *The Social Ideas of American Educators.* Curti views the history of education as primarily a conflict between people who wanted to use education to maintain their power and those who wanted education to be a means of improving conditions for all people. Curti argues that the colonial use of education as an instrument for preserving existing economic and social arrangements was rooted in European traditions. In England, for instance, the sons of the nobility were educated in the great endowed public schools, while the well-to-do middle class studied at the local grammar schools. The vast number of children of the poor were apprenticed, and the minimal instruction they received in reading and writing was for the purpose of maintaining religious conformity and the power of existing authority.

In New England, as well as in the other colonies, Curti argues, the identity of interests between the dominant religious group and the ruling authorities was even closer than in Europe, which resulted in education serving to protect the existing authority structure. Curti identifies two distinct schemes of education in the colonies. One served the elite, which included merchants, planters, clergy, and lawyers. The other scheme served the rest of the population. In the southern colonies, he argues, the class system was most in evidence; there the children of the rich were educated by private tutors or attended private schools, while other children received only a minimal education. In New England the class distinctions began in the reading and writing schools, with the children of the elite attending private dame schools and the children of the poor attending the town schools. According to Curti, the sharpest distinction was between children in apprenticeship and those attending grammar schools and colleges. The majority of boys were placed in apprenticeship, but the sons of the elite were sent to grammar schools and on to college. As stated earlier, the minimal instruction in reading and writing given apprentices was solely for the purpose of teaching religious conformity and understanding the laws of the colony. In Curti's words, "Apprentices were taught to respect their superiors and the sons of their superiors who were conning Latin verbs and acquiring the other requisites of the culture and polish that characterized the class to which they belonged."[10]

To understand Curti's argument, the history of reading and writing instruction and the development of grammar schools must be examined. The primary content in colonial reading and writing instruction was religious and moral, whereas the grammar school emphasized the teaching of Latin and Greek as part of a Renaissance conception of the educated person.

Both reading and writing schools and grammar schools were products of an educational revolution that had swept England in the sixteenth century. This revolution embodied the emphasis of the Protestant Reformation on the individual's responsibility to know the word of God and learn proper religious behavior. Reading and writing schools, often called petty schools, concentrated on the teaching of reading, with some teaching of writing and ciphering. This instruction took place in a variety of places, including households, churches, and schools. Instruction was conducted using a hornbook—a piece of wood with a thin layer of horn on top bearing the letters of the alphabet and a brief prayer. A majority of these schools were conducted by a single master or mistress.

A popular form of the petty school in the colonies was the dame school for neighborhood children. The dame school often was conducted in the kitchen or living room of the teacher's home. These schools primarily gave instruction in reading and writing, whereas writing schools provided a more advanced level of instruction in writing and also instruction in arithmetic and the simple elements of merchants' accounts. Instruction in these schools became a prerequisite for admission to grammar schools.

The content of instruction in the petty schools was primarily religious and authoritarian. The best example of this was the *New England Primer,* which became the most popular text for primary instruction. Primers were originally published in England, beginning in the fifteenth and sixteenth centuries, to provide Christian instruction for children. Early editions included the alphabet, the Lord's Prayer, the Hail Mary, and the Ten Commandments. These early primers were not schoolbooks but manuals for church services. Beginning in the sixteenth century, printers began to see the economic advantage of combining the church manuals with schoolbooks and began to publish instructional primers.[11]

One problem for New Englanders was that the primers published in England contained catechisms that conflicted with Puritan beliefs. To correct this problem, the General Court in the Massachusetts Bay Colony in 1641 ordered the church elders to prepare a catechism for the instruction of the colony's youth. This resulted in many religious disputes among the followers of the various types of Protestantism that had begun to appear on the New England landscape, but eventually most churches accepted the Shorter Catechism of the Westminster Assembly. It was this catechism that was reproduced in the *New England Primer.* Historians have not been able to determine the exact date of the printing of the first *New England Primer;* the best guess is that the first edition was printed between 1687 and 1690 in Boston by writer and printer Benjamin Harris. The book proved to be such a success in New England that when Harris returned to England in 1701 he continued its publication. For more than a hundred years the *New England Primer* was the schoolbook of America. An estimate of the actual number of copies published is that for a period of 150 years the average annual sale was 20,000 copies, for a total sale of 3 million copies. One estimate showed that a Philadelphia firm sold 37,100 for the 17-year period between 1749 and 1766.

The content of the *New England Primer* reflects the strong religious and authoritarian nature of colonial education. It opens with the alphabet and a guide to spelling. This section is followed by the short statement, "Now the child being entered in his letters and spelling, let him learn; these and such like sentences by heart, whereby he will be both instructed in his duty and encouraged in his learning." The authoritarian context of the child's duty is presented in the first lines of the following verse, which the student was required to memorize.

> I will fear God, and honour the KING.
> I will honour my Father & Mother.
> I will obey my Superiors.
> I will Submit to my Elders.

After this verse comes "An Alphabet of Lessons for Youth"—an alphabetic listing of statements containing religious and moral maxims that the student was required to memorize.

> A wise son makes a glad Father, but a foolish son is the heaviness of his Mother.

B etter is little with the fear of the Lord, than great treasure and trouble therewith.

C ome unto CHRIST all ye that labour and are heavy laden, and He will give you rest.

This list is followed by the Lord's Prayer, the Creed, the Ten Commandments, a section called the "Duty of Children Towards Their Parents," a list of the books of the Old Testament and New Testament, and a list of numbers. Numbers are introduced with the statement, "The numeral letters and figures, which serve for the ready finding of any Chapter, Psalm and Verse in the Bible." After the section on numbers comes a long exhortation given by John Rogers to his nine children in 1554 at the time the entire family was burned at the stake. The *Primer* ends with the Shorter Catechism.

A catechism is a series of questions with a set of correct answers. The child was required to memorize both the questions and the answers. The catechism in the *New England Primer* provided lessons in the basic tenets of Protestant faith. It opens with the question, "What is the chief end of Man?" This question was to be answered, "Man's chief end is to glorify God, and to enjoy him forever." The next question is:

Q. What rule hath God given to direct us how we may glorify and enjoy him?

A. The Word of God which is contained in the Scriptures of the Old and New Testament, is the only Rule to direct us how we may glorify and enjoy him.

The catechism then proceeds to take the student through a series of religious lessons to a final question on the meaning of the conclusion of the Lord's Prayer.[12]

After a reading of the *New England Primer* it is not difficult to understand why a historian like Rush Welter would consider colonial education a false start on the road to a democratic education. The content of colonial education emphasized not only submission to authority but also a particular method of instruction. Students were required to memorize the entire text. The method used to teach reading and writing was not one that taught individuals to give direction to their own lives but a method by which individuals would learn to submit to the laws of religion and the government. Students were not asked to analyze and give their opinions about religious texts but were taught to accept official interpretations as correct.

Chapter 6 in this book includes a discussion of the reaction in the nineteenth century to both the content and the method of this type of instruction. It is important to understand at this point in the history of education that this method of instruction and content were part of a world view whose adherents believed the good society could be achieved only through obedience to the word of God. In other words, educational practices were consistent with the philosophy and organization of society at that time. It is also important to understand the continuity in history. For example, in the nineteenth century the most important schoolbook was Noah Webster's spelling book, which has many of the characteristics of the *New England Primer*.

The grammar school provided a strikingly different type of education than the reading and writing schools. The purpose of the grammar school, in contrast to that of the petty school, was to educate the leaders of society. For instance, the typical goal of grammar school was stated by the Hopkins Grammar School at New Haven in 1684 as "[the education] of hopeful youth in the Latin tongue, and other learned languages so far as to prepare such youths for the college and public service of the country in church, and commonwealth."[13]

Historian Lawrence Cremin, in his monumental study *American Education: The Colonial Experience 1607–1783*, links the development of grammar schools to the Renaissance ideal of the educated public leader. During the Renaissance in the sixteenth century, intellectual leaders began to argue for the proper education of future leaders as the means of producing the just society. Foremost among these thinkers was Desiderius Erasmus, who in the early sixteenth century wrote a treatise titled *The Education of the Christian Prince*. This work calls for the education of a just and wise prince through the study of the Scriptures and the selected works of Plutarch, Seneca, Aristotle, Cicero, and Plato. Of great importance for the development of grammar schools is the emphasis on the study of classical Greek and Roman writers, which would, it was believed, lead to the development of civic character and preparation for leadership.

Cremin argues that it was a logical step for the middle class in England to see the type of education proposed by Renaissance writers such as Erasmus as a method of enhancing the status in society of the middle class. This argument highlights an important distinction between education as a means of conferring status and education as a means of confirming status. In the education of a prince, the status of the prince is to be confirmed by the type of education he receives. If the middle class receives the same type of education, it enhances their social position and confers an improved status.[14]

Therefore, the grammar school became an important institution in England and the colonies for the improvement of middle-class status. This represented an important shift in the role of education, one that would have lasting results. First, by conferring status, education assumed the role of providing a degree of upward mobility. By the nineteenth century, increasing numbers of individuals began turning to education as a means of enhancing their social status. In modern times, this role for education was born with the grammar school. Second, grammar schools represented a direct threat to aristocratic control because their existence suggested that individuals could be educated to rule. An issue of concern to aristocratic leaders is the source of the society's leadership. The suggestion that an educated leadership might be superior to an inherited leadership opened the door for consideration of republican forms of government. The argument that a systematic study of Greek and Latin authors would produce superior leaders in government and church contributed to the rapid expansion of grammar schools in England in the sixteenth century. By the time of the settlement of North America, grammar schools had become an established part of the educational landscape in England. In the colonies, as previously mentioned, the Massachusetts Law of 1647 required the establishment of a grammar school in every town with 100 or more households. By 1700, 39 grammar schools had been founded in New England.

The typical grammar school, as described by Lawrence Cremin, provided a seven-year education with major emphasis on the study of Latin and minor emphasis on Greek and Hebrew. The schools were divided into eight forms and concentrated on the study of Latin grammar, Latin conversation and composition, and Latin readings. In addition, students studied Greek and Hebrew grammar and Greek literature. Cremin writes, "As a rule, mornings were devoted to grammar, afternoons to literature, Fridays to review and the testing of memorization, Saturdays to themes and Sundays to catechizing and other religious exercises."[15]

It is important to remember that the purpose of the classical education in the grammar school was to provide instruction in the wisdom of the Greeks and Romans as preparation for civic and religious responsibilities and leadership. Another step in this preparation was to receive a college education. It is significant to note that after the American Revolution, many leaders, including Thomas Jefferson, began to view American colleges as the source of republican leadership; this idea had its roots in sixteenth- and seventeenth-century educational arguments.

A first act by colonists in the Massachusetts Bay Colony was to establish Harvard College in 1636. Its founding is described in a pamphlet, *New England's First Fruits*, published in London in 1642:

> *After God had carried us safe to New England, and we had build our houses, provided necessaries for our liveli-hood, rear'd convenient places for Gods worship, and settled the Civil Government: One of the next things we longed for, and looked after was to advance* Learning, *and perpetuate it to Posterity.*[16]

To advance learning, the colonists accepted money and books from John Harvard for the founding of Harvard College.

New England's First Fruits states clearly that the purpose of Harvard College was to assure an educated ministry for the colony. It was feared that no replacements would be forthcoming for the religious leaders who had led the colonists from England. In the words of *New England's First Fruits*, there was a "dreading to leave an illiterate Ministry to the Churches, when our present Ministers shall lie in the Dust."[17] Thus the goal for Harvard College was to guarantee continuity in the social organization and leadership of the colony.

Studies of the occupations of Harvard graduates in the seventeenth century confirm the role of the college in educating religious and civic leaders. Roughly half, or 180, of the 368 Harvard alumni completing their studies between 1642 and 1689 became clergymen. The next largest group of alumni, 42, became public servants—governors, councilors, judges, and permanent government officials. Twenty-seven of the alumni became physicians and 13 became schoolmasters and college tutors. Occupations for 68 of the alumni could not be determined and 27 died at a young age. The remaining alumni were classified as merchants, planters, gentlemen, soldiers, mariners, and miscellaneous.[18]

After reviewing the purposes and history of reading and writing schools and of grammar schools and the establishment of Harvard College, one can understand historian Merle Curti's argument that the educational system in New England was designed to protect existing authority by providing a class system of education. Reading and writing schools, which the majority of the school-going population attended, provided an authoritarian education and taught only the skills necessary to read and understand religious and civil decrees. On the other hand, grammar schools and Harvard College trained society's future leadership by providing an education in the classics. It is important to understand that the latter type of education provided knowledge that was ornamental but was not necessarily useful. In other words, education in the classics became a means of conferring and identifying social status.

Education in colonial New England must be understood in the context of a group of people struggling for survival in an unknown wilderness. The colonists faced many problems and experienced labor shortages that blurred social-class lines. The different forms of schooling were not a closed system in which all individuals below a certain level of social status were excluded from attendance at a grammar school. Nor was education the chief and only means of improving one's position in society. In fact, when dealing with education from the perspective of the twentieth century, one always faces the problem of attributing too much importance to its past social role. What is described here is only the early beginnings of a system that rapidly increased in importance and size during the nineteenth century.

Colonialism and Educational Policy

In the seventeenth century, marked differences existed among the colonial policies of the various nations with colonies in North and South America. In fact, national policies differed during the various periods of colonization. The differences in colonial policies were reflected in the educational practices of the North American colonies. The result was sharp variations in educational practices among the different regions of North America in the seventeenth and eighteenth centuries, and, in the nineteenth century, differences among the states.

Historian Lawrence Cremin's *American Education* provides insight into the effects of colonial policies. Cremin believes that educational history has been too narrowly defined as the history of schooling. He has written educational history as the history of all institutions that have shaped American thought and character, including families, churches, libraries, museums, publishers, newspapers, and benevolent societies. As part of this general approach, Cremin emphasizes the importance of colonial policy in the transmission of culture to the New World.

The differences in English colonial policy in different regions can be understood by comparing Virginia with New England. The Virginia companies chartered in 1606 were primarily concerned with the establishment of plantations that would yield a profit. During the early years of the Virginia settlement, education was in the hands of ministers for the purposes of maintaining discipline and order and controlling the native Americans. During these early years Virginia was above all viewed as a trading post in the wilderness. In 1609, this colonial policy changed, when families were transported from England to settle on small plots of land. The colony was governed like a military outpost as opposed to an agricultural community. Education consisted of little more than colonists going to church twice daily. By the 1620s, more settlers were brought to Virginia and an ordered community was established. Several unsuccessful attempts to establish schools occurred between 1618 and 1622.

The regional differences in early colonial policies created different educational traditions in Virginia and New England. As discussed earlier, the Massachusetts Bay Colony was established with a particular religious purpose and as a colony of self-sustaining families. Unlike the colony of Virginia, its major goal was not to provide a profit for English-based companies. Consequently, schooling became important as a means of sustaining a well-ordered religious commonwealth. In Virginia, on the other hand, less attention was paid to the education of the average colonist. Reading and writing schools were established in Virginia in the seventeenth century, but their numbers were small compared with those in New England. By 1689, Virginia had 6 reading and writing schools, while Massachusetts had 23.[19]

Most historians of colonial education have depicted early education in Virginia and the rest of the South as being aristocratic. Only a few pauper schools and apprenticeship training were available for the poor, but for the elite there were private pay schools and opportunities for education in the mother country. It can be argued that, within the context of colonial policy, Virginia most represented the educational policies of England in contrast to the colonies in New England. This was a result of more direct control from the mother country and the emphasis on colonization for profit.

Colonial policy in New Netherland represents a different and more complex situation. By the time of the English conquest of New Netherland in 1664, it had a population of over 5,000, living in a dozen Dutch villages and a few Puritan, Swedish, and Finnish settlements. The Dutch villages had less self-government than the New England towns and less of a sense of educational mission.

Before the English conquest of New Netherland, the Dutch West Indies Company had founded schools in 11 of the 12 Dutch communities. A struggle within the Dutch West Indies Company over schools in New Amsterdam resulted in the company's paying the cost of the schoolmaster, the city's paying for the schoolhouse and teacher's dwelling, and control administered by the local government. The English continued the practice of letting local officials and the courts hire, remove, and supervise teachers in local schools.

A major result of the more diverse population that settled in New York was the emergence of a variety of educational institutions. New York City (New Amsterdam) developed a system of private schools that dominated the educational scene until the early nineteenth century. These private schools offered a broad range of subjects, including instruction in practical arts. They also served the particular needs of several religious interests and therefore avoided any major clash among the different religious factions over the content of schooling. This would become a major issue in New York in the nineteenth century, when public support for education was expanded. Therefore, in New York, English colonial policy involved a certain degree of respect for religious and ethnic differences. This allowed for the development of more diversity in educational institutions.

A similar development occurred in the settlement of Pennsylvania, but with a major clash between German and English settlers over language usage. In many respects, the problems encountered in Pennsylvania foreshadowed conflicts in the nineteenth and twentieth centuries over which language should be used in the schools. Pennsylvania is also a good example of how colonial policy viewed education as a means of establishing the superiority of one ethnic group over another. Here the language used in the schools was thought to be the means by which one ethnic group could gain cultural ascendancy over another.

William Penn, the Quaker founder of Pennsylvania, actively recruited the oppressed from England and the Continent to settle in the New World. An original settlement of English Quakers and Anglicans was followed by a large German settlement of religious minorities, including Mennonites, Dunkers, and Amish. Both the Amish and the Mennonites were to be in conflict with civil authorities over the issue of schooling through the twentieth century. Groups of other religious minorities from Scotland, Ireland, England, and Germany also settled throughout Penn's colony. By 1766, Benjamin Franklin estimated that the colonial population of 160,000 consisted of one-third Quakers, one-third German, and one-third religious minorities from a variety of places in Europe.[20]

Cremin points out that some major differences existed between English control in New York and in Pennsylvania. In New York, the English attempted to Anglicize the administration of the colony while allowing diversity in cultural and social institutions. In Pennsylvania, the English embarked on what Cremin calls a policy of "cultural Anglicization."[21] This policy was directed in particular at the Germans, who caused the greatest fears among the English settlers. Cremin quotes a letter to John Penn in 1727 warning him about German immigration: "At this rate you will soon have a German colony here, and perhaps such a one as Britain once received from Saxony in the fifth century."[22] Concern was so great that the Pennsylvania assembly passed a law in 1727 requiring all male German immigrants to swear an oath of allegiance to the British Crown.

The great fear was that the culture and language of the settlers would become German. As a result, proposals began to appear that would prohibit German printing houses, the publication of German government documents, and the importing of German books. Of great importance were the recommendations for the establishment of English-language schools. These were viewed as a means to counter and suppress the expansion of German culture.

Benjamin Franklin was a major proponent of English-language schools and opponent of the expansion of German culture. He played a significant role in the establishment of charity schools, which were to be used for Anglicization. The schools originated as religious institutions for educating the poor German children of the province. Appeals for funds for the schools spread to London, where in 1753 an enthusiastic supporter of the endeavor, William Smith, proclaimed: "By a common education of English and German youth at the same schools, acquaintances and connections will be formed, and deeply impressed upon them in their cheerful and open moments. The English language and a conformity of manners will be acquired."[23]

In early 1755, the first schools were organized and a press was purchased from Franklin. Immediately, the German community attacked the schools for giving a false picture of German culture. This attack caused the failure of the schools. At their peak in 1759, the schools served only 600 to 750 children, of whom two-thirds were German. By 1764, the effort was considered a failure.[24]

This brief history of the attempt to Anglicize the Germans in Pennsylvania illustrates a continuing theme in American educational history: The use of the school as a means of spreading a particular culture has resulted in tensions between organized school systems, on one side, and immigrant groups, native Americans, Mexican-Americans, and blacks, on the other. In the nineteenth century, many of the religious tensions caused by Catholics' perception of the public school system as Protestant could also be considered a result of cultural differences.

Although Germans eventually did become Anglicized in Pennsylvania, they retained their own separate German schools and churches throughout the colonial period. The result was an educational system in the colony that relied on a combination of apprenticeship, private schools, and schools operated by the different religious denominations. The attempt to Anglicize the German population through charity schools was one of the first attempts in America to use education as a means of cultural imperialism.

The educational goals of many of the religious schools in Pennsylvania and New York were similar to those of the schools in New England. Memorization, submission, and authority were all emphasized in the instruction and the curriculum, and the *New England Primer* was used throughout these colonies. However, the pattern of development of the educational system in Pennsylvania and New York was distinctively different from that in New England and the southern colonies. New England placed an emphasis on the establishment of town schools to assure the perpetuation of religious values and obedience to the government. The southern colonies displayed little interest in the development of educational institutions except for private schools and tutors for the planter class.

These regional differences were a function of England's colonial policies. The most lasting of these differences was between the North and the South. Throughout the nineteenth century, the South lagged behind the North in the development of government-operated systems of education, and in the late nineteenth and twentieth centuries, the regions continued to be divided on the issue of segregated education. It was not until the 1950s and 1960s that the major differences between the educational systems of the North and the South began to fade.

Freedom of Thought and the Establishment of Academies

An intellectual revolution occurred in the seventeenth and eighteenth centuries that changed the purposes of education and made possible a secular school system. This revolution encompassed two major developments. The first was the emergence of the argument that freedom of ideas is essential for the development of society. The second was a growing awareness that education and learning can be instrumental and useful in improving the conditions of society.

These developments reflected changes in political thinking that were integral in shaping the American Revolution. The belief that the maintenance of a republican society requires freedom of thought and beliefs became embodied in American political life in the words of the First Amendment to the Constitution, which prohibits Congress from making any laws that would abridge freedom of speech and the press. Both of these intellectually revolutionary concepts also were related to new developments in science and technology that promised to enhance the quality of human existence.

In England, the struggle for intellectual freedom found its outlet in the establishment of dissenting academies. The idea of the academy was brought to the colonies, where it underwent changes to meet the practical needs of the New World. An important aspect of the academy movement was that it provided a clear alternative to the classical education of the grammar schools and colleges of the seventeenth and eighteenth centuries. The academies also provided an early model for the development of the high school.

The curriculum of the academy, with its dissenting tradition and its emphasis on practical skills, made the school something more than an institution to cultivate religious and civic obedience or to shape future leaders. The academy taught ideas and skills directly related to the practical side of life and provided intellectual tools for the development of new knowledge about the material world.

The changes in thinking about schooling and freedom of ideas were part of the ideological justification of the American Revolution that appeared in pamphlets and newspapers distributed in England and the colonies during the seventeenth and eighteenth centuries. Historian Bernard Bailyn describes his study of these pamphlets and newspapers:

> It confirmed my belief that intellectual developments in the decade before Independence led to a radical idealization of the previous century and a half of American experience, and that it was this intimate relationship between Revo-

lutionary thought and the circumstances of life in eighteenth-century America that endowed the Revolution with its peculiar force and made it so profoundly a transforming event.[25]

An early work in this revolutionary tradition, and the one most directly related to schools, was Robert Molesworth's *Account of Denmark as it was in the Year, 1692*. Molesworth's book is one of the first criticisms of the use of schooling to create obedient and submissive citizens. The purpose of his study was to find elements that had been most important in transforming Denmark into a system of hereditary absolutism. A key to explaining this transformation was the gaining of absolute obedience of the people to the state.

Molesworth believed that obedience had been gained by linking religion to the state and making education a function of religion. He argued that religious orders preached and taught a doctrine of submission and obedience to both heavenly and earthly rulers. When religion linked arms with government, religious doctrines were used to justify tyranny, and when education was a function of a state-established religion, religious doctrines were used to justify the power of the state and to mold future citizens into a condition of obedience.

In his study of tyranny in Denmark, Molesworth writes, "Enslaving the Spirits of the People, as preparative to that of their Bodies; . . . those Foreign Princes think it their Interest that Subjects should obey without reserve, and all Priests, who depend upon the Prince, are for their own sakes obliged to promote what he esteems his Interest." After establishing the interrelationship of interests, he goes on to lament, "'Tis plain, the Education of Youth, on which is laid the very Foundation Stones of the Public Liberty, has been of late years committed to the sole management of such as make it their business to undermine it."[26]

According to Molesworth, a major service that religion performed for the state through education of youth was "to recommend frequently to them what they call the Queen of all virtues, Viz. Submission to Superiors, and an entire blind Obedience to Authority." Of even greater importance, this educational system caused the people to forget that government was a product of human actions—not divine intervention. By making government appear divine in origin, religiously controlled education could teach obedience to government as if it were obedience to divine authority. Such education taught "that the People ought to pay an Absolute Obedience to a limited Government; fall down and worship the Work of their own Hands, as if it dropt from Heaven."[27]

A major conclusion of Molesworth's study is that education, in order to contribute to liberty and freedom, must be secular and separated from religion. He called for the professor to replace the priest and for students to learn the content of their classical studies rather than just the grammar. He believed that education must be free of religious dogma in service to the state and free to lead the learner down the path of reason. Molesworth's criticisms of education could easily have been applied to the type of education provided in the *New England Primer* and to the reading and writing schools of the seventeenth and eighteenth centuries. His study became part of a general discussion with his two friends John Trenchard and Thomas Gordon, who provided the broadest defense of freedom of ideas and learning that had so far been offered. Their essays were distributed between 1720 and 1723 as *Cato's Letters* and were many times reprinted during the subsequent 25 years. These essays, which are considered a primary source for the justification of the American Revolution, provided topics for endless political discussions in public houses on both sides of the Atlantic Ocean.[28]

The essays defend freedom of thought and speech as essential for the economic and social development of a nation. In making the link between social progress and freedom, the *Letters* offer their defense in concrete terms, not merely as an appeal to abstract justice: A country needs freedom because without freedom there can be no growth in human wisdom and invention and, consequently, no progress in economic development. The authors of *Cato's Letters* believed that tyranny and slavery stop social development and improvement in human well-being, whereas freedom and liberty lead people down the road to progress and happiness.[29]

Cato's Letters define freedom of thought and speech as a right that can be abridged only to protect the freedom of others: "Without Freedom, there can be no such Thing as Wisdom; and no such Thing as public Liberty, without Freedom of Speech: Which is the Right of every Man, as far as by it he does not hurt and control the Right of another." This one limitation on freedom, they declared, "is the only Check which it ought to suffer, the only Bounds which it ought to know."[30]

In linking freedom of thought to human progress, the authors of *Cato's Letters* argue that humans in their original state of nature contented themselves with "the Spontaneous Productions of Nature," but these "spontaneous" supplies proved insufficient to support increasing numbers of humans. The next step was "to open the bosom of the Earth, and, by proper Application and Culture, to extort her hidden stores." The differing degrees of prosperity that existed among nations are considered largely a product of different levels of advancement in the state of learning, which allowed the more advanced nations to enjoy greater productivity. Wisdom and art, the authors argue, promote prosperity, which in turn provides full employment, economic well-being, and a general elevation of the spirit and culture of a people. If the advancement of wisdom and learning fails to occur, unemployment will come, and resulting human misery. In describing the conditions that produce human misery, they write, "People, in most countries, are forced, for want of other Employment, to cut the Throats of one another, or of their neighbors; and to ramble after their Princes in all their mad conquests . . . and all to get, with great Labour, Hazard, and often with great Hunger and slaughter, a poor precarious, and momentary subsistence."[31]

The equation made in *Cato's Letters* between freedom of ideas and the good life is this: Freedom of thought and speech promotes wisdom, which in turn provides the basis for prosperity and the elimination of the crime that grows from hunger and poverty. Within the framework of this argument, tyranny must be avoided because it hinders the growth of wisdom, prosperity, and social happiness. "Ignorance of Arts and Sciences, and of everything that is good, together with Poverty, misery, and desolation, are found for the most part all together, and are all certainly produced by Tyranny."[32]

The arguments in *Cato's Letters* and in Molesworth's writings give an entirely different perspective on the nature of schooling and the role of schooling in society. In the context of their arguments, if education took place in an environment free of ideological restraints, particularly those of religion, it would be the source of material benefits for society. These arguments reflect the scientific revolution that emerged in the seventeenth century as the result of work by individuals like Francis Bacon.

Bacon was one of the first people to see in science hope for the progress of humanity. During his life as a barrister, essayist, and scientist, he envisioned a utopia made possible by the use of the scientific method. In his book *Novum Organum* (1620), he argues that scientific experimentation would unlock the secrets of nature and usher in a golden era. His utopian novel *New Atlantis* describes a society in which the central institution is a College of Six Days Works, devoted to the scientific study of nature.[33]

Bacon's early arguments were accepted by intellectuals such as Molesworth and the authors of *Cato's Letters*. In the eighteenth century, this group of English political thinkers, scientists, inventors, and early industrialists was known as *commonwealthmen*. The scientists and inventors in the group included Matthew Boulton, James Watt, Erasmus Darwin, Samuel Galton, and Joseph Priestly.[34] All of these persons had contact with leading members in Glasgow and Edinburgh of the important intellectual centers of the day and interacted freely with the leading philosophical societies in England.

This group of intellectuals took the argument for freedom of ideas one step further than would their counterparts in North America. They objected to government-provided systems of education as a threat to intellectual freedom. English historian Brian Simon has written about Joseph Priestly and this group of intellectuals: "In common with . . . all other dissenters, Priestly was adamantly opposed to education becoming a function of the state. Should it do so, it would not achieve the object he desired, on the contrary, it would be used to promote uniformity of thought and belief."[35] Joseph Priestly used specific examples to show the negative results of government-controlled education. For instance, he often referred to the attempt at Oxford University to discourage the reading of John Locke's *Essay on Human Understanding*. Priestly believed that any group that gained control of the educational system could greatly increase its power over the rest of society. He argued that education should encourage free inquiry and inspire the love of truth, and that state-endowed education would be more committed to instilling a particular set of religious, moral, or political principles than to training the mind for the free use of reason.

Historian Caroline Robbins summarizes Priestly's ideas about state-provided education as follows:

The chief glory of human nature, the operation of reason in a variety of ways and with diversified results would be lost. Every man should educate his children in his own manner to preserve the balance which existed among the several religious and political parties in Great Britain.[36]

In England, the institution through which the advocates of intellectual freedom expressed their beliefs became the dissenting academies established in the latter half of the seventeenth century. These academies served as refuges for Nonconformist ministers and others dissenting against the major religious and educational institutions in England. Their growth was a direct result of the closing in 1662 of Oxford and Cambridge to non-Anglicans. The dissenting academies became centers of intellectual and educational innovation as they promoted science and rejected a strictly classical curriculum. In fact, the academies introduced English as the language of instruction.

Although various types of academies served numerous purposes, many of the academies accepted the idea that science and politics were suitable subjects for the curriculum and that freedom of inquiry should be encouraged. Some academies were run by individuals; others were operated by religious denominations. The variety of schools and the commitment of most of them to intellectual freedom made the academies an important source of educational innovation in the eighteenth century. In England, they were considered an alternative to older forms of higher education. When the academy idea was introduced into the colonies it served as a model both for newly established colleges and, in the nineteenth century, for the development of the American high school.

In conclusion, the intellectual revolution that fostered the importance of freedom of ideas had two significant consequences for schooling: First, it led to a different concept of the purposes of education and institutional organization. Within this framework, education was viewed as providing the intellectual tools, scientific knowledge, and inventions required to create a better society. Second, this intellectual revolution attacked the notion that the primary purpose of education was to bring people into obedience to a church or government.

The Useful and the Ornamental in Learning

The academy movement in North America was primarily a result of the desire to provide a more utilitarian education as compared with the education provided in classical grammar schools. The North American academies were modeled after the English dissenting academies, but unlike those in England, they were not a response to exclusion from other educational institutions nor did they place as much emphasis on intellectual freedom. In North America, these institutions served two needs: They provided a useful education and at the same time they transmitted the culture required for entrance into the middle class. In other words, they were institutions that could provide social mobility for the average citizen. They were often called *people's colleges*.

The academy movement spread rapidly in the eighteenth and nineteenth centuries. In 1855, United States Commissioner of Education Henry Barnard reported the existence of 6,185 academies in the United States, with a total enrollment of 263,096. As in England, the academies in North America were varied in curriculum and organization. In general, a mixture of public and private control and financing was used. Often, small towns would provide financial support to local academies under the control of a private board of trustees. The curricula of the academies tended to be flexible and adaptable to the needs of the student, although, of course, this varied from institution to institution.[37]

One of the earliest and most famous plans for an academy was Benjamin Franklin's *Proposals Relating to the Education of Youth in Pennsylvania* (1749). Ironically, the institution established to carry out his plans, which eventually became the University of Pennsylvania, failed to teach his curriculum, but nonetheless it became a widely discussed model for other academies. In many ways, Franklin's model academy embodied the elements of the life experiences that had gone into his own education. A famous phrase from his proposal states that "it would be well if [students] could be taught every Thing that is useful, and every Thing that is ornamental: But Art is long, and their Time is short. It is therefore propos'd that they learn those Things that are likely to be most useful and most ornamental."[38]

Franklin's life was a model for getting ahead in the New World. He was exposed early in life to the major types of educational institutions that existed in the colonies. Benjamin Franklin was born in Boston in 1706 and at the age of eight was sent by his father to grammar school to prepare to be a minister. His father, who became financially unable to carry through with this plan, later withdrew Franklin from the grammar school. He was sent to a school for writing and arithmetic and was made an apprentice to his brother in the newspaper trade. Eventually, he rebelled and left Boston, going to Philadelphia in 1723 to pursue his trade of printer.

Although his life in Philadelphia demonstrated the opportunities available in the New World for upward mobility, Franklin's ability to eventually become an internationally recognized scientist and statesman was dependent on his self-education.

The "useful" elements in Franklin's education were the skills learned in apprenticeship and through his reading. The "ornamental" elements, on the other hand, were the knowledge and social skills learned through reading, writing, and debating, which provided him with the culture needed to advance in the world. A main source of his ornamental education was a club he organized in Philadelphia called the Junto. The Junto met every Friday evening, and its members were required to prepare questions dealing with morals, philosophy, and politics. Every three months, they had to write an essay and defend it to the other members. As Franklin wrote in his *Autobiography*, the purpose of the club was "mutual improvement."[39] Mutual improvement and self-education were also Franklin's reasons for founding the first subscription library in America. He recommended to the members of the Junto that they place all their individually owned books into a common library for the benefit of all members. Out of this grew the idea of a subscription library to which library members would pay a fee for expenses and the purchase of new books. Franklin believed that these libraries improved the general culture of the average citizen:

> These libraries have improved the general conversation of the Americans, made the common tradesmen and farmers as intelligent as most gentlemen from other countries, and perhaps have contributed in some degree to the stand so generally made throughout the Colonies in defense of their privileges.[40]

The academy Franklin proposed was an institutionalized version of both his own formal schooling and his self-education. The academy proposal can also be viewed as a model of an educational system that would confirm one's status in the middle class or prepare one for entrance into the middle class in eighteenth-century North America. Certainly, Franklin's *Autobiography* can be considered a guide for social mobility in the world as he knew it.

The educational content that Franklin proposed reflects the influence of the radical English writers who did so much to spark the American Revolution. His plan includes the study of English through reading *Cato's Letters* and the writings of the English radical Algernon Sidney. It should be noted that *Cato's Letters* had been published only a few decades before the publication of Franklin's proposal, but in his proposal Franklin refers to them as classics.

Franklin placed a great deal of emphasis on the teaching of style in both writing and speaking. Proper style, for Franklin, included writing clearly and concisely and "pronouncing properly, distinctly, emphatically, not with an even Tone, which under-does, nor a theatrical, which over-does Nature."[41] It was style in writing and speaking that would allow an individual to move through the social world with grace.

According to Franklin, the substance behind the style would emerge from the study of history, which in its broadest sense would be the vehicle for learning the "most useful" knowledge. In Franklin's words, "But if History be made a constant Part of their Reading . . . may not almost all Kinds of useful Knowledge be that Way introduc'd to Advantage, and with Pleasure to the Student?"[42] For Franklin, history was a vehicle for teaching morality, oratory, geography, politics, philosophy, human affairs, agriculture, technology, science, and invention. The teaching of history, combined with the teaching of style in writing and speech, would provide the "most useful and most ornamental" in learning.

Franklin's proposal heralded the beginning of the academy movement in North America. Although academies came in many forms and were governed by a variety of public and religious groups, they all were considered to be distinct from the classical grammar school. Unlike the grammar schools, the academies were conceived as institutions to provide a practical education. This is best exemplified in the wording of the constitution of the Phillips Academy, founded in 1778. It states that the founding of the academy was "for the purpose of instructing Youth, not only in English and Latin Grammar, Writing, Arithmetic, and those Sciences, wherein they are taught; but more especially to learn them the GREAT END AND REAL BUSINESS OF LIVING."[43]

Over the years the identity of the academies fluctuated: They sometimes were considered to be small colleges and at other times, high schools. By the latter part of the nineteenth century, however, academies had established a primary identity as institutions providing a secondary education. Also by the end of the nineteenth century, they had become identified as institutions for educating the elite. This view of the academy had not yet emerged in the eighteenth and early nineteenth centuries.

A direct contribution by the academy movement to the development of high schools in the United States was made in 1821, when the English Classical School was founded in Boston. At that time, most academies were country boarding schools. A group of parents in Boston complained about having to send their children either outside the city to attend an academy or—the only alternative—to the Boston Latin School, where a traditional grammar school curriculum was taught. The city responded to the complaints by founding the English Classical School, which offered a curriculum typical of academies of the time, including English, geography, arithmetic, algebra, geometry, trigonometry, history, navigation, and surveying. Within a few years, the school was renamed English High School and became the first high school in the United States.

The history of dissenting academies in England and academies in North America demonstrates the interrelationship among politics, the organization of society, and education. The dissenting academies, born in the midst of revolutionary talk that quickly spread to the North American continent, were institutions reflecting the new spirit of science and industrial development. Transplanted to the New World, they became institutions for teaching what was considered useful knowledge and for providing social mobility. A real irony of history is that by the late nineteenth century, the academies in the United States primarily served to confirm the social status of elite members of society.

The Family and the Child

A popular interpretation of historical change in the United States is to view it as a process of institutional expansion and contraction. In this framework, the institution of the family is portrayed as contracting while other institutions assume roles once performed by it. In terms of the history of education, this means the school has assumed tasks previously performed by the family as educational responsibilities have shifted from the parents to the schoolteacher. In addition, changes in commonly held concepts of childhood and of women have had a fundamental effect on the organization of education. Changes in the concept of childhood provided a basis for the belief that the proper education of children could create the ideal political and social world.

In *American Education*, Cremin interprets educational history mainly as a shifting set of institutional arrangements wherein the family had the basic responsibility for education. Cremin writes, "The household remained the single most fundamental unity of social organization in the eighteenth-century colonies and, for the vast majority of Americans, the decisive agency of deliberate cultural transmission."[44] In frontier areas, he argues, the family often assumed functions of the church and the school, whereas in more settled areas it shared these responsibilities with other institutions.

The importance of the socializing role of the family in colonial life is highlighted in John Demos's study *A Little Commonwealth: Family Life in Plymouth Colony*. Demos ascribes a variety of functions to the colonial family. First, it was a business; work was a natural part of family life and most households were self-sufficient. Second, it was a school; parents and masters were required by law to attend to the education of their children. Third, it was a vocational institution; it transmitted skills for earning a living. Fourth, it was a church; family worship supplemented the work of formal religious institutions. Fifth, the family was a house of correction in which idle and even criminal persons were sentenced to live as servants. And last, the family was a welfare institution that functioned at various times as hospital, orphanage, old peoples' home, and home for the poor.[45]

Within this broad-ranging institution was a strict hierarchy, with the father at the top and the children at the bottom. The colonial family operated on a simple premise: "He for God only, she for God in him." This meant that women were to bow to the God in men, and men were to assume the spiritual care of women. In legal matters, the married woman was at the mercy of her husband—she was without rights to own property, make contracts, or sue for damages.

Although women were dependent on men, they still had to assume responsibility for their own individual salvation, and in order to do so, they had to learn how to read. This created an ambivalent situation regarding the education of women. The education of women was under-taken purely for purposes of religious control, but, ironically, even though women were considered the weaker sex with regard to intellectual capacities, they not only assumed responsibility for teaching reading within the household but also functioned as neighborhood teachers in the dame schools and, during the summer, in district schools of New England.

In general, the education of women was limited to basic reading, writing, and arithmetic, but their role as teachers in the family and in dame schools foreshadowed their dominant role as teachers in public schools in the late nineteenth and the twentieth centuries. This role of teacher opened the door to further education for women and provided a career for them that became an important stepping stone on the road to greater equality and rights.

Children in the colonial family were in a position of complete subordination to their parents. The requirement to honor one's parents even extended into adulthood. This is best exemplified by a statute of the Plymouth Colony that stated,

If any Childe or Children above sixteen years old, and of competent Under-standing, shall curse or Smite their Natural Father or Mother; he or they shall be put to Death, unless it can be sufficiently testified that the Parents have been very Unchristianly negligent in the Education of such Children.[46]

Of major importance to the family was the economic function of the child. In a world where most families were financially self-sufficient, each new pair of helping hands was welcomed. After infancy, the colo-nial child usually helped with agricultural chores during the summer and attended school in the winter. Between the age of seven and pu-berty, children were fully integrated into the work force. Many times, the family would apprentice out to another family boys over the age of seven. The economic value of the child was clearly demonstrated by the requirement in families that if the boy left home to work he was ex-pected to pay for a substitute for his labor. Often families considered the child's value during the winter to be no more than the cost of providing board, but during the summer months the child's labor was considered essential. It is not surprising that families would resist child labor laws in the nineteenth and twentieth centuries, given the deep roots of this traditional view of the economic worth of the child to the family unit.[47]

The primary responsibility of colonial parents to their children was to raise them to live according to God's commandments. This meant caring for their physical and spiritual needs. Parental strictness was required because of a belief that all children at birth shared in the common sins of humanity. This is best exemplified by the alphabet in the *New England Primer* that begins,

A In Adam's Fall We Sinned All
B Thy Life to Mend This Book Attend.[48]

The "Book" referred to is the Bible, which was presented as the source for correction of the Original Sin in which all children were believed to have been born.

The emphasis in child rearing was to prevent children from leading a life of sin. In other words, parents had an obligation to make sure their children were good. What this meant is expressed in the following verse from the *New England Primer:*

Good Children Must

Fear God all Day,	Love Christ Alway,
Parents Obey,	In Secret Pray,
No False thing Say,	Mind Little Play,
By no Sin Stray,	Make no delay,

In doing Good.[49]

This attitude toward children can be understood more clearly by contrasting it with other concepts of childhood that began to be popularized in the eighteenth century. For instance, the French philosopher Jean-Jacques Rousseau believed that the child is born good and that the greatest danger in childhood is corruption by the outside world. He popularized this concept of childhood in his book *Emile* (1762). *Emile* is Rousseau's plan for the ideal education of a child. To provide Emile, the protagonist, with the best education, Rousseau isolates him from society until the onset of adolescence and places him in a country home under the supervision of a tutor who allows Emile to discover what is necessary and useful for living. The concept of education that permits the child to learn through experience and discovery was a major departure from schooling that emphasized memorization and subordination to authority.[50]

A major contrast exists between colonial ideas about child rearing and Rousseau's theory that moral education should not take place until the child has reached the age of social reasoning—adolescence. Rousseau calls this *negative education,* by which he means that learning is to be a product of experience, not moral and verbal instruction. According to Rousseau, during the early period of their development, human beings are incapable of reasoning about morality and social relations. Thus, it is important to avoid placing a child in situations requiring moral choices before the child is old enough to handle them with his or her own powers of social reasoning. Rousseau felt that books are a great plague in childhood. He did not mean by this that children should not be taught how to read, but that learning to read should be attached to experience and necessity. For example, Emile receives invitations to dinners and parties but cannot find anyone to read them to him. These experiences lead Emile to learn how to read out of self-interest and necessity. Rousseau's method of teaching reading avoids moral instruction; it is not based on a sense of duty or on a belief in an abstract good. For Rousseau, learning and knowledge are tools to be used by the individual—not tools enabling society to use the individual.

Emile demonstrates how a theory of childhood can influence actual child rearing and instruction. The colonial concept that the child is born in a state of sin required restraining children from doing evil and subjecting them to authoritarian instruction to assure a godly life. On the

other hand, according to Rousseau, children are born in a state of goodness and need to be protected from the sins of the world and allowed to
freely develop their basic good nature. Rousseau's concept of childhood
means more freedom for the child and a more permissive form of instruction.

Emile heralded the beginning of a romantic concept of childhood,
which, in the nineteenth and twentieth centuries, sparked educational
trends emphasizing instructional techniques to allow the free development of the child. In modern times, the major rival to this concept is the
idea that the child is born as a blank slate (*tabula rasa*) and is completely
molded by the environment. In this theory of childhood, which can be
traced to the eighteenth century, can be found the roots of modern
behavorial psychology.

The book most closely identified with the origins of the concept of the
child as a blank slate is English philosopher John Locke's *Some Thoughts
Concerning Education* (1693). For Locke, the adult is primarily a product of
his or her education in the world, and this education is a result of rewards and punishment received during childhood. Consequently,
Locke argues that the most important factor in education is the development of correct habits, which depends on proper manipulation of
rewards and punishment. Locke writes, "I grant, that good and
evil, reward and punishment, are the only motives to a rational
creature; these are the spur and reins, whereby all mankind are set on
work and guided, and therefore they are to be made use of to children
too."[51]

According to Locke, the most powerful reward for children is esteem
and the most powerful punishment is disgrace (as opposed to corporal
punishment). In a sense, Locke calls for the manipulation of parental
love as a means of shaping the character of the child. He also expresses
concern about children's learning bad habits from other children, and he
warns parents that sending their offspring to school might lead to such
contagion.

Locke's solution to the influence that children exert on one another in
school is to have teachers who are able to both teach subject matter and
shape proper habits. He advises parents to keep their children out of
school until they find a school "wherein it is possible for the master to
look after the manners of his scholars, and . . . show as great effects of
his care of forming their minds to virtue, and their carriage to good
breeding, as of forming their tongues to the learned languages."[52] In one
sense, this echoes the traditional view that the teacher is responsible for
the virtue of students. In another sense, however, Locke envisioned
what we might call the modern concept of the teacher—a teacher who is
given not only the responsibility for imparting subject matter but also
responsibility for consciously shaping character. For Locke, the child is

not viewed as being either good or evil, but as a person to be molded for the future.

Locke's concept of childhood, like Rousseau's, led to rejection of traditional methods of instruction. Locke criticized what he called the ordinary method of instruction, which fills the mind with rules and precepts that are not understood and are quickly forgotten, and considered memorization to be the poorest method of instruction. Locke advocated instead that the child learn through performance until the object of the lesson is mastered: "By repeating the same action, till it be grown habitual in them, the performance will not depend on memory, or reflection, the concomitant of prudence and age, and not of childhood; but will be natural in them."[53]

Locke's concept of childhood greatly influenced the development of public schools in the nineteenth and twentieth centuries. The concept of the child as a blank slate allowed educational leaders to believe they could create the good society through the proper molding of children. Nineteenth-century common school reformers such as Horace Mann specifically rejected the Calvinist view of the child born in sin for a concept of the child as a lump of clay that can be shaped for the future. This allowed school reformers to dream of creating the perfect school— one that would produce the perfect political citizen, the perfect moral person, and the perfect worker.

The romantic view that children are born good had the most influence on dissenters in the nineteenth and twentieth centuries against the controlling power of the public school. One model of education in the twentieth century, the "free school," called for opposing this power by encouraging the natural unfolding of the child. The romantic concept of childhood also played a role in the development of adolescent psychology and child study.

These concepts of childhood have never been as distinct in real life as they are in a historian's conceptualization, but they do provide a basis for understanding the effect of different concepts of childhood on the organization of education. The colonial view of childhood created an environment that was controlling and authoritarian. Major changes in education occurred with the rejection of the idea that the child is born in a state of sin and therefore must be controlled and made submissive. The viewpoint that the child is neither good nor evil and is a product of the environment allowed educators to view the school as a panacea for social, economic, and political problems.

Conclusion

What distinguishes education in pre-Revolutionary and post-Revolutionary America is the concept of service to the broader needs of govern-

ment and society. After the American Revolution, many Americans began to believe that a public system of education was needed to build
nationalism, to shape the good citizen, and to reform society. In other
words, education in the post-Revolutionary period was brought into the
service of public policy.

Before the Revolution, education mainly served to prepare an individual to live a godly life and to confer status. The major goal of education
was to ensure that the public knew how to read the Bible, religious
tracts, and laws. Status was conferred by the classical education of the
grammar school and college through the teaching of a particular cultural
style and body of knowledge.

Although the colonists thought education was important, they did not
believe the creation of an extensive and well-organized system of education was necessary. It was not until education was viewed as a government function, as opposed to a family function, that organized systems
of schooling appeared. This occurred when government leaders began
to see education as a useful tool for governing society. The closest any of
the colonies came to creating a system of education was the town
schools in New England. However, even though these schools were
established according to law, they were never organized into an educational system. The Middle Colonies contained a diversity of religious and
private schools, and the southern colonies for the most part neglected
the education of the general public.

The forces behind the changes that took place after the Revolution
were in evidence in the pre-Revolutionary colonies. The academy movement stimulated thinking about education's serving the practical needs
of humanity as well as religious needs. Changing concepts of childhood
made it possible for educators to dream of schools as institutions for
creating the perfect society. And, more important, the general population began to realize the value of learning as a tool for gaining independence, not just for instilling subservience. For instance, as mentioned
previously, Benjamin Franklin believed the rebellious spirit of the population was a result of the wide availability of libraries. In fact, the political tracts read by the colonists were instrumental in setting the stage for
the American Revolution. As the history of schooling in the colonial
period demonstrates, education can be brought into the service of either
authority or independence.

Notes

1. A good study of this faith in education is Henry Perkinson, *The Imperfect
Panacea: American Faith in Education, 1865–1965* (New York: Random House,
1968).
2. One book that stresses this view of colonial education is Merle Curti, *The*

Social Ideas of American Educators (Paterson, N.J.: Pageant Books, 1959). This interpretation of nineteenth-century education can be found in Michael Katz, *Class, Bureaucracy, and Schools: The Illusion of Educational Change in America* (New York: Praeger, 1971).

3. Lawrence Cremin, *The Wonderful World of Ellwood Patterson Cubberley* (New York: Teachers College Press, 1965).

4. Ellwood Cubberley, *Public Education in the United States: A Study and Interpretation of American Educational History* (Boston: Houghton Mifflin, 1934), p. 14.

5. Carl F. Kaestle, *Pillars of the Republic: Common Schools and American Society, 1780–1860* (New York: Hill and Wang, 1983).

6. Rush Welter, *Popular Education and Democratic Thought in America* (New York: Columbia University Press, 1962), p. 9.

7. Quoted in Lawrence Cremin, *American Education: The Colonial Experience 1607–1783* (New York: Harper & Row, 1970), p. 15.

8. Reprinted in Ellwood Cubberley, ed., *Readings in Public Education in the United States: A Collection of Sources and Readings to Illustrate the History of Educational Practice and Progress in the United States* (Cambridge, Mass.: Riverside Press, 1934), p. 16.

9. Ibid., pp. 18–19.

10. Curti, *Social Ideas*, pp. 23–24.

11. Paul Leicester Ford, ed., *The New-England Primer* (New York: Teachers College Press, 1962), pp. 1–53.

12. All the quotes from the *New England Primer* are from the edition reprinted in ibid.

13. Quoted in Cremin, *American Education*, p. 186.

14. Ibid., pp. 58–79.

15. Ibid., p. 175.

16. Reprinted in Cubberley, *Readings in Public Education*, p. 13.

17. Ibid.

18. Cremin, *American Education*, pp. 220–221.

19. Ibid., p. 183.

20. Ibid., p. 259.

21. Ibid.

22. Quoted in ibid., p. 260.

23. Quoted in ibid., p. 261.

24. Ibid., p. 262.

25. Bernard Bailyn, *The Ideological Origins of the American Revolution* (Cambridge, Mass.: Harvard University Press, 1967), pp. vi–vii.

26. Robert Molesworth, *An Account of Denmark as it was in the Year, 1692* (Copenhagen: Rosenkilde and Bagger, 1976). None of the pages of the preface are numbered; all quotations are taken from the preface.

27. Ibid.

28. *Cato's Letters: Unabridged Reproduction of 6th Edition 1755*, ed. Leonard Levy (New York: Da Capo Press, 1971).

29. Ibid.

30. Ibid., Vol. I, p. 96.

31. Ibid., Vol. II, pp. 306–309.

32. Ibid., p. 312.

33. Cremin, *American Education*, pp. 94–96.
34. Caroline Robbins, *The Eighteenth-Century Commonwealthman* (Cambridge, Mass.: Harvard University Press, 1959).
35. Brian Simon, *Studies in the History of Education, 1780–1870* (London: Lawrence & Wishart, 1960), pp. 34–35.
36. Robbins, *Eighteenth-Century Commonwealthman*, p. 350.
37. Theodore Sizer, ed., *The Age of the Academies* (New York: Teachers College Press, 1964), pp. 1–48.
38. Quoted in ibid., pp. 70–71.
39. L. Jesse Lemisch, ed., *Benjamin Franklin: The Autobiography and Other Writings* (New York: Signet, 1961), p. 72.
40. Ibid., p. 82.
41. Quoted in Sizer, *Age of the Academies*, p. 71.
42. Quoted in ibid.
43. Quoted in ibid., pp. 77–78.
44. Cremin, *American Education*, p. 480.
45. John Demos, *A Little Commonwealth: Family Life in Plymouth Colony* (New York: Oxford University Press, 1970), pp. 183–186.
46. Reprinted in ibid., p. 100.
47. Joseph F. Kett, *Rites of Passage: Adolescence in America, 1790 to the Present* (New York: Basic Books, 1977), pp. 1–38.
48. Ford, *New-England Primer*. Pages are unnumbered in the reproduction of the original work contained herein.
49. Ibid.
50. Jean-Jacques Rousseau, *Emile* (New York: Dutton, 1911).
51. Peter Gay, ed., *John Locke on Education* (New York: Teachers College Press, 1964), p. 36.
52. Ibid., p. 48.
53. Ibid., p. 50.

2
Freedom and Order

None of the educational proposals that appeared after the American Revolution were ever enacted in their entirety, but all contained arguments that would become part of the ongoing debate in the nineteenth and twentieth centuries about the role of education in a democratic and republican society. It is important to understand the impact of these early arguments on the evolution of a philosophy of American education.

The proposals varied in their content and emphasis, but certain central themes ran through all of them. One theme was nationalism, an important issue after the American Revolution because of the feeling that America needed to be distinguished from its European origins. A search began for an American language, literature, and culture that would unify a nation whose diverse population encompassed a multitude of languages, religions, and cultures. The use of education as a means of creating a unified population became a major theme in the history of American education.

An important aspect of nationalism is patriotism—"love of country," or emotional attachment to symbols of the country. The use of education during the post-Revolutionary period to promote feelings of patriotism was not unique to the United States. Leaders of many European countries, particularly Prussia, had realized the importance of building feelings of patriotism as a means of unifying the citizenry and building military strength. The ultimate end of patriotism was to strengthen emotional ties to the country so that the common citizen would be willing to die in military service to the government.

Methods of teaching patriotism included studying a national literature and language, singing nationalistic songs, honoring the flag, and participating in patriotic exercises. In the United States, the most popular promoter of nationalism and patriotism was Noah Webster, often called the "Schoolmaster of America." Webster's spelling book, with its nationalistic themes, replaced the *New England Primer* in importance and use during the post-Revolutionary period.

Another theme that appeared in post-Revolutionary educational literature and has been continually debated up to present times is how to establish a balance between freedom and order. On the one hand, the rhetoric of the American Revolution stressed the idea of freedom, but on the other hand, the strong religious and political feelings of many citizens of the new republic caused them to fear that uncontrolled freedom would lead to a decadent and chaotic society.

For many Americans, the balance of freedom and order was to be achieved through education. They argued that individuals could be allowed to be free if they were educated to be virtuous. In other words, freedom could be allowed if controls over behavior were internalized within the citizen. Stated in a different manner, freedom meant freedom to do good and act virtuously. Educational proposals by post-Revolutionary leaders such as Benjamin Rush and Noah Webster emphasized the importance of educating citizens to be virtuous and thus to exercise their freedom in a correct manner.

A debate also took place about the type of knowledge needed by the citizen of the new republic. Most writers on education realized the importance of an educated citizenry, but varied in important ways on their definition of the nature of that education. Two major positions on this issue emerged during the late eighteenth and early nineteenth centuries.

One position held that all citizens should be educated to read and write and that political opinions should be formed outside of educational institutions. This position was taken by Thomas Jefferson in his various writings on education. The other position argued that educational institutions needed to teach basic principles of a republican form of government. This position was taken by the common school reformers (see Chapter 3).

The differences between these two positions are important. The first position relegates the shaping of political opinions to the free marketplace of ideas and places faith in the ability of individual citizens to form their own political beliefs, whereas the second position posits that it is necessary to have a single institution form correct political ideas. This particular argument entangled the schools in a continuing debate over who should define the political beliefs to be taught in the schools.

Finally, educational writers in the post-Revolutionary period were concerned about the sources of leadership for a republican government. For Europeans, this issue was often answered by the existence of an aristocracy. In the new republic, however, educational institutions were frequently considered to be a means for selecting and educating future leaders, thus placing education in the United States in a pivotal role in the political and social process. Within this framework, education was given the task of consciously selecting talent. By the twentieth century, the selection process had broadened to encompass occupational as well as political concerns, so that selection became one of the most important social purposes of education.

Educating Republican Machines

The educational writings of Benjamin Rush, the leading American physician of the post-Revolutionary period, exemplify the concern at the time with educating virtuous citizens and republican leaders through traditional colonial educational methods of imposition and control. A primary emphasis in Rush's writings is on the necessity to maintain order in a republican society by educating virtuous citizens in a system of government-operated schools.

Benjamin Rush was born in Pennsylvania in 1746 and served as an apprentice to a Philadelphia doctor between 1760 and 1766. From 1766 to 1769, he studied at what was considered the most advanced school of medicine, the University of Edinburgh. Upon returning to the colonies, he established his medical practice in Philadelphia and began teaching chemistry at the College of Philadelphia.

A unique feature of Rush's writings is his translation of political problems into medical problems. He has been called the "father of American psychiatry" because he often defined political and social problems as mental problems. At the heart of his conceptual framework is the belief that all human beings have a moral faculty that leads them instinctively to avoid evil. Evil acts, he believed, are the result of physical factors weakening the moral faculty. Thus, he prophesizes, it might eventually "be as much the business of a physician as it is now of a divine [minister] to reclaim mankind from vice."[1]

Rush's belief in the existence of a moral faculty was widely shared by important educational leaders in the nineteenth century. For instance, the major leader of the common school movement in the nineteenth century, Horace Mann (see Chapter 3), believed in the existence of a number of different mental faculties. This notion made it possible to believe in the ability of education to mold the future citizen by training different faculties in different groups of students.

The concept of mental faculties did not affect the traditional belief that the function of education is to control behavior and to impose ideas. In his 1786 plan for the establishment of public schools in Pennsylvania, Rush writes: "I dissent from one of those paradoxical opinions with which modern times abound: that it is proper to fill the minds of youth with religious prejudices of any kind and that they should be left to choose their own principles." He states flatly,

It is necessary to impose upon them [youth] the doctrines and discipline of a particular church. Man is naturally an ungovernable animal, and observa-

tions on particular societies and countries will teach us that when we add the restraints of ecclesiastical to those of domestic and civil government, we produce in him the highest degrees of order and virtue.[2]

Rush believed that public schools should impose on the individual a system of values that would create what he called "republican machines": "I consider it . . . possible to convert men into republican machines. This must be done if we expect them to perform their parts properly in the great machine of the government of the state."[3] He believed education could train the individual to be obedient and submissive to the will of the government and to be willing to give up ownership of self to the state: "Let our pupil be taught that he does not belong to himself, but that he is public property. Let him be taught to love his family, but let him be taught at the same time that he must forsake and even forget them when the welfare of his country requires it."[4]

Two related concepts—that the child is the property of the government and that the state's interest in the child is greater than the family's—were becoming popular during this period. These beliefs justified the right of government to educate the child even against the wishes of the family.

Rush was one of the first writers to argue for the superiority of public schools over the family. By the end of the nineteenth century, a recurrent refrain was that the family was collapsing or failing in its duties, and thus the school had to assume the role of the family. Rush made a similar argument in 1786 when he wrote, "Society owes a great deal of its order and happiness to the deficiencies of parental government being supplied by those habits of obedience and subordination which are contracted at schools."[5]

Rush believed that a goal of public schooling should be the inculcation of republican duties, including the sacrifice of property to the state: "He [the student] must be taught to amass wealth, but it must be only to increase his power of contribution to the wants and needs of the state."[6]

For Rush, the social order of the new republic depended on control exerted over the student in school. By making the student subordinate to the power of the teacher and the rules of the school, Rush argued, the student would be prepared to obey the laws of government. Within this conceptual framework, freedom could be maintained in society if all citizens were educated to be obedient.

Rush supported the goals of his educational plan with a belief in highly authoritarian methods of instruction. In the education of youth, he argued, "The authority of our masters [should] be as absolute as possible. . . . By this mode of education, we prepare our youth for the subordination of laws and thereby qualify them for becoming good citizens of the republic." He demanded very strong control over youth and wrote that the most useful citizens were formed from those youths who "have never known or felt their own wills till they were one and twenty years of age."[7]

Rush envisioned a uniform system of education for Pennsylvania, with a single university, at the top of a pyramid of schools, located in the state capital. In this structure, an individual would attend a free school in a local township, proceed from there to a county academy, and then to one of four regional colleges. The best students from the colleges would be sent to the university.

All schools in this system were to be uniform in their teachings and conform to a single state philosophy: "The same systems of grammar, oratory, and philosophy will be taught in every part of the state, and the literary features of Pennsylvania will thus designate one great and equally enlightened family."[8]

The principle of uniformity in Rush's proposed educational system reflects the interest at the time in creating national unity out of a diverse population. His emphasis on educating submissive "republican machines" highlights the general concerns with balancing freedom and order.

Rush's educational philosophy is similar to that expressed in two educational proposals that won prizes in an essay contest held by the American Philosophical Society in the 1790s. Although only two essays from the competition survive, it is reasonable to assume that they reflect what the members of the society thought were the best educational ideas of the time.

The American Philosophical Society was formed in 1769, from Benjamin Franklin's Junto. Franklin was the first president and was followed by David Rittenhouse. After Rittenhouse's death in 1796, Thomas Jefferson became head of the group. The general purpose of the organization was to provide a forum for the spread of "all philosophical experiments that let light into the nature of things, tend to increase the power of man over matter, and multiply the conveniences or pleasures of life."[9]

The two winning essays, like Rush's proposals, advocate centralization, uniformity, censorship, and control of the diffusion of knowledge. One essay, by Samuel Harrison Smith, proposes that a board of literature and science be established to organize a system of national education including primary schools, colleges, and a national university. Also, the board would be given the power to judge all literary and scientific productions "and in case they shall pronounce any such work worthy of general perusal . . . it shall be printed at the public expense and the author rewarded."[10] Because the material would be reproduced at public expense, the board would have the power to force public financial support of certain creative works.

Smith gave the board control of the diffusion of knowledge: "It shall be the especial duty of the board to determine what authors shall be read or studied in the several institutions and at any time to substitute one author for another." The board was also given control of a national system of libraries: "It shall be in the power of the board to establish them [libraries] wherever it shall see fit and to direct all original productions of merit to be introduced into them."[11]

The second prize-winning essay, by Samuel Knox, also proposes a national board of education, which would supervise primary schools, academies, and colleges. Under his system, each state government would have its own printer, who would produce for the school "such school books and other literary publications as should be recommended or directed by the board of education." In this manner, Knox writes hopefully, throughout the United States would be the "same uniform system of the most approved school books."[12]

Like Rush's, Knox's emphasis on uniformity was part of a desire to build a sense of nationalism through unity. Also like Rush, he wanted to control the exercise of liberty through the education of a virtuous character. In other words, the republican citizen, according to Knox, needed instruction about government and morality: "It is certainly of the highest importance in a country like this that even the poorest and most uninstructed of its citizens be early empressed with a knowledge of the benefits of that happy constitution under which they live and of the enormity of their being corrupted in their right of suffrage." To aid in achieving this goal, Knox proposed the use "of a well-digested, concise moral catechism."[13]

Clearly, the educational proposals of Benjamin Rush, Samuel Harrison Smith, and Samuel Knox reflect concerns with nationalism and with maintaining order in a free society. The proposals demonstrate the extreme positions taken by some people on these issues. It was easy for individuals filled with anxieties about nationalism and social order to advocate an authoritarian educational system that emphasized uniformity and practiced censorship. Throughout the history of American education, this has been one of the extreme positions on these issues.

The Schoolmaster of America

Nationalism was a major theme in the work of Noah Webster. A prolific writer of political and social essays, he left as a legacy a standardized American dictionary of the English language, an American version of the Bible, and his famous spelling book. The wide use of Webster's speller and dictionary throughout the United States cast a lasting mold on American language.

Webster also made a political contribution to the development of the

American common school system. Between 1815 and 1819, he served in the Massachusetts legislature and worked actively for a state school fund. One of his speeches to the legislature captures the flavor of what he believed would be the result of a system of common schools:

> *I should rejoice to see a system adopted that should lay a foundation for a permanent fund for public schools, and to have more pains taken to discipline our youth in early life to sound maxims of moral, political, and religious duties. I believe more than is commonly believed may be done in this way towards correcting the vices and disorders of society.*[14]

One historian has claimed that Webster's activities in the state legislature initiated the movement for common schools that culminated in Horace Mann's work in the 1830s.[15]

Born in Connecticut in 1758, Webster began his early career as a country schoolmaster. While teaching in 1779, he conceived the idea of developing a new system of instruction. He completed one spelling book in 1783, the first of three volumes in a series titled *A Grammatical Institute of the English Language*. In 1784, he completed a grammar book, the second volume in the series, and a reader, which was the third. In 1785, he packed his bags and rode through the country as an itinerant lecturer, selling his instructional system.

Both his salesmanship and the content of his textbooks proved a success. One and a half million copies of the speller had been sold by 1801; 20 million, by 1829; and 75 million, by 1875. The speller became a model used by other spelling book authors. Its extreme popularity was demonstrated by the publication in 1863 of a Civil War edition in the South that was adapted "to the youth of the Southern Confederacy."[16]

Webster believed that, in addition to teaching reading and writing, his texts should produce good and patriotic Americans, develop an American language, and create a unified national spirit. As his biographer, Harry Warfel, states, "This unified series of textbooks effectually shaped the destiny of American education for a century. Imitators sprang up by the dozen, and each echoed Websterian nationalism. The word 'American' became indispensable in all textbook titles; all vied in patriotic eloquence."[17]

Like Benjamin Rush, Webster believed that moral and political values had to be imposed on the child: "Good republicans . . . are formed by a singular machinery in the body politic, which takes the child as soon as he can speak, checks his natural independence and passions, makes him subordinate to superior age, to the laws of the state, to town and parochial institutions."[18]

One method used to instill proper political values was the Federal Catechism, which appeared in the early versions of Webster's spelling book. The inclusion of a catechism in a spelling book was not an original idea. The *New England Primer* contained one, but it was mainly religious in content. However, a catechism with political content was probably Webster's original idea. The use of a catechism required children to memorize questions and answers, which perpetuated an authoritarian method of instruction.

The content of Webster's Federal Catechism reflected his own concern—that the new republican government remain primarily a representative institution and not become democratic. For example, the Federal Catechism contains the following question and answer to be memorized by the reader:

Q. What are the defects of democracy?

A. In democracy, where the people all meet for the purpose of making laws, there are commonly tumults and disorders. A small city may sometimes be governed in this manner; but if the citizens are numerous, their assemblies make a crowd or mob, where debates cannot be carried on with coolness and candor, nor can arguments be heard: Therefore a pure democracy is generally a very bad government. It is often the most tyrannical government on earth; for a multitude is often rash, and will not hear reason.[19]

Webster's spelling books also contained a Moral Catechism, to teach the moral values Webster considered necessary for maintaining order in a republican society. Like most Americans of this period, Webster equated public virtue with Christian morality. In other words, a good citizen is one who lives a Christian life. This attitude is similar in some ways to the goals of the early settlers in New England. The first part of the Moral Catechism illustrates the type of Christian morality people like Webster believed necessary in a republican society.

Q. What is moral virtue?

A. It is an honest upright conduct in all our dealings with men.

Q. Can we always determine what is honest and just?

A. Perhaps not in every instance, but in general it is not difficult.

Q. What rules have we to direct us?

A. God's word contained in the Bible has furnished all necessary rules to direct our conduct.

Q. In what part of the Bible are these rules to be found?

A. In almost every part; but the most important duties between men are summed up in the beginning of Matthew, in Christ's Sermon on the Mount.[20]

An aspect of Webster's concern with nationalism and virtue included the building of an emotional feeling of patriotism. In an essay entitled

"On the Education of Youth in America," published in 1790, Webster writes,

It is an object of vast magnitude that systems of education should be adopted and pursued which may not only diffuse a knowledge of the sciences but may implant in the minds of the American youth the principle of virtue and of liberty and inspire them . . . with an inviolable attachment to their country.[21]

What he meant by an "inviolable attachment" is an emotional bond between citizen and government: Webster believed that "every class of people should know and love the laws" and that attachment to the law "may be formed by early impressions upon the mind." This emotional bond was to be forged by creating a national language and by widely disseminating the patriotic content of his textbooks. The following statement about Webster's method of selecting material for his readers illustrates his patriotic objectives:

In the choice of pieces, I have not been inattentive to the political interests of America. Several of those masterly addresses of Congress, written at the commencement of the late revolution, contain such noble, just and independent sentiments of liberty and patriotism, that I cannot help wishing to transfuse them into the breasts of the rising generation.[22]

Illustrative of his patriotic themes was the cover of his 1787 reader, which contained the words, "Begin with the infant in the cradle; let the first word he lisps be Washington."[23] His readers contained Washington's Farewell Orders to the Army, patriotic poems, and (for the first time in a schoolbook) a history of the Revolutionary War.

For Webster, patriotism, nationalism, and virtue were the central foci of educating the republican citizen. These educational values clearly emphasize representative as opposed to democratic government. Noah Webster's importance in the history of American education is twofold: He represented widely held opinions of his times, and he had a major effect on the education of children in the United States in the late eighteenth and the nineteenth centuries.

The Natural Aristocracy

Thomas Jefferson's opinions on education in the new republic were quite different from those of his contemporaries and of later leaders of the common school movement. Unlike Benjamin Rush and Noah Webster, Jefferson did not believe that schooling should impose political values or mold the virtuous republican citizen. Rather, he believed that education should provide the average citizen with the tools of reading and writing and that political beliefs would be formed through the exercise of reason. For Jefferson, the most important means of political education was the reading of history and newspapers. In one of his more famous statements, he argues:

> *The basis of our government being the opinion of the people, the very first object should be to keep that right; and were it left to me to decide whether we should have a government without newspapers, or newspapers without a government, I should not hesitate a moment to prefer the latter.*[24]

Jefferson was concerned with the education of future republican leadership. He believed that the new republic needed to identify its future leaders in the early years of their schooling and provide them with an education through college. This educated leadership would form a natural aristocracy.

Jefferson was born in 1743 in Shadwell, near Charlottesville, Virginia. His father was a Virginia magistrate and surveyor and his mother was a member of one of the most prominent families in the colony. After graduating from the College of William and Mary, Jefferson was admitted to the Virginia bar in 1767. Between 1769 and 1775, he served as a member of the Virginia legislative assembly, and in 1776, as a member of the Continental Congress, Jefferson drafted the Declaration of Independence. As a strong proponent of individualistic democracy, he championed legislative proposals and constitutional amendments protecting freedom of speech and religion. In 1800 he was elected president of the United States.

One reason for Jefferson's opinion that democracy is possible was his belief in the existence of an inborn moral sense, which he refers to as "common sense." For this reason, his educational writings do not emphasize the shaping and controlling of students' moral behavior as preparation for citizenship. Jefferson wrote to his friend Peter Carr in 1787 that the individual is "endowed with a sense of right and wrong. . . . This sense is as much a part of his nature as the sense of hearing, seeing, feeling; it is the true foundation of morality." Jefferson argues that this innate sense of right and wrong can be improved through exercise, like any other part of the body, and can be guided by reason. On the other hand, the study of moral rules can interfere with the proper functioning of this innate sense of morality. He writes, for example, "State a moral case to a ploughman and a professor. The former will decide it as well, and often better than the latter, because he has not been led astray by artificial rules."[25]

Jefferson's belief in reason and a moral sense did not cause him to reject the importance of knowledge and learning. In a letter to John Adams in 1814, he comments on his disgust with his recent reading of

Plato's *Republic*. In simple terms, Plato argues that individuals are born with the world's knowledge and that the role of education is to reveal that inner knowledge to the individual. Jefferson complains in his letter that post-Revolutionary youth seemed to have a similar idea that they had acquired "all learning in their mother's womb and bring it into the world ready made." He goes on to attack the shallow education provided at academies, which committed "pupils to the theatre of the world, with just taste enough of learning to be alienated from industrious pursuits, and not enough to do service in the ranks of science." Jefferson then describes his dream for the establishment of a university that would teach every branch of science to its "highest degree."[26]

Jefferson's ideas on the role of education and knowledge in society reflect a belief in the possibility of improving the human condition: Individuals are born with reason and a moral sense, and education can improve the workings of these faculties and contribute to the increase of human knowledge. In his 1818 *Report of the Commissioners Appointed to Fix the Site of the University of Virginia,* Jefferson likens this process to that of creating a new and better tree by grafting a cultivated tree onto a wild and uncultivated tree. "Education, in like manner, engrafts a new man on the native stock, and improves what in his nature was vicious and perverse into qualities of virtue and social worth." In addition, he argues, each generation adds to the store of human knowledge, and this "constant accumulation must advance the knowledge and well-being of mankind, not *infinitely,* as some have said, but *indefinitely,* and to a term which no one can fix and foresee."[27]

Jefferson's belief that education can provide the tools and knowledge for the improvement of the exercise of morality and reason is evident in his most famous educational proposal, *A Bill for the More General Diffusion of Knowledge,* made to the Virginia legislature in 1779. This bill proposes that schools be established to provide tuition-free education for three years for all male and female children. In these schools, children were to be taught "reading, writing, and common arithmetick, and the books which shall be used therein for instructing the children to read shall be such as will at the same time make them acquainted with Graecian, Roman, English and American history."[28] This was to be the basic education of the citizens of the new republic.

Jefferson elaborates the reasons for the content of this education in *Notes on the State of Virginia.* He rejects the teaching of the Bible in reading instruction, stating "Instead, therefore, of putting the Bible and Testament into the hands of the children at an age when their judgments are not sufficiently matured for religious inquiries, their memories may here be stored with the most useful facts from Grecian, Roman, European, and American history." The development of morality, he argues, should be postponed until reason matures. The first elements of moral instruction should be for the purpose of teaching children "how to work out their own greatest happiness, by shewing them that it does not depend on the condition of life in which chance has placed them, but is always the result of a good conscience, good health, occupation, and freedom in all just pursuits."[29]

The most important part of moral instruction, according to Jefferson, is the study of history, which guides reason by providing the individual with knowledge about human actions. "History, by apprising them of the past, will enable them to judge of the future; it will avail them of the experience of other times and other nations; it will qualify them as judges of the actions and designs of men."[30]

For Jefferson, education contributes to the balance between freedom and order by providing all citizens with the basic tools of learning, a knowledge of history, and the ability to work out their own happiness and morality. He believed that knowledge, reason, and a developed moral sense would result in a natural order in a free society.

A Bill for the More General Diffusion of Knowledge also contains a plan for the selection and education of a natural aristocracy. The bill proposes the establishment of grammar schools in every county. An overseer of the reading and writing schools would choose "the boy of best genius in the school, of those whose parents are too poor to give them further education, and . . . send him forward to one of the grammar schools." After every one or two years in the Latin School, the best student of the group would be selected and given six more years of education. "By this means," Jefferson writes in *Notes on the State of Virginia,* "twenty of the best geniuses will be raked from the rubbish annually, and instructed, at the public expence, so far as grammar schools go." Out of the selected group of grammar school graduates, half of the best would be sent at public expense for three years to the College of William and Mary.[31]

The talent selected through this three-tier system of education was to provide the leadership for the republic. According to Jefferson, the purpose of higher education is to "form statesmen, legislators and judges, on whom public prosperity and individual happiness are so much to depend." In addition, higher education should teach the principles and structure of government, promote the interests of agriculture and business, and advance the sciences.[32]

Jefferson's educational plan combines two ideas: preparing the citizen and preparing the political leader. Of the two goals, Jefferson believed the instruction of the citizen was the more important: "But of all the views of this law none is more important, none more legitimate, than that of rendering the people the safe, as they are the ultimate, guardians of their own liberty."[33]

From Jefferson's educational writings emerges the following portrait of the ideal citizen. Guided by a knowledge of history and the reading of newspapers, the individual would exercise reason and moral common sense to make political decisions. One of the most important decisions would be the selection of republican leadership. Ideally, the choice would be among members of the natural aristocracy that had been selected by the school system and given a university education.

Conclusion

Most historians emphasize the conservative educational views of these early theorists of the role of education in a republican society. Rush Welter writes in *Popular Education and Democratic Thought in America* that those hoping to find a democratic orientation in the Founding Fathers' views on education are often disappointed. Welter notes that these early writings have a "tendency to stress the conservative role of educational institutions in overcoming an excess of popular liberty."[34]

The same interpretation of the period is given by Carl Kaestle in *Pillars of the Republic*. For Kaestle, the main concern of the period was to balance freedom and order: "Political theorists and policy makers were therefore concerned not only with protecting liberty, for which the Revolution had been fought, but also with maintaining order, without which all might be lost."[35] The purpose of education, according to Kaestle, was to maintain the balance between order and freedom by producing virtuous, well-behaved citizens.

Kaestle places his interpretation in the broader framework of republicanism. According to him, during the post-Revolutionary period, *republicanism* meant a combining of the concepts of virtue, balanced government, and liberty. By *virtue*, "republican essayists meant discipline, sacrifice, simplicity, and intelligence." Many of the early leaders believed in the natural virtue of the landed yeoman—virtue that did not depend upon deliberate instruction. However, the problem for these leaders was the increasing population of citizens who did not belong to the class of landed yeomen. For this group, natural virtue could not be assumed and deliberate instruction was needed.[36]

Kaestle indicates that educational proposals were motivated by factors other than fear of the disorder that would result from liberty. He argues that Revolutionary leaders were also captured by the idea of the perfectability of humans and human institutions. They wanted to create a society that would be an alternative to the corrupt society of Europe and believed that education, by perfecting virtue, would contribute to achieving this utopian goal.

Kaestle does not draw a clear distinction between Jefferson's belief in individual reason and virtue and the more authoritarian ideas of leaders like Rush and Webster. On the other hand, in *The Social Ideas of American Educators*, Merle Curti considers educational leaders like Webster to represent a clearly conservative viewpoint on the organization of society. Curti writes that Webster's spelling book contains a social philosophy "appropriate to a system which attached great value to acquiescence on the part of the poor in their poverty and at the same time promised ultimate success to those who would practice the virtues of frugality, industry, and submissiveness to moral teachings and to God's will."[37]

Curti concludes from his review of the moral maxims in Webster's speller that they were primarily designed to protect the property of the wealthy, and that "other half-truths, equally fitting to a society in which some had more and others less, were read and re-read by American youth who learned their letters from the old 'blue-back.' "[38] In general, Curti finds that most post-Revolutionary educational practices and proposals continued, with minor changes, the colonial class system of education.

Curti does think that Thomas Jefferson's ideas on education contrast sharply with others of the period. Curti argues that Jefferson displayed little sympathy for authoritarianism in education and that the ideas he advanced were hostile to the class character of existing educational practice. According to Curti, Jefferson's educational plan was a major step in the direction of breaking down class barriers in education. Specifically, he contends that Jefferson's proposal to select leaders from the masses through his three-tier system of education was the beginning of more democratic thinking about education: "Jefferson's quest for genius among the poor was far more democratic than anything that existed then, or was for a long time to exist."[39]

Nonetheless, Curti argues that Jeffersonian thought was limited by aristocratic pretensions. Without taking into account Jefferson's beliefs regarding the exercise of virtue and the role of history, Curti criticizes Jefferson for proposing a mainly literary education for the lower and middle schools and argues that education of this type would be of little benefit "to common folk struggling on the less fertile soils and to frontiersmen with their peculiar problems."[40] He also criticizes Jefferson for displaying more interest in the organization of university studies than of schools for the common folk. Despite these reservations, Curti hails Jefferson as the first American "to emphasize public education as an instrument for the realization of democracy and for the furthering of social reform."[41]

While these grand schemes for republican forms of education were being proposed, schooling continued in the same pattern that had existed during colonial times. Submission and authority continued as the dominant elements in the classroom pattern. In the decades immediately after the Revolution, the only major changes were the growth of opportunities for the education of women and the expansion of charity schools.

The differing historical interpretations presented in this chapter high-light the important issues in the early debate about the role of education in a free society. The major tension in this debate was between those who believed schooling should mold the virtuous citizen and those who believed schooling should provide the tools for the exercise of freedom. From the nineteenth century until the present, some have argued that a democratic society needs a school system that imposes morality, empha-sizes patriotism, teaches respect for authority, and inculcates certain basic political values.

At the same time, others have argued that schooling in a democratic society should provide the intellectual tools to all people that will enable them to select their own moral and political values. American educa-tional philosophy has evolved as a blend of these two arguments.

Notes

1. Quoted in David Hawke, *Benjamin Rush: Revolutionary Gadfly* (New York: Bobbs-Merrill, 1971), pp. 108–109.
2. Benjamin Rush, "Thoughts upon the Mode of Education Proper in a Repub-lic," in Frederick Rudolph, ed., *Essays on Education in the Early Republic* (Cam-bridge, Mass.: Harvard University Press, 1965), p. 5.
3. Ibid., p. 17.
4. Ibid., p. 14.
5. Ibid., p. 16.
6. Ibid., p. 14.
7. Ibid., p. 16.
8. Benjamin Rush, "Plan for the Establishment of Public Schools," in Rudolph, *Essays on Education*, pp. 4–6.
9. Allen Oscar Hansen, *Liberalism and American Education in the Eighteenth Cen-tury* (New York: Macmillan, 1926), pp. 105–110.
10. Samuel Harrison Smith, "Remarks on Education," in Rudolph, *Essays on Education*, p. 213.
11. Ibid., p. 214.
12. Samuel Knox, "An Essasy on the Best System of Liberal Education," in Rudolph, *Essays on Education*, p. 323.
13. Ibid., p. 332.
14. Quoted in Harry Warfel, *Noah Webster: Schoolmaster to America* (New York: Macmillan, 1936), p. 335.
15. Ibid., pp. 335–336.
16. Ibid., pp. 71–75.
17. Ibid., p. 93.
18. Quoted in ibid., p. 21.
19. "Noah Webster's Federal Catechism (1798)," in Sol Cohen, ed., *Education in the United States: A Documentary History* (New York: Random House, 1974), pp. 769–770.
20. "Noah Webster's Moral Catechism," in Cohen, *Education in the United States*, p. 771.

21. Noah Webster, "On the Education of Youth in America," in Rudolph, *Essays on Education.*
22. Quoted in Warfel, *Noah Webster*, p. 86.
23. Quoted in ibid., p. 90.
24. Thomas Jefferson, "To Edward Carrington," in Gordon Lee, ed., *Crusade against Ignorance: Thomas Jefferson on Education* (New York: Teachers College Press, 1961), p. 102.
25. Thomas Jefferson, "To Peter Carr, With Enclosure," in Lee, *Crusade against Ignorance*, pp. 145–146.
26. Thomas Jefferson, "To John Adams," in Lee, *Crusade against Ignorance*, pp. 109–112.
27. Thomas Jefferson, "Report of the Commissioners Appointed to Fix the Site of the University of Virginia, &c.," in Lee, *Crusade against Ignorance*, p. 119.
28. Thomas Jefferson, "A Bill for the More General Diffusion of Knowledge," in Lee, *Crusade against Ignorance*, pp. 83–92.
29. Thomas Jefferson, "Notes on the State of Virginia," in Lee, *Crusade Against Ignorance*, p. 95.
30. Ibid., p. 96.
31. Ibid., p. 94.
32. Jefferson, "Report of the Commissioners," in Lee, *Crusade against Ignorance*, pp. 117–118.
33. Jefferson, "Notes," in Lee, *Crusade against Ignorance*, p. 96.
34. Rush Welter, *Popular Education and Democratic Thought in America* (New York: Columbia University Press, 1962), p. 27.
35. Carl F. Kaestle, *Pillars of the Republic: Common Schools and American Society, 1780–1860* (New York: Hill and Wang, 1983), p. 5.
36. Ibid.
37. Merle Curti, *The Social Ideas of American Educators* (Paterson, N.J.: Pageant Books, 1959), p. 32.
38. Ibid., p. 34.
39. Ibid., p. 41.
40. Ibid., p. 43.
41. Ibid., p. 44.

3

Institutions and Reform: Schools and Colleges in the New Republic

In the early part of the nineteenth century, Americans organized institutions for the moral reformation of society and began to make an important distinction between public and private institutions. These developments set the stage for the evolution of the common school system in the 1830s and the multiplication of colleges in the early nineteenth century. The organization of the common school system in different states in the 1830s and 1840s provided the basis for the modern system of public schooling in the United States. This chapter will consider the important institutional changes that foreshadowed the development of the common school system and the modern system of higher education.

The history of institutions for moral reformation can create the impression that educational change primarily was the result of elite reformers trying to find a means of controlling the population. For example, the establishment of most charity schools fits that image. But certain educational developments during the early period of the nineteenth century represented attempts by people to create institutions that would serve their educational interests. The best example of this kind of grass-roots movement in education is the schools organized by black people to serve their community.

Moral Reform and Faculty Psychology

Americans in the early nineteenth century were taken with the idea that institutions could perfect the good person and create the good society. This pattern of thinking made it possible for educational leaders to envision a system of common schooling that would lead to a moral and political reformation of society. The belief that institutional structures could be used to develop the good society was reflected in the expansion of charity schools in the early part of the nineteenth century and in the establishment of special institutions for delinquent youth.

Charity schools were the first to be based on the Lancasterian system of school organization and instruction, which revolutionized the concept of schooling. Prior to the introduction of the Lancasterian method, the main purpose of education was to develop the moral character of the child through memorization and recitation of didactic readings. The *New England Primer* is a good example of this type of instruction.

What was new about the institutional changes in the early part of the nineteenth century, and the Lancasterian system of instruction, was the idea that institutional arrangements were important in developing moral character. A belief developed that moral character could be shaped by how students interacted in the school as well as through the learning of didactic material. In later years, this would be referred to as the *process of socialization*.

In the early nineteenth century, the belief in the importance of institutional arrangements in shaping moral character contributed to the already developing idea that schooling of the entire population was necessary for social and political order. As discussed in Chapter 2, post-Revolutionary leaders viewed education as important in promoting nationalism and balancing freedom and order. These ideas, combined with a belief in the necessity of particular institutional arrangements, easily led to the conclusion that all children of the republic should be educated in a single common school system.

The acceptance of the notion of malleability of character provided the basis in the early nineteenth century for the belief that the good society could be created through schooling and through other institutional changes. Of primary importance was the widespread belief in some form of faculty psychology. Chapter 1 shows how behavioral and romantic concepts of childhood had begun to develop in the eighteenth century. The behavioral concept of human psychology stressed the importance of the environment in shaping character, whereas the romantic concept stressed the unfolding of the inner nature of the individual.

Faculty psychology contained elements of both behaviorism and romanticism. The human mind was said to be divided into several different parts, such as intelligence and morality. These different faculties were natural components of the individual and could be influenced by the environment. For instance, Benjamin Rush (see Chapter 2) argued in 1786 that a moral faculty was a natural part of the human mind. Rush's influence in promoting this idea was significant because of his standing as the leading physician of the post-Revolutionary period and as the father of American psychiatry.

Rush believed that the moral faculty had the function of "distinguishing and choosing good and evil." From this perspective, moral actions were dependent on the degree of development of the moral faculty. Rush argued that the moral faculties of some individuals were developed out of proportion to other faculties. He referred to these individuals as benevolent idiots and gave as an example an individual who "spent several hours of every day in devotion, in which he was so careful to be private that he was once found in the most improbable place in the world for that purpose, vz. in an oven." Rush also described individuals in whom all faculties except the moral faculty were highly developed. For instance, he cited the Duke of Sully, who was very learned, creative, and athletic, but who "died in the flower of his age, in a common brothel, perfectly corrupted by his debaucheries, and expired with the glass in his hand, cursing and denying God."[1]

People adhered to many different forms of faculty psychology during the early part of the nineteenth century. For instance, Horace Mann, often called the "father of the common school," was a phrenologist, and his educational writings often refer to the different faculties of the mind (see Chapter 4 for a fuller discussion). In a report to the Massachusetts State Board of Education in 1848, for example, he likened an uneducated republic to an obscene giant "whose brain has been developed only in the region of the appetites and passions, and not in the organs of reason and conscience."[2]

One common characteristic of all varieties of faculty psychology was a belief that the virtuous functioning of the moral faculty is dependent on how it is cultivated. For instance, the prescription given by Rush for a well-functioning moral faculty included sunshine, a plain diet, water, and cleanliness. Rush also included with these physical remedies "mechanical means of promoting virtue," such as odors, eloquence from the pulpit, music, and solitude.[3]

Also, discipline and exercise of the various faculties of the mind were considered necessary for their proper development. This type of reasoning would often appear in educational reports. Yale College's famous report in 1828, which will be discussed in more detail later in this chapter, states, "In laying the foundation of a thorough education, it is necessary that all the important mental faculties be brought into exercise. . . . If the student exercises his reasoning powers only, he will be deficient in imagination and taste, in fervid and impressive eloquence."[4]

Faculty psychology in all its various forms reflected the growing belief in the perfectability of the human being. This belief provided the intellectual basis for the reform movements in the early part of the nineteenth century that produced modern systems of education and other institutions designed to improve human character. Of major importance was the idea of controlling the institutional environment affecting the individual as a means of achieving perfection.

Charity Schools, the Lancasterian System, and Prisons

Charity schools and juvenile reformatories developed in the United States in the early part of the nineteenth century as part of a general attempt to reduce crime and poverty. Both institutions sought to perfect human character through some form of education. The beginnings of the idea that educational institutions can solve the problems of society can be seen in this early reform movement. From the early nineteenth century to present times, the school continually has been called on to solve the problems of poverty and crime.

The charity school movement is important because it was the first major attempt to use the school as a means of socializing children into an industrious way of life. Common school reformers of the 1830s and 1840s would use the same arguments as did charity schools for the ameliorating power of education. In addition, in some places charity schools provided the basic institutional structure for the development of common schools.

In general, charity schools and juvenile reformatories in the early nineteenth century sought to create good moral character by replacing a weak family structure and by destroying criminal associations. An individual, it was believed, became a potential criminal when the family failed to provide adequate moral training and eventually was led astray through contact with a criminal community.

For instance, the failure of the family structure is emphasized in the petition for incorporation in 1805 of the organization that became the major promoter of the Lancasterian system—the New York Free School Society. The incorporation statement declares that the condition of the children of the poor "is deplorable indeed; reared up by parents who . . . are become either indifferent to the best interests of their offspring, or, through intemperate lives, are rendered unable to defray the expense of their instruction." The petition goes on to argue that the neglect of education had resulted in "ignorance and vice, and all those manifold evils resulting from every species of immorality."[5] This society, which was organized to provide education for the poor, within a short time dominated charity schooling in New York City. By the 1840s, the schools of the New York Free School Society came under public control and became the core of the early system of public schools in New York City.

Like those involved with charity schools, reformers involved with juvenile reformatories linked waywardness with the failure of the family. The first reformatories, called houses of refuge, were founded in New York in 1824, in Boston in 1826, and in Philadelphia in 1828. The organization responsible for opening the New York House of Refuge was the New York Society for the Prevention of Pauperism, founded in

1815. This organization changed its name in 1823 to the Society for the Reformation of Juvenile Delinquents. Its report for 1822 states that children became wayward because no "moral standard of conduct has been placed before their eyes. No faithful parent has watched over them and restrained their vicious propensities."[6]

Arguing in the same manner, the Boston House of Refuge went so far as to advocate the use of their institution by any child who was considered to have an improper family life. Its report to the city of Boston in 1829 argues that to avoid the evils arising from the neglect of family government, the city's laws should be extended so that any "parents, or guardians, or friends of children, who are unable to exercise any moral government, might place them in this institution."[7]

Thus, the purpose of charity schools and reformatories was to correct the problems caused by the failure of parental government. In addition, they were to keep children and youth from exposure to immoral education by isolating them from criminal contacts. Members of the New York Free School Society believed that criminal associations were one of the major problems of raising children in a city. De Witt Clinton, president of the New York Free School Society, issued this warning in 1809: "Great cities are, at all times the nurseries and hotbeds of crimes . . . . And the dreadful examples of vice which are presented to youth, and the alluring forms in which it is arrayed . . . cannot fail of augmenting the mass of moral depravity."[8]

The preceding arguments provided the rationale for the charity schools. In essence, they were supposed to eliminate crime and poverty by replacing the failed government of the family with the government of the school and by keeping the children off the streets and out of contact with potential criminal associates. The argument that an important function of schooling is to keep children off the streets continued into the twentieth century.

Reformers involved in charity schools and juvenile reformatories believed the solution for crime and poverty to be education and provision of the proper institutional environment: Education was supposed to provide the tools by which an individual could function in a social role, and the institutional environment was supposed to teach an individual how to use these tools in a moral manner.

The charity school movement spread rapidly in the 1790s and the early 1800s. These schools, which provided the basic framework for the later development of public schools, were mainly organized by private associations such as the New York Free School Society. The existence of charity schools created a division between social classes—the poor attended charity schools and the more well-off attended other private and public institutions.

Although the stated intention of charity schools was to save the children of the poor from a life of crime and poverty, their creation also had important effects on existing private schools and, later, on the development of public schools. The best history of the early effects of the development of charity schools is Carl Kaestle's *Evolution of an Urban School System: New York City, 1750–1850*. Kaestle examined the registers of the private schools in New York City in the 1790s and found that they were not exclusive or limited to the education of the children of the wealthy. In fact, he argues, the private schools were common in several respects. First, they were the most common or prevalent system of education. Second, they all provided what was called a common system of education. And third, they were attended in common by children from a wide range of families with differing incomes and occupations.[9]

As Kaestle indicates, this last point is most important because school reformers at a later time would argue for the necessity of common public schools as a means of mixing the children of the rich and poor in the same classroom, in order to eliminate social-class divisions in education: "This third fact is the most important, for it is this sense of the word that was central to the ideology of the 'common school' reformers of the nineteenth century. The data . . . suggest that their reform, whether they knew it or not, was an attempt to restore the social mixing that had existed, at least in New York, before the creation of the free schools."[10] Private schools were attended by a variety of children from different social classes because a practice existed of adjusting tuition according to the income of the parents. Furthermore, Kaestle found little difference between the percentage of children annually attending school in the 1790s and the percentage attending free public schools in the mid-1800s.

Kaestle also found that attempts in the 1790s to systematize the private schools in New York City failed and that these schools were unable to accommodate the influx of immigrants, particularly from Ireland and France. The result was that private schools in the early nineteenth century became, in Kaestle's words, "restricted more and more to the wealthy minority. Meanwhile, the city's public school system arose from the charity schools, which had played a traditional but numerically slight role in the colonial period."[11]

In addition to laying the foundation for later public schooling, charity schools provided the first organized educational opportunities for the increasing number of freed slaves settling in the North. Kaestle details these developments in *Pillars of the Republic*. He states that a school for freed blacks was opened in Philadelphia in 1770, in New York in 1787, and in Baltimore in 1792.[12]

The Lancasterian system, introduced into charity schools in the United States and England in the early nineteenth century, was revolutionary in its emphasis on the process of schooling as a means of developing moral character. It was considered ideally suited for charity schools because it was inexpensive and provided training in character development.

The New York Free School Society was mainly responsible for introducing and spreading the fame of the Lancasterian system in the United States. Most of De Witt Clinton's dedicatory speech for the new Free School Society building in 1809 was devoted to praising the new instructional system. He was so enraptured with its potential that he stated, "I consider his [Joseph Lancaster's] system as creating a new era in education, as a blessing sent down from heaven to redeem the poor."[13] The system spread rapidly throughout the country, and its adoption was not limited to charity schools. Ellwood Cubberley found the system in use in the early nineteenth century from Massachusetts to Georgia and as far west as Detroit, Cincinnati, and Louisville. In 1822, the Pennsylvania state legislature, in an act reorganizing the Second School District, required the use of the Lancasterian system.[14]

The popularity of the system in the United States eventually caused its English developer, Joseph Lancaster, to make his home here. He died in 1838 when he was run over by a horse and carriage after inspecting a New York Lancasterian school. At the time of his death, he had plans to push his system to a new height of educational efficiency. He had contracted with the New York Society to run an experiment in which a system of instruction would be used that was supposed to teach 40 children to read and spell accurately in four to six weeks.

Claims were made that civilization owed Joseph Lancaster a debt for coining the pregnant mottoes "A place for everything and everything in its place" and "Let every child at every moment have something to do and a motive for doing it."[15] These were the mottoes of a system designed to handle large numbers of pupils in an efficient and inexpensive manner. The system supposedly could handle as many as 1,000 students at a time. Under the Lancasterian system, pupils were seated in rows and received their instruction from monitors, who received their instruction from the master, who sat at the end of the room. Monitors were selected from among the better students in the class, and they wore badges indicating their rank.

The discipline and orderliness required by the Lancasterian system were meant to provide the moral training. An engraving of a Lancasterian schoolroom in Pennsylvania illustrates how the training in orderliness was inherent in the system of classroom management. This particular room was designed to accommodate 450 students. The teacher sits at the head of the room on a raised platform. Beneath and in front of the teacher are three rows of monitors' desks placed directly in front of the pupils' desks. The pupils' desks are divided into three sections, each of which is divided into two parts, and each section is in line with one of the rows of monitors' desks. Arrows on the engraving indicate that a group of pupils would march to the front of the room and stand around the monitors' desks, where they would receive instruction from the monitors. When they finished, they would march to the rear part of their particular section and recite or receive further instruction from another monitor. While this group was marching to the rear, another group would be marching up to the front to take their places around the monitors. When finished, these pupils would march to the rear, and the group in the rear would move forward to the second part of their section to receive instruction from yet another monitor. Because each of the three sections had a group in front, one in the rear, and one in the middle, working on different things, a total of nine different recitations could be carried on at one time.

Educators of the period made an analogy between the Lancasterian system and a factory. An unidentified French writer was quoted as saying, "It is a masterpiece which must produce a revolution in popular education . . . . It may be styled a manufactory of knowledge."[16] De Witt Clinton described it as "a system which is, in education, what the neat finished machines for abridging labor and expense are in the mechanic arts."[17] Undoubtedly, the greatest selling point of the system was its cheapness. It provided a system for educating poor children inexpensively. Those promoting the system also believed that it provided character training for the child.

A student's submission to this factory system of education was supposed to lead to a sense of orderliness and obedience. The periodic movement of pupils and materials required order and discipline. Each student had an assigned place in the educational machine, and the machine was kept oiled by a distribution of awards and punishments. Virtue was rewarded by a system of badges, the highest being the Order of Merit. Virtue and ability led to appointment to the rank of monitor. Lancaster developed a unique system of punishments. Children who talked frequently or were idle were punished by having a wooden log placed around their necks. Extreme offenders were placed in a sack or basket suspended from the roof of the school in full view of the rest of the pupils.

The constant activity, regimentation, and lock-step marching were supposed to indelibly imprint the virtues of orderliness and obedience on the student's mind. Clinton hailed Lancaster as the benefactor of the human race: "I contemplate the habits of order which it [the Lancasterian system] forms, the spirit of emulation which it excites, the rapid improvement which it produces, the purity of morals which it inculcates—when I behold the extraordinary union of celerity in instruction and economy of expense."[18]

The virtues of submission, order, and industriousness were considered necessary for functioning in the world of business. The Boston School Committee investigated the New York Lancasterian schools in 1828 and reported that the system kept students attentive and interested by permitting no moments of idleness. The committee praised the method and declared that "its effects on the habits, character, and intelligence of youth are highly beneficial; disposing their minds to industry, to readiness of attention, and to subordination, thereby creating in early life a love of order, preparation for business."[19]

The Lancasterian system was supposed to help the pauper child escape poverty and crime by imparting formal knowledge and by instilling the virtues needed in the world of work. Within this framework of reasoning, the qualities of submission, order, and industriousness made the child moral by making him or her useful to and functional in society. In addition, the very act of attending school kept the pupil off the streets and out of contact with the kind of learning believed to occur through contact with criminals.

Concern with the evil influence of the criminal community on the molding of human character was the basis for the establishment of houses of refuge for juvenile delinquents. At first, the New York Society for the Reformation of Juvenile Delinquents only wanted separate buildings within prisons for youthful offenders, but in 1824, after deciding this did not provide complete enough separation, it founded the New York House of Refuge.

Just as charity school reformers viewed cities as colleges of vice, promoters of juvenile reformatories viewed prisons as systems of criminal education. This attitude is clearly stated in the 1828 report of the New York House of Refuge, which called prisons "so many schools of vice . . . so may seminaries to impart lessons and maxims, calculated to banish legal restraints, moral consideration, pride of character, and self-regard."[20]

Like the charity schools, the juvenile reformatories sought to provide an institutional replacement for what was believed to be a failed family structure. The Lancasterian system was used in attempts to create an ideal family structure within the institutional setting of the reformatory. The ideal family government would separate the juvenile from evil and teach the habits of order and discipline. The Boston Prison Discipline Society's report in 1832 claims, "How much may parents, and all who have the care of youth, learn from the Houses of Refuge for Juvenile Delinquents." What could be learned, according to this report, was the morally rewarding effect on youth of "regular hours for solitude and sleep; regular hours for promoting cleanliness; regular hours for exercise and recreation; regular hours for obtaining knowledge human and divine; and regular hours for manual labor." The report goes on to state that the significance of the houses of refuge was their "unspeakably important lessons of instruction to the world, on these every day duties of parents and others."[21]

The houses of refuge emphasized regimentation and order. The New York House of Refuge instituted a rigorous schedule of Lancasterian instruction and labor. The first two hours of the morning were devoted to classroom instruction, followed by four hours of labor in workshops. Then came lunch and a "little time . . . [for] recreation." In the afternoon, four hours were devoted to labor. Then came supper, followed by two more hours of Lancasterian instruction. Religious exercises were given in the early morning and before retirement at night.[22]

Both the New York and the Philadelphia houses of refuge followed similar scheduling. In both systems, each child was placed in a separate cell at night. During the day, the children were not allowed to communicate while receiving instruction or performing work. Conversation was allowed only during free time.

In this manner, the juvenile offender was to be isolated from evil and trained in the habits of order, obedience, and industriousness. The 1833 annual report of the New York House of Refuge states that "obedience and industry are necessary to make good boys good men and useful citizens." The report goes on to hail its own success at being able "to implant principles of virtue and habits of industry, where the vilest and wickedest associations have pre-occupied the mind."[23] The education and training received by the inmates was intended to prepare them to fit into the social structure. Basic occupational skills were to be learned in the classrooms and workshops. The virtues instilled by the system were considered necessary in the world of work.

The development of charity schools, the Lancasterian system, and the houses of refuge reflected a growing faith in the power of schooling to solve the problems of society. They all contained within them, in varying degrees, institutional procedures that provided the individual with moral examples, habituated the student to moral conduct, and disassociated the pupil from evil influences. What is most important about these institutions is that they embodied the belief that education could end poverty and crime in society.

This belief in the ameliorating power of schooling became an essential part of the common school movement of the 1830s and 1840s. Charity schools provided a working model and, in some places, the basic institutional structure for the establishment of a common school system. In addition, they became a target of attack by some common school reformers who believed the existence of charity schools resulted in the separation of the children of the rich and the poor. This, it was believed, reenforced social-class differences. The hope of the common school was to overcome the problems of social class by mixing together all children in the same schoolhouse. A major result of this argument was the extension of the moral training provided in the charity schools to the children of all social classes.

The Quest for an Education

In studying attempts to use educational institutions for social reform, it is easy to lose sight of the fact that many people wanted an education for their own personal improvement and advancement. It would be easy to form the impression, from the previous discussion of charity schools, that one group of people was trying to impose its values on an unwilling population. That impression is difficult to prove or disprove because we lack information about the attitudes of parents who sent their children to those schools. Because there were no compulsory-education laws, one can assume a certain willingness to attend on the part of the students and parents.

The actions of one group—the free blacks living in the northern states—provide an example of people seeking the establishment of schools to meet their own personal needs. Their story also illustrates the early development of segregated schooling and demonstrates the lack of clear distinction between public and private schools in the early part of the nineteenth century.

The best historical account of early black schools in the North is given by Stanley Schultz in *The Culture Factory: Boston Public Schools, 1789–1860*.[24] Boston had organized the first comprehensive system of urban schools after the passage of the Massachusetts Education Act of 1789. This law required towns to provide elementary schools for six months of the year and grammar schools in communities with over 200 families. An important feature of this act is that it required the education of girls at public expense. The law allowed girls to go to school with boys and study the same subjects. Prior to this time, some girls received their education in private schools or at home and some received no education at all.

It was in the context of this newly developing urban educational system that blacks in Boston began their struggle for a quality education. According to Schultz, the black population in Boston in 1790 was 766, among a total population of 18,038. At the beginning of the nineteenth century, no law or tradition excluded black children from the public schools. Some did attend public schools and some attended private schools.[25]

According to Shultz, however, very few black children actually attended school. The low attendance rate, he argues, was a result of the poor economic conditions of the black population and the hostile reception given black children in the public schools. Partly as a result of prejudice in the existing public schools, in 1798 a group of black parents asked the city for a separate system of schools for their children. The Boston School Committee rejected this request, with the reasoning that if it provided separate schools for blacks, it would also need to provide separate schools for other ethnic groups. The black parents then requested and received financial help from white philanthropists and opened a school that survived for only a few months. In 1800, a group of 36 blacks again asked the Boston School Committee to establish a separate school for their children. Again, the answer was no. Two years later the black community opened another separate private school.[26]

Finally, Schultz reports, the School Committee accepted the idea of supporting a segregated school. A permanent black school was established in 1806 with funds from white philanthropists and the School Committee. In 1812, the School Committee voted permanent funds for the school and established direct control over it.[27]

The Boston School Committee's decision created a complex situation. First, the committee supported and controlled a segregated school, although no law in existence required segregation. In theory at least, black children were free to attend public schools other than the one established for them. Second, the black community supported the segregated school as an alternative to the prejudice existing in the other schools. And last, the school was supported by a combination of private and public monies. Private contributions to the school became a major factor when Abiel Smith died in 1815 and left the entire income from his shares in New England turnpikes and bridges and from United States bonds to be used for the support of black schools. The School Committee assumed trusteeship of the estate, which meant that it controlled the school and the majority of private funds supporting the school.[28]

By the 1820s, some people in the black community began to question their earlier request for segregated schools. One major problem was the quality of teachers hired by the School Committee for the black schools. Other complaints began to appear as well. In 1833, a subcommittee issued a report on the conditions of the schools. The major conclusion of this report was that black schools were inferior to other schools in the quality of education and the physical conditions of the schools. According to Schultz, the report argued that "a classroom better than a basement room in the African Church could be found. After all, Black parents paid taxes which helped to support white schools. They deserved a more equal return on their share of the city's income."[29]

The most important conclusion in the report was that segregated education was not benefitting either race. The School Committee did not deal with this repudiation of the original reasons for establishing segregated schools and concentrated instead on building a new school. However, this activity did not answer the concerns of the black community, which was beginning to believe that only integrated education would provide equal educational opportunity.

Concerns about the quality of education in segregated schools were heightened by the writings of a local black abolitionist, David Walker. Walker was born in North Carolina in 1789 of a free mother and a slave. According to North Carolina law, Walker was born free. He moved to Boston in the early 1820s and became a contributor to and local agent for the nation's first black newspaper, *Freedom's Journal*, published in New York.

According to Schultz, Walker argued in his writings that four principal factors were responsible for the poor situation of blacks in the nation. Slavery, the use of religion to justify slavery and prejudice, and the African colonization movement designed to send free blacks back to Africa were three of the factors. The fourth factor was education. Walker argued that white Americans were trying to keep black Americans from receiving any significant amount of education. As proof, he cited the laws in the South making it illegal to educate slaves. In the North, according to Walker, the inferior education blacks received in the schools was designed to keep them at a low level of education.

Most of the coloured people when they speak of the education of one among us who can write a neat hand, and who perhaps knows nothing but to scribble and puff pretty fair on a small scrap of paper, immaterial whether his words are grammatical, or spell correctly, or not; if it only looks beautiful, they say he has as good an education as any white man.[30]

After studying the conditions of the Boston schools, Walker reached the conclusion that segregated education in the city was a conspiracy by whites to keep blacks in a state of ignorance. Walker claimed that the School Committee forbade the teaching of grammar to black children. Although this was not true, Shultz does point out that black children did receive a poorer education than did white children and that the New Testament was the basic text used in black schools.

Walker's arguments added fuel to the fire. Demands by the black community for integrated education intensified, and for almost two decades more the black community struggled with the School Committee to end segregated education. Part of the issue was the loss of control of black schools by the black community. This was one of the problems causing the lines between public and private education to be unclear. Originally, the black community had sought segregated schools as an alternative to the prejudice black children experienced in existing schools and was able to exercise control over its early private educational endeavors. Over the years, however, the School Committee had gained complete control, so that any complaints the black community had about its schools had to be resolved by the committee. The black community might have found segregated schools satisfactory if it could have exercised control over its schools and if it had received the same financial support as the white community did for its schools.

In 1849, the protests over segregated schools finally reached the Massachusetts Supreme Judicial Court when Benjamin Roberts sued the city for excluding his five-year-old daughter from the schools. In this particular case, his daughter had to pass five white primary schools before reaching the black school, so Roberts tried to enroll her in one of the closer white schools. He lost the case on a decision by the court that the school system had provided equal schools for black children. This was one of the first separate-but-equal rulings in American judicial history.

The issue of segregation in Massachusetts schools was finally resolved in 1855, when the governor signed into law a requirement that no child be denied admission to a public school on the basis of race or religious opinions. In September of that year, the Boston public schools were integrated without any violent hostilities.

The story of black education in Boston illustrates the struggles by various groups in American society to gain a quality education. It is the other side of the picture from that of elite reformers trying to use education as a means of social control. The workingmen's parties (see Chapter 4) represented the same type of popular movement for an expansion of common schooling.

Institutional Change and the American College

Although the charity schools and houses of refuge served a different social strata than did the colleges, similar arguments were given in support of a traditional collegiate life. The *Yale Report of 1828*, regarded as the standard for the maintenance of colleges in the nineteenth century, argued that it was necessary for the residential college to provide a family form of control over students, and it used faculty psychology to defend a traditional liberal arts curriculum against pleas for more practical studies and electives.

In the early nineteenth century, American colleges were established at an incredible rate in response to denominational rivalries, local boosterism, and public demand. Concerns about the nature of the college curriculum and the differences between public and private institutions were sparked by this growth. The resolution of these institutional issues was to have an important effect on the history of the college in the nineteenth century.

Nine colleges had been established in the colonies prior to the Revolutionary War. Between the Revolutionary War and the Civil War, approximately 250 colleges were established, and 182 of these survived into the twentieth century. The growth of the American college was highlighted in a striking comparison made in 1880 between American and British institutions of higher learning. It pointed out that England had 4 universities to serve a population of 23 million, and Ohio had 37 institutions of higher learning to serve a population of 3 million.[31]

The rapid expansion of American colleges created many institutional problems. A major issue was the nature of the college curriculum. Public demand for higher education placed pressure on colleges in the early part of the nineteenth century to achieve a balance between what Benjamin Franklin had referred to as the useful and the ornamental in learning. The traditional classical curriculum of Latin and Greek was still considered an ideal for the education of gentlemen. On the other hand, the study of science and modern languages, along with a demand for education in practical subjects, created conflict over the nature of the college curriculum.

The increased number of institutions of higher education led to an inevitable problem of separating public and private control. Colonial colleges developed during a period when few distinctions were made between public and private schools. Public and private financing combined with public and private control to blur the status of colleges in relationship to government. This issue was finally resolved in *Dartmouth College v. Woodward* (1819), which affected not only the later history of colleges but also the development of American corporations.

The curriculum issues faced by colleges in the early nineteenth century reflected a general concern about the role of higher education in society and the proper education of the individual. As discussed in Chapter 1, higher education during the early colonial period was primarily concerned with the education of ministers and public leaders. The classical curriculum of Latin and Greek was considered appropriate to serve these two social functions. Latin was the traditional education for the ministry, and the study of Greek was part of the Renaissance ideal for the education of the gentleman ruler.

During their early years, all the colonial colleges reflected these social goals and educational ideals. This was certainly true for the early years of Harvard, as discussed in Chapter 1, and was true also for the College of William and Mary, established by royal charter in 1693 in Virginia to assure a steady supply of Anglican clergymen. Yale and Princeton were established to serve religious purposes, but in a spirit of denominational rivalry. Yale was established in 1701, in reaction to what was believed to be the more liberal theological orientation of Harvard. In 1746, Princeton was established through support given by one branch of the Presbyterian church that had been affected by the religious Great Awakening of the eighteenth century. Baptists established the College of Rhode Island (Brown University) in 1764; the Dutch Reformed church established

Queen's College (Rutgers University) in 1766; the Congregationalists founded Dartmouth in 1769; and King George III appealed for funds for the founding of what would later become the University of Pennsylvania and Columbia University.

The curriculum of colonial colleges did not remain static. Both science and the emphasis of the Enlightenment on reason found their way into the curriculum under the general label of natural philosophy. The works of Locke and Newton and Copernican theory began to appear in the readings at Yale in the eighteenth century. In 1734, Yale imported a telescope, a microscope, and a barometer. The growth in the influence of science is reflected in the curriculum changes made at Yale: In 1726, mathematics was required only in the fourth year, but by 1745 arithmetic was made an entrance requirement, and mathematics was required in the second, third, and fourth years. At King's College (Columbia University) in New York, an attempt was made in 1754 to introduce a course of study in navigation, surveying, geography, and natural history that would teach "the knowledge . . . of every Thing useful for the Comfort, the Convenience and Elegance of Life . . . and everything that can contribute to . . . true Happiness."[32] These are only a few examples of the changes that began to take place in the college curriculum of the eighteenth century.

Richard Hofstadter argues in *Academic Freedom in the Age of the College* that the college boom in the early nineteenth century caused a major regression in the progress of the college curriculum and academic freedom. As discussed in Chapter 1 in regard to the development of academies, freedom of thought was considered an essential element in the development of science and the progress of society. Hofstadter writes, "During the last three or four decades of the eighteenth century the American colleges had achieved a notable degree of freedom, vitality, and public usefulness and seemed to have set their feet firmly on the path to further progress."[33]

On the other hand, he describes the opening decades of the nineteenth century as the great retrogression in collegiate education and academic freedom. Hofstadter argues that this retrogression occurred because colleges came to serve narrow religious interests. In the eighteenth century, the small number of colleges in existence had begun to move away from serving narrow sectarian interests, but the multiplication of colleges in the nineteenth century primarily reflected particular denominational concerns. Added to these religious concerns was local boosterism, which resulted, according to Hofstadter, in an intense denominational rivalry "to supply every locality with a cheap and indigenous institution that would make it possible for local boys who desired degrees to get them easily."[34]

In addition to the problems caused by the creation of a large number of colleges serving narrow sectarian interests, there was the problem of quality. Many of these institutions employed a limited number of faculty members, who were required to teach a maximum number of courses. Quality declined as, for example, the teaching of the classics was reduced to the teaching of grammar, so that the culture of antiquity was no longer conveyed.

Colleges started in the spirit of local boosterism often made little attempt to plan academic quality. Historian Frederick Rudolph describes the college-building mania: "Often when a college had a building, it had no students. If it had students, frequently it had no building. If it had either, then perhaps it had no money, perhaps no professors; if professors, then no president, if a president, then no professors." Rudolph portrays college building during this period as an activity that was undertaken with the same zeal as "canal-building, cotton-ginning, farming, and gold-mining."[35]

In the midst of the college boom, a search for a guiding standard was in progress. For many colleges, this standard came in the form of the *Yale Report of 1828,* which used faculty psychology to defend a traditional curriculum. In part, the *Yale Report* was a reaction to other proposed reforms in the college curriculum. Theodore Crane writes: "For decades after 1828 the Yale Report sustained traditionalists. Its assumptions seemed to reflect a realistic appraisal of the role played by American colleges and of the expectations of the public."[36] Rudolph argues that the *Yale Report* satisfied the established elites because it withstood demands for reforms that would have given American colleges a more practical and popular curriculum: "The religious, the very pious, the privileged—were the people who ran the colleges, people who also knew that the American college was running on a shoestring and that the old course of study, while the best, was also the cheapest."[37]

The *Yale Report,* like the charity schools and other reforms of the period, placed a great deal of importance on maintaining a family structure within an institutional setting. In defining the appropriate goal of a college, the report states its goal is "to LAY THE FOUNDATION of a SUPERIOR EDUCATION: and this is to be done, at a period of life when a substitute must be provided for *parental superintendence.*" The report argues that students, when removed from the family, need to be protected against "untried scenes of temptation," and this protection would result from providing a substitute for parental control. These regulations "should approach as near to the character of parental control as the circumstances of the case will admit."[38]

To achieve this form of parental control, the report argues strongly for the necessity of a residential college: "The parental character of college government, requires that the students should be so collected together, as to constitute one family; that the intercourse between them and their instructors may be frequent and familiar."[39] To accomplish this objective, the report calls for the establishment of residence halls on college campuses.

Discussion took place during this period about the need to arrange the institutional environment of residence halls at colleges and academies. For example, in 1829 the Boston Prison Discipline Society gave full support to the dormitory plans of an unnamed "important school in Massachusetts." These plans called for three stories of galleries along which individual rooms would face a large open space in the middle. Each room was to have a glass window. The master of the school could stand in the middle of the building and observe all the rooms. In this building, the society reported, the student would have time to read and reflect in his own room, and, more important, "the idle, profane and vicious youth is effectually prevented from corrupting his fellows, during those hours of darkness, in which there is the greatest danger."[40]

Within the residential environment of college life, students were to develop an intellectual culture—referred to in the *Yale Report* as "the *discipline* and the *furniture* of the mind"—through the study of a general curriculum. The *Yale Report* rejects the idea of college's providing practical and professional studies.

> *The great object of a collegiate education, preparatory to the study of a profession, is to give that expansion and balance of the mental powers, those liberal comprehensive views, and those fine proportions of character, which are not to be found in him whose ideas are always confined to one particular channel.*[41]

Within the framework of the preceding statement, collegiate education was to provide a general background of knowledge and an exercise of mental powers so that the individual would be able to participate in a wide range of intellectual activities. In the words of the report, "Wherever he [the college graduate] goes, into whatever company he falls, he has those general views, on every topic of interest, which will enable him to understand, to digest, and to form a correct opinion, on the statements and discussions he hears."[42]

In addition to knowledge, a collegiate education was supposed to provide a balanced exercise of the different mental faculties. The *Yale Report* uses faculty psychology to explain the processes involved in achieving the goal of balanced mental training: "In laying the foundation of a thorough education, it is necessary that all the important mental faculties be brought into exercise." The report goes on to argue that if exercising any particular mental faculty were neglected, the mind would not reach full perfection. Full perfection was to be achieved through bringing each mental faculty to "the fair proportions which nature designed."[43]

The reasoning used in the report was that balanced mental faculties would result in a balanced character. The general studies offered by the college were to provide the exercise necessary for achieving a balance of mental faculties and character. As stated in the report, "In the course of instruction in this college, it has been an object to maintain such proportion between the different branches of literature and science, as to form in the student a proper balance of character."[44] Each subject-matter area would contribute to the exercise of a different part of the mind. For instance, the report claims that mathematics would teach demonstrative reasoning, physical sciences would teach inductive reasoning, ancient literature would provide finished models of taste, English reading would teach speaking and writing, philosophy would teach thinking, and rhetoric and oratory would teach the art of speaking.

The *Yale Report* has often been viewed as a conservative response to reforms proposed during the 1820s for electives and specialization in the college curriculum. Its attraction might have been the promise it offered of providing a general education that would confirm or confer social status. Implicit in the idea of education to develop the balanced character that could fit into any intellectual conversation and gathering was the assumption of easy movement between social classes. Receiving a general collegiate education might not have guaranteed access to any particular occupation, but it did promise to inculcate the culture and manners that might be useful in achieving any social advancement.

The *Yale Report* did seem to reflect general sentiments about the type of education required for the development of moral character. Similar arguments for parental government and for the training of mental faculties could be found in the charity school movement: Charity schools sought moral development through classroom management and instruction that replicated family government and exercised mental faculties, whereas the *Yale Report* sought to use residential colleges and a general curriculum to achieve a similar purpose. The differences, of course, were that charity schools wanted to uplift the children of the poor from a life of poverty and crime, and the colleges wanted to confer or confirm a social status. In either case, however, education was being used to shape the moral character of the individual for social purposes.

The *Yale Report* is important because it set the tone for collegiate education in the nineteenth century. The importance of the *Dartmouth College* case of 1819 lies in the fact that it began to define the lines between private and public education. In the seventeenth and eighteenth centuries, colleges, academies, reading and writing schools, and grammar schools were often established with little concern for distinctions between public and private education. As mentioned previously, most of these institutions received a combination of public and private money and were governed through a mixture of public and private control. Even a charity school organization—the New York Free School Society—received both public and private monies and was controlled by a private board of trustees, and eventually the schools established by this society came under complete public control.

The *Dartmouth College* case was the result of a dispute between Dartmouth president John Wheelock (son of Dartmouth's founder, Eleazor Wheelock) and an absentee board of trustees. To protect his power against the board of trustees, John Wheelock asked the New Hampshire state legislature to investigate the college. The board of trustees fired Wheelock, who immediately won support of the state Republican party. The Republican governor charged the board of trustees with being a self-perpetuating group of aristocrats and worked with the state legislature to pass a bill that would change the name of the institution from Dartmouth College to Dartmouth University and, more important, bring the institution under state control.

The board of trustees immediately went to the Superior Court of New Hampshire to contest the state's action. Part of the state of New Hampshire's case rested on the fact that it had originally chartered the college. The question that quickly emerged in this case was whether Dartmouth was a public or a private corporation. On November 6, 1817, the superior court ruled that Dartmouth was a public corporation and was subject to legislative control. On March 10, 1819, the case was heard before the United States Supreme Court.

The lawyer for the board of trustees was Dartmouth graduate Daniel Webster (class of 1801), who argued his case for five continuous hours. His eloquence, it was reported, brought Chief Justice John Marshall to tears. Webster presented his case in the form of an argument that asked, "Shall our state legislature be allowed to take that which is not their own, to turn it from its original use, and apply it to such ends or purposes as they, in their discretion shall see fit?"[45] Embodied in this question is the fundamental issue of the extent to which government power should be allowed to operate in the management of institutions. This question reaches beyond a consideration of educational institutions alone to encompass all institutions, including corporations.

Certainly in colonial times there would have been little debate about the right of government to intervene in the affairs of institutions serving the public. Society was viewed as an integrated whole in which government had the responsibility to assure correct actions by all its parts. However, the early nineteenth century was still influenced by the Revolutionary War, which had sought to limit the power of government, and by a rising capitalistic ideology that sought to eliminate all government involvement in the economic system. In fact, the major conflicts about expansion of the common school system in the 1830s and 1840s centered on the political issue of the extent to which government should be involved in the educational system. The significance of the *Dartmouth College* case was in delineating the lines between government control and private institutions.

Webster's famous statement before the Supreme Court—"It is, sir, as I have said, a small college, and yet there are those that love it"—may have influenced the Court's decision in favor of the board of trustees. The Supreme Court ruled that the charter granted by the New Hampshire legislature was a contract protected by the federal Constitution against alteration by the state.

The decision, written by Chief Justice Marshall, made a sharp distinction between private and public educational institutions. Recognition was given to the importance of education as a national concern and to the notion that this concern could be reflected in "an institution founded by government, and placed entirely under its immediate control, the officers of which would be public officers, amenable exclusively to government."[46] But, the argument continued, did this mean that all education should be entirely in the hands of government and every teacher a public employee? Did it mean that all donations for education became public property?

The Court's response to these questions was given in the form of a description of a corporation. Marshall's decision described a corporation chartered by a state as having immortality and individuality. These properties, given to a perpetual succession of persons or boards of trustees that acted as a single person, allowed a corporation to hold property and manage its own affairs. "It is chiefly for the purpose of clothing bodies of men, in succession," Marshall wrote, "with these qualities and capacities, that corporations were invented, and are in use."[47] Furthermore, the chief justice argued, a corporation did not participate in civil government unless that was the reason for its creation.

Therefore, according to the Court's decision, a corporation "is no more a state instrument than a natural person exercising the same powers would be."[48] This meant that a college chartered by the state had the same rights against government interference as did an individual. It also meant that if a state wished to promote education to serve its own purposes, it would need to create its own institutions and hire its own faculty. The same argument, of course, would apply to institutions for elementary and secondary education. Thus a sharp distinction was drawn between private and public institutions as a result of the *Dartmouth College* case, and a precedent was set that privately created educational institutions could not be forced to serve the purposes of government; this could be done only through institutions owned and operated by the government. Although court decisions in the twentieth century would allow for state regulation of private schools, the *Dartmouth College* case clearly drew the line between private and public schooling.

The college boom of the early nineteenth century was characterized by an emphasis on shaping individual character through a system of private, residential colleges. In the mid-nineteenth century, reform movements began to expand public colleges to serve public purposes. The most important factor in this reform movement was the Morrill Federal Land Grant Act of 1862.

Conclusion

The expansion of urban charity schools, the developing faith that education can solve social problems, the increased desire among different parts of the population for public schools, and the growing distinctions between private and public colleges set the stage for the common school movement of the 1830s and 1840s. A variety of historical interpretations of the common school movement have been offered. The differences in interpretations reflect the tension between the desire of elite social reformers to create schools that would reform the population and the quest of common people for increased schooling. This tension, which is seen in this chapter in the differences between the organizers of charity schools and the educational desires of the black population of Boston, is an important theme in the history of schooling in the nineteenth and twentieth centuries.

Notes

1. Benjamin Rush, "The Influence of Physical Causes upon the Moral Faculty," in Dagobert D. Runes, ed., *Selected Writings of Benjamin Rush* (New York: Philosophical Library, 1947), p. 186.

2. Horace Mann, "Twelfth Annual Report," in Lawrence Cremin, ed., *The Republic and the School: Horace Mann on the Education of Free Men* (New York: Teachers College Press, 1957), p. 92.

3. Rush, "Influence of Physical Causes," in Runes, *Selected Writings*, pp. 198–202.

4. "The Yale Report (1828)," in Theodore Crane, ed., *The Colleges and the Public, 1787–1862* (New York: Teachers College Press, 1963), p. 86.

5. "Incorporation Statement of the New York Free School Society," reprinted in William O. Bourne, *History of the Public School Society of the City of New York* (New York: Wood, 1870), p. 3.

6. "1822 Report of the New York Society for the Prevention of Pauperism," in *Report of the Prison Discipline Society, Boston, 1828* (Boston: Press of T. R. Marvin, 1855), p. 174.

7. "1829 Boston House of Refuge Report to the City of Boston," in *Report of the Prison Discipline Society, Boston, 1829* (Boston: Press of T. R. Marvin, 1855), p. 246.

8. Quoted in Bourne, *History of the Public School Society*, p. 17.

9. Carl F. Kaestle, *The Evolution of an Urban School System: New York City, 1750–1850* (Cambridge, Mass.: Harvard University Press, 1973).

10. Ibid., p. 42.

11. Ibid., p. 187.

12. Carl F. Kaestle, *Pillars of the Republic: Common Schools and American Society, 1780–1860* (New York: Hill and Wang, 1983).

13. Quoted in Bourne, *History of the Public School Society*, p. 19.
14. Ellwood Cubberley, *Public Education in the United States: A Study and Interpretation of American Educational History* (Boston: Houghton Mifflin, 1934), p. 129.
15. David Salmon, *Joseph Lancaster* (London: McKay, 1904), p. 9.
16. Quoted in George H. Martin, *The Evolution of the Massachusetts Public School System* (Englewood Cliffs, N.J.: Prentice-Hall, 1901), p. 138.
17. Quoted in Bourne, *History of the Public School Society*, p. 18.
18. Ibid., p. 19.
19. "Report on Monitorial Instruction to the Boston School Committee; Boston, 1828," in Ellwood Cubberley, ed., *Readings in Public Education in the United States: A Collection of Sources and Readings to Illustrate the History of Educational Practice and Progress in the United States* (Cambridge, Mass.: Riverside Press, 1934), p. 137.
20. "1828 Report of the New York House of Refuge," in *Report of the Prison Discipline Society, Boston, 1828*, p. 174.
21. *Report of the Prison Discipline Society, Boston, 1832* (Boston: Press of T. R. Marvin, 1855), p. 570.
22. Ibid.
23. "1833 Report of the New York House of Refuge," in *Report of the Prison Discipline Society, Boston, 1833* (Boston: Press of T. R. Marvin, 1855), p. 694.
24. Stanley Schultz, *The Culture Factory: Boston Public Schools, 1789–1860* (New York: Oxford University Press, 1973).
25. Ibid.
26. Ibid.
27. Ibid.
28. Ibid.
29. Ibid., p. 169.
30. Quoted in Ibid., p. 173.
31. Frederick Rudolph, *The American College and University* (New York: Knopf, 1962), pp. 48–49.
32. Quoted in Ibid., pp. 31–32.
33. Richard Hofstadter, *Academic Freedom in the Age of the College* (New York: Columbia University Press, 1955), p. 209.
34. Ibid., p. 214.
35. Rudolph, *American College*, pp. 47–48.
36. Crane, *Colleges and the Public*, pp. 17–18.
37. Rudolph, *American College*, p. 135.
38. "Yale Report (1828)," in Crane, *Colleges and the Public*, p. 88.
39. Ibid.
40. *Report of the Prison Discipline Society, Boston, 1829*, p. 290.
41. "Yale Report (1828)," in Crane, *Colleges and the Public*, p. 90.
42. Ibid., p. 89.
43. Ibid., p. 86.
44. Ibid.
45. Quoted in Rudolph, *American College*, p. 209.
46. *Dartmouth College v. Woodward* (1819), quoted in Crane, *Colleges and the Public*, p. 70.
47. Ibid., p. 71.
48. Ibid.

4

The Ideology and Politics of the Common School

The 1830s and 1840s are known in educational history as the decades of the common school movement in the United States. It was during this historical period that the modern American school system began to take form. Obviously, schools and public school systems existed in the United States before the 1830s. What was different about the common school movement was the establishment and standardization of state systems of education designed to achieve specific public policies.

Historians have offered various interpretations of the common school period. No other period in American educational history has stimulated as extensive a debate about its meaning and goals. In part, this debate reflects the importance of the common school movement in understanding the American educational system. This chapter begins with a discussion of the various social and political groups that supported the common school movement, including the full-time educational reformers who devoted their lives to the common school ideal. Political, economic, and religious groups that opposed the establishment of the common school are considered next. Last, the meaning of the common school movement for the later development of the American school is explored.

Before the common school period, a variety of public and private school organizations existed. Massachusetts had laws requiring the provision of education and, as discussed in Chapter 3, had established the first system of urban education in Boston in the 1790s. On the other hand, many states, like New York and Pennsylvania, supported charity schools while a majority of children in those states attended private schools. Newer states had passed laws allowing for the development of schools but had not actively created organized systems of education. For instance, Ohio, after its admission to the Union in 1802, passed legislation in 1806 and 1816 allowing for the organization of schools supported by rents from lands and tuition. Beginning in 1821, Ohio law permitted the taxation of all property in a district for the support of schools. The state created a permanent school fund in 1827.

Although all these actions provided some support for education, they did not approximate the very distinctive features of the common school movement. Probably the most important difference between the common school movement and previous educational developments in the United States was the concept underlying the common school movement of a school under state control teaching a common body of knowledge to students from different social backgrounds. This concept of schooling was to serve distinct social and political goals.

Three distinctive aspects of the common school movement made it different from past educational developments. The first was an emphasis on educating all children in a common schoolhouse. It was argued that if children from a variety of religious, social-class, and ethnic backgrounds were educated in common, there would be a decline in hostility and friction between social groups. In addition, if children educated in common were taught a common social and political ideology, a decrease in political conflict and social problems would result. Obviously, this aspect of the common school movement can be traced to educational advocates in the late eighteenth and early nineteenth centuries who wanted to teach nationalism as a means of promoting national unity and to those supporters of charity schools who wanted to use education as a means of eliminating poverty and crime. The idea of using education to solve social problems and build a political community became an essential concept in the common school movement. The term *common school* came to have a specific meaning: a school that was attended in common by all children and where a common political and social ideology was taught.

The second important aspect of the common school movement was the idea of using schools as an instrument of government policies. Certainly, this aspect of education had existed in the past. Colonial schools had been maintained to train a population that would understand and obey secular and religious laws. Writers after the Revolution had advocated systems of schools to provide leaders and a responsible citizenry. What was different about the common school movement was the acceptance of the idea of a direct linkage between government educational policies and the solving and control of social, economic, and political problems. Within this concept, the common school was to be a panacea for society's problems.

The third distinctive feature of the common school movement was the creation of state agencies to control local schools. In part, this was necessary if schools were to carry out government social, political, and economic policies. In the past, states, like Massachusetts, had passed laws requiring the establishment of schools in local communities or, like New

York and Pennsylvania, had established state school funds for charity schools. In these situations, an official position had not been established to oversee the state educational system. In 1812, New York was the first American state to create the position of state superintendent of schools. In the 1820s, some other states followed New York's lead and created the office of state superintendent of education. But it was during the 1830s that state supervision and organization of schools became a major educational reform. In part, this was the work of the "father of the common school," Horace Mann, who became the first secretary of the Massachusetts Board of Education in 1837.

These three distinct features of the common school movement do not constitute a revolution against previous ideas about schooling, but they do represent ideas that were gaining increasing currency in the early nineteenth century. Probably the most important of these ideas was the belief that human nature can be formed, shaped, and given direction by training within formally organized institutions. This thinking was embodied in faculty psychology and in the charity schools. It was a logical step for common school reformers to apply this reasoning to the entire society and to argue that government-operated schools could create the perfect society. Also, various social groups, such as the black community discussed in Chapter 3, began to believe that schooling could be a means for economic and social improvement. They began to demand common schools, but often for reasons quite different from those given by full-time common school reformers. Although these differences existed within the common school movement, the final outcome of its reforms was the beginning of the modern American school system.

Varieties of Historical Interpretation

The different historical interpretations of the common school era reflect the more general debate about the role of education in American society. On the one hand, there are those who see the common school period as a battle between liberals and conservatives for the establishment of a school system that would be of great benefit to all members of society. On the other hand, some historians argue that common schools were established to protect privileged economic and religious positions in society. These broad differences in historical interpretation contain elements of the debate that continues to this day about whose interests are served by the public schools. Therefore, understanding the differences in historical interpretation of the common school period is important for understanding both common school reforms and current debates about schooling.

The first major educational historian to portray the common school movement as a battle between liberals and conservatives over extending the benefits of schooling to all people was Ellwood Cubberley in his text first published in 1919, *Public Education in the United States: A Study and Interpretation of American Educational History.* Cubberley describes liberals as good people who struggle for education for all people against avarice-minded conservatives. He wrote lists of characteristics and arguments that divided those in favor of from those opposed to the expansion of common schools. His divisions and descriptions reflect his bias in favor of the common school. For instance, supporters are described as citizens of the republic; opponents are described as belonging to an old aristocratic class. Philanthropists and humanitarians in favor of common schooling were put in opposition to conservatives. Cubberley indicates his real bias when he places "public men of large vision" in opposition to "politicans of small vision." In addition, he describes the differences between supporters and opponents, respectively, as city residents versus rural residents; intelligent workingmen versus the ignorant and narrow minded; nontaxpayers versus taxpayers; Calvinists versus Lutherans, Mennonites, and Quakers; and New Englanders versus southerners. (Cubberley's description is not correct in all cases; for example, Quakers were strong supporters of the common school.) Cubberley locates further opposition to the common school movement among owners of private schools and non–English-speaking groups.[1]

Each of these groups supported or opposed the common school for a variety of reasons. Again, Cubberley creates a list of these differing reasons, which reflects his own support of the common school movement. The arguments he lists as those given in support of the common school movement include prevention and reduction of poverty and crime; increased work force productivity; elimination of "wrong ideas as to the distribution of wealth"; reduction of tensions between social classes; elimination of charity schools because they stigmatized a certain class in society; assimilation of immigrants; and preparation of the citizenry for the exercise of the right to vote. Of course, these arguments not only supported the common school movement, but also became the traditional arguments for the support of public schooling in the United States.

Cubberley also lists arguments for the expansion of state control over education. In one sense, these arguments can be viewed as part of the continuing debate about the rights of parents versus the rights of the state over the education of children. In Cubberley's words, the major arguments were as follows: "That a State which has the right to hang has the right to educate"; that "the taking over of education by the State is not based on considerations of economy, but is the exercise of the State's inherent right to self-preservation and improvement"; and finally, as a reflection of the common school emphasis on education serving government policies, "that only a system of state-controlled schools can be free to teach whatever the welfare of the State may demand."[2] Cubberley's list of the arguments favoring state control of education describes the actual political divisions that occurred during the 1830s and 1840s over the degree of government intervention in social and economic issues.

He lists the following as arguments given in opposition to the expansion of state power: "That taxes would be so increased that no state could long meet such a lavish drain" and "that there was a priestcraft in the scheme, the purpose being first to establish a State School, and then a State Church." As discussed in more detail later in this chapter, Cubberley's list greatly oversimplifies the political debate about the extension of state control.[3]

Cubberley lists the arguments of those opposed to the social and economic reform arguments for the common school, which, according to his interpretations, centered around aristocratic ideas of social class: fear that common schools would destroy desirable social-class differences and educate people out of their proper place in society; fear that the industrious would be taxed to pay for the education of the indolent; fear that people without children would be forced to pay for the education of other peoples' children; fear that native language instruction of non–English-speaking students would supplant English-language instruction in the schools; concerns of religious groups that the common school would hinder their advancement; and fear that private schools would be forced to close.

In general, Cubberley's interpretation is one that depicts the common school movement as the correct historical route to the development of an educational system that would benefit the majority of people by solving economic, political, and social problems. This vision of the common school movement received added support in Merle Curti's *Social Ideas of American Educators*, first published in 1935. As mentioned previously, Curti's history of education was written during the Depression, when there was a great deal of concern over the historical struggle between the haves and the have-nots.

For Curti, the common school movement was a major democratic movement designed to extend social benefits to the lower social classes in society. His description of the period is given in large part in the two chapters devoted to Horace Mann and Henry Barnard respectively. He portrays Horace Mann as a great equalitarian and reformer. For Curti, Mann's primary motivation was a desire to assure that all classes of society had equal access to knowledge. Curti states that Mann's "social vision remained undimmed to the end, and all his work in the educational field was an effort to introduce into that field a more humane and democratic spirit."[4]

Curti is equally glowing in his tribute to Henry Barnard, who was secretary of the Connecticut Board of Education from 1839 to 1842 and was later editor of the *American Journal of Education*. Although Curti protrays Barnard as being more conservative than Mann, he still pays tribute to Barnard's career. Barnard, like Mann, is described as the educational reformer trying to democratize knowledge.

Unlike Cubberley, Curti is highly critical of the conservative economic and social ideas held by both Mann and Barnard, which puts a critical edge to Curti's praise of the common school movement. Criticism of the social and economic opinions of common school reformers became an important factor in the revision of educational history that occurred in the 1960s. The most dramatic revision came with the publication in 1968 of Michael Katz's *Irony of Early School Reform*, which deals with the decision in 1860 by Beverly, Massachusetts, voters to abolish their high school. In examining voting patterns, Katz found that working-class groups resisted the establishment of the high school, while the elite of the community worked actively for its creation.[5] A later analysis found that wealth and occupation correlated with voting patterns, but that neighborhood location was the more important determinant of voting. In this case, those who lived in areas outside of the town opposed the existence of a high school serving the entire township.[6]

Katz used his discovery of resistance to the establishment of a high school in Beverly as a vehicle for providing a new interpretation of common school reforms. In the opening statement of his introductory chapter, "Educational Reform: The Cloud of Sentiment and Historiography," he states: "For the most part historians have helped to perpetuate this essentially noble story, which portrays a rational, enlightened working class, led by idealistic and humanitarian intellectuals, triumphantly wresting free public education from . . . selfish, wealthy elite and from the bigoted proponents of orthodox religions."[7] This, of course, is the interpretation given to the period by Ellwood Cubberley.

But, Katz argues, one should immediately begin to question this historical interpretation when one considers that by the end of the nineteenth century most urban schools were "cold, rigid, and somewhat sterile bureaucracies." He goes on to ask: "Could a truly humanitarian urge to help realize widely diffused aspirations have turned so quickly into the dispassionate ethos of red tape and drill?"[8] In answering this question, Katz paints an entirely different picture of the evolution of the common school.

For Katz, the most important factors in explaining the common school movement are the social and economic changes associated with the building of factories, the increase in immigration, and the growth of cities. Within the context of these events, upper-class reformers were seeking to assure that they would benefit from these changes by imposing a common school system that would train workers for the new factories, educate immigrants into acceptance of values supportive of the ruling elite, and provide order and stability among the expanding populations of the cities.

From this perspective, the rigid and bureaucratic schools that Katz claims existed by the end of the nineteenth century were not accidental, but were the logical result of a school system designed to discipline a population to serve the needs of an urban and industrial society. The emphasis on attendance, disciplined study, and order was designed to socialize the student, particularly the immigrant child, to the requirements of the new factory systems. Learning to behave in school was preparation for learning to work in the factory. Also, Katz argues, the bureaucratic structure of education, which evolved from common school reforms, was designed to assure upper-class control of schooling. In his conclusion, Katz states that the common school movement was "a coalition of the social leaders, status-anxious parents, and status-hungry educators to impose educational innovation, each for their own reasons, upon a reluctant community."[9]

Katz's interpretation does not change the identity of the leaders of the common school movement, but it does change their motivations. According to Katz, their actions were not the result of disinterested humanitarian impulses but were caused by a desire to protect their social positions and to provide the new industrial system with disciplined workers.

What became the most controversial aspect of this interpretation is the argument that common school reforms were imposed on an unwilling working class–an argument that posed an important challenge to traditional ways of viewing American schools. This interpretation suggests that the vast majority of people in the nineteenth century did not want the type of organization of schooling that became standard in the nineteenth and twentieth centuries. It is important to understand that this attitude did *not* reflect a general opposition among the populace to education and schooling, but a rejection of common school reforms that sought to organize schools under central state control for the purposes of serving the social, political, and economic goals of government.

Katz's interpretation challenges not only Cubberley's benign view of the reformers but also interpretations that emphasize the importance of working-class support of the common school movement. Traditional labor history, beginning with the work of John R. Commons at the University of Wisconsin in 1918, stresses the key role of workingmen's parties in the late 1820s and 1830s in fighting for common school reforms. This interpretation places the American worker at the forefront of the battle for common schools. Of particular importance in this interpretation is the opposition of workers to the existence of charity schools, which they felt reinforced social-class distinctions. According to Commons's interpretation, members of the workingmen's parties supported the common school because it provided the children of the poor with equal educational opportunity by mixing the rich and poor. Equality of educational opportunity, it was believed, would provide the children of the poor and the working class with an equal opportunity to compete with the children of the more affluent classes.

Rush Welter emphasizes the role of workingmen's parties in *Popular Education and Democratic Thought in America* (1962), but his discussion minimizes their contribution to common school reform and stresses their contribution to later thinking about the democratic role of education. Welter, discussing the organized workingmen of the late 1820s and early 1830s, states, "Their numbers were few and their direct political influence was slight, but they first spelled out the educational perspective in which several generations of American democrats would see their society and their politics."[10]

A more complicated picture of common school reform emerges from Welter's interpretation of the workingmen's contribution to democratic educational theory: Although the workingmen's parties accepted the common school ideal of eliminating social-class distinctions and providing equality of opportunity, they also supported public schooling as a means of providing the working class with knowledge to protect itself against the interests and power of the privileged in society. This concept of political education in the common school, according to Welter, was different from the concept of education as a means of maintaining order in a free society. On the contrary, the workingmen's parties saw political education as a means of arming the working class against the authority and power of the upper class. In Welter's words, "In their [workingmen's] eyes political knowledge was useful, not because it supported the exercise of governmental authority, but because it provided an intellectual resource against authority."[11]

The importance of Welter's interpretation is his emphasis on the workingmen's support of school reform and his argument that the workingmen supported the common school for different reasons than did other members of society. Within this framework, the common school did not arise from a consensus of values about what the common school should accomplish but was a result of different social groups' each hoping that the common school would fulfill particular educational goals.

Katz's argument for imposition of common school reforms on an unwilling working class is in direct opposition to these traditional arguments. Interestingly, the major attack on Katz's thesis comes from radical Marxist historians who feel that his interpretation denies the role of the working class in progressive historical change. Marxist historian

Philip Foner led the attack in an article titled "The Role of Labor in the Struggle for Free Compulsory Education." For Foner, "the organized working class . . . was the driving force for universal compulsory and free public education."[12] Foner argues that the working class did not get the type of school system it wanted but that, from the time of the American Revolution, the working class was in the forefront of the struggle for public education.

Although recognizing the role of the workingmen's parties in the struggle for public education, historians have continued to emphasize the role of common schools in protecting the interests of certain groups in society. The scope of this interpretation was broadened in 1983 with the publication of Carl Kaestle's *Pillars of the Republic: Common Schools and American Society, 1780–1860*. Kaestle argues that the common school movement was primarily designed to protect the ideology of an American Protestant culture. Most of the common school reformers, he states, were native-born Anglo-American Protestants, and their public philosophy, "called for government action to provide schooling that would be more common, more equal, more dedicated to public policy, and therefore more effective in creating cultural and political values centering on Protestantism, republicanism, and capitalism."[13]

Kaestle identifies 10 major propositions as constituting the American Protestant culture the common school was designed to protect. These 10 propositions can be divided into 4 groups: The first group includes the belief in the fragility of the republican form of government, the importance of developing individual character to achieve social morality, and the role of personal effort in defining merit. This group of beliefs can be traced back to the early proponents of republican education, who believed that order could be maintained in a free republican society only through the education of responsible citizens. Kaestle argues that by the 1830s a certain confidence had developed that the experiment in republican government would survive, but there was still concern that actions had to be taken to assure its survival. In the common school movement, stress was placed on protecting the fragility of the republican form of government by providing a political education that taught a common set of political beliefs, emphasized the exercise of intelligence, and promoted a respect for laws. Or, as Kaestle states, the implication of native Protestant ideology was that "schooling should stress unity, obedience, restraint, self-sacrifice, and the careful exercise of intelligence."[14]

Also, as discussed in Chapter 3, the belief that social morality was achieved through improving the quality of individual morality was a central theme of the charity school movement. As part of Protestant ideology and the common school movement, Kaestle argues, it resulted in a belief that a good moral education would produce a moral society. In addition, this aspect of Protestant ideology stressed that poverty could be eliminated if the children of the poor were taught that they could advance in society through their own individual effort.

The second group of factors in Kaestle's discussion is the role of women in society and the importance of the family and social environment in building character. According to Kaestle, Protestant ideology defined three central roles for women in middle-class families: to provide a sanctuary for the hard-working husband, to intelligently manage the household, and to nurture children. Of crucial importance was the role of women in child rearing because this role involved education for the political and moral well-being of the nation. The arguments given for the importance of this social role for women provided a justification for recruiting women as teachers in common schools—an important aspect of common school reforms—because of their supposed skills in nurturing and developing morality. Another important factor, which will be discussed in more detail in Chapter 5, is the fact that women were cheaper to employ as teachers than men were.

As noted in Chapter 3, during this period emphasis was also placed on the importance of the environment and family on the development of individual character. This was an important theme in faculty psychology and in the establishment of charity schools and houses of refuge. The stress on the importance of the family structure reinforced the importance of the domestic role of women.

In the third group of themes characterizing Protestant ideology, Kaestle includes a belief in the virtue of property and the availability of economic opportunity in the United States. Both Protestant ideology and the common school ideology contain the belief, according to Kaestle, that "property was to be respected because it taught virtue. Everyone should be taught to desire property and to respect property."[15] Related to this belief was a vision of America as the land of economic opportunity: The availability of property and education would make it possible for all people to achieve economic success.

The last group of themes Kaestle identifies includes a belief in the superiority of American Protestant culture, in the manifest destiny of American society, and in the necessity of unifying America's population. In the context of these beliefs, American Protestants believed that their religious values were the central core of the American experiment with republicanism. As noted in Chapter 2, educational writers after the Revolutionary War, like Noah Webster, equated Protestant-Christian values with republican values. Kaestle argues that this same theme appears in the Protestant ideology associated with the common school movement. Kaestle also argues that the belief in the superiority of Protestantism combined with a belief in America's unique destiny to "suggest to Americans that their nation was destined to reach the peak of human civilization."[16] The assumption of the superiority of Protestantism logically led to the belief that all people should be united by being educated into a Protestant culture.

Kaestle's description of early nineteenth-century Protestant ideology, which will be elaborated later in this chapter, provides a good summary of the basic tenets of the common school movement of the 1830s and 1840s. From Kaestle's perspective, this ideology was shared by a majority of Americans. Of course, Catholics, an important group whose importance increased as their population increased in the United States, rejected many parts of this Protestant ideology. Catholics felt it necessary to organize their own private school system in the 1840s in opposition to the common school system.

These different interpretations highlight the complex factors involved in the common school movement. No single interpretation provides an adequate explanation. Rather, the common school appears to have been a result of a complicated set of often-conflicting social and economic factors that included a humanitarian impulse to create the good society; a desire by the working class to enhance its political and economic position in society; a desire by manufacturers to have a disciplined and well-trained work force; a desire of the upper classes to protect their economic and social privileges; and a desire to maintain an American Protestant culture.

These themes are explored in this chapter by examining the goals and ideology of the common school reformers, the activities of the working-men's parties, the actions of organized political parties and interest groups, and Catholic rejection of the common school.

The Ideology of the Common School Movement

The creation of a popular ideology and justification for the common school movement was mainly the work of a class of individuals who were able to devote the majority of their time to educational causes. These individuals occupied newly created government positions that gave them the time and authority to articulate the principles of the common school movement and conduct a campaign to spread the common school ideology. The most prominent of these individuals were Horace Mann and Henry Barnard.

For the purpose of understanding the basic ideology of these full-time common school reformers, this section concentrates on the life and ideas of Horace Mann. It is important to understand that the popularly stated common school ideology did not necessarily reflect the reality of the changes taking place in American education or reflect the positions held by all supporters of the common school. For instance, as mentioned briefly and as will be discussed in a later section of this chapter, the workingmen's parties supported the establishment of common schools for different reasons from those given in the more popular rhetoric of the common school movement.

What is important about the ideology of the common school movement, as stated by its major leaders, was that it established the basic framework, from the nineteenth century to the present, for popular and official discussions about the goals and purposes of public schooling in American life. Within these early arguments for common schools can be found most of the hopes and aspirations that many American people have had for the public schools. These early justifications for public schooling not only claimed that schools could solve the major social, economic, and political problems of society, but also argued that common schools were necessary for its very survival.

Two important mechanisms spreading the popular ideology of the common school were educational periodicals and newly created educational organizations. Between 1825 and 1850, over 60 periodicals devoted to education were established. The most important of these journals were the *Massachusetts Common School Journal*, edited by Horace Mann; the *Connecticut Common School Journal*, edited by Henry Barnard; and the *Ohio Common School Director*, edited by Samuel Lewis. As historian Sally Wertheim states:

> One of the purposes of the journals was to build support for the common school movement in communities where the proper climate for acceptance of the idea of universal education did not exist. The periodicals represented leading educational ideas of the times, as perceived by their editors and publishers, and provided a forum for these educational leaders to advance their philosophies about education.[17]

According to Lawrence Cremin, the most important organizations for spreading the ideals of the common school were the American Lyceum, organized in 1825; the Western Literary Institute and College of Professional Teachers, founded in 1829; and the American Institute of Instruction, established in 1830. For common school reformers, Cremin claims, these organizations were an important "means of enunciating and pressing their demands."[18] They held countless lectures, public discussions, and conventions at which common school advocates were able to spread their ideas.

In many ways, the spread of the common school ideology was a fascinating example of the diffusion of ideas. But, it should be remembered, the spread of new ideas required a public that was willing to accept them. In many ways, the public had been made ready for the acceptance of the basic ideas of the common school movement by the educational writers of the post-Revolutionary period, such as Noah Webster and Benjamin Rush, and by the arguments for social and moral reform made by the leaders of the charity school movement and the

Lancasterian system. In addition, the various types of faculty psychology made it possible for many Americans to believe in the common school as the panacea for the social, political, and economic problems of society.

Those who created and spread the ideology of the common school worked with as much fervor as leaders of religious crusades. And, in fact, there are striking parallels between the two types of campaigns. Both promised some form of salvation and moral reformation. In the case of the common school, the promise was the salvation of society.

In fact, the life and writings of Horace Mann can be characterized as a constant search for a means of social salvation. During his life he rejected Calvinism and adopted law as the means of social redemption, and after finding little hope in saving society through the establishment of proper laws, he turned to education. Mann was born in 1796 into a harsh Calvinistic environment in Franklin, Massachusetts. He claimed throughout his life that he abandoned Calvinism when, at the funeral of his 12-year-old brother, who had died of drowning, the family's Calvinist minister used the occasion to warn other young people of the dangers of dying unconverted. Mann described this minister as one who

> *expounded all the doctrines of total depravity, election, and reprobation, and not only the eternity, but the extremity, of hell-torments, unflinchingly and in their most terrible significance; while he rarely if ever descanted upon the joys of heaven, and never, if ever, upon the essential and necessary happiness of a virtuous life.*[19]

For Mann, phrenology and the common school became substitutes for his youthful experience with Calvinism. Calvinism had created for him a living hell that "spread a pall of blackness . . . beyond [which] . . . I could see the bottomless and seething lake filled with torments, and hear the wailing and agony of its victims."[20] In a series of letters to his sister in 1836, one year before becoming secretary of the Massachusetts Board of Education, he describes his rejection of this haunting vision of hell for a belief in good works in the present life. "My nature revolts at the idea of belonging to a universe in which there is to be never-ending anguish . . . while we are one earth, the burden of our duties is toward man."[21]

Mann entered the practice of law with the same fervor that would later characterize his involvement in common school reform. He was educated at Brown University and in 1823 was admitted to the bar and practice of law at Dedham, Massachusetts. Between 1827 and 1833, he served in the Massachusetts state legislature, where concerns with reforming society made him instrumental in enacting laws limiting the sale of alcohol and lottery tickets, establishing hospitals for the insane, and creating the Massachusetts State Board of Education.

While serving in the state legislature, he was surrounded by political and social events that affected his belief in the importance of common school reform and helped to shape his justification of the movement. A good way of understanding the social context of his decision to accept common school reform as the answer to society's problems is to read his description in his journal of the events between the time he was asked to serve as secretary of the Board of Education and his acceptance of that position.

On May 18, 1837, Mann received a letter proposing his nomination to the newly created State Board of Education and urging him to lead the board as secretary. He wrote in his journal on that date that, could a person be successful in that office, "what a diffusion, what intensity, what perpetuity of blessings he would confer! How would his beneficial influence upon mankind widen and deepen as it descended forever!"[22] He did not communicate his acceptance of that position until the end of June. During that time, according to his journal entry for May 25, he read "Combe on the Constitution of Man." This was his basic text in phrenology, which provided him with the scientific hope that the mental faculties could be developed and shaped to create a moral and good individual and, consequently, a moral and just society. His continued involvement in general social reform was reflected by his attendance at meetings of the Massachusetts Temperance Society. This society believed that the ending of alcohol consumption would contribute to the elimination of poverty and crime and add stability to the family. Mann noted on May 25, after attending a meeting of the society: "The faith [temperance] is now in a forward state of realization; and what a triumph it will be! not like a Roman triumph that made hearts bleed, and nations weep, and reduced armies to captivity, but one that heals hearts, and wipes tears from a nation's eyes, and sets captivity free."[23]

Mann's fear of growing social disorder in the United States was heightened when, on May 30, someone tried to start a fire next to his hotel room. He says about the event, "Fortunately it was discovered early, and extinguished. A gang of incendiaries infest the city. What a state of morals it reveals." He wonders how a group or individual could be driven to such an act. In the closing line of his description of the event, he touches on what would be an important theme in the common school movement: The hope for eliminating this type of crime, as he argued in his later writings on education, was the training of the young child. Or, as he asks in his closing line, "When will society, like a mother, take care of all her children?"[24]

His fear of social disorder and religious conflict was further intensified when on Sunday, June 11, a riot took place in Boston between Catholics and Protestants. Tension between the two religious groups had been increasing in the United States with the immigration of large numbers of

Irish. Irish Catholics generally were widely discriminated against in housing and employment. One of the more popular songs of the time was "No Irish Need Apply." In his description of the riot, Mann says,

> As I sit down to write, martial music is playing in the streets. A riot of almost unheard-of atrocity has raged for several hours this afternoon between the Irish population . . . and the engine-men and those who rallied to their assistance. . . . It is said lives are lost: it is certain that great bodily injury has been inflicted.

Mann goes on to reflect that the real problem was public opinion, which played a major role in the power of American government. The key, he felt, to eliminating this type of riot would be the proper education of public opinion.[25]

Three days after the riot, Mann worried in his journal over whether or not to accept the leadership of the Board of Education. Finally, on June 30, after reflecting on phrenology, attending temperance meetings, experiencing a fire-bombing, and observing a religious riot, he accepted the position. His journal for the date contains a statement of his belief in the ameliorating power of the school. With almost a religious passion, he states, "Henceforth, so long as I hold this office, I devote myself to the supremest welfare of mankind upon earth. . . . I have faith in the improvability of the race."[26]

Horace Mann believed that he was moving from the profession of law, which he felt had failed to save society, to a field of endeavor that promised universal salvation. A month after his acceptance he wrote to a friend that he had abandoned the practice of law for a higher calling. He explained that law had failed because it dealt with adults whose character had already been shaped, but the hope was in molding the child: "Having found the present generation composed of materials almost unmalleable, I am about transferring my efforts to the next. Men are cast-iron; but children are wax. Strength expended upon the latter may be effectual, which would make no impression upon the former."[27]

Mann's hopes and dreams for the common school unfolded in the pages of the reports he wrote as secretary of the Massachusetts State Board of Education. The most important was the *Twelfth Annual Report*, written in 1848 after Mann had resigned his educational post for a seat in the United States Congress. This report contained a summary of his ideas on the purposes of the common school.

In the *Twelfth Annual Report*, Mann returned to the reasoning he had used 11 years earlier for abandoning law for education. Again he argued that the hope for ridding society of evil actions was not in the law but in moral education. The increasing complexity of society, he felt, continually expanded the possibilities for moral transgressions. He even dismissed as futile his earlier involvement in the passage of laws against the sale of alcohol, because "the government sees the evils that come from the use of intoxicating drinks, and prohibits their sale; but unprincipled men pander to depraved appetites, and gather a harvest of dishonest profits."[28]

The answer to this steady expansion of crime, he maintained, was to educate the child. In language reflecting his ardent belief in the moral power of the school, he stated that there was one experiment society had not tried in its attempt to control crime: "It is an experiment which, even before its inception offers the highest authority for its ultimate success. Its formula is intelligible to all; and it is as legible as though written in starry letters on an azure sky." This formula, and the key to the good society, he stated, was "best expressed in these few and simple words:—'*Train up a child in the way he should go, and when he is old he will not depart from it.*'"[29] Mann claimed that all attempts to reform humanity had failed to realize the possibilities for shaping the character of children and youth.

In a broader sense, Mann put his hope in the schoolteacher, who, by educating children so that they would not transgress the law, would replace the police. This concept made schools the central institution for the control and maintenance of the social order. Also, it opened the door for the explosive political issue of whose morality would be taught in the public schools.

Mann walked a delicate tightrope in his advocacy of moral education in the schools. Given the temper of the times, moral education, which for most people meant a religious education, was considered an essential part of education. On the one hand, this meant that if Mann did not advocate a moral education with religious foundations he faced the possibility of being called irreligious and of having the common school condemned as a secular institution without religious foundations. For most people during this period, the education of character had to be linked to religious doctrines. If not, it could be accused of being antireligious. On the other hand, if he did link moral education to religion, he had to make a choice about the religious tenets to which moral education should be linked. Given the fierce denominational rivalries of the time, any choice he made opened the possibility that the common school might be destroyed by competing religious groups.

Mann defended his position on this issue in the *Twelfth Annual Report* by arguing that the presence and use of the Bible in the schools provided instruction in the fundamental doctrines of Christianity without reference to denominational differences, and this provided the basis for all creeds.

Is it not, indeed, too plain, to require the formality of a syllogism, that if any man's creed is to be found in the Bible, and the Bible is in the schools, then that

man's creed is in the schools? . . . If a certain system, called Christianity,
were contained in . . . the Bible, then wherever the Bible might go, there the
system of Christianity must be.[30]

In addition to the use of the Bible in the schools, Mann claimed that
the laws of Massachusetts required the teaching of the basic moral doctrines of Christianity, which he listed as instruction in piety, justice, love
of country, benevolence, sobriety, industry, frugality, chastity, modera-
tion, and temperance. "Are not these virtues and graces," asked Mann,
"part and parcel of Christianity?"[31] Within the framework of this reasoning, religious education in the common schools was to be based on a
nonsectarian use of the Bible with the teaching of broad religious principles common to all Christian denominations.

Mann envisioned four destructive alternatives to this form of nonsectarian moral education. The first was to exclude all religious instruction
from the schools. This, he argued, would make the schools "un-Chris-
tian," and the schools would receive no support from the general population. The second alternative was for the law to define and prescribe a
system of religion for the schools, which, according to Mann, would
involve the government in the establishment of religion and force a
particular religion on all children. The third alternative was to give each
religious sect with a majority in a community the power to define the
religion of the schools. Mann strongly felt that this would result in the
destruction of the common school by the heat of religious rivalries as all
denominations fought for the inclusion of their doctrines. The last alternative was for the government to abandon all interference in the education of the young. As an advocate of the common school system, Mann
quickly rejected this last possibility.

In the context of these arguments, the term *common* took on added
meaning. Children in the common school were to receive a common
moral education based on the general principles of the Bible and on
common virtues, and such education was to eliminate crime and corruption in society.

Mann used the same type of reasoning in defining his goals for political education in the common schools. Like religious instruction, political
instruction opened the door for groups with differing political ideas to
fight over the content of political instruction. Mann stated in his *Twelfth
Annual Report*, "It is obvious . . . that if the tempest of political strife
were to be let loose upon our Common Schools, they would be over-
whelmed with sudden ruin." His answer was to have schools teach only
those articles of republican faith that were approved by "all sensible and
judicious men, all patriots, and all genuine republicans." This political
education, he proclaimed, would contain "articles in the creed of repub-

licanism, which are accepted by all, believed in by all, and which form the common basis of our political faith."[32]

To avoid political controversy in the schoolroom, Mann proposed that the teacher avoid any discussion or comment that touched on political disputes. However,

> *when the teacher, in the course of his lessons or lectures on the fundamental law, arrives at a controverted text, he is either to read it without comment or remark; or, at most, he is only to say that the passage is the subject of disputation, and that the schoolroom is neither the tribunal to adjudicate, nor the forum to discuss it.*[33]

In this manner, Mann hoped to provide instruction in the fundamentals of politics without destroying the common school in the fury of political controversy.

Within the context of political education, the *common* in common school meant the teaching of a common political creed. The combination of moral and political instruction meant that the student leaving the common school would share with fellow students a set of moral and political beliefs; the result would be the creation of a society with a consensus of political and moral values.

For Mann, the inculcation of a common set of political beliefs would reduce the level of political violence in society as a whole. He hoped that a common school education would lead to political discussions based on a shared set of political beliefs. Thus, even though some disputes over political issues might arise, these disputes would take place in the context of a common political faith. Mann envisioned that political violence would be avoided because of the adherence to common articles of republican faith.

According to Mann, it was necessary to teach the importance of using the vote, as opposed to revolution and violence, to bring about political change. This was a particularly important issue during Mann's time because the extension of universal male suffrage had taken place in the 1820s. Prior to that time, the vote had been restricted by property requirements. In reference to the vote replacing political violence, Mann stated: "Had the obligations of the future citizen been sedulously inculcated upon all children of this Republic, would the patriot have had to mourn over so many instances, where the voter, not being able to accomplish his purpose by voting, has proceeded to accomplish it by violence."[34]

Mann wished to avoid not only political violence but also violence between social classes. Like Karl Marx in Europe, Mann was concerned with the creation of divisions between social classes caused by the growth of modern industry. *The Communist Manifesto* by Karl Marx and

Friedrich Engels was published in 1848, the same year that Mann wrote his final and summary *Twelfth Annual Report* for the Massachusetts State Board of Education. Unlike Marx and Engels, Mann believed that the answer to social-class conflict was a common school education—not revolution by the working class.

Like Marx and Engels, however, Mann recognized that modern industrial development had created a major split between capital and labor and thus the intensification of class consciousness. Writing in the *Twelfth Annual Report* about industrial development in Massachusetts, he poses a warning question: "Are we not in danger of . . . those hideous evils which are always engendered between Capital and Labor, when all the capital is in the hands of one class and all the labor is thrown upon another?" He goes on to argue that if one class possesses all the wealth and education, and the other is poor and ignorant, then the latter will be "servile dependents and subjects of the former."[35]

"Now, surely," Mann writes with a great deal of conviction about the social power of the common school, "nothing but Universal Education can counter-work this tendency to the domination of capital and servility of labor." He believed that two alternatives existed through which common schooling could eliminate the problems between capital and labor. The first was to eliminate the friction caused by class consciousness. Mann admits that "a fellow-feeling for one's class or caste is the common instinct of hearts not wholly sunk in selfish regards for person, or for family." For Mann, the problem was not elimination of class consciousness but its expansion across social boundaries. Mann hoped that a common school education would spread feelings of class consciousness among all members of society: "The spread of education, by enlarging the cultivated class or caste, will open a wider area over which the social feelings will expand; and, if this education should be universal and complete, it would do more than all things else to obliterate factitious distinctions in society." In Mann's words, the expansion of class consciousness would "disarm the poor of their hostility towards the rich."[36]

The second way common schooling would eliminate the conflict between capital and labor was by increasing the general wealth of society. Mann felt that common schooling, by improving the general wealth of society, would be the answer to those reformers who were calling for a redistribution of property from the rich to the poor. His argument is one of the earliest considerations of schooling as capital investment and of teaching as the development of human capital. Within his framework of reasoning, education would produce wealth by training intelligence to develop new technology and methods of production. Investment in education is a form of capital investment because it leads to the production of new wealth, and teaching is a means of developing human capital because it provides the individual with the intellectual tools for improved labor.

In other words, according to Mann, common schooling would eliminate the problems of the unequal distribution of property by increasing the general wealth of society and, consequently, improving the economic conditions of the poor. It would prevent poverty by giving individuals the tools for enhancing their economic position in society. Therefore, as Mann states in one of his more famous passages in the *Twelfth Annual Report*, "Education, then, beyond all other devices of human origin, is the great equalizer of the conditions of men—the balance-wheel of the social machinery."[37]

Mann's arguments regarding the conflict between labor and capital added another meaning to the word *common*. Common schooling was to create a common social class by the extension of a common class consciousness among all members of society. By mixing the rich and poor within the same schoolhouse, social-class conflict would give way to a feeling of membership in a common social class and thus would provide society with a common set of political and moral values.

Mann uses arguments about education as capital investment to justify public financial support of the common school. One of the questions asked during the period was why those without children, or those who sent their children to private schools, should pay for the education of other people's children. Mann's answer is that the value of property is dependent on the work of previous generations and on the general level of prosperity of the community. He argues that property is held in trust by each generation, which through its labors increases its value. In other words, even a family without any children benefits from common schooling because common schooling increases the wealth of the entire community, which, in turn, increases the value of the family's property. Therefore, all members of society benefit economically from common schooling, whether or not they make any direct use of the schools.

With minor variations, Mann's statement of the goals and purposes of common schooling in his reports to the Massachusetts Board of Education were shared by the leading educational reformers of the time. This does not mean that they were shared by all members of society during this period. In a sense, Mann's reports represented the official justification for the creation of a common system of education. Involved in this justification was the hope that all the social, economic, and political problems of society would be solved by putting together in a common school the children of all members of society and by teaching them a common set of political and moral beliefs.

But this utopian vision of the good society created by a system of common schooling had certain inherent problems. First was the real problem of agreement on a common set of political and moral values to

be taught in the classroom. Such agreement concerning religious values
never occurred, and, as a result, a private parochial system of education
developed side by side with the common school. In the simplest terms,
the common school never became common to all students. In addition,
no proof existed that education would eliminate crime. In fact, one could
argue that increased education simply meant improving the educational
level of the criminal. Nor was there any real proof that a common school
education could eliminate social, political, and economic unrest. It is
possible, for instance, that social unrest is rooted in real economic and
political problems that cannot be solved without dealing directly with
the problems themselves. In this sense, the official ideology of the common school might be considered as essentially conservative because it
did not call for any basic changes in the economic and political structure
of society, but placed its hope for social improvement on the education
of the individual. In fact, the official ideology of the common school
accepted the existing political and economic organization of society and
argued that any problems were the result of individual deviance or
failure. Therefore, it was argued by common school reformers, the common school could create a utopian world by educating the individual to
conform to the needs of existing political, social, and economic organizations.

Although there were obvious flaws in the reasoning of common
school reformers, their faith in the power of the school continued into
the twentieth century. The ideology of the common school became a
standard part of the beliefs held by most Americans: Since the mid-
1800s, the school has continually been seen as a means of eliminating
poverty, crime, and social problems. In addition, the idea of education
as capital investment and as a means of developing human capital has
became one of the major justifications for schooling in the twentieth
century. Horace Mann and other common school reformers made a
lasting contribution to the ongoing debate about the relationship between school and society.

The Workingmen and the Struggle for a Republican Education

The educational demands made by the workingmen's parties between
1827 and 1835 provide an important example of how support of similar
ideas and institutions by different groups and for different reasons can
contribute to the advancement of an important social reform. Clearly,
workingmen's parties wanted common schools, but for different reasons from those given by common school reformers. Nonetheless, the
result of the combined efforts of the workingmen's parties and the common school reformers gave the appearance of a popular struggle for the
establishment of a common school system.

Although the political impact and social composition of workingmen's parties between 1827 and 1835 has been debated, there has been no dispute about the importance of education in the political campaigns of the workingmen's parties. Their educational arguments shared many of the characteristics of the ideology of common school reformers, particularly a general demand for free common public schooling to serve political and economic purposes. But the reasons given by workingmen's parties for the establishment of common schools were distinctly different from those given by Horace Mann and other common school reformers. The reformers stressed the necessity of teaching a common moral and political creed as a means of eliminating crime, poverty, and social unrest and providing for equal economic opportunity, whereas the workingmen's parties argued for the necessity of education as a means by which workers could protect themselves from economic and political exploitation. Common school reformers emphasized education as a mechanism of social control, while the workingmen's parties emphasized education as a mechanism for gaining political and economic power. Both groups agreed that a common education was necessary to eliminate the distinctions between the rich and the poor and to promote equality of economic opportunity.

The workingmen's political movement began in Philadelphia in 1827 with a demand by the Mechanics Union of Trade Associations for worker influence on legislative action. In the spring of 1828, the Philadelphia Workingmen's Party nominated and campaigned for candidates to the state legislature. The organization of labor parties quickly spread through Pennsylvania, Delaware, Massachusetts, and New York. For most of these workingmen's parties, education became a central theme of their political campaigns.

Representative of the workingmen's parties' concern about education was the establishment in 1829 by the Philadelphia Mechanics Union of Trade Associations of a committee to investigate educational conditions in the city and state. The committee found that for all areas of the state except Philadelphia, Lancaster, and Pittsburgh, little support could be found for public instruction. The committee also attacked the existence of charity schools. First, there was a concern that private individuals were using government money to provide education of questionable quality for the poor. In his excellent study *Education and the Working Class: The Expansion of Public Education during the Transition to Capitalism,* historian William Russell quotes the committee as claiming that a large number of charity schools were "irresponsible institutions, established by individuals, from mere motives of private speculation or gain, who are destitute of character, and frequently, of the requisite attainments and abilities." In addition, the schools suffered from "ignorance, inattention and immorality." Criticisms were also raised that charity schools offered a limited curriculum and led to a loss of pride among parents.[38]

In general, the committee believed that government monies were primarily being used to support colleges and universities—a situation it argued was "exclusively for the benefit of the wealthy, who [were] thereby enabled to procure a liberal education for their children, upon lower terms than it could otherwise be afforded them." If this condition persisted, the committee reported, knowledge would be mostly in the hands of the privileged few and would "[consign] the multitude to comparative ignorance, and [secure] the balance of knowledge on the side of the rich and the rulers."[39] The answer to this situation was to make equal knowledge a common property of all groups in society.

In New York, a similar complaint was voiced about the private control of charity schools by the New York School Society (originally the New York Free School Society). The New York Workingmen's Party believed that the existence of charity schools and the lack of adequate funding of schooling were increasing social-class differences. The lack of education among workingmen, it was argued, kept them ignorant of their rights and allowed for exploitation by the privileged.

One of the most important points made in the arguments of the New York Workingmen's Party was that knowledge was power in an industrial society. Thus, keeping knowledge from the masses was considered one method of assuring the upper classes a monopoly of power. Russell explains the general view of the workingmen's parties: "Kept in ignorance, workers could be deprived of their rights, cheated in their daily business, and 'gulled and deceived' by 'designing schemers,' 'parasitic politicians,' 'greedy bank directors,' and 'heartless manufacturers.'"[40] In summary, workingmen's parties believed that the lack of a common school system was an attempt to deny them their rights and their share of economic and political power.

Workingmen's groups believed that common schooling was essential for the protection of their rights—that knowledge was necessary for the *equal* exercise of power in a democratic system of government. This argument is best expressed in an 1830 statement in the *Workingmen's Advocate:* "The right of self government implies a right to a *knowledge* necessary to the exercise of the right of self government. If all have an *equal* right to the first, all must consequently have an equal right to the second; therefore, *all* are entitled to *equal education.*"[41]

In addition, access to knowledge meant protection of rights against what was considered the tyranny of the upper class. One statement in the *Workingmen's Advocate* in 1831 stresses that education was the only sure "defense against not only an infringement, but a total usurpation of the native rights of the people, by the monopolizing demagogues of the land."[42] An editorial in 1830 in the *Sentinel*, a workingmen's newspaper, wishfully claims that if the previous generation had been properly educated, it would not have been cheated and blinded by those currently wielding political and economic power.

Differences and similarities existed between the arguments of the workingmen's parties for the necessity of education in a republic and those of the common school reformers like Horace Mann. Both groups agreed that education was necessary for the maintenance of a republican and democratic form of government, but the common school reformers emphasized political education as a means of making individuals worthy of democratic rights and as necessary for maintaining political harmony, whereas workingmen's groups emphasized the necessity of education for the equal sharing of power and the protection of rights. These differences suggest a different content in the political instruction to be offered in the schools. As a means of achieving his objectives, Mann wanted the basic principles of government and a common republican creed to be taught, while workingmen's groups called for the teaching of how to exercise power in the political system, the nature of political rights, and the protection of those rights as the means to achieve their goals.

With regard to crime and poverty, workingmen's groups and common school reformers shared an equal faith in the power of the school. In fact, in response to the issue of why a person without children should pay for the education of other people's children, workingmen's groups often advanced the argument that education increased the security of all people from criminal activities.

Common school reformers and workingmen's groups also shared a belief that equal education for all was necessary to reduce distinctions among economic classes, but, again, their reasons were different. The reason common school reformers wanted a common education was to reduce friction between capital and labor. Workingmen's groups wanted equal education as means of assuring that capital did not maintain a monopoly over knowledge and as a means of protecting their economic interests. As an editorial in the *Workingmen's Advocate* of 1834 states, education would provide workers with "a correct knowledge of their value as producers . . . [and of their] general interest as productive laborers." This knowledge, it was hoped, would destroy the causes for the dependency of workers on owners and the unjust accumulation of capital.[43]

Because knowledge was viewed as power and as a means by which capital maintained its grip over labor, it was logical for workingmen's groups to support equal education as a means of providing equal economic opportunity. The relationship between equality of educational opportunity and equality of economic opportunity has been stressed throughout the nineteenth and twentieth centuries.

The most extreme, but logical, linkage between equal education and equal economic opportunity was made by the New York Workingmen's Party in its state guardianship plan. The basic argument behind this plan was that equality of educational opportunity could not be achieved if one child went from school to an impoverished home life and another child went home to a life that was rich and offered many advantages. To achieve true equality of educational opportunity, the state guardianship plan argued, all children must be taken from their families and placed in state boarding schools where they would receive equal treatment, equal clothes, equal food, and an equal education. Although the radicalism of this proposal split the party, it did highlight the extreme importance workingmen's groups gave to the connection between equality of educational opportunity and equality of economic opportunity.[44]

The question remains as to whether or not workingmen, as represented by these early labor parties, gained the type of education they wanted through the establishment of a common school system. As discussed in later chapters, a tension existed in the nineteenth and twentieth centuries between organized labor and the public school system over the content of instruction. Labor often claimed that public school instruction was conservative and taught principles opposed to the organization of workers into unions. Whether or not this was the case does not detract from the very important effect workingmen's parties had on spreading ideas favoring common school education and winning support for the establishment of common schools. In fact, when one considers the dates of the activities of the workingmen's parties and the common school reformers, it is clear that the workingmen's parties paved the way for reformers like Barnard and Mann.

The differences between the common school reformers and the workingmen's parties highlight the differences in meaning that can exist over commonly used words. One cannot assume that if all people say they favor education, they all favor the same thing. The word *education* has meant different things to different people. This is particularly true of the way the word was used in the different arguments given in support of the establishment of common schools.

The Whigs and the Democrats

The common school movement was born during a period of intense political change and rivalry. Of primary political importance in the 1820s was the ending of property qualifications for voting and the establishment of universal male suffrage. In addition, modern political parties were born in 1828 when the Jacksonian Democrats competed against the National Republican Party (which died in the early 1830s and was replaced by the Whigs). The Whigs and the Democrats had almost equal shares of the nation's voters.

These political changes were related to the common school movement in several ways. First, universal suffrage created a concern with the education of the future voter. Many supporters of the common school movement stressed the importance of education in assuring the maintenance of political order as democratic rights were extended. Second, political affiliation was the most important difference between groups advocating different forms of school organization. Most leaders of the common school movement were Whigs who believed that government should intervene to maintain social order through a centrally managed school system designed to educate moral and responsible citizens. On the other hand, members of the Democratic Party believed that social order would occur naturally, and, therefore, they believed in minimal government intervention and local control of the schools.

In their analysis of voting patterns in six states, Herbert Ershkowitz and William Shade show that between 1833 and 1843 the voting patterns of the members of each party were clearly different. By 1840, 80 to 100 percent of both Whigs and Democrats adhered to the point of view of their party. With regard to educational legislation, in most cases there were significant differences in party voting patterns.[45]

The differences between each party's political philosophy highlight important aspects of the common school and the continuing controversy over the political structure of schooling. Both political groups believed that education was a necessity but differed over the goals and structure of the educational system. In general, Whigs were concerned with morality, duty, and the reduction of social conflict and thus wanted an educational system that would shape moral character, teach social and political duties, and reduce conflict among social classes and political groups. Whigs believed these goals could best be achieved through centralized supervision by state governments. Democrats resisted the trend toward centralization of government control and talked mainly about rights and a society of conflicting interests.

In *The Concept of Jacksonian Democracy*, Lee Benson describes the differences between these two political groups as positive versus negative liberalism. Within this framework, Whigs were advocates of a positive liberalism that called for government intervention to assure the workings of a free marketplace economy. Therefore, Whigs believed that government should provide money for education and for internal improvements to guarantee the establishment and functioning of institutions and economic organizations essential for the development of the country. For instance, Whigs argued that because private capital was not available for the development of canals and railroads essential for economic growth, the government should supply the needed capital. Benson quotes New York governor William Seward's 1839 message as a summary of the Whig position on internal improvements and education. Seward argued that government action and spending were necessary "to enlarge . . . national prosperity, while we equalize its enjoyments and direct it to the universal diffusion of knowledge."[46]

The Democrats represented negative liberalism and argued that government governed too much. They believed that the economy should function without any state intervention and that state monies should not be used to support a common school system. Benson states that John Bigelow, a leading writer for the Democrats in New York, "believed that the common school fund should be applied to the present crippling state debt and that thereafter the state should cease to propagate any science, art, trade, or religion among any class of people."[47]

In *The Political Culture of the American Whigs,* Daniel Howe argues that faculty psychology had the strongest influence on the moral philosophy of the Whigs, who believed that the balancing and regulating of the moral faculties was essential for the maintenance of social order. From this perspective, schools were necessary for assuring harmony within the individual. Whigs believed that if moral faculties were

> *left to themselves, the lower powers would escape control and wreck havoc. An unregulated faculty—whether pride, licentiousness, or some other appetite or emotion—was called a "passion." The good life entailed continual self-discipline, as one sought to "suppress his passions" or "cultivate and improve his virtues."*[48]

As Howe indicates, this philosophical perspective ruled out the idea of a laissez-faire society completely free of some form of regulation and "implied an active, purposeful central government, 'administering the affairs of the nation according to its best judgment for the good of the whole, and all parts of the whole.'"[49] According to this political ideology, the government was to play an active role in maintaining the economy, regulating morality, and assuring political and social order. Consequently, Whigs supported not only government funding of internal improvements (such as canals) but also the passage of laws to regulate morality. For instance, the temperance movement received strong support from Whigs.

For Whigs, schooling was the key to an ordered society. Howe summarizes the Whigs' political campaigns as being part of "a cultural struggle to impose on the United States the standards of morality we usually term Victorian. They were standards of self-control and restraint, which dovetailed well with the economic program of the party, for they emphasized thrift, sobriety, and public responsibility."[50] Whigs believed these values were necessary to bring discipline to voters.

The Whig idea that society requires a consciously arranged order and the Democratic free-market ideas reflected two different concepts of freedom. In turn, these differing concepts of freedom were reflected in attitudes about the political and social role of the school. For Whigs, true freedom occurred only when the balance of mental faculties within an individual assured that passion did not reign over reason. In addition, Whigs contended that social conditions must be organized so that the individual was not tempted into activity that would disrupt the harmony of the mind. In other words, the Whig position was that true freedom was possible only if individuals received a proper education and social temptations were removed. This explains why many common school reformers were active in the temperance movement while working for greater centralization and uniformity in the school system.[51] Democrats, on the other hand, believed that true freedom was possible only in a society in which there was a minimum of government interference in the social order. Democrats viewed government attempts to order society as attempts to promote and protect the special privileges of the upper class.

Not all members of American society in the 1830s and 1840s complacently accepted the moral-reform efforts of the Whigs. For example, Howe reports that many thought the Whigs' assumption of moral responsibility for others meddlesome. He tells the story of the burning of the church of Lyman Beecher, who was a Whig, temperance advocate, and minister.

When Lyman Beecher's church on Hanover Street burned down, the volunteer fire companies, who hated his temperance crusading, refused to fight the flames. Instead, it is reported, they watched and sang: "While Beecher's church holds out to burn / The vilest sinner may return"—a parody of a hymn.[52]

The best study of the differences in educational philosophy between the Democrats and the Whigs was conducted by Carl Kaestle and Maris Vinovskis for their book *Education and Social Change in Nineteenth-Century Massachusetts.*[53] They studied the attempt in 1840 to abolish the Massachusetts State Board of Education and, of course, Horace Mann's position as its secretary. This action was considered a direct attack on the common school movement.

Kaestle and Vinovskis report that in the year preceding the attempt to abolish the board, a leading Massachusetts Democrat, Orestes Brownson, had attacked the board for trying to "Prussianize" education by centralizing control over the schools. Brownson contended that the board was a vehicle for Whig ideas about education and maintained that control should remain at the local level.

In 1840, a legislative committee composed of three Whigs and two Democrats was established to investigate the work of the Board of Education. Surprisingly, given the majority of Whigs on the committee, its report attacked the board as an unnecessary expense and, quoting Kaestle and Vinovskis, as "a danger to political and religious freedoms." The committee report argues: "District schools, in a republican government need no police regulations, no systems of state censorship, no checks of moral, religious, or political conservatism, to preserve either the morals, the religion, or the politics of the state. 'Let them ever be kept free and pure.'"[54] Obviously, this reasoning was almost the exact opposite of that given by Mann for establishing a common school system.

The committee's report provoked a series of other investigations that eventually led to a vote by the members of the state legislature on the abolition of the board. The attempt to abolish the board failed by a vote of 182 to 245. The legislative vote provided Kaestle and Vinovskis with data by which they could analyze the nature of the supporters and opponents of the common school system in Massachusetts.

Kaestle and Vinovskis classified the members of the legislature according to religion, occupation, the geographical area they represented, and party affiliation. They hoped to determine which factors were most important in determining support or nonsupport of the board. The assumption was made that a legislator's position on this issue reflected that individual's support or nonsupport of the common school movement.

After analyzing the data, Kaestle and Vinovskis concluded that party affiliation was the most important factor in determining a legislator's support or nonsupport of the board. They also found that religion was not an important factor in legislative action. Of course, the legislature did not include a large Catholic faction, so the rift between Catholics and Protestants was not represented in their findings. They did find that legislators from manufacturing areas tended to support the board, unlike those from rural areas.

The fact that party affiliation was the most important factor does not mean that all Whigs supported the existence of the board and that all Democrats stood in opposition. One-fifth of Whigs and one-third of Democrats did not follow the general voting pattern of their respective parties. But even with these defections from the positions of both political parties, political ideology was the most important factor in differentiating between supporters and nonsupporters of the Board of Education.

The differences between the political parties in Massachusetts reflected more general differences between the two political groups throughout the nation. According to Kaestle and Vinovskis, "the Whigs argued that positive government intervention was a necessary and useful means of improving the quality of public schools throughout the commonwealth." On the other hand, Democrats felt "that any increased state interference in local educational matters created the potential, if not the reality, of a centralized state school system that would dictate how children were to be educated."[55]

Another way of interpreting these differences between Whigs and Democrats is advanced by Michael Katz in *Class, Bureaucracy, and Schools*. Katz argues that the issue of local versus state control was part of a more general concern about who should control the schools. According to Katz, in the early nineteenth century there were four models for the control of educational institutions, any one of which could have become the dominant method in the nineteenth and twentieth centuries. He labeled the four models paternalistic voluntarism, democratic localism, corporate voluntarism, and incipient bureaucracy. One particular model became dominant, he maintains, because it reflected the realities of changing social conditions and because it served the interests of a particular social group.

His example of paternalistic voluntarism is the New York Free School Society, which controlled and administered charity schools by a self-perpetuating board of leading citizens who volunteered their time and were unpaid. Katz states that this type of organization "rested on faith in the individual talented amateur and, at an over-all administrative level, scorned the need for elaborate organization, state control, or professional staff."[56] The supporters of this type of organization claimed that it entailed little administrative expense, provided a great deal of financial integrity and efficiency, and demonstrated success in the existence of an extensive network of charity schools maintained for several decades. Paternalistic voluntarism, Katz argues, was a method of organization that allowed the social elite to exert its control and social goals over educational institutions. This form of organization and control was suitable for serving the interests of elites in preindustrial mercantile cities.

In contrast, supporters of democratic localism, which had been current in rural areas in the early nineteenth century, tried to adapt it to urban centers in the 1840s and 1850s. Advocates of democratic localism wanted to divide large urban school districts into smaller districts, each having its own administrative unit controlled by the local residents, instead of having one school board and a large bureaucracy administrating an urban school system. Katz argues that democratic localism would have given the general public greater control over the educational system.

According to Katz, it was Orestes Brownson who formalized the theory of democratic localism. Brownson argued that the state should be composed of distinct communities that were the smallest units possible for protecting local interests. With regard to education, the local school district was to remain more powerful than the state, and each individual school was to be "under the control of a community composed merely of the number of families having children in it." Obviously, this form of organization served the interests of the middle and lower classes. Katz contends that "democratic localists . . . subordinated both efficiency and organizational rationality to an emphasis on responsiveness, close public control, and local involvement."[57]

The third model, corporate voluntarism, is the organizational model that was mainly used by colleges and academies. This model of control involves a self-perpetuating board of trustees administering a single institution. A great deal of variety among educational institutions is allowed by this form of organization, as exemplified by the many different types of academies that came into existence in the nineteenth century. Unlike democratic localism, this model assumes that the public does not have the knowledge requisite for governing an educational institution and that the board of trustees is to provide enlightened management. This type of management serves the educational interests and opinions of local elites.

The death blow to corporate voluntarism, according to Katz, came with the emergence of sharper differences between public and private institutions. Katz argues that academies lost the distinction of being public because they were not initiated by government and were not administered by government officials.

The fourth model of organization, incipient bureaucracy, is the one advocated by common school reformers like Horace Mann and Henry Barnard. The chief characteristics of this model are centralization of control, elimination of local variations, and standardization of schooling. Obviously, common school reformers rejected democratic localism because of the potential conflict among different religious and political factions over the content of instruction. In fact, the idea of a local school reflecting the point of view of its particular constituency was antithetical to the basic ideas of the common school movement. Common school reformers did not want schools to offer different courses of instruction but wanted all instruction to be the same in order to achieve the goal of providing a common education to all people.

The creation of a system of common schooling required centralization to assure uniformity of practices. This is best exemplified by the establishment of state boards of education and the appointment of state secretaries or superintendents of education. To a certain extent, the struggle between Whigs and Democrats was a struggle between incipient bureaucracy and democratic localism. An aspect of the emphasis on uniformity of practice was the creation of graded schools in which children were grouped according to age. Common school reformers believed that replacing the system of having children of all ages in the same classroom with the system of graded schools would result in increased efficiency.

In addition, standardization of instruction would be ensured by the hiring of full-time professionals to supervise the teachers. Katz argues that this model of organization is characterized by "professionalism and system," which "like the obsession with punctuality, reflected industrial values. Newly industrialized people must learn to reward a man for what he can do rather than for who he is." Thus, according to Katz, "graded schools, regulated promotions, and trained staff were designed to counter problems created by a populace accustomed to gaining privileges by means that had little to do with capacity to perform."[58]

Katz argues in more general terms that incipient bureaucracy, with its emphasis on standardization, was primarily a mechanism for protecting middle-class Protestant values against the onslaught of an increasingly diverse population. Bureaucracy was to be the mechanism for assuring that the content of the common school education would reflect in the main the values of the original settlers' Protestant culture.

Katz's argument is similar to that given by Kaestle in *Pillars of the Republic*. As discussed earlier, Kaestle makes a case that the ideology of the common school movement centered primarily on republicanism, Protestantism, and capitalism. Katz argues that bureaucracy is an organizational form that ensured that these three values became standard in the common school. The opposite organizational model, democratic localism, left open the door for other values to gain dominance in particular schools.

For these reasons, Catholics supported democratic localism as a means by which their values might be reflected in local public schools. Bear in mind that the fear of common school reformers of the growth of pluralism was fueled by the increase in the number of Catholics in the United States and by the growth of an industrial proletariat. The triumph of bureaucracy over democratic localism in education made it necessary for Catholics to organize their own school systems.

The struggle between Whigs and Democrats over the common school reflected a more general concern about how schools should be controlled and whose values should be taught in a school's curriculum. This debate, which has continued into the twentieth century, has reflected in varying degrees the tension between those wanting popular control of the schools and little government intervention and those believing that government should work actively to assure that the schools serve general social, political, and economic goals.

The Catholic Issue

The contradiction between the attempt to make schooling common to all children and the Protestant values that dominated common schools resulted in major disputes between Catholics and Protestants over the use of state educational funds. In large part, this conflict resulted from strong anti-Catholic feelings in the Protestant community. In the end, Catholics felt excluded from the common schools and found it necessary to establish their own system of independent parochial schools, which meant that the common schools never became common to all American children.

New York City was the scene of a major conflict in the 1840s over school funds, when Catholics demanded a share of the state educational funds that were being monopolized by the Public School Society (originally the New York Free School Society). Until this time, Catholics had been operating their own schools in an attempt to provide children of Catholic parents with an alternative to the Protestant-dominated schools of the Public School Society. Catholics objected to the use in the schools of the King James Version of the Bible and of textbooks that contained anti-Catholic statements.

The smoldering conflict between Catholics and Protestants in New York City erupted into a major conflict with the 1838 election of William Seward as governor of New York. Seward was a Whig and, like all good Whigs, was a strong advocate of government-sponsored internal improvements and increased state support of education. But his Whig philosophy had an important twist when it came to the issue of education. Although he believed that a centrally controlled and expanded system of education was necessary for the health of society, he also believed that state money for the support of Catholic schools was necessary to achieve this goal. It was this proposal that fanned the flames of conflict between Catholics and Protestants.

Seward indicated in his first message to the state legislature in 1839 that education would be an important part of his legislative agenda. He argued before the legislature that improved educational facilities were necessary for the development of responsible citizens and claimed that during his administration, "improvement in our system of education will be wider and more enduring than the effects of any change of public policy."[59] As reflected in his other speeches and correspondence, one of his major concerns was to educate Catholic immigrants, particularly the Irish, for citizenship. He resisted the strong anti-Irish feeling that existed in the 1830s and 1840s and denounced American hatred of "foreigners."

Seward discovered, while visiting New York City, that large numbers of immigrant children were not attending school, and by 1840 he concluded that many of New York's Catholic children were not attending public schools because of their anti-Catholic atmosphere. His concern was that immigrant children might grow up to be adult illiterates who would become public burdens and never enter the mainstream of American life. He therefore proposed before the state legislature in 1840 that Catholic schools should become part of the state school system while retaining their private charters and religious affiliation. As historian Vincent Lannie writes in *Public Money and Parochial Education*, "Seward urged the establishment of schools that would be acceptable to this minority group and staffed with teachers who spoke the same language and professed the same religious faith as their pupils. Such schools would be administered by Catholic officials but supported with public funds."[60]

Many Protestant Whigs were outraged by Seward's proposal and raised strong opposition to the plan. In a letter to a friend in 1840, Seward reasoned that any Whig who withheld support from him because of his proposal did not really support the "Whigism we derived from our forefathers of the Revolutionary Age nor is such the Whigism that I shall teach my children." He argued that it was necessary for the state to provide a moral and religious education to all children in order to maintain social stability and "if it cannot be otherwise conferred, may rightly be conferred by the employment for the purpose of teachers professing the same language and religious creed."[61]

The immediate response of the Catholic community in New York to Seward's proposal was to petition the Board of Aldermen of New York City for a portion of the common school fund. Historically, this petition was important because it enumerated Catholic complaints about the Protestant dominance of the public schools. First, the Catholic petitioners attacked the supposed nonsectarianism of the schools operated by the Public School Society. Of course, most common school reformers had claimed that the schools could be nonsectarian if they taught the basic principles of Christianity. The petition cited a number of instances in which the reports of the Public School Society either called for religious instruction or demonstrated the existence of religious instruction in the schools. This religious instruction included the reading and study of the Bible, which the petition claimed made the school sectarian. The petitioners argued:

> *Even the reading of the Scriptures in those schools your petitioners cannot regard otherwise than as sectarian; because Protestants would certainly consider as such the introduction of the Catholic Scriptures, which are different from theirs, and the Catholics have the same ground of objection when the Protestant version is made use of.*[62]

In addition, the petitioners complained of anti-Catholic statements in selections used for elementary reading lessons. They argued that historical and religious portions of the reading lessons were selected from Protestant writers who were prejudiced against Catholics. The petition stated: "The term 'Popery' is repeatedly found in them. This term is known and employed as one of insult and contempt towards the Catholic religion, and it passes into the minds of children with the feeling of which it is the outward expression."[63]

The petition recognized that the members of the Public School Society had tried to remove anti-Catholic sentiments from textbooks, but, according to the petitioners, they had failed because they were incompetent in their ability to identify anti-Catholic statements. As an example, the petition quoted the following passage from a textbook approved by the Public School Society.

Huss, John, a zealous reformer from Popery, who lived in Bohemia, towards the close of the fourteenth, and the beginning of the fifteenth centuries. He was bold and persevering; but at length, trusting himself to the deceitful Catholics, he was by them brought to trial, condemned as a heretic, and burnt at the stake.[64]

The petitioners argued that the anti-Catholic atmosphere of the schools operated by the Public School Society had forced them to open their own schools for the education of the poor and that this amounted to a system of double taxation, whereby they were taxed to support the schools operated by the Public School Society and had to use their own money for support of an alternative school system. In the words of the petition, "The expense necessary for this [establishment of Catholic schools], was a second taxation, required not by the laws of the land, but by the no less imperious demands of their conscience."[65] Catholic claims that they had to assume the burden of double taxation for the maintenance of Catholic schools continued into the twentieth century.

The petitioners recognized that public monies should not be used for the support of religion but claimed that this was precisely what was happening through public support of the Public School Society. The petitioners were willing to remove all religious instruction from their schools during school hours. To assure that money was not used for religious instruction they recommended that the organization of their schools and the control of the disbursement of money "shall be conducted, and made, by persons unconnected with the religion of your petitioners, even the Public School Society. . . . The public may then be assured that the money will not be applied to the support of the Catholic religion."[66]

Both Governor Seward's proposal and the Catholic petition brought a storm of protest from the Protestant community. The "great debate" began within a month of the presentation of the petition before the Board of Aldermen in the city's Common Council chambers. The Protestant community responded to the Catholic petition with the argument that if Catholics were willing to postpone religious instruction until after school hours, they should be willing to instruct the children attending the Public School Society schools after school hours. The Reverend Mr.

Knox of the Dutch Reformed Church claimed that the public schools were not "adverse to feelings of reverence for Catholic peculiarities." The Reverend Mr. Bangs of the Methodist Church argued that all poor and wayward children should be forced to attend public schools. Bangs argued, in the words of Vincent Lannie: "This coercive action of the state would really be an act of compassion, since these vagrants would be snatched from the streets and their concomitant vices, and taught to become Christian gentlemen and competent citizens." And last, Gardner Spring of the Presbyterian Church told the aldermen that he viewed the petition "with more alarm on account of the source from which it comes . . . if there was no alternative between infidelity and the dogmas of the Catholic Church, I would choose, sir . . . , to be an infidel tomorrow."[67]

The issue pitted Catholics against Protestants and forced realignments in the political parties. A Whig-nativist coalition developed in opposition to state support of Catholic schools and in favor of state support of public schools. Some Catholics remained in the Whig Party and gave their support to Governor Seward. On the other hand, Democrats had decided to support the Catholic school position and attracted a large following of independent Catholics. The actions of the Democratic Party were consistent with the principle that schools should reflect the desires of the local community.

The school issue so inflamed public feelings that riots between anti-Catholics (a coalition of nativists and Irish Protestants) and Irish Catholics broke out during the 1842 election. The riot began in front of the city prison and quickly spread to attacks on unsuspecting Catholic individuals and Catholic homes. Some Catholics took refuge in a hotel, but it also was attacked by anti-Catholic mobs. Rioters even attacked the residence of Bishop Hughes located behind St. Patrick's Cathedral.

Although emotions remained high, the state legislature in 1842 passed compromise legislation ending the existence of the Public School Society and turning over control of its schools to the public. In hopes of winning Catholic support for the public schools, the legislation established a central, elected school board that shared power with local boards at the ward level. It was hoped that in local wards that were primarily Catholic, ward control would result in the schools' reflecting Catholic sentiments. In the end, Catholics found this an unsatisfactory method of resolving their complaints.

New York City was not the only place where conflict erupted between Catholics and Protestants over the content of public schooling. In *Pillars of the Republic*, Carl Kaestle details Protestant and Catholic conflicts around the country. For instance, in Philadelphia in 1843 the public school board ruled that Catholic children could read their own version of the Bible in public schools and be excused from other religious instruction. Protestants claimed that this was an attempt by Catholics to exclude the Bible from the schools. The result of this conflict was the Philadelphia Bible Riots, in which 13 people died and a Catholic church was burned to the ground. Conflicts of this type but not of this intensity occurred around the country.[68]

In the end, Catholics found it necessary to establish their own system of schooling, the organization of which emerged from the work of plenary councils held in Baltimore in 1852, 1866, and 1884. A major theme of these councils was that religious instruction should not be separated from other forms of instruction. At the First Plenary Council, church leaders told parents that they had a responsibility to "watch over the purity of their [children's] faith and morals with jealous vigilance." To avoid neglecting their children's upbringing, Catholic parents were urged to give their children a Christian education "based on religious principles, accompanied by religious practices and always subordinate to religious influence." The council urged that all possible sacrifices be made for the establishment of Catholic schools.[69]

The idea that religion must be an integral part of instruction ran counter to the increasingly secular quality of common school instruction in the mid-1800s and the increasing importance of science. The Second Plenary Council meeting, in 1866, again emphasized the principle "that religious teaching and religious training should form part of every system of school education." In addition, concern was expressed about the large number of delinquent Catholic youth who were being sent to Protestant reformatories. The council admitted, "It is a melancholy fact, and a very humiliating avowal for us to make, that a very large proportion of the idle and vicious youth of our principal cities are the children of Catholic parents." It recommended the establishment of Catholic industrial schools to care for delinquent Catholic youth.[70]

The Third Plenary Council, in 1884, sent forth decrees for the establishment of a system of Catholic schools. The council warned that the continued trend toward secular education was resulting in the undermining of Christianity and argued that all religious groups were calling for a Christian education in the schools, reflecting a common concern with the preservation of religious faith. The council claimed it was not condemning the state "for not imparting religious instruction in the public schools as they are now organized; because they well know it does not lie within the province of the State to teach religion." In fact, it considered the creation of Catholic schools as beneficial to the state because such schools would create better citizens by educating better Christians. It declared: "Two objects therefore, dear brethren, we have in view, to multiply our schools, and to perfect them."[71]

To achieve the objective of assuring a Catholic education, the council decreed that every church establish a parish school and that all Catholic parents send their children to Catholic schools. The following decrees of the Third Plenary Council established the ideals of Catholic education in the United States.

I. That near every church a parish school, where one does not yet exist, is to be built and maintained in perpetuum within two years of the promulgation of this council, unless the bishop should decide that because of serious difficulties a delay may be granted.

IV. That all Catholic parents are bound to send their children to the parish school, unless it is evident that a sufficient training in religion is given either in their own homes, or in other Catholic schools; or when because of sufficient reason, approved by the bishop, with all due precautions and safeguards, it is licit to send them to other schools. What constitutes a Catholic school is left to the decision of the Bishop.[72]

The establishment of a Catholic school system suggests that the dream of establishing a school system common to all children was impossible in a country settled by a wide variety of cultural and religious groups. It also demonstrates that some groups viewed the common school system as an attempt to impose a particular set of religious and cultural values on all American people. The Catholic rebellion against public school reformers gave proof to the argument that the common school reflected a primarily Protestant ideology. Beginning in the nineteenth century and continuing into the twentieth, many Catholics would refer to public schools as Protestant schools.

Conclusion

The common school movement provided the basic ideology and structure for the modern American school system. No single set of reasons or social forces brought it into existence. Rather, it was a product of a combination of political, economic, and social concerns that existed in the early part of the nineteenth century.

Politically, the success of the common school movement represents the victory of one political philosophy over another. Most individuals who supported and worked for a common school system believed that government should play an active role in assuring the success of the economic and social system and that this was best achieved by centralizing and standardizing governmental processes. Many who opposed the development of the common school system believed that the government that governed best governed least, that the success of the economic and social system depended on the absence of government intervention, and that the free actions of the marketplace guaranteed the most equitable distribution of economic benefits. They opposed the centralizing tendencies of government and hoped to maximize popular control of the political process by maintaining local control.

In the 1830s, these differences in political philosophy separated the Whigs from the Democrats: Most Whigs favored the centralization of control over education and the intervention of government, while most Democrats resisted the expansion of government power and fought to retain democratic localism. The tension and struggle between these two different political philosophies has continued into the twentieth century under different political labels and represents one of the major areas of disagreement in American political thought. By the middle of the twentieth century, conflict over this issue was expressed as concern with centralization of educational control at the federal level—the Democratic Party supported this trend because of the promise it held for a more just and equitable school system, whereas the Republican Party resisted continued federal intervention and argued for local control and the benefits of the free marketplace. Throughout the history of the modern American school, differences in political philosophies have had a major impact on the development and organization of education.

Culturally, the common school movement attempted to assure that one set of cultural values remained dominant, as large groups of immigrants with differing religious and cultural values entered American life. During the early period of common school reforms, this primarily meant protecting a Protestant ideology against an influx of Irish Catholics. In the latter part of the nineteenth and early part of the twentieth centuries, Americanization programs for immigrants in the public schools served the same function.

The protection of a particular set of cultural and religious values was made possible by the way in which control of the school system was organized. The growth of centralized and bureaucratic control, as opposed to democratic localism, assured that the dominant values of the school system would be Protestant and middle class. Beginning in the nineteenth century and continuing into the twentieth, the shifting patterns of control usually reflected the desire of one or more groups in society to ensure that the schools served particular political, social, and economic interests.

The development of the common school also reflected changing economic conditions. The early growth of industrialism placed a premium on education as preparation for work. From the standpoint of employers, common schooling could serve the useful function of socializing and training workers for the factory. From the workers' perspective, as reflected in the workingmen's parties, common schooling was a means of assuring that employers did not maintain a monopoly over knowledge. Knowledge was power in the evolving modern industrial setting, and workers did not want to be kept from that source of power.

Also, the promise of American life was improved economic opportunities for all people. In fact, one could argue that the concept of equality of economic opportunity is a theme that has united all American people. For the worker, equality of economic opportunity was a means for improving personal economic condition. For the school reformer, such as Horace Mann, equality of economic opportunity was a means of reducing friction among social classes. For the employer, equality of economic opportunity was a means of ensuring a supply of the best possible workers by creating competition among workers in the labor market. For most members of society, the common school became the hope for providing and maintaining a society based on equality of economic opportunity.

Most social groups believed that the common school was the best means of controlling crime, social unrest, and political disruptions. In the early nineteenth century, workingmen, Protestants, Catholics, reformers, urban dwellers, and others shared a belief that the school was the key to social control and social stability. This belief became a standard fixture in the rhetoric surrounding the American school in the nineteenth and twentieth centuries.

In summary, by the middle of the nineteenth century most of the major themes of the modern American school had emerged. Persistent political divisions over schooling would occur, and dissent in certain areas would continue. Also, hope would continue that common schooling would bring forth the good society by improving economic conditions, providing equality of opportunity, eliminating crime, and maintaining political and social order.

Notes

1. Ellwood Cubberley, *Public Education in the United States: A Study and Interpretation of American Educational History* (Boston: Houghton Mifflin, 1934), pp. 164–165.
2. Ibid., pp. 165–166.
3. Ibid., p. 166.
4. Merle Curti, *The Social Ideas of American Educators* (Paterson, N.J.: Pageant Books, 1959), p. 138.
5. Michael B. Katz, *The Irony of Early School Reform* (Cambridge, Mass.: Harvard University Press, 1968).
6. Carl Kaestle, *Pillars of the Republic: Common Schools and American Society, 1780–1860* (New York: Hill and Wang, 1983), pp. 146–148.
7. Katz, *Irony*, p. 1.
8. Ibid., p. 2.
9. Ibid., p. 218.
10. Rush Welter, *Popular Education and Democratic Thought in America* (New York: Columbia University Press, 1962), p. 45.

11. Ibid., p. 48.
12. Philip S. Foner, "The Role of Labor in the Struggle for Free Compulsory Education," in Marvin Berlowitz and Frank Chapman, eds., *The United States Educational System: Marxist Approaches* (Minneapolis: Marxist Educational Press, 1980), p. 93.
13. Kaestle, *Pillars*, p. 103.
14. Ibid., p. 81.
15. Ibid., p. 90.
16. Ibid., p. 94.
17. Sally Wertheim, "Educational Periodicals: Propaganda Sheets for the Ohio Common Schools" (Ph.D. dissertation, Case Western Reserve University, 1970), p. 1.
18. Lawrence Cremin, *The American Common School: An Historic Conception* (New York: Teachers College Press, 1951), p. 49.
19. Horace Mann's edited letters and journal are reprinted in Mary Peabody Mann, ed., *Life of Horace Mann* (Washington, D.C.: National Education Association, 1907), p. 13.
20. Ibid., p. 14.
21. Ibid., pp. 49–50.
22. Ibid., p. 71.
23. Ibid., pp. 71–72.
24. Ibid., pp. 72–73.
25. Ibid., pp. 74–75.
26. Ibid., pp. 80–81.
27. Ibid., p. 83.
28. Edited copies of Horace Mann's reports can be found in Lawrence Cremin, ed., *The Republic and the School: Horace Mann on the Education of Free Men* (New York: Teachers College Press, 1957), p. 98.
29. Ibid., p. 100. Italics in original.
30. Ibid., p. 106.
31. Ibid.
32. Ibid., pp. 94–97.
33. Ibid., p. 97.
34. Ibid., p. 93.
35. Ibid., p. 86.
36. Ibid., p. 87.
37. Ibid.
38. Quoted in William Russell, "Education and the Working Class: The Expansion of Public Education during the Transition to Capitalism" (Ph.D. dissertation, University of Cincinnati, 1981), pp. 274–275.
39. Quoted in ibid., pp. 276–277.
40. Ibid., p. 291.
41. Quoted in ibid., p. 294. Italics in original.
42. Quoted in ibid., p. 295.
43. Quoted in ibid., p. 300.
44. Welter, *Popular Education,* pp. 51–52.
45. Herbert Ershkowitz and William G. Shade, "Consensus or Conflict? Political Behavior in the State Legislatures during the Jacksonian Era," in Edward Pes-

sen, ed., *The Many-Faceted Jacksonian Era: New Interpretations* (Westport, Conn.: Greenwood Press, 1977), pp. 212–231.

46. Quoted in Lee Benson, *The Concept of Jacksonian Democracy: New York as a Test Case* (New York: Atheneum, 1966), p. 107.

47. Ibid.

48. Daniel Walker Howe, *The Political Culture of the American Whigs* (Chicago: University of Chicago Press, 1979), p. 29.

49. Ibid., pp. 29–30.

50. Ibid., p. 33.

51. Major L. Wilson, "What Whigs and Jacksonian Democrats Meant by Freedom," in Pessen, *Jacksonian Era*, pp. 192–212; Howe, *Political Culture*, pp. 23–43.

52. Howe, *Political Culture*, pp. 34–35.

53. Carl F. Kaestle and Maris Vinovskis, *Education and Social Change in Nineteenth-Century Massachusetts* (New York: Cambridge University Press, 1980).

54. Quoted in ibid., p. 215.

55. Ibid., p. 230.

56. Michael Katz, *Class, Bureaucracy, and Schools: The Illusion of Educational Change in America* (New York: Praeger, 1971), p. 9.

57. Ibid., p. 17.

58. Ibid., p. 36.

59. Quoted in Vincent Lannie, *Public Money and Parochial Education: Bishop Hughes, Governor Seward, and the New York School Controversy* (Cleveland: Press of Case Western Reserve University, 1968), p. 16.

60. Ibid., p. 21.

61. Quoted in ibid., p. 24.

62. "To the Honorable the Board of Aldermen of the City of New York," in Neil McCluskey, ed., *Catholic Education in America: A Documentary History* (New York: Teachers College Press, 1964), pp. 70–71.

63. Ibid., p. 71.

64. Ibid., p. 72.

65. Ibid., p. 73.

66. Ibid., p. 76.

67. Quoted in Lannie, *Public Money*, pp. 85–87.

68. Kaestle, *Pillars*, pp. 167–172.

69. "First Plenary Council (1852)," in McCluskey, *Catholic Education in America*, pp. 78–81.

70. "Second Plenary Council (1866)," in McCluskey, *Catholic Education in America*, pp. 82–85.

71. "Third Plenary Council (1884)," in McCluskey, *Catholic Education in America*, pp. 86–92.

72. Ibid., p. 94.

5

Organizing the American School: The Nineteenth-Century Schoolmarm

The organization of the common school system focused on the development of elementary schools. It is important to understand that common school reform was primarily organizational and did not necessarily result in the expansion of educational opportunities. According to the statistical work reported by Carl Kaestle and Maris Vinovskis in *Education and Social Change in Nineteenth-Century Massachusetts*, the percentage of people under 20 years of age attending school in Massachusetts declined between 1840 and 1880. In addition, the amount of money spent per $1,000 of state valuation increased only slightly during this period. On the other hand, the average child in the same period increasingly received more days of instruction, and the length of the average school year in Massachusetts increased from 150 days in 1840 to 192 days in 1880. Kaestle and Vinovskis examine the earlier work of economic historian Albert Fishlow and find that one of the primary effects of the common school reform was a shift of student population from private to public schools. Therefore, the primary result of common school reform in the middle of the nineteenth century was not the education of increasing percentages of children, but the creation of new forms of school organization.[1]

The real heroines of the common school movement were the schoolmarms. Actualization of the common school dream required three important steps that involved a complex relationship among a number of factors: the struggle of women for education and careers; the development of concepts of republican motherhood and of women as symbols of charity; the inclusion of sex-role differences in the organization of education; and the economic exploitation of women. The first, and probably most important, step was to create a stable and inexpensive teaching force that would uphold in the classroom the moral ideals of the common school movement. The creation of this teaching force began with the pioneering efforts of women educators that resulted in the establishment of the first teacher-training institutions. Common school reformers aided these efforts because they believed women would provide the schools with a stable, inexpensive, and moral teaching force.

Second, common school reformers believed that standardization of the organization of education was required to assure that the schools taught a common moral and political philosophy. Of great importance was the function of supervision of instruction. In rural areas, the county superintendent became a major figure, riding from schoolhouse to schoolhouse checking on the quality of instruction and the adherence of teachers to a standard curriculum. In urban areas, city superintendents began to take over the functions of school committees in the supervision and evaluation of teachers and students. As larger schools replaced the one-room schoolhouse, two roles—principal teacher and assistant teacher—began to appear; the teaching functions of the principal teacher were slowly replaced with administrative duties. The emerging hierarchical system of supervision and administrative control made possible a uniform system of education.

An important factor in creating this hierarchical system was the subservient status of women. Hierarchical organization required a division of duties and subordination to authority. The emerging pattern in nineteenth-century education, which reflected more general social patterns, was for men to manage and women to teach. What was considered the natural subordination of women to men provided a social basis for creating a hierarchical educational system in which role expectations were the same as those in more general social situations. Thus, the function of women in the common school system was to be moral, nurturing, and loving teachers, guided and managed by men holding positions of authority as superintendents and principals.

The creation of a uniform common school system also required standardization of curriculum and instruction. Again, like the other organizational changes, this process was in only embryonic form in the decades before the Civil War. Of primary importance was the development of the graded school and graded textbook series. In addition, an early science of education developed around new methods of instruction. Also of major importance during these early years were Pestalozzian methods of instruction, which originated in Europe and upheld the ideal of woman as mother and teacher. Johann Pestalozzi's methods provided further justification for the subordinate role of women in teaching. In the most popular texts used during the development period of the common school, the McGuffey Readers, females are depicted as models of charity. The concept of charity justified the increasing economic inequalities occurring with the expansion of industrialism. Combined with the other organizational changes, Pestalozzian techniques and McGuffey's Readers added the final touches to the portrait of the nineteenth-century schoolmarm as the inexpensive, moral, nurturing, stable, kind, charitable, and subordinate backbone of the common school system.

The American Teacher

Early attempts to develop a professional teaching corps for the common schools involved a complex relationship among the struggle by women for education and careers, popular concepts of the role of women in the new republic, and the desire by common school reformers for a stable and moral teaching force. In addition, women were welcomed into the ranks of teaching by local school boards because they could be hired at lower wages than men. As a result, by the end of the Civil War women dominated the ranks of teaching, and teacher education centered on the education of women.

Traditional histories of education identify the Reverend Samuel Hall's private school, established in 1823 in Concord, Vermont, as the first teacher-training institution. However, a good argument can be made that the first teacher-training institution in the United States was the Troy Female Seminary, officially opened by Emma Willard in 1821 but with earlier beginnings, in 1814. Willard opened the seminary for the specific purpose of educating women for responsible motherhood and teaching. Her thoughts on the education of women can be traced to the American Revolution, when new ideas about the public role of women opened the door to new educational opportunities. These ideas provided women with the necessary leverage for increasing both their level of formal education and their opportunities as teachers and also provided later common school reformers with a justification for the increased utilization of women as teachers.

One effect of the American Revolution was to link the domestic responsibilities of women with broader public purposes. During colonial times, little consideration was given to the relationship between the domestic role of women and their role in the public sphere. Personal salvation and service to other members of the family were the major purposes of education for women during this period. As Mary Norton states in *Liberty's Daughters: The Revolutionary Experience of American Women, 1750–1800,*

> Prior to the Revolution, when the private realm of the household was seen as having little connection with the public world of politics and economics, wom-

*en's secular role was viewed solely in its domestic setting. . . . no one, male
or female, wrote or thought about the possibility that women might affect the
wider secular society through their individual or collective behavior.*[2]

During and immediately after the Revolution, male and female writers
began to link the domestic role of women with the development of
republican citizens. Women, as mothers, were seen as having the responsibility for shaping the character of their sons as future republicans.
This perception of the role of mothers logically led to the conclusion that
women needed to be educated to assume the role of republican motherhood. In Norton's words:

*And so citizens of the republic set out to discover and define woman's public
role. They found it not in the notion that women should directly participate in
politics. . . . Rather, they located woman's public role in her domestic responsibilities, in her obligation to create a supportive home life for her husband, and particularly in her duty to raise republican sons who would love
their country and preserve its virtuous character.*[3]

The acceptance of the concept of republican motherhood allowed
greater educational opportunities for women. Prior to the Revolution,
the education of women was limited to reading and writing and, for
some young girls, to education at "adventure schools," which taught
music, dancing, drawing, needlework, and handicrafts. After the Revolution, some academies began to open their doors to women, and
schools began to be established for the specific purpose of educating
young girls. These new educational opportunities for women included
academic instruction in subjects such as geography, history, philosophy, and astronomy, which had been taught in the past only to boys. In
addition, charity schools for girls were started during this period, and
urban school systems—for instance, Boston's—began admitting girls.

One of the results of the expanding educational opportunities for
women was that charity schools began to seek female graduates as
teachers. This was different from colonial times, when women without
any particular qualifications operated dame schools. After the Revolution, school authorities began to recruit young female academy graduates. In turn, educated women began to realize that teaching offered
career possibilities. "Teaching," Norton argues, "was the first profession opened to women on a regular basis, and as such it attracted, albeit
for only a few years of their lives, a large number of intellectually aware
young women, many of them products of the republican academies."[4]

It was against this background that Emma Willard opened the Troy
Female Seminary. In an address to the New York legislature in 1819, she
declared the hopes of republican motherhood: "Who knows how great
and good a race of men may yet arise from the forming hands of mothers, enlightened by the bounty of that beloved country,—to defend her

liberties, to plan her future improvements and to raise her to unparal-leled glory?"[5] In all her public statements, she supported the existence of a patriarchal family. She argued that women needed to be educated to be teachers both because of a shortage of male schoolmasters and to function as responsible mothers.

According to Anne Scott, as an encouragement for women to be self-supporting and educated, Willard provided "'instruction on credit' for any woman who would agree to become a teacher, the debt to be repaid from her later earnings." To facilitate this process, Willard maintained a teacher placement agency, which had difficulty meeting the demand for teachers. In Scott's words, "Someone commented that Emma Willard's signature on a letter of recommendation was the first form of teacher certification in this country."[6]

The curriculum at the Troy Female Seminary included a full range of academic subjects from Latin to geography. Furthermore, like other teacher educators in the early nineteenth century, Willard believed that development of character was the first aim of education and placed a great deal of emphasis on that development and on moral virtues. As discussed later in this section, in the development of teacher institutes in the late 1830s, both she and Henry Barnard placed the same strong emphasis on education of character.

As Paul Mattingly demonstrates in *The Classless Profession: American Schoolmen in the Nineteenth Century*, the overriding concern of those inter-ested in the reform of teaching in the 1830s and 1840s was the develop-ment of moral character.[7] As women began to be educated in larger numbers, schoolmen began to seek them out as teachers because of the belief in the inherent moral character of females. The teacher was to be a paragon of moral virtue whose influence would be felt and imitated by the students in the common school. If the schools were to reform and morally uplift society, it was reasoned, it was of fundamental impor-tance for the teacher to function as a model of morality. Consequently, along with education in the subject matter to be taught, a major goal of teacher training was to link methods of instruction, classroom manage-ment, and the character of teachers to the moral character development of students.

The emphasis on moral character had a lasting effect on the teaching profession. Through the nineteenth century and into the twentieth, teachers were expected to live exemplary lives, with their social activities constantly under public scrutiny. This is still true in some places. Wil-lard Elsbree in *The American Teacher: Evolution of a Profession in a Democ-racy:* "The teacher's private life has always been open to public scrutiny like a goldfish in a glass bowl. Tradition has given teachers a place in society comparable to that accorded to ministers and the restrictions placed upon their conduct have been many and varied."[8] The control of the social life of teachers contributed to the low status of teaching as a profession.

The ideal characteristics of teachers for the common school are stated by Horace Mann in his *Fourth Annual Report* (1840) to the Massachusetts State Board of Education. First, he lists as a qualification for teaching a "perfect" knowledge of the subjects to be taught in the common schools. He complains that the major defect in instruction in existing schools is the teacher's lack of knowledge of the subject matter. The second qualification he lists is an aptness for teaching, which he believed could be learned. He feared that inadequate or erroneous methods of teaching could destroy the moral character of students. As an example, he describes the custom in surveying in feudal Scotland of tying boys to landmarks and whipping them so they would retain a knowledge of the boundaries of the land and could be used as witnesses in any litigation. He states, "Though this might give them a vivid recollection of localities, yet it would hardly improve their ideas of justice. . . . But do not those, who have no aptness to teach, sometimes accomplish their objects by a kindred method?" A third essential qualification listed by Mann is the ability to manage and govern a schoolroom and to mold moral character. Mann believed that the primary source of moral instruction in the classroom was the moral character of the teacher. He lists "Good Behavior" and "Morals" as the fourth and fifth characteristics of a good teacher. With regard to good behavior, he states:

If, then, the manners of the teacher are to be imitated by his pupils—if he is the glass, at which they "do dress themselves," how strong is the necessity, that he should understand those nameless and innumerable practices, in regard to deportment, dress, conversation, and all personal habits, that constitute the difference between a gentleman and a clown.

Mann goes on to argue that one could accept eccentricities in a friend, "but it become quite a different thing, when the oddity, or eccentricity, is to be a pattern or model, from which fifty or a hundred children are to form their manners." In other words, a major requirement of a schoolteacher was to conform to accepted social customs.[9]

Under "Morals," Mann emphasizes the importance of having teachers "of pure tastes, of good manners, [and] of exemplary morals." He gave the responsibility for assuring the morality of teachers to local school committees or school boards. He writes that "the school committee are sentinels stationed at the door of every schoolhouse in the State, to see that no teacher ever crosses its threshold, who is not clothed, from the crown of his head to the sole of his foot, in garments of virtue."[10]

It was the nineteenth-century schoolmarm who was to fulfill the requirements of high morality and social conformity demanded by common school reformers. The reason women were recruited into teaching was candidly stated by the board in Boston in 1841. Its annual report notes that within the previous year the number of male teachers in the system had declined by 33, while the number of female teachers had increased by 103. The report gives three reasons for supporting this trend. The first is a belief that women are better teachers of young children because of their natural child-rearing talents: "They [women] are endowed by nature with stronger parental impulses, and this makes the society of children delightful, and turns duty into pleasure."

Second, the report argues that because female minds are less distracted by wordly forces, and because women have no other possibilities of employment, they can more easily concentrate on teaching:

> *As a class, they never look forward, as young men almost invariably do, to a period of legal emancipation from parental control, when they are to break away from the domestic circle and go abroad into the world, to build up a fortune for themselves; and hence, the sphere of hope and of effort is narrower, and the whole forces of the mind are more readily concentrated upon present duties.*

As statistics show, a major concern of the times was that men remained in teaching for only a short period of time. Because this created a great deal of instability in the teaching force, it was hoped that the narrow range of opportunities for women would keep them in teaching and thus provide a stabilizing influence.

The third reason for favoring women, the report argues, is because "they are also of purer morals." The report goes on to argue: "In the most notorious vices of the age, profanity, intemperance, fraud, &c., there are twenty men to one woman . . . on this account, therefore, females are infinitely more fit than males to be guides and exemplars of young children."[11]

The concern of educational leaders with creating a moral and nurturing teaching force complemented the notion of republican motherhood. The conjunction of these ideas provided justification for the increased use of women as teachers, while the social and economic conditions of teaching convinced school leaders of the wisdom of the idea. The compatibility of republican motherhood with the needs of common school systems received explicit attention in a famous report on education distributed in the United States in the late 1830s and the 1840s.

The author of that report was Calvin Stowe, a founder of the Western Literary Institute, one of the earliest associations for professional teachers in the United States. Stowe's wife, Harriet Beecher Stowe, the author of *Uncle Tom's Cabin*, provided a model of woman extending her concerns beyond the domestic family into the arena of political and social issues. Calvin Stowe placed sharp limits in his own public statements on the proper role of women in the public sphere.

In 1836, Calvin Stowe departed for Europe to purchase books for the Lane Theological Seminary in Cincinnati, Ohio. Before he left, the state legislature passed a resolution requesting him to report on European systems of education. On his return in 1837, he presented his statement, *Report on Elementary Public Instruction in Europe*, to the governor and state legislature. One important aspect of the report, discussed in more detail in the next section of this chapter, is his discussion of Pestalozzian educational methods as practiced in Prussia. The report received a great deal of attention and was widely circulated in the United States. The Ohio legislature printed 10,000 copies and distributed them to every school district in the state. Copies were also reprinted and distributed by the governments of Massachusetts, Michigan, North Carolina, Pennsylvania, and Virginia.

In the concluding section of his report, Stowe addresses the problem of recruiting and training teachers. First, he argues that, given the economic conditions in the United States, there was little hope of finding enough male teachers for all the schools. Therefore, the education of young children must be placed in the hands of women. Then, in one sentence he ties together several strands of the arguments supporting women as teachers: "There is not the same variety of tempting employment for females as for men, they can be supported cheaper, and the Creator has given them peculiar qualifications for the education of the young."[12]

Stowe continues by alluding to the more advanced place of women in American society as compared with women in Europe and links this condition to American women's greater involvement in the public arena: "There is no country in the world where woman holds so high a rank, or exerts so great an influence, as here; wherefore, her responsibilities are the greater, and she is under obligations to render herself the more actively useful." He makes clear to his readers that although he supports a greater role for women in society, he believes that role should be limited. In reference to women of the period who were seeking political equality with men, he states,

> I think our fair countrywomen, notwithstanding the exhortations of Harriet Martineau, Fanny Wright, and some other ladies and gentlemen, will never seek distinction in our public assemblies for public discussion, or in our halls of legislation; but in their appropriate work of educating the young, of forming the opening mind to all that is good and great, the more they distinguish themselves the better.[13]

Stowe's statement illustrates how the emphasis on the domestic role of women could be used to severely limit the role of women in the public sphere.

A major reason for employing women was the lack of stability in the male teaching force. In the early nineteenth century, the typical pattern was for young men to enter teaching for a few years before continuing on to some other career. Consequently, the teaching force was young and inexperienced, with a high turnover rate, which made selection of teachers and control of their moral character difficult. Although the number of women teachers did increase (and by the end of the Civil War they dominated the ranks of teaching because men were called to military action), their teaching careers tended to be as short as those of men. In part, this was caused by continuing low salaries.

Before the Civil War, the increase in the number of women in teaching varied from state to state, with females becoming a majority in the teaching force in some states. For example, in Connecticut, 56 percent of the total teaching force was female by 1846, and the percentage increased to 71 in 1857. In 1862, the state superintendent in New Jersey reported that in 1852 there had been twice as many male teachers as female, but within 10 years, female teachers had come to outnumber male teachers. In Vermont, 70 percent of the teaching force was female by 1850, and in Pennsylvania, the proportion of female teachers increased from 28 percent in 1834 to 36 percent in 1856. The dramatic effect of the Civil War was felt in states like Indiana, where the percentage of male teachers dropped from 80 percent in 1859 to 58 percent in 1864, and in Ohio, where the number of male teachers declined from 52 percent in 1862 to 41 percent in 1864. New York reported a loss of 1,119 male teachers between 1862 and 1863, and in 1862, Iowa reported that female teachers exceeded male teachers for the first time.[14]

The teaching force remained unstable despite the increased number of women in it because many women entered teaching for only a few years before being married. This is seen in the ages of female teachers. Kaestle reports that in 1860 in southeastern Michigan, 77 percent of female teachers were between 17 and 24 years of age, and in Dane County, Wisconsin, 27 percent of female teachers were under 18.[15] Still, the caricature of the late nineteenth-century teacher is the prudish, pedantic, spinster schoolmarm.

Statistics gathered by Elsbree indicate a continued problem for school leaders in the youth and inexperience of the teaching force: "The average age of teachers in Maine in 1866 was twenty-one and three quarters years; in Pennsylvania it was under twenty-four in 1856. In this latter state, of 7428 teachers in thirty-eight counties, 2328 or nearly one third of the total were under twenty-one years of age." In many cases, teachers remained in teaching only one year. It was reported that in Connecticut in 1858, two-thirds of the teachers were new to the system. New York reported in 1853 that of 20,000 teachers in the state, one-third would leave their positions and be replaced with new teachers. The *Pennsylva-*

Table 1   *Average Weekly Salaries of Teachers, 1841 to 1864*

	Rural		City	
Year	Men	Women	Men	Women
1841	$4.15	$2.51	$11.93	$4.44
1845	3.87	2.48	12.21	4.09
1850	4.25	2.89	13.37	4.71
1855	5.77	3.65	16.80	5.79
1860	6.28	4.12	18.56	6.99
1864	7.86	4.92	20.78	7.67

Source: Adapted from Willard Elsbree, *The American Teacher: Evolution of a Profession in a Democracy* (New York: American Book Company, 1939), p. 274.

nia School Report for 1856 tabulated the amount of experience of teachers in 34 counties and found the following range of experience:

Those who have taught less than one year	1,793
Those who have taught between 1 and 3 years	2,035
Those who have taught between 3 and 6 years	1,058
Those who have taught over 6 years	1,124
Total	6,010[16]

Although the increased number of female teachers did not seem to fulfill the common school reformers' hopes of creating an experienced and stable teaching force, there was ample evidence that female teachers made education less expensive. In fact, from a look at the differences in salaries between male and female teachers in the nineteenth century, one could argue that the primary reason for the acceptance of women into the ranks of teaching was that they were inexpensive to employ. Table 1, compiled in 1920 by Warren Burgess, indicates not only the differences between the salaries of men and women but also the differences between the salaries of rural and urban teachers. The figures give some indication of the economic position of teachers during this period. In his compilation, Burgess estimated that weekly wages for common laborers were $4.86 in 1841 and $7.98 in 1864, while artisans earned an average of $8.28 in 1841 and $12.66 in 1864. This means that male urban teachers earned more during this period than either common laborers or artisans. On the other hand, urban and rural female teachers and rural male teachers earned less than common laborers.

Burgess's statistics were supported by a survey conducted by Horace Mann for the *Common School Journal* in 1843, in which Mann claims to have ascertained the wages of "journeymen, shoemakers, carpenters, blacksmiths, painters, carriage-makers, wheelwrights, harness-makers, cabinet and piano-forte makers and some others." He reports that all these occupations paid more than teaching and that the salaries of some were from 50 to 100 percent higher than the average salary of teachers.[17]

In addition to indicating why school boards increasingly hired female teachers, Burgess's figures provide some explanation for the high turnover in teaching. Compared with the wages of laborers and artisans, it would appear that perhaps only urban male schoolteachers earned enough to support a family and that both urban and rural female teachers earned barely a subsistence wage. For women, marriage would most certainly have been an attractive economic alternative to the income earned as a teacher, and for male rural teachers, other occupations certainly would have appeared to be economically more attractive.

The problem of stability in the rural teaching force was compounded by the practice of supplementing salaries with the custom of "boarding 'round." Before the Civil War, it was the practice in most rural areas for teachers to spend a week or more each in the homes of all the children attending their schools. This meant that rural teachers had to pack their belongings and move frequently during the school year. Students' families provided food and housing as part of their contribution to the teacher's salary. Vermont reported in 1862 that 68 percent of the state's teachers boarded around, and Connecticut reported in 1846 that 84 percent of its teachers engaged in this practice.[18]

The practice of boarding around was not conducive to maintaining a stable teaching force. It is hard to imagine that many people would want to spend their lives moving from house to house. Also, this practice certainly was more suited for the young and inexperienced than for the older person.

In addition to the utilization of women in teaching, common school reformers hoped to improve teaching through the establishment of teacher institutes and normal schools, both of which introduced the novel idea that methods of instruction could be taught and learned. In a broader sense, this marked the beginning of the study of pedagogy and the investigation of various methods of instruction. Also, normal schools opened a new arena for the education of women. Female students dominated the classes in normal schools, and, in turn, normal schools contributed to the increase in the number of female teachers.

Before the Civil War, the most important type of organization for the training of teachers was the teacher institute. The idea for teacher institutes was developed by Emma Willard and Henry Barnard in Connecticut in 1839. This uniquely American experiment in teacher education spread rapidly throughout the country. The typical teacher institute met once or twice a year for two to four weeks. At first, teachers paid the cost of the institute, but later private citizens and the government covered the expenses. The primary objective of the institutes was to provide a brief course in the theory and practice of teaching. As Paul Mattingly argues, the institutes were conducted very much like religious revivals. Concepts of methods of instruction were vague, and the greatest emphasis was placed on elevating the moral character of the teachers. Of course, the stress on moral character was in keeping with the general tone of common school reform. Mattingly states:

> For this generation of professional educators this institution [the teacher institute] made explicit, more than any other educational agency, how determined schoolmen were to equate professionalization with "awakening" of moral character rather than with the training in communicable skills and the standard techniques of teaching.[19]

Mattingly underlines a distinctive feature of the concern with development of moral character. Those involved with teacher training were interested not in producing moral crusaders who would engage in open public conflict over moral and social issues but in producing teachers who would limit their moral campaigns to shaping student character. In other words, teacher education did not encourage or train teachers to confront directly the products of "weak moral character," such as corrupt political structures, economic injustice, or actual criminal activities.

This approach to the education of teachers safely removed discussions of moral character from the political arena. Like the education of common school students, the stress in teacher education was on motives, not consequences. As Mattingly states, "Out of a political necessity to avoid controversial issues in the act of instruction, schoolmen developed their own rituals of moral inquiry and proper maneuvers. The moral sphere dealt primarily with motives which were treated both as aspirations and as embryonic consequences."[20] The result was a passive quality to the moral training of teachers and students, as opposed to preparing them to take active public positions on moral issues. What was important to common school reformers was to ensure that training for both teachers and students would stifle all desire to do anything morally incorrect.

This approach to the training of moral character was in keeping with general social attitudes about women. The majority of students at teacher-training institutions in the nineteenth century were women. It would not have been in keeping with the temper of the times if these institutions had trained women to become public crusaders because active political and social endeavors were not considered a proper part of the social role of women in the nineteenth century. As stated earlier, the proper role for women was to connect with the public sphere by nurturing moral character in the family and the school. Thus, both in the common school and in teacher-training institutions, there was little discussion of the major social, economic, and political problems confronting society. Discussion was limited to individual motives and desires.

Ironically, although the nineteenth-century schoolmarm was given responsibility for the morality of society, she was limited in political and social activities. This had consequences for the development of both the profession of teaching and the concept of citizenship in the schools. A passive type of morality was expected of teachers, not socially active moral behavior. They were expected to prevent social problems but not to actively engage in solving existing problems. Students were also included in this concept of passive citizenship. They were to learn to not break the law, but they were not taught how to actively deal with injustice.

The result was that teachers in the nineteenth century were expected to live exemplary moral lives and avoid active participation in political, social, and economic issues. These expectations would change (as discussed in Chapter 9) when female teachers organized to improve the economic rewards of their profession. By the middle part of the twentieth century, their union activity had resulted in active teacher participation in political and social campaigns.

Although teacher institutes were the primary means of teacher education before the Civil War, formally organized teacher-training institutions became more important by the end of the nineteenth century. The establishment of Emma Willard's Troy Female Seminary, with its emphasis on academic education and the education of moral character, was quickly followed in the 1820s and 1830s by other experiments in teacher-education institutions. The most important of these experiments was the first state normal school, opened in Lexington, Massachusetts, in July 1839. Soon after, normal schools were established at Barre, Massachusetts, in September of the same year, and at Bridgewater, Massachusetts, the following year.

Normal schools were supposedly modeled on Prussian institutions, but the term *normal* was of French derivation. The early normal schools prepared teachers to teach in what would later be considered the elementary school grades. The ordinary practice was for normal school students, who were mostly female, to graduate from elementary or common schools and directly enter normal schools. As the pattern developed in the nineteenth century and clearer distinctions were made between elementary and secondary education, important differences emerged in teacher education for the two levels. Teachers in secondary institutions, high schools, and academies tended to be graduates of colleges and universities, whereas elementary school teachers tended to be graduates of normal schools. These differences contributed to the justification for paying secondary school teachers more than elementary school teachers. This difference in salaries has continued into the twentieth century.

The low salaries of normal school graduates as compared with those of secondary school teachers also denoted the primarily female composition of normal schools. In 1856, the four normal schools in Massachusetts reported a student population of 332, 290 of whom were girls. Between 1862 and 1886, the Oswego State Normal and Training School in New York had 1,245 female graduates and 128 male graduates.[21] The same enrollment pattern existed at the Bridgewater Normal School in Massachusetts, from where between 1854 and 1904 2,075 females, as compared with 546 males, graduated.[22]

Although normal schools became a major source of female education in the nineteenth century, they provided a very abbreviated form of education. After graduating from elementary schools but before being sent back to elementary schools as teachers, normal school students received a one- or two-year course that included a review of material learned and to be taught in the elementary school grades and instruction in classroom management and methods of teaching. Overriding this formal curriculum was the concern with moral character. As Mattingly states, "In a sense, the nineteenth-century normal school always determined as its first priority the creation of a common, moral purpose out of the diverse needs and interests of school teachers."[23] In considering the development of the normal school, it is important to remember that a majority of teachers in the nineteenth century were not graduates of normal schools. In some places, even in 1900 and even in reform-minded Massachusetts, only a bare majority of teachers had attended normal schools.

These early attempts to create a professional corps of teachers in the United States linked the educational concerns of common school reformers with the desires of women for further education and for careers. Women, as republican mothers and vessels of virtue, were considered the ideal teachers for a system of schooling that emphasized moral development. However, the second-class citizenship of women and the low salaries in teaching contributed to the generally low status of teaching as a profession in the nineteenth and early twentieth centuries. Indeed, even the earliest professional teacher training, with its limited preparation for elementary school instruction, its mainly female student population, and its emphasis on moral exhortation, further contributed to the low-status professional image of teaching.

The Maternal Model of Instruction

Given the attitudes about morality and women in the early and middle nineteenth century, it is not surprising that the first widespread theory of instruction was based on the concepts of maternal love and the cultivation of the moral faculty. Like the belief in the importance of the role of republican motherhood, the educational theories of Johann Pestalozzi gave to the mother and the household the main responsibility for the salvation of society. Pestalozzi's conception of maternal instruction in the home became his model for instruction in the school.

Any discussion of educational ideas must give recognition to the difference between theory and practice. Usually there is a time lag between the development of a theory and its impact on practices in the school. For instance, Barbara Finkelstein, in her study of elementary school classrooms in the nineteenth century, found that the majority of teachers had students recite, work at their desks, or listen to verbal instruction by the teacher: "North and south, east and west, in rural schools as well as urban schools, teachers assigned lessons, asked questions and created standards of achievement designed to compel students to assimilate knowledge and practice in a particular fashion." Finkelstein argues that teachers during this period were of two major types: the "intellectual overseer" who stressed memorization and punished failures in assignments, and the "drillmaster," who had the students repeat material in unison.[24]

Many common school reformers hoped that those types of classroom practices would be replaced by what they considered the more humane educational methods of Pestalozzi. The major impact of Pestalozzian theory was its emphasis on relating instruction for learning in the early years to objects in the real world, to learning by doing, and to the importance of activity, as opposed to sitting at a desk. By the end of the nineteenth century, these Pestalozzian practices had become an important part of progressive instructional theory, and by the twentieth century, they were an important part of elementary classroom practice.

A maternal and moral model of instruction complemented the goals of common school reformers and the growing role of women in education. In addition, one of the major intellectual revolutions to accompany the development of teacher training was the idea that people could be taught how to teach. This meant that the process of teaching was open to study and inquiry and that methods of instruction could be developed and imparted to future teachers. Joseph Lancaster and his monitorial system (see Chapter 3) provided the first systematic method of classroom management; Johann Pestalozzi popularized the first systematic method of instruction.

The development of a system of instruction involved the formulation of theories of learning, or, to state it another way, it involved an attempt to match the laws of the mind to the process of learning. Most early attempts in the United States to teach methods of instruction disregarded theories of the mind and systematized only traditional instructional techniques. For instance, in a letter to Henry Barnard in 1841, Cyrus Peirce, the head of the first normal school, in Lexington, Massachusetts, describes the method of instruction he imparted to future teachers as involving four different methods of recitation: "I have four different methods of recitation. 1st, by question and answer; 2d, by conversation; 3d, by calling on one, two, three more or less, to give an analysis of the whole subject contained in the lesson; and 4th, by requiring written analyses."[25] Peirce considered these methods to be "the best way of teaching the same things effectually to others." This explication of the methods of instruction incorporated traditional school recitations.

In contrast, by 1861, when the Oswego State Normal and Training School was established in Oswego, New York, Pestalozzian ideas were considered the basis for relating the development and functioning of the mind to learning in the classroom. In fact, the Oswego State Normal and Training School launched the Oswego movement, which helped to spread Pestalozzian concepts throughout the United States.

Johann Pestalozzi (1746–1827) was born in Zurich, Switzerland, and in 1781, after dabbling in journalism and education, he wrote his classic and popular description of domestic education, *Leonard and Gertrude*. His ideas on education quickly spread throughout the Western world. Many American visitors to Prussia in the early nineteenth century were impressed by the use of Pestalozzian methods in the schools. The English Home and Colonial Institution, organized in 1836, became a forum for the dissemination of Pestalozzian ideas in England, the United States, and Canada. This organization had developed from the work of Charles Mayo, who, beginning in 1818, adapted Pestalozzian ideas to English infant schools.

Pestalozzi's theories of maternal education paralleled in time and content the development of concepts of republican motherhood in the United States. *Leonard and Gertrude* is the story of moral and social reform that occurs as a result of the extension of maternal influence and education from the home to the public sphere. The story is set in the small village of Bonnal. The main characters are Leonard, an alcoholic husband, and Gertrude, a brave and pious wife. It is a tale of moral struggle between the forces of evil and idleness and the forces of maternal love and nurturing. The opening lines of the tale describe the social conditions that could be remedied if education were based on maternal values. The reader is told that "his [Leonard's] trade would have enabled him to support his family of a wife and seven children, if he could have resisted the temptation to frequent the tavern, where there were always idle loafers to entice him in, and induce the good-natured, easygoing man to squander his earnings in drink and gambling."[26]

The struggle by women to redeem their men from the pitfalls of demon rum and gambling became a classic tale by the end of the nineteenth century. In Pestalozzi's story, Leonard and the village are re-deemed because domestic relationships are maintained by Gertrude's becoming a public model. To symbolize the connection between the domestic role of women and the public sphere, Pestalozzi has three male leaders of the village visit Gertrude's home and study her system of household management. Their analysis of Gertrude's actions provides the basis for the development of a pedagogical theory.

In the story, the visit by the three village leaders occurs just as the family is completing breakfast. After the children wash the dishes, they immediately engage in a variety of tasks, including spinning and gardening. What is most impressive for the visitors is Gertrude's ability to integrate instruction into the activities of the household. A trademark of the Pestalozzian method is the use of common objects in instruction and the development of the child's powers of observation, as opposed to abstract teaching that has little connection to the realities of life. For instance, the *New England Primer* (see Chapter 1) taught numbers without any reference to real objects, whereas Gertrude gives instruction in arithmetic by having her children

> count the number of steps from one end of the room to the other, and two of the rows of five panes each, in one of the windows, gave her an opportunity to unfold the decimal relations of numbers. She also made them count their threads while spinning, and the number of turns on the reel, when they wound the yarn into skeins.[27]

Shortly after departing from Gertrude's home, one of the visitors dashes back and proclaims that he will be the schoolmaster of Bonnal. The next day, after returning to further observe Gertrude's family, the village leaders ask Gertrude to help the newly self-appointed school-master. "Then they explained to her that they regarded the proper education of the youthful population as the only means of elevating the condition of the corrupt village; and full of emotion, Gertrude promised them she would do anything in her power to forward the good cause."[28]

Pestalozzi later declared that "maternal love is the first agent in education."[29] In *How Gertrude Teaches Her Children*, written between 1799 and 1804 while Pestalozzi was a schoolmaster, he draws a direct connection between maternal love and individual moral development. He argues that people must love and trust other people before they are able to love and trust God and that the germ of love and trust is developed in the mother's nurturing of the child. The mother's lack of response to irregular desires of the infant teaches the first lessons in obedience; in addition, the infant learns to be grateful for the mother's actions. The combination of trust, gratitude, love, and obedience forms the early beginnings of a conscience.

According to Pestalozzi, the development of conscience and moral feelings that is learned from interaction with the mother depends on the art of instruction. He argues that society does not provide the child with moral instruction because such instruction is a distortion of nature. It is the responsibility of the teacher to arrange the world encountered by the child so that the early beginnings of moral ideas will be developed.

Like all aspects of Pestalozzian instruction, the development of morality depends on the education of the senses: "The first instruction of the child should never be the business of the head or of reason; it should always be the business of the senses, or the heart, of the mother." What he declares as the second law of instruction is to move slowly from the exercise of the senses to the exercise of reason. In accord with the general attitudes of the time, he associates the senses, or heart, with women, and reason with men. "It is for a long time the business of the heart," Pestalozzi states with regard to instruction, "before it is the business of the reason. It is for a long time the business of the woman before it begins to be the business of the man."[30]

Pestalozzi always declared that he was trying to psychologize the education of humanity, by which he meant adapting methods of instruction to human development and the laws of the mind. He was greatly influenced by Jean-Jacques Rousseau's *Emile* (see Chapter 1), in which the inability of children to reason until the age of adolescence is stressed. Before that time, Rousseau argues, the child should not be given verbal instruction but should learn from experience and nature. Pestalozzi emphasizes that the young child should receive no verbal instruction and that learning should be a result of experience. In addition, he accentuates the importance of educating the senses. From the education of the senses, one is to move to an understanding of ideas and eventually to a knowledge of God and morality.

The concentration on education of the senses, the use of objects in instruction, and the replacement of corporeal discipline with control through love revolutionized methods of instruction. Certainly a major contrast exists between the type of instruction of young children provided by the recitation of the *New England Primer* and Pestalozzi's statement that the best general methods of instruction "are speech, the arts of drawing, writing, reckoning and measuring."[31]

Americans returning from visits to Europe in the early nineteenth century helped to acquaint fellow Americans with Pestalozzian methods of instruction. One of the earliest visitors was John Griscom, who was active in social and educational reform in New York. His visit to Europe in 1818 included tours of hospitals, schools, prisons, and charitable institutions. *A Year in Europe*, the story of his trip, includes glowing reports of Lancasterian schools in England and Pestalozzian schools in Prussia. After the publication of this book, Griscom became actively involved in social and educational reform by serving, among other positions, as chairman of the committee that established the New York House of Refuge and as a leader in the establishment of a monitorial high school in New York in 1825.

On his trip, Griscom visited Pestalozzi at the educational institution he had established at Yverdun in 1805. Griscom was warmly greeted by Pestalozzi and was given a tour of the school, which at that time had 90 boys from a variety of European countries. In the classroom visited by Griscom, the teacher did not use books but relied solely on the use of objects. Griscom claimed that the constant interaction between students and the instructor made it too difficult to write a detailed account of the type of instruction provided in the classroom. His more general description states:

> We saw the exercises of arithmetic, writing, drawing, mathematics, lessons in music. . . . To teach a school, in the way practised here, without book, almost entirely by verbal instructions, is extremely laborious. The teacher must be constantly with the child, always talking, questioning, explaining, and repeating. The pupils, however, by this process, are brought into very close intimacy with the instructor.[32]

In general, Griscom was most impressed by the moral aspects of the Pestalozzian methods: "But the greatest recommendation of the Pestalozzian . . . plan of education, is the moral charm which is diffused throughout all its operations."[33] He felt that children educated under this method would become more moral and intelligent members of society.

Many Americans learned about Pestalozzian methods of instruction while visiting schools in Prussia, where Pestalozzi became very popular in the nineteenth century. Another visitor was Calvin Stowe, whose widely circulated *Report on Elementary Public Instruction in Europe* is discussed in the previous section with regard to hiring women as teachers. Stowe included in his report a description of a classroom in a Berlin school using Pestalozzian methods. Like Griscom, Stowe was struck by the amount of verbal exchange between the teacher and the students. The use of objects for instruction and the education of the senses are very evident in Stowe's description:

> He [the teacher] first directs their [students'] attention to the different objects in the school-room, their position, form, color, size, materials of which they are made, &c., and requires precise and accurate descriptions. He then requires them to notice the various objects that meet their eye on the way to their respective homes; and a description of these objects and the circumstances under which they saw them, will form the subject of the next morning's lesson. Then the house in which they live; the shop in which their father works; the garden in which they walk, &c., will be the subject of the successive lessons; and in this way for six months or a year, the children are taught to study

things, to use their own power of observation, and speak with readiness and accuracy, before books are put into their hands at all.[34]

After giving a detailed description of the structure of Prussian schools, Stowe strongly recommends the system as moral and practical. He argues that it educates all faculties of the mind and demonstrates to the student the practical value of knowledge. In addition, he claims it elevates the moral condition of all children.

By the 1840s in the United States, most educational leaders had some aquaintance with Pestalozzian ideas. A major attempt to implement these ideas occurred with the establishment of the Oswego State Normal and Training School in New York in 1861. Its founder and principal, Edward Sheldon, claimed to have first become acquainted with Pestalozzian methods in 1859 while visiting a display in Toronto of educational materials created by the English Home and Colonial Institution. At the time, Sheldon was superintendent of the Oswego school system. In 1860, he purchased English instructional materials and proposed the establishment of a teacher-training institution. The following year, the Oswego Board of Education hired Margaret Jones, who had 18 years' experience working with the London Pestalozzian materials, to head the primary teacher-training school. Jones left the following year and was replaced by another worker from the English organization, Herman Krusi, whose father had worked with Pestalozzi.

The establishment of the normal school at Oswego launched what was known in the nineteenth century as the Oswego movement. According to Ned Dearborn's study *The Oswego Movement in American Education*, school records show that students were attracted from throughout the South, Midwest, and East, and the graduates taught around the country. In addition, 11 books and other learning materials based on Pestalozzian principles were written at Oswego.

The Pestalozzian methods taught at Oswego had been filtered through American and English institutions. Even so, the methods retained a stress on student activity, the training of senses, and the use of objects in instruction. The following list of the Pestalozzian principles was copied by Edward Sheldon in 1861, while attending a class at Oswego taught by the English Pestalozzian Margaret Jones.

1. Begin with the senses.
2. Never tell a child what he can discover for himself.
3. Activity is a law of childhood. Train the child not merely to listen, but to do. Educate the hand.
4. Love of variety is a law of childhood—change is rest.
5. Cultivate the faculties in their natural order. First, form the mind, then furnish it.

6. Reduce every subject to its elements, and present one difficulty at a time.[35]

The stress on activity and on learning by doing became the hallmark of progressive educational methods in the late nineteenth and early twentieth centuries. How much the Oswego movement contributed to these later developments in methods of instruction is difficult to determine, but there is little doubt that the discussion and use of Pestalozzian methods by American educators in the nineteenth century set the stage for later developments.

The model of mother as teacher had a profound impact on textbooks, classroom equipment, and methods of teaching. Just as Gertrude used the objects of her household for purposes of instruction, by the late nineteenth century, textbooks and teachers began to use real objects to illustrate lessons. For example, map work became important in the study of history and geography; the counting of objects became a method of learning arithmetic; and the study of nature became a source of scientific understanding for young children. In *How Teachers Taught: Constancy and Change in American Classrooms, 1890–1980*, Larry Cuban includes a set of three photographs depicting elementary school classrooms in Washington, D.C., in 1900. In two of the photographs, students are shown working alone at individual desks. In the third, students are gathered around a table at the head of the classroom examining, with the teacher, models of parts of the body. On the blackboard is a drawing of the heart, and leaning against the wall is a full-sized drawing of the human body with its inner parts illustrated. Although a direct connection cannot be made between the work of Pestalozzi and the student activity depicted in this classroom, Pestalozzi's work and the spread of his ideas must be given some credit for the illustrations, objects, and teaching activities shown in that photograph.[36]

The Evolution of the Bureaucratic Model

David Tyack states in *The One Best System: A History of American Urban Education* that as the organization of American schools developed, "the employment of women appears to correlate highly with the pace of bureaucratization."[37] This correlation can be explained by the relationship between the values inherent in bureaucratic organizations and the attributes ascribed by nineteenth-century society to males and females.

As discussed in Chapter 4, bureaucratic organization triumphed in the public schools in the nineteenth century over paternalistic voluntarism, corporate voluntarism, and democratic localism. By the late nineteenth century, the following elements composed the bureaucratic organization of the typical school system:

1. A hierarchy with a superintendent at the top and orders flowing from the top to the bottom of the organization
2. Clearly defined differences in roles of superintendent, principals, assistant principals, and teachers
3. Graded schools in which students progressively moved from one grade to another
4. A graded course of study for the entire school system to assure uniformity in teaching in all grades in the system
5. An emphasis on rational planning, order, regularity, and punctuality

Michael Katz argues in *Class, Bureaucracy, and Schools* that incipient bureaucracy was favored by the middle class because it assured their control of the educational system and the success of their children in the new industrial society (see Chapter 4). However, this argument is only one among many reasons in the complex process of historical change. For instance, Tyack cites a number of other causes for the adoption of a bureaucratic organization. He argues that "the pressure of numbers was a main reason for the bureaucratization that gradually replaced the older decentralized village pattern of schooling."[38] According to Tyack, this pressure forced school leaders to seek some method of achieving system and efficiency in school systems that had grown up haphazardly. In addition, many nineteenth-century school leaders believed that bureaucratic ogranization taught students values necessary for functioning in an industrial society. Tyack quotes a statement made in 1871 by William T. Harris, a superintendent of schools and U.S. commissioner of education: "The first requisite of the school is *Order:* each pupil must be taught first and foremost to conform his behavior to a general standard." Harris claimed that modern industrial society required "conformity to the time of the train, to the starting of work in the manufactory. . . ," and therefore "the pupil must have his lessons ready at the appointed time, must rise at the tap of the bell, move to the line, return; in short, go through all the evolutions with equal precision."[39]

In more general terms, it appears natural that school people would turn to bureaucratic organization as a model for the most advanced system of school organization. In the minds of nineteenth-century educators, it also seemed logical to socialize a student for the type of organization that was developing in business and industry. For instance, one of the major requirements of developing industrial organization was regularity of attendance by the work force. The factory system as it was developing could not operate unless every worker was assigned a specific task, had his or her tasks coordinated, and was on the job at a specific time.

Just as regular attendance and punctuality became important for factories, these behaviors were considered important by school people for the management of educational systems and as values to be taught to schoolchildren in preparing them to function in society. Nothing more clearly demonstrates this relationship between the requirements of organization and the desire to teach organizational values than the mania that developed among nineteenth-century educators over student attendance and punctuality. Because of the need for organization and the desire to teach industrial values, tardiness to class became a major student offense within this bureaucratic system.

Although the motivation to protect middle-class values and status, the increasing size of school systems, and the desire to teach bureaucratic values are all important explanations for the adoption by schools of a bureaucratic model, the increased feminization of the teaching force is what made it possible to link social roles outside the school with roles within the educational bureaucracy.

The feminization of teaching and the development of bureaucratic organization involved two interrelated nineteenth-century social beliefs. First, it was widely believed that women are naturally subordinate to men. Thus it was natural as bureaucratic school systems evolved that men managed and women taught. Second, a theme that ran through Pestalozzian methods of instruction and the arguments for having women instruct young children was the attribution of rational activity to males and emotional activity to females—men were responsible for the head, and women were responsible for the heart.

The importance of the subordination of women to men in the evolution of bureaucratic school systems is demonstrated by the history of the graded school. One of the major organizational changes in the schools in the nineteenth century, considered important for introducing efficiency and uniformity of instruction, was the separation of students by age into separate classrooms. Prior to this development, students were taught in ungraded classrooms in which teachers were responsible for simultaneously teaching a variety of subjects to students at different levels of knowledge. For example, Ellwood Cubberley includes in *Public Education in the United States* a sketch of a Providence, Rhode Island, grammar school in 1840, where each floor seated 228 students in a single room and was conducted as a single school.[40] A master teacher and assistant teachers combined their efforts to teach the entire group within this large ungraded classroom. In 1823, Boston schools were being built with rooms that seated 300 pupils, on the premise that three large groups would be taught by one master teacher and two assistant teachers. And, of course, monitorial schools (see Chapter 3) were conducted in large ungraded groups.

The major inspiration for the creation of graded schools came from accounts of visitors to Prussia of school organization in that country. After visiting Prussia in 1843, Horace Mann wrote in his *Seventh Annual*

Report that "the first element of superiority in a Prussian school, and one whose influence extends throughout the whole subsequent course of instruction, consists in the proper classification of the scholars." Mann went on to describe how schoolhouses were constructed so that each group of students, divided by age and attainment, could be housed in a single classroom. The ungraded large classroom, Mann argues, created the difficulty for the teacher of trying to teach a variety of subjects at one time. On the other hand, he says,

> *All these difficulties are at once avoided by a suitable classification, by such a classification as enables the teacher to address his instructions at the same time to all children who are before him, and to accompany them to the playground at recess or intermission without leaving any behind who might be disposed to take advantage of his absence.*[41]

When the first school based on the Prussian method of classification was built in the United States, it incorporated not only graded classrooms but also what Tyack refers to as the "pedagogical harem" of a male principal and female teachers. The establishment of the first graded school, the Quincy School, is credited to John Philbrick, who became its first principal. Philbrick had worked hard to convince the Boston School Board of the wisdom of applying Horace Mann's ideas on pupil classification.

When the Quincy School was opened in 1848, its radical design attracted national attention. Rather than the usual school construction of the period—large rooms accommodating hundreds of students—the Quincy School contained a greater number of schoolrooms, each of which could hold 56 students. What was considered its greatest improvement was the provision of a separate room for each teacher and a desk for each student.

Philbrick's description of the relationship between the staffing of the school and the unique design of the building indicates how perceived differences in sex roles fit the new concept of school organization. After stating that all scholars in a single classroom would attend to the same lesson, Philbrick specifies the following type of arrangement among staff members: "Let the Principal or Superintendent have the general supervision and control of the whole, and let him have one male assistant or sub-principal, and ten female assistants, one for each room."[42]

The very architecture of the Quincy School established the sex-role and authority differences in the new system of graded schools. The Quincy School had four floors; the first three contained classrooms and the top floor was a large assembly hall. More important, with regard to symbols of authority, a separate office for the principal was included in the design. According to Ellwood Cubberley, writing in the early twentieth century, the design for the Quincy School became the standard for urban elementary schools throughout the country in the twentieth century.[43]

The adoption of this plan for elementary school organization based on the classification of students and the self-contained classroom is inextricably linked with the system of staffing that placed the male principal in charge of a "pedagogical harem." This pattern of administrative control within the school had been evolving in the early nineteenth century as schools became larger. Originally, a teacher would be designated as head teacher and given the responsibility of observing assistant teachers and reporting directly to the board of education. The position of head teacher was also referred to as principal teacher. As the size of schools increased, the duties of the principal teacher became more administrative and less involved with direct classroom instruction. One important duty of the principal became the supervision of other teachers in the school. The Cincinnati school report for 1858 cited by Willard Elsbree illustrates the evolution of the position of principal: "The most efficient agency in the improvement of the schools has been the constant and active supervision of the Principals over the labors of their Assistants." The report notes that this was a recent phenomenon. "They [the principals] were, till within the last two years, only teachers of the highest classes of their respective schools." However, with the assignment of new responsibilities, changes had been made in room arrangements to reflect the new role of the principal. The Cincinnati school report describes how, "By a regulation of your Board . . . the Principals . . . have small recitation rooms assigned to them, where they keep records, examine classes, and transact the general business of their schools."[44]

As this pattern of graded elementary schools spread into other American cities, the grade system became more clearly defined. Once the general category of elementary students was established, it was necessary to determine how many levels of classification should exist in a school. The average duration of common school eduation at the time the Quincy School was built was seven to nine years. A survey of 45 cities conducted by the U.S. commissioner of education in 1870 indicates that by that time, the majority of elementary schools classified students into eight separate grades. The eight-year elementary school remained the standard until the junior high school was developed in the early twentieth century.[45]

The development of the eight-year elementary school and its accompanying "pedagogical harem" was part of the more general growth of hierarchical bureaucratic organization in education. As previously mentioned, these organizational developments reflected not only differences between sex roles, but also differences in characteristics attributed to each sex. Studies of organizational forms conducted in the latter part of the twentieth century show that a hierarchical bureaucracy embodies characteristics most often associated with males. Sociologist Rosabeth Kanter argues that this form of organization specifies that the ideal manager is one who is rational and objective. In the nineteenth and early twentieth centuries, these characteristics have most often been ascribed to males. Kanter states:

> This *"masculine ethic"* elevates the traits assumed to belong to men with educational advantages to necessities for effective organizations: a tough-minded approach to problems; analytical abilities to abstract and plan; a capacity to set aside personal, emotional considerations in the interests of task accomplishment; and a cognitive superiority in problem-solving and decision-making.[46]

In other words, organizational forms specify certain characteristics for leadership, and if these characteristics are associated by society with a particular gender, then sex bias is built into the organizational model. According to Kanter, it has been assumed in the nineteenth and twentieth centuries that women are governed by emotions and are prone to "petty" concerns with interpersonal relationships and responsibilities. In terms of the managerial requirements of a hierarchical bureaucracy, this means that women do not make good managers and that their role in this type of organization is to be supportive of male leaders.

The evolution of the graded elementary school supports Kanter's analysis. Women were considered to be more effective in the education of young children because of their emotional nature and nurturing qualites, characteristics not ascribed to men. Men, on the other hand, were not considered ideal for teaching young children because of their supposed lack of emotional qualities and their reliance on the use of reason. The graded school with a single male principal in power and subordinate female teachers in self-contained classrooms fit nicely into these social stereotypes. From the perspective of nineteenth-century society, the rational male should govern the school and provide limits and order to the emotional nature of the female schoolteacher.

Within the framework of Kanter's analysis, an important, but not the only, reason for the development of hierarchical bureaucracy in education is that it was compatible with the hiring of large numbers of female teachers to fill the lower ranks of the hierarchy. For instance, the role of school superintendent, an important element in the school bureaucracy as it developed in the nineteenth century, evolved with a clear understanding by most participants that the role would be filled by males who would control a primarily female work force. In *The One Best System*, Tyack quotes statements that illustrate the existence of this attitude. He cites an 1878 article in *Harper's* that states that "women teachers are often preferred by superintendents because they are more willing to comply with established regulations and less likely to ride headstrong hobbies" and a nineteenth-century superintendent of the Denver school system who claimed that when teachers have advice to give to their superiors, "it is to be given as the good daughter talks with the father."[47]

The development of the role of superintendent was important in the evolution of a hierarchical educational organization. The primary reason for creating the position was to have a person work full time at supervising classroom instruction and assuring uniformity in the curriculum. As discussed in Chapter 4, an important common school reform was the creation of the office of state superintendent, whose purpose was to organize a uniform system of common schools. Direct classroom supervision evolved along with the positions of city and county superintendents. The creation of these local positions paralleled the establishment of the office of state superintendent. In addition, they were associated with the district system of organizing schools.

In the nineteenth century, the district system became the most widespread method of organizing state systems of education, but by the twentieth century, it became an obstacle to providing equal educational opportunity. The creation of the district system allowed wealthy school districts to exist side-by-side with poor school districts. Thus, it often was difficult to accomplish the common school dream of mixing the rich and the poor in the same schoolhouse.

The idea of the school district originated with the Massachusetts Law of 1789, which affirmed the Old Deluder Satan Law of 1647 (see Chapter 1) and authorized towns to establish boundaries for school support and attendance that would be called *districts*. Later laws, in 1800, 1817, and 1827, gave members of a school district the right to hold meetings, choose officers, collect school taxes, select schoolbooks, and hire teachers. The New England states of Maine, Vermont, New Hampshire, Rhode Island, and Connecticut instituted the district system early in the nineteenth century. The idea spread to New York in 1812 and westward to Ohio in 1821, Illinois in 1825, Tennessee in 1830, Indiana in 1833, Michigan in 1837, and Kentucky and Iowa in 1838.

Depending on the exact political organization of the state, the development of local supervision was associated with the development of the role of district or county superintendent. Willard Elsbree provides colorful examples of the work of these early superintendents. A Bucks County, Pennsylvania, school superintendent states in his report in 1856, "In one school, where I had drawn the map of Pennsylvania on the black board, the same diagram had remained for a year, the board never having been used in the interim." In another situation, the county superintendent describes how "not a scholar in the school could tell me in what country he lived, and when I held up Holbrook's five inch globe, the oceans on which were painted blue, and asked what it was, a large boy, at least seventeen years of age, replied, 'a bird's egg!'" The activities of the Bucks County superintendent reflect the primary duty of these early superintendents, which was to supervise instruction. For instance, the state superintendent of New York reported that "the schools of the state were visited during the year 1854 by the several town and city superintendents 22,082 times."[48]

The evolution of the office of city school superintendent paralleled the establishment of district and county offices. Buffalo, New York, was the first city to establish the position, in 1837, and was quickly followed by Louisville, St. Louis, Providence, Springfield, Cleveland, Rochester, and New Orleans. One of the major functions of the early city school superintendents was to write a uniform course of study for their school systems. This course of study naturally paralleled the establishment of graded schools. For instance, Tyack reports that William Wells, superintendent of the Chicago schools from 1856 to 1864, published *A Graded Course of Instruction with Instructions to Teachers* in 1862 based on his efforts to institute a citywide uniform system of instruction related to the classification of students by grade. Wells's graded course of study specified topics to be covered in each grade and appropriate methods of instruction. Tyack describes the contents of this course of study: "Children began with the alphabet at the age of five, learned to count to 100 and do simple addition in the next grade, and proceeded in the next years to learn about the mysteries of Roman numerals, the hanging gardens of Babylon, the Crusades, and the Trojan War." According to Tyack, Wells's course of study was adopted by many cities as an official curriculum.[49]

The graded school, the uniform course of study, the district system, and the positions of principal and of city, district, county, and state superintendent were all elements in the early development of a hierarchical and bureaucratic organization for the administration of American education. In the twentieth century, the bureaucratic organization of the schools became more clearly defined as the professionalization of school administration developed. Many factors contributed to the development of this type of organization, including the real problems created by the increased size of schools and school districts; the common school ideal of a uniform curriculum for all children; the desire of the middle class and native groups to protect their values and power; and the need for socialization of students for an industrial workplace. The creation of a hierarchy was facilitated by the use of female teachers. In Lotus Coffman's 1911 study of teachers, he argues that the increasing number of women in the teaching force was

due in part to the changed character of the management of the public schools, to the specialization of labor within the school, to the narrowing of the intellectual range or versatility required of teachers, and to the willingness of women to work for less than men. . . . all of the graded school positions have been preempted by women; men still survive in public school work as "managing" or executive officers.[50]

McGuffey's Readers and the Spirit of Capitalism

The popularity and importance of William McGuffey's readers in the latter half of the nineteenth century can be compared with the role of the *New England Primer* during colonial times and Noah Webster's *Spelling Book* in the first half of the nineteenth century. The *New England Primer* prepared readers for submission to the authority of the family, the Bible, and the government, and Webster's *Spelling Book* taught republican values designed to maintain order in a free society. McGuffey's readers contain numerous moral lessons designed to teach appropriate behavior in a developing industrial society with increasing concentrations of wealth and expanding social divisions between the rich and the poor. Within this context, the readers provide an example of the actual meaning given to attempts to reduce social-class tensions by mixing the rich and the poor in the common school.

The growth in popularity of McGuffey's readers paralleled the development of the common school. Ironically, as the nineteenth-century schoolmarm took over the schoolroom, girls occupied little space in the new reading series. Females are seldom-discussed characters in these moral tales dealing with social behavior in a developing industrial society. If the McGuffey Readers were our sole source for understanding human conduct in the latter half of the nineteenth century, we would have the impression that the only role for women in the development of a capitalistic and industrial society was to serve as models of charity. The concept of charity is important because it justifies the concentration of wealth by making the rich the stewards of wealth for the poor. Even in their role as models of charity, however, girls were less frequently portrayed in that role than boys were. As depicted in the moral tales in McGuffey's readers, girls are almost invisible in the social relationships of developing capitalism.

The McGuffey Readers were written in the heart of what was considered the West in the 1830s. William Holmes McGuffey was born in 1800 near Washington, Pennsylvania, and was raised on a homestead in Trumbell County, Ohio. In 1825, after a period of education and teaching in the schools of the frontier, McGuffey accepted a teaching post at Miami University in Oxford, Ohio, near the booming city of Cincinnati. Through his work as an educator, McGuffey became an active member of the Western Literary Institute and College of Professional Teachers and a friend of Calvin Stowe and Harriet Beecher Stowe at the Lane Seminary in Cincinnati. As a result of his educational contacts in Cincinnati, the Cincinnati publishing firm of Truman and Smith asked McGuffey in 1834 or early 1835 to prepare a series of textbooks.

The McGuffey Readers were prepared specifically for use in the developing common school systems. The series, first published between 1836 and 1838, contains a primer, a speller, and four readers. A fifth reader was added in 1844. The series was revised between 1841 and 1849 and again in 1853, 1857, and 1879. The changes in 1857 and 1879 were primarily in gradation of material and in binding. Sales figures for the series are indicative of its use and popularity. Between 1836 and 1922, approximately 122 million copies were sold, with the strongest sales, as indicated by the following figures, occurring between 1870 and 1890.[51]

1836–1850	7,000,000
1850–1870	40,000,000
1870–1890	60,000,000
1890–1920	15,000,000

The content of the McGuffey Readers varies in length and difficulty, from short and simple stories in the first, second, and third readers to selected literary writings by a variety of authors in the fourth and fifth readers. Each story and poem in the less-advanced readers is preceded by a spelling list and by definitions of words used in the selection and is followed by several related questions.

The goal of the stories in the McGuffey Readers is to teach reading and, like the general goal of the common school, to impart moral lessons. An analysis of the content of the stories in the 1843 edition of *McGuffey's Newly Revised Eclectic Second Reader* reveals the range of moral values, the importance given to certain moral themes, and the different expectations for boys and for girls in dealing with moral issues.[52]

McGuffey's Newly Revised Eclectic Second Reader contains 104 readings of from one to three pages. Some of the readings are religious selections like the Lord's Prayer, the Story of Joseph, and the Child's Prayer. There are also a number of historical sketches, poems, and tales about animals and birds. Some stories, like "Story of the Coat" and "Story of Buttons," are designed to convey information about objects. Of course, many of these writings about history, nature, and objects are designed to teach a particular moral lesson.

The largest group of writings in the second reader, about 35 percent of the 104 selections, deals directly with problems of moral character. Given the primacy of moral education in the common school movement, this emphasis is not surprising. Of these didactic stories, 29 center on the character of boys and only 8, on the character of girls.

There are several ways to explain the neglect of girls in these didactic tales. One could assume it reflects the subordinate and secondary role of women in society. In other words, McGuffey's attitude toward females reflects the more general vision men had of women's place in society. Another explanation could be that the female character was considered to have few moral defects. This explanation is supported by one of the major reasons given for recruiting women into teaching, namely, the purity of their moral character. In fact, in the stories in the second reader, the range of moral problems for girls is very narrow as compared with that for boys. In 2 of the stories dealing with girls, "Mary and Her Father" and "The Little Letter Writer," the theme is learning and the value of education. In another story, "The Greedy Girl," the moral problem is gluttony, which is illustrated by a little girl who eats so much that she constantly gets sick. Untidiness is the central theme in "A Place for Every Thing," a story about a girl who constantly loses things and learns from another girl to put everything in its proper place.

One could conclude from these stories that in the nineteenth century the central problems in the character of girls were considered to be overeating, a lack of appreciation for learning, and untidiness. The other 4 stories dealing with girls do not present problems in character, but models of charity. In "The Kind Little Girl," the central female character shares with animals and hungry people; in "A Dialogue on Dress," a girl refuses new clothes so that she can save to buy clothes for the poor; in "The Two White Doves," a girl and boy give their doves to a sick child; and in "The Last Two Apples," a girl gives the last apples to her siblings. Thus, in half the stories dealing with female character, girls are presented as acting charitably in certain situations.

The theme of charity is also important in the stories dealing with boys. As mentioned previously, this was an important theme in the developing social relationships of capitalism. The range of character problems exhibited by boys in the McGuffey Readers is much greater than that associated with girls. In the 29 stories dealing with boys, the themes include relationship to nature, value of learning, gluttony, mercy, pranks, charity, industriousness, honesty, courage, envy, alcoholism, insolence, and thrift.

Interestingly, the most frequent theme in *McGuffey's Newly Revised Eclectic Second Reader*, which appears in 6 of the stories, is a boy's relationship to nature. This probably reflects the importance of the expanding West and the role of nature in nineteenth-century life. In the second story of the reader (the first of which deals with the importance of reading), a boy is depicted reflecting on the loveliness of the sun and the goodness of God. In contrast to the boys who love nature are the boys in "The Bird Set Free" who rob birds' nests.

The second most frequent theme, which appears in 5 of the stories about male character, is charity, and the third most frequent theme is the value of education. To understand the importance of charity, consideration must be given to the general social and political messages in all the McGuffey Readers. This analysis is done by Richard Mosier in *Making the American Mind: Social and Moral Ideas in the McGuffey Readers*. As the title suggests, Mosier approaches his analysis from the perspective that the wide use of the McGuffey Readers had a profound impact on average Americans by shaping their attitudes toward political, social, and economic institutions.

In general, Mosier argues that the political messages found in the pages of the McGuffey Readers are conservative and express a distrust of popular participation in government. Within this conservative framework, the primary purpose of government is the protection of property. Mosier contends that most of the political ideas in the readers express the values of the Whig Party as opposed to the Democratic Party of the early nineteenth century. This, of course, means that the books agree with the political values of the leadership of the common school movement. The fear of spreading democracy, or suffrage, is expressed in the McGuffey Readers' support of the common school system. In Mosier's words, "The antidote for these new forms of demagoguery and radicalism [Jacksonian democracy] was religion and education, the fire engines of Church and State, to which conservatives turned in their darkest hours." He argues that the purpose of education, as reflected in the readers and in conservative political thought, was

for education . . . [to] be linked particularly with a call to return to the stern moral code of the Puritan fathers . . . [when] the objects of education were considered largely in terms of religious and moral culture. . . . the McGuffey readers voiced their fear for the corrupting influences of the new age that had come upon them, and hinted that in the metaphysical subtleties of the great New England theologians lay the appropriate foundations for state, school, church, and society.[53]

The treatment of economic issues in the McGuffey Readers, Mosier maintains, is premised on the Calvinist concept that wealth is an outward sign of inner salvation. This economic argument allowed for an acceptance of a society that was experiencing increasing concentrations of wealth and an expanding social distance between the rich and the poor. Wealth was a sign of God's blessing and poverty was a sign of God's disapproval. Within this economic argument, for the poor to gain wealth they had to be godly and industrious, and for the rich to continue receiving the blessings of God they had to use their wealth in a godly fashion.

Therefore, charity was a means for the rich to remain worthy of their wealth in the eyes of God and a justification for a concentration of wealth in their hands. Mosier states about the contents of the McGuffey Readers, "Those who are wealthy are reminded that they are so by the grace of God, and that this grace and concession implies a responsibility toward the poor. . . . Many are the lessons that praise the charitable activities of the merchant, and many are those that show the kindness of the rich to the poor."[54] This conceptual framework gave the wealthy a stewardship over the riches of the earth and the destiny of the poor.

Within this context of this gospel of wealth, the poor were placed in a paradoxical situation. On the one hand, the existence of the poor was considered inevitable and, therefore, an acceptable part of the social order. On the other hand, some argued that poverty existed because the poor did not have the virtues of the rich and that the poor could escape poverty by being industrious, thrifty, and moral. As Mosier summarizes the dominant attitude in the McGuffey Readers: "It was argued that the poor would always be with us, that the best for them was charity and benevolence, but that no one need be poor. There are, argued the apostles of acquisition, numerous avenues to success that stand open for the sober, and frugal, the thrifty, and the energetic."[55]

The best examples of this gospel of wealth are two successive stories in the 1843 edition of *McGuffey's Newly Revised Eclectic Second Reader* having the descriptive titles "The Rich Boy" and "The Poor Boy." The reader is informed in the first story that the rich boy knows "that God gives a great deal of money to some persons, in order that they may assist those who are poor." In keeping with the idea that the rich are elected by God, the rich boy is portrayed as being humble, kind to servants, and "careful not to make a noise in the house, or break any thing, or put it out of its place, or tear his clothes." The reader is also told that this model of virtue "likes to go with his parents to visit poor people, in their cottages, and gives them all the money he can spare. He often says: 'If I were a man, and had plenty of money, I think no person who lived near me should be very poor.'" The story ends with the rich boy dreaming of how he would use his future wealth:

I would build a great many pretty cottages for poor people to live in, and every cottage should have a garden and a field, in order that the people might have vegetables, and might keep a cow, and a pig, and some chickens; they should not pay me much rent. I would give clothes to the boys and girls who had not money to buy clothes with, and they should all learn to read and write, and be very good.[56]

Certainly, a child reading "The Rich Boy" would easily conclude that God is just and that the rich boy deserves to inherit his parents' wealth.

In a similar fashion, the reader of "The Poor Boy" might conclude that poverty is good because of its effect on moral character. The poor boy is portrayed as industrious, helpful, moral, and eager to learn. The story opens, "The good boy whose parents are poor, rises early in the morning; and all day long, does as much as he can, to help his father and mother." It goes on to explain that the poor boy studies hard so that when he grows up, he can read the Bible and find gainful employment. The story makes a clear distinction between the poor boy who is good and poor boys who are bad. In the story, the poor boy hurries home from his lessons to help his parents. On the way, the reader is told,

he often sees naughty boys in the streets, who fight, and steal, and do many bad things; and he hears them swear, and call names, and tell lies; but he does not like to be with them, for fear they should make him as bad as they are; and lest any body who sees him with them, should think that he too is naughty.

Unlike the rich boy wanting to help the poor, he dreams of earning his own living. The poor boy likes his food of bread and bacon and does not envy the rich little boys and girls "riding on pretty horses, or in coaches." At the end of the story, the poor boy states his acceptance of his social position:

I have often been told, and I have read, that it is God who makes some poor, and others rich;—that the rich have many troubles which we know nothing of; and that the poor, if they are but good, may be very happy: indeed, I think that when I am good, nobody can be happier than I am.[57]

In summary, the two stories provide a justification for economic inequality and a rationale for accepting one's position in life. After reading the stories, poor boys might have been pleased to learn that they could be happy if they were good and that they were free of the burdens and responsibilities of the wealthy. Rich boys might have been pleased to learn that their good fortune was a blessing from God that required them only to adopt paternalistic attitudes toward the poor.

The economic arguments embodied in the McGuffey Readers provide another means of understanding the goals of the common school. One of the basic reasons given for the establishment of a common school system, as discussed in Chapter 4, was that it would reduce antagonisms between the rich and the poor. In addition, consciousness of one's particular social class was to be changed into a consciousness of belonging to the more general social class of humanity.

Because McGuffey's readers were written for the common schools and were one of the most popular texts during the time the common school system was growing, it can be assumed that they offer an important perspective on how the reduction of tension between the rich and the poor would take place. In other words, the readers provided part of the real content of the more general educational rhetoric. From this perspective, one might conclude that the common school was supposed to solve the problem of social-class tension by educating children to accept their positions in society and the existing economic arrangements. The poor were educated to accept the existence of the rich; to learn that the rich would take care of them and that they were free of the responsibilities that accompanied wealth. Indeed, the poor were taught that their happiness depended on behaving in a manner that would not antagonize the wealthy. For their own good and, obviously, for the good of the wealthy, the poor were taught to be free of envy, thrifty, industrious, and moral.

From the standpoint of the rich, social-class tensions would be reduced by learning humility and charity toward the poor. They were not to disdain the poor, but were to learn to love them. Therefore, educating the rich in the common school was meant to reduce social-class antagonisms in two ways: first, by disarming the rich of negative feelings about the poor, and second, by teaching the rich acts of charity as a means of disarming the poor of hostility.

The McGuffey Readers' concerns with morality and with developing virtuous character made them an ideal companion for the growth of the common school and an industrial society. In the readers, the concept of republican motherhood is enlarged to include behaviors considered important in a society of increasing economic and social tensions. In the early nineteenth century, men and women considered the traits of motherhood to be ideal as methods for educating good republicans. In the latter half of the century, it was easy to extend the nurturing qualities of motherhood to include acts of charity. Furthermore, charity, as discussed earlier, was an essential concept for justifying inequalities in the distribution of wealth. Therefore, females, particularly women teachers, became symbols of the virtues needed to maintain order in a republican society and of the kindness and the acts of charity required to maintain order in a capitalistic society.

Conclusion

The organization of the common school in the middle of the nineteenth century established certain patterns of development that would begin to change and take on new direction by the late nineteenth and early twentieth centuries, when women began to rebel against their subservient status in the educational hierarchy and to seek a greater voice in educational policy through unionization and participation in the administration of the schools. These changes occurred as schools modeled themselves on industry and became more bureaucratic.

The schools developed an expanded economic role in the increasingly urban and industrial society of the late nineteenth century, and as this happened, the high school joined the elementary school as an institution at which attendance was considered essential for all people. Pedagogy—the science of education—changed during this period to meet the needs of the corporate model of the school and the new economic role of schooling. But even with all these changes, the schoolmarm remained the backbone of the educational system. As models of republican motherhood and sisters of charity, they continued to toil in the factories of education.

Notes

1. Carl F. Kaestle and Maris Vinovskis, *Education and Social Change in Nineteenth-Century Massachusetts* (New York: Cambridge University Press, 1980), pp. 9–46.

2. Mary Beth Norton, *Liberty's Daughters: The Revolutionary Experience of American Women, 1750–1800* (Boston: Little, Brown, 1980), p. 297.

3. Ibid., pp. 297–298.

4. Ibid., p. 293.

5. Quoted in Anne Firor Scott, "The Ever Widening Circle: The Diffusion of Feminist Values from the Troy Female Seminary, 1822–1872," *History of Education Quarterly* (Spring 1979): 7.

6. Ibid., p. 8.

7. Paul H. Mattingly, *The Classless Profession: American Schoolmen in the Nineteenth Century* (New York: New York University Press, 1975).

8. Willard Elsbree, *The American Teacher: Evolution of a Profession in a Democracy* (New York: American Book Company, 1939), p. 296.

9. Horace Mann, "Fourth Annual Report (1840)," in Lawrence Cremin, ed., *The Republic and the School: Horace Mann on the Education of Free Men* (New York: Teachers College Press, 1957), p. 47.

10. Ibid., pp. 50–52.

11. Quoted in Elsbree, *American Teacher*, p. 201.

12. Calvin Stowe, "Report on Elementary Public Instruction in Europe," in Edgar Knight, ed., *Reports on European Education* (New York: McGraw-Hill, 1930), p. 311.

13. Ibid.

14. Elsbree, *American Teacher*, pp. 202–208.

15. Carl F. Kaestle, *Pillars of the Republic: Common Schools and American Society, 1780–1860* (New York: Hill and Wang, 1983), p. 126.

16. Elsbree, *American Teacher*, pp. 293–294.

17. Quoted in ibid., pp. 280–281.

18. Elsbree, *American Teacher*, p. 288.

19. Mattingly, *Classless Profession*, pp. 62–63.

20. Ibid., p. 57.

21. Ned Dearborn, *The Oswego Movement in American Education* (New York: Teachers College Press, 1925), p. 32.

22. Mattingly, *Classless Profession*, pp. 154–155.

23. Ibid., p. 135.

24. Quoted in Larry Cuban, *How Teachers Taught: Constancy and Change in American Classrooms, 1890–1980* (White Plains, N.Y.: Longman, 1984), p. 19.

25. "Cyrus Peirce to Henry Barnard," in Merle Borrowman, ed., *Teacher Education in America: A Documentary History* (New York: Teachers College Press, 1965), pp. 60–61.

26. Johann Pestalozzi, *Leonard and Gertrude*, trans. Eva Channing (Lexington, Mass.: Heath, 1901), p. 11.

27. Ibid., pp. 130–131.

28. Ibid., p. 135.

29. Johann Pestalozzi, "How a Child Is Led to God through Maternal Love," in J. A. Green, ed., *Pestalozzi's Educational Writings* (London: Edward Arnold, 1916), p. 266.

30. Johann Pestalozzi, *How Gertrude Teaches Her Children: An Attempt to Help Mothers to Teach Their Own Children and an Account of the Method*, trans. Lucy Holland and Francis Turner (Syracuse, N.Y.: Bardeen, 1898), p. 294.

31. Ibid., p. 317.

32. John Griscom, "A Year in Europe," in Knight, *Reports*, p. 60.

33. Ibid., p. 55.

34. Stowe, "Report on Elementary Public Instruction," in Knight, *Reports*, p. 277.

35. Quoted in Dearborn, *Oswego Movement*, p. 69.

36. Cuban, *How Teachers Taught*, pp. 20–21.

37. David Tyack, *The One Best System: A History of American Urban Education* (Cambridge, Mass.: Harvard University Press, 1974), p. 61.

38. Ibid., p. 38–39.

39. Quoted in ibid., p. 43.

40. Ellwood Cubberley, *Public Education in the United States: A Study and Interpretation of American Educational History* (Boston: Houghton Mifflin, 1934), p. 308.

41. Horace Mann, "Seventh Annual Report to the Massachusetts State Board of Education, 1843," in Ellwood Cubberley, ed., *Readings in Public Education in the United States: A Collection of Sources and Readings to Illustrate the History of Educational Practice and Progress in the United States* (Boston: Houghton Mifflin, 1934), pp. 287–288.

42. Quoted in Tyack, *One Best System*, p. 45.

43. Cubberley, *Public Education*, p. 312.

44. Quoted in Elsbree, *American Teacher*, pp. 174–175.

45. Tyack, *One Best System*, p. 45; Cubberley, *Public Education*, pp. 306–315.

46. Rosabeth Kanter, "Women and the Structure of Organization: Exploration in Theory and Behavior," in Marcia Millman and Rosabeth Kanter, eds., *Another Voice* (Garden City, N.Y.: Doubleday [Anchor Books], 1975), p. 43.

47. Quoted in Tyack, *One Best System*, p. 60.

48. Quoted in Elsbree, *American Teacher*, p. 49.

49. Tyack, *One Best System*, pp. 45–46.

50. Quoted in ibid., p. 61.

51. Richard Mosier, *Making the American Mind: Social and Moral Ideas in the McGuffey Readers* (New York: Russell & Russell, 1965), pp. 167–170; Harvey C. Minnich, *William Holmes McGuffey and His Readers* (New York: American Book Company, 1936), pp. 30–89.

52. William H. McGuffey, *McGuffey's Newly Revised Eclectic Second Reader* (Cincinnati: Winthrop B. Smith, 1843).

53. Mosier, *Making the American Mind*, p. 31.

54. Ibid., p. 161.

55. Ibid., p. 162.

56. McGuffey, *McGuffey's*, pp. 47–48.

57. Ibid., pp. 48–50.

6

Schooling and the New Corporate Order

In the last two decades of the nineteenth century, American society and the educational system were transformed by the impact of urbanization, industrialization, and immigration. As the concentration of population shifted from rural to urban areas, large factories and business organizations began to dominate the economic system. From a country that had been largely agricultural and centered in rural areas and small towns, there emerged a nation learning to adapt to the complex patterns of living required by urban life, large corporate organizations, and unions. Adding to the complexity of the situation were large numbers of immigrants from southern and eastern Europe who served as inexpensive labor for the new industrial plants and filled the ghettos in expanding urban areas. These new immigrants frightened older immigrant groups and created concern among industrial leaders who feared that they were bringing in radical ideologies and creating unrest among American labor.

The American educational system changed by taking on broader social and economic functions. In urban areas, schools expanded their social functions by adding school nurses and health programs, introducing showers, providing after-school and community activities, and attaching playgrounds to school buildings. Educators tried to change the school curriculum to solve the perceived social problems caused by the loss of the values of a small-town, rural society. Special Americanization programs were instituted for the new waves of immigrants.

Of profound importance to the future of American education was the decision to organize the school system to improve human capital as a means of economic growth. In fact, the development of human capital as a means of solving problems in the labor market became a major educational goal of the twentieth century. It resulted in the acceptance of vocational education as a legitimate part of the educational system and the establishment of the comprehensive high school designed to provide students with differing curricula to meet their various interests in a complex and specialized society. In the twentieth century, the high school became an institution serving the majority of youth.

Complementing the goal of developing human capital was the evolution of the science of education, an important part of which was the measurement of intelligence, interests, and abilities. It was with the tools of measurement that the school attempted objectively to match the student with an educational program and future occupation. Vocational guidance developed at the same time as another means of helping students select a course of study and a future job. Vocational education, the comprehensive high school, the junior high school, and vocational guidance were all viewed as means of adapting the educational system to the new economic order.

Also, the political structure of schooling changed as corporate models of organization became popular. The modern school bureaucracy emerged as educators emulated factories and businesses. As this process occurred, educational administration became professionalized and new concepts of educational control emerged. In addition, teachers modeled their teaching on forms of industrial organization and initiated the first teachers' unions.

As these changes took place, questions were raised about which groups in society were receiving the most educational benefits. Some historians claim that these changes benefited all of society, whereas others argue that corporate wealth attempted to organize the school system to meet its economic needs. The issue of political power has been of primary importance in this debate.

In this chapter, we first examine the varieties of historical interpretation of this major period in the history of American education. Woven through the analysis of the various interpretations is a description of the social and economic changes of the period. A discussion of the expanding role of the school in dealing with the problems of immigration and urbanization follows. Finally, there is a description of the attempts to change the organization of the classroom to meet the new social conditions.

Public Benefit or Corporate Greed?

At one end of the scale, historians have described the major educational changes occurring in the late nineteenth and early twentieth centuries simply as responses to the problems caused by the collapse of traditional institutions and the influx of immigrants unfamiliar with American democratic ways of living. At the other end of the scale, the argument has been made that the schools were brought under the control of the new corporate elite to serve its social and economic interests. In the middle of this debate has been the claim that immigrants and workers helped to define their own educational future through rational economic choices.

One early interpretation of this period is that given by Ellwood Cubberley, who was both a chronicler of the period and a participant in many of its educational changes, in *Public Education in the United States: A Study and Interpretation of American Educational History.* First published in 1919, Cubberley's work reflects the attitudes of many educators about social and economic conditions in the late nineteenth and early twentieth centuries and the thinking of some educational reformers of this period. His interpretation is that the schools had to change to meet the threat posed to democratic institutions by immigrants from southern and eastern Europe and to instill the social values lost with the passing of small-town rural life.

Cubberley portrays the immigrants from southern and eastern Europe as being politically, socially, and educationally backward as compared with earlier immigrants from northern and western Europe. He states that these newer immigrants were

largely illiterate, docile, often lacking in initiative, and almost wholly without the Anglo-Saxon conceptions of righteousness, liberty, law, order, public decency, and government, [and] their coming has served to dilute tremendously our national stock and to weaken and corrupt our political life.

He includes in this category Italians immigrating after 1870; Poles, Bohemians, Hungarians, Slovaks, and Austrians arriving after 1880; and Jews, Russians, Japanese, Koreans, and residents of the Balkans. According to Cubberley, these immigrant groups were a threat to the American way of life.[1]

Cubberley argues that in the past the assimilation of immigrant groups was easier because most spoke English (except for the Germans), had common values, and were free "of a priesthood bent on holding nationalities together for religious ends." On the other hand, the assimilation of newer groups had been retarded because of their large numbers, their settlement in urban areas, and various language and religious differences. Cubberley argues that these conditions made it necessary for the schools to consciously institute Americanization programs "to so assimilate the foreign-born that they come to have our conceptions of law and order and government, and come to act in harmony with the spirit and purpose of our American national ideals."[2]

After detailing the technological and industrial changes after the Civil War and the growth of urbanization in America, Cubberley goes on to maintain that the influence of the home and church had been seriously weakened, and, consequently, traditional values of courtesy, respect, obedience, and honesty were not as widely taught to children as in the past. In addition, the homogeneous community of the American past was dissolving, so that it no longer exercised restraint over individual actions; and the nature of employment also had changed to meet the growing requirements of specialization in the factory system.

Cubberley argues that, against the background of these changes, the school changed to meet the needs of society:

> As modern city-life conditions have come more and more to surround both boys and girls, depriving them of the training and education which earlier farm and village life once gave, the school has been called to take upon itself the task of giving training in those industrial experiences and social activities which once formed so important a part of the education of American youths.

Also, he claims, the growth of divisions among social classes as a result of industrialization required the schools to build a new social consciousness and unity.[3]

Therefore, Cubberley's interpretation of the educational changes of the late nineteenth and early twentieth centuries is that the school changed simply to solve social and economic problems. Within this framework, the school is seen as a mere captive of social conditions. There is little or no discussion by Cubberley of the school as a political institution shaped by the competition of various interest groups in society.

Lawrence Cremin uses the same interpretative framework, but without the attitude of Anglo-Saxon superiority found in Cubberley's description of the new immigrants, in his landmark study published in 1961, *The Transformation of the School: Progressivism in American Education, 1876–1957*. Cremin places all major educational changes of the late nineteenth and the twentieth centuries under the label of progressivism and states that this movement began as "a many-sided effort to use the schools to improve the lives of individuals." Cremin lists as elements in this "many-sided effort" the expansion of the social functions of the school "to include direct concern for health, vocation, and the quality of family and community life"; the use of principles of psychology and the social sciences in classroom instruction; and the attempt to have instruction meet the needs of "different kinds and classes of children."[4]

Like Cubberley, Cremin does not deal with political conflicts or with the issue of whose interests were being served by the changes in educational institutions. His basic assumption is that the school was a benign institution and that most educational changes were the result of attempts to improve the quality of life for all people.

Unlike Cubberley, however, Cremin presents a broader view of the educational community's reaction to the new immigration. He identifies one school of thought, which he associates with Cubberley, as believing that Americanization meant Anglicization. Cremin argues that others believed the promise of national unity was in the creation of a new nationality that would result from a melting together of the old and new immigrants. Another group believed that cultural pluralism was possible, allowing ethnic identity to be maintained in the framework of shared American values. Cremin also provides in-depth and scholarly interpretation of the school's response to industrialization and urbanization.

Many scholars have opposed the view that most educational change in the late nineteenth and early twentieth centuries was primarily a product of altruism. One set of interpretations argues that the political and administrative structure of education changed to assure elite and corporate control of the educational system and to produce cooperative and docile workers. Another set of interpretations portrays the educational change of the period as a result of the dynamic interplay between the demands of industry and the demands of workers. This interpretative framework makes historial change a product of conflict—not the manipulation of passive workers by powerful business leaders.

The earliest historical study to span both interpretative frameworks is Merle Curti's *Social Ideas of American Educators*. Unlike Cubberley, who views industrial evolution as a matter of technological triumph, Curti discusses the major clashes and wars between workers and capitalists in the late nineteenth century. Curti contends that the majority of educational changes that occurred at that time were designed to serve the interests of the owners of industrial enterprises. For instance, he argues that vocational education and manual training were attempts to control and counteract radicalism among American workers: "An increasing number of educators advocated manual training and industrial education as the best specific means of counteracting radicalism on the part of the working masses." According to Curti, vocational education, the differentiated curriculum of the comprehensive high school, and other educational reforms were designed specifically to improve the industrial efficiency of America for competition in world markets. Even the values of cooperation and interdependence that were to be taught in the classroom are considered by Curti attempts to deny the inevitable conflict between labor and capital. Curti maintains that values of most leading educators were economically conservative: "Hardly an annual meeting of the National Education Association was concluded without an appeal on the part of educators for the help of the teacher in quelling strikes and checking the spread of socialism and anarchism." The educators who were developing moral training for the schools, he states, "turned . . . increasingly to the social sciences as means by which schools might inculcate respect for law and order, and suspicion for the doctrines of socialism and anarchism."[5]

Although Curti paints a picture of the public schools as institutions enlisted by the power of organized wealth to train and select workers and inculcate values supportive of their control, he does recognize the efforts of organized labor to influence educational policy. Of special importance, from Curti's viewpoint, was the founding of the Chicago Federation of Teachers—the predecessor of the American Federation of Teachers—in the early twentieth century by classroom teacher Margaret Haley. Curti sympathetically relates Haley's belief that "public school teachers must recognize the fact that their struggle to maintain the efficiency of the schools through better conditions for themselves was part of the same great struggle which manual workers had been making for humanity through their efforts to secure living conditions for themselves and their children." Haley fought against the tendency to turn schools into factories and children into future factory workers (see Chapter 9). To a certain extent, Curti views militant teachers as being allied with organized labor against school administrators who were allied with business interests.[6]

Another school of historical interpretation places the idea that business controlled and used the school in the broader conceptual framework of the rise of the corporate liberal state. Clarence Karier, Paul Violas, and Joel Spring's *Roots of Crisis: American Education in the Twentieth Century,* Joel Spring's *Education and the Rise of the Corporate State,* and Clarence Karier's *Shaping the American Educational State* advance the idea that schools in the late nineteenth and early twentieth centuries were shaped as instruments of the corporate liberal state for maintaining social control. Karier states that there was a belief that the corporate liberal state "could be used as a positive vehicle to reconcile the competing interest of capital, labor and the public welfare. They further surmised that such conflicting interest could be reconciled by effectively rationalizing and stabilizing an ever expanding economy of production and consumption of goods and services."[7] In other words, the government was to intervene in the economy and social system to maintain balance and rational order. The public schools were seen as an important instrument used by the government to aid in the rationalization and minimization of conflict by selecting and training students for their future positions in the economy and by imbuing the population with a sense of cooperation and national spirit.

According to this interpretation, the corporate liberal state was operated by expert managers using scientific methods, which in the case of the public schools meant psychologists armed with tests to measure intelligence, abilities, and interests. Within this interpretative context, the expanded social functions of the school, the socialized classroom with its emphasis on cooperation, vocational education, vocational guidance, testing, and a differentiated curriculum were all instruments to be used to provide rationality and order in society.

This group of historians emphasizes the concept of social control—a concept born during the late nineteenth and early twentieth centuries and used by the architects of corporate liberalism to justify their actions. This idea is most clearly stated by sociologist Edward Ross in a series of articles that appeared in the *American Journal of Sociology* between 1896 and 1898. In these articles, Ross defines social control as the means of maintaining social order and divides the means of control into external and internal forms. External forms of control involve direct confrontation between individuals and the police or government. Internal forms of control, which Ross considers more democratic and to be most relied upon, involve psychic control—control of the conscience of individuals. In America's past, Ross argues, internal forms of control were established through the community, family, and church. The problem for the future, he maintains, was that these traditional instruments of internal control were collapsing with the growth of industrialization and urbanization.

Ross suggests that these traditional instruments of social control be replaced with new forms, such as mass media, propaganda, and education, and argues that reliance on education as a means of control was becoming characteristic of American society as the school began to take the place of the church and family: "The ebb of religion is only half a fact. The other half is the high tide of education. While the priest is leaving the civil service, the schoolmaster is coming in. As the state shakes itself loose from the church, it reaches out for the school."[8]

Within the framework of the corporate liberal state, education, through the utilization of social science, was seen as the ideal mechanism for engineering social control for the benefit of all. The traditional forms of social control exercised through the church, family, and community were considered inadequate for modern society because they could not be scientifically managed, whereas the school could be used as an instrument of rational planning. Ross believed that modern civilization was learning this important lesson. He argues that the advantage of the school over the home as a means of control was in the fact that a public official was substituted for a parent: "Copy the child will, and the advantage of giving him his teacher instead of his father to imitate, is that the former is a picked person, while the latter is not." In the school, the child learned "the habit of obedience to an external law which is given by a good school discipline." In rather interesting language, Ross refers to education in the context of social control as collecting "little plastic lumps of human dough from private households and shap[ing] them on the social kneadingboard."[9]

In summary, those who argue within the framework of the corporate liberal state interpret educational changes in the late nineteenth and early twentieth centuries as an attempt to scientifically engineer a specialized and cooperative society. According to these educational historians, the major problem in this effort is that science and claims of objective social engineering were only masks for values that were racist and designed to control the majority of people. On the other hand, some argue that controllers of the liberal corporate state were merely trying to engineer a society that would protect their interests and that educators, the schools, social science, psychologists, and other engineers of the human mind were merely servants of power.

A variation on the theme of the corporate liberal state is used by David Tyack in his well-written, scholarly study *The One Best System: A History of American Urban Education*. An important element in Tyack's history is the development of modern urban educational bureaucracies and power structures. Like Merle Curti, Tyack concludes that education was controlled by business and corporate elites, and like Karier, Violas, and Spring, he believes that an alliance existed between the new corporate leaders and the intellectuals who served as their instruments of power. Regarding the campaign from 1890 to 1920 to reform urban education, Tyack states: "At that time an interlocking directorate of urban elites—largely business and professional men, university presidents and professors, and some 'progressive' superintendents—joined forces to centralize the control of schools."[10]

Using the corporate model developed by the historians of the corporate liberal state, Tyack argues that the administration of schools during this period was patterned after that of the modern corporation and factory. He calls these centralizers of organizational control and power "administrative progressives," in contradistinction to the political progressives who had organized the corporate liberal state.

A major problem with both Tyack's interpretation and that of the historians of the corporate liberal state is that they treat the worker, the immigrant, and the average citizen as pawns in a power game played by a ruling elite of business people and intellectuals. According to this view of history, the masses of humanity were mere objects of decisions made by conspiratorial seekers of control; thus the average citizen is depicted as not wanting or caring about the educational reforms of the period and as not having an effect on the system.

An important corrective to this point of view came with the publication of David Hogan's article "Education and the Making of the Chicago Working Class, 1880–1930," for which he received a History of Education Society award. The purpose of Hogan's study was to determine why school attendance among immigrant children increased dramatically in the first half of the twentieth century. Hogan's figures for 1910 to 1930 show that school attendance for the 14 to 15 age cohort increased "for native white children of foreign or mixed parentage, from 66.3 to 94.4 percent," and "for white foreign-born children, from 54.9 to 94.3

percent." The age-cohort group of 14 to 15 used by Hogan represents the age at which children were most likely, despite child-labor laws, to leave school and enter the labor market.[11]

In studying these changes in school attendance, Hogan was interested in assessing the demand by common people for an education. In other words, was schooling imposed on people, or was it given in response to public demand? He notes that

> *David Tyack, for example, in discussing the Americanization movement, acknowledged the xenophobia of Americanizers, but insisted that Americanization was part of a "general pattern of socialization" or the "modernization of behavior and beliefs which has been world wide during the past century." Moreover, he added, "No brigades of attendance [officers] could have coerced . . . [immigrant] masses of children into school if their parents had strongly opposed public education."*[12]

Hogan maintains that Tyack's view is simplistic and that decisions made by immigrant families about school attendance or nonattendance were rational economic decisions. To prove his argument, Hogan studied the school-attendance patterns of Chicago's immigrant groups and reached the conclusion that the increase in Chicago's population between 1880 and 1930 was primarily the result of an influx of immigrants from southern and eastern Europe. In 1880, the "first five countries of birth of Chicago's foreign-born population were Germany, Ireland, Canada, England, and Sweden." As a reflection of the shift in immigration patterns from western and northern Europe, in 1910 the first five countries were Germany, Poland, Russia, Austria, and Ireland. Indicative of the immigrant nature of Chicago's population is the fact that in 1930 approximately "65 percent of the population were foreign-born or first-generation immigrant children."[13]

Hogan concludes that school-attendance patterns paralleled the economic conditions and requirements of immigrant life. In the first stage of immigrant life, poverty required families to send their children into the labor market. In other words, children were removed from the educational system to help meet the family's economic needs, not because of a lack of desire for schooling. In the second stage of immigrant life, the purchase of a home was considered necessary protection against the uncertainty of renting. Children's labor was required at this stage of immigrant life also. In the final stage, immigrant children received prolonged schooling as a means of gaining better employment opportunities. According to Hogan, "In effect, immigrant parents experienced a tension between survival and schooling, a tension produced by two conflicting forms of economic necessity—the necessity to survive on a day-to-day basis through home ownership on the one hand, and surviving through educational certification on the other hand."[14]

Hogan's study gives a more dynamic role to workers and immigrants in the structuring of the educational system and tempers the image that schooling was mainly a product of elite imposition. A much stronger attack on this idea is made by historian Julia Wrigley in *Class Politics and Public Schools: Chicago, 1900–1950*. One of her main concerns is the lack of attention given by historians of the liberal corporate state to the impact of conflict between labor and capital on the shaping of the schools: "In their readiness to call attention to the successes of the social elite in dominating and socializing those below . . . [historians of the liberal corporate state] have given little weight to the social conflicts that have occurred over the creation and shaping of public institutions."[15]

Wrigley argues that attention must be given to the double-edged character of education: On the one hand, it can be used to promote docility, and, on the other hand, it can heighten criticism of the system. She finds that Chicago business leaders resisted increased spending for education because of a fear of an "over-educated" work force, but when faced with the prospect of increased school attendance by working-class children, they began to demand a differentiated curriculum that emphasized character development and vocational training. In contrast, Wrigley states, organized labor promoted increased education for working-class children and supported a broad liberal education for all children.

Wrigley's book highlights the continual struggle between business and organized labor. The picture she presents is one of constant attempts by both groups to promote educational policies that matched their own economic interests. Business struggled to maintain a school system that was inexpensive and produced students trained and socialized to meet the requirements of the labor market, whereas organized labor struggled to force business to spend more on education that would produce students capable of protecting their economic, political, and social rights. For Wrigley, the educational institutions of the twentieth century are not a product of elite imposition but were shaped by this social struggle.

The range of interpretations of this important period of educational history provides different ways of viewing schooling as a social and political institution. At one end of the spectrum is the view of schools as benign institutions shaped by well-intentioned individuals to solve social problems, and at the other end of the spectrum is the interpretation that the school has developed as a product of group conflicts over economic interests. These differences in interpretation reflect the individual political philosophies of their proponents: Conservatives tend to see the history of schooling as a process that has been free of conflict, with educational leaders working for the general good, whereas radicals emphasize sharp differences in educational policies based on economic interests.

Extending the Social Role of the School

In the late nineteenth century, immigration and industrialization expanded urban areas and created a host of social problems. Crowded ghettos, inadequate urban services, and a population primarily rural in origin contributed to unsanitary living conditions and the spread of disease. Added to these real conditions was a belief held by many Americans that a sense of community was being lost with the growth of urban America and that this loss would cause the urban population to suffer alienation, a breakdown in traditional forms of social control, and, as a consequence, increased crime and poverty. A fear also arose that the new immigrants would destroy traditional American values and create a strong following for radical economic and political ideas.

The school was considered a logical institution to prevent these problems by providing social services, teaching new behaviors, and creating a community center. Nurses, health facilities, and showers were added to schools in order to control the spread of disease, and special instructional programs were introduced to educate children about sanitary conditions. Americanization programs were offered as a means of assimilating children of immigrants in American life and preventing the spread of radical ideologies. Playgrounds were attached to schools to provide after-school activities for children that, it was hoped, would reduce juvenile delinquency. To curb a sense of alienation caused by urban living, auditoriums and special facilities for adults were provided by schools to serve as centers for community activities.

All these educational changes expanded the social functions of the school. Of course, ending poverty and crime had been a traditional goal of the school since the early nineteenth century, but common school reformers at that time saw those goals being achieved through instruction in the classroom. The changes in the late nineteenth century made the school more than a center of instruction by turning it into a major social agency.

John Dewey, the great educational philosopher of the period, explained the new social functions of the school to educators who gathered in 1902 for the annual convention of the National Education Association. He told the school people gathered from around the country that education must provide a "means for bringing people and their ideas and beliefs together, in such ways as will lessen friction and instability, and introduce deeper sympathy and wider understanding." Using the schools as social centers, he argued, would morally uplift the quality of urban living by replacing brothels, saloons, and dance halls as centers of recreation. More important, he considered the school to be a potential clearinghouse of ideas that would interpret to the new urban industrial worker the meaning of his or her place in the modern world. Through an exchange of ideas and the establishment of relationships with a variety of people, an understanding of others and the bonds of an interdependent society would develop. The school as social center, Dewey told his audience, "must interpret to [the worker] the intellectual and social meaning of the work in which he is engaged; that is, must reveal its relations to the life and work of the world." For Dewey, therefore, the new role of the school was to serve as an agency providing social services and a community center that would solve the problem of alienation in an urban industrial society.[16]

A major educational movement that combined the expansion of the social role of the school with an emphasis on improving urban living was the movement to establish public kindergartens. Kindergartens had originally served upper-class families, but by the 1880s and 1890s they were considered a primary educational method of dealing with the problems of urban poverty. In a broader context, one could argue that early-childhood education, as represented by the kindergarten movement, originated in concerns with urban problems.

The concept of kindergarten as introduced in the United States in the 1860s and 1870s by Carl Schurz and Elizabeth Peabody was almost mystical in nature. The original kindergarten was opened in Germany in 1840 by Friedrich Froebel (1782–1852) as a method of early-childhood education that was to lead the child from a world concentrated on self to a society of children. As the name implies, the kindergarten was conceived as a garden of children to be cultivated in the same manner as plants. Like Johann Pestalozzi, Froebel advocated a model maternal teacher whose method "should be passive and protective, not directive and interfering." Froebel believed that the divine spirit existed in all humans and that it was the key to social harmony. By cultivating the garden of children, the kindergarten teacher was to bring forth their divine spirits and create a sense of unity among all humans.[17]

The first public school kindergarten in the United States was opened in St. Louis, Missouri, in 1873 for the specific purpose of dealing with urban poverty. In his excellent history of the St. Louis school system, *The Public and the Schools: Shaping the St. Louis System, 1838–1920,* Selwyn Troen describes how that system's famous superintendent, William Torrey Harris, analyzed the distribution of children in the city according to the locality of "haunts of vice and iniquity" and decided that the only way of saving slum children from corruption was to get them into school at an early age. Harris first requested that the school board lower the minimum age of school attendance. After being refused by the school board, he recommended the establishment of kindergartens as a permanent part of the school system. Harris claimed that kindergartens were necessary because traditional socializing agencies like the family, church, and community had collapsed:

> *Living in narrow, filthy alleys, poorly clad and without habits of cleanliness,*
> *"the divine sense of shame," which Plato makes to be the foundation of civili-*
> *zation, is very little developed. Self respect is the basis of character and virtue;*
> *cleanliness of person and clothing is a sine qua non for its growth in the child.*
> *The child who passes his years in the misery of the crowded tenement house or*
> *alley, becomes early familiar with all manner of corruption and immorality.*

Within this context, the kindergarten was to be a substitute for the habits of living and moral training formerly taught by the family organization that supposedly had been lost in the slums of the new urban areas.[18]

The curriculum established for the kindergarten in the St. Louis school system was intended to redeem the slum child by, in Troen's words, bridging "the 'nurture' of the family with the established program of the district school." A major effort of the kindergarten program was to teach virtues and manners considered necessary for community living. Emphasis was placed on teaching moral habits, cleanliness, politeness, obedience, regularity, and self-control. Thus, the kindergarten was to be not only a substitute for the socialization that supposedly was no longer offered by the family, but also preparation for the habits required by the school.[19]

This same relationship between urban reform and the kindergarten is found by Marvin Lazerson in his brilliant history of the Boston school system, *Origins of the Urban School: Public Education in Massachusetts, 1870–1915*. According to Lazerson, the first director of Boston's kindergartens, Laura Fisher, saw them as being directly concerned with elevating the home life of the urban poor. In an article published in 1904, she states:

> *The mere fact that the children of the slums were kept off the streets, and that*
> *they were made clean and happy by kind and motherly young women; that the*
> *child thus being cared for enabled the mother to go about her work in or outside*
> *the home—all this appealed to the heart of America, and America gave freely*
> *to make these kindergartens possible.*[20]

Lazerson found that a major goal of the early kindergarten movement was to teach children habits that would reform the home. In other words, the early kindergarten was viewed as a method of educating the parents, particularly the mother. According to Lazerson, an early example of this thinking can be seen in Lucy Wheelock's tale "A Lily's Mission," in which two slum children bring a flower home

> *to their dingy apartment. The mother has failed to keep the house clean; the*
> *father is out drinking. Overjoyed at seeing the flower, the mother places it on a*
> *windowsill only to discover that dirt prevents any sunlight from shining*

through the window to the flower. With the window clean, sunlight reveals
the filth of the apartment, which is then quickly cleaned, the mother is washed
and dressed, and father, overcome by his new environment upon his return
home, vows to give up the bottle.[21]

The concept of parental education introduced by the kindergarten
movement extended the role of the school in a new direction that gave
the kindergarten a social role far beyond anything originally intended by
Froebel. As a new educational institution, the kindergarten was to compensate for the supposed loss of socialization within the slum family, to
protect the young child from the influences of the street, to provide
preparation for entrance into regular elementary school classes, and to
educate the parents, particularly the mother.

Lazerson argues that these extended social goals resulted in the kindergarten's losing its original emphasis on creative play and self-expres-
sion. In place of these activities, the kindergarten stressed creating order
and discipline in the child's life as compensation for family life and as
preparation for school. Lazerson found that as the kindergarten evolved
in Massachusetts in the twentieth century, it became less involved in
parental education and that, in the end, discipline, order, and protection
from the urban environment became its primary objectives.

The play movement, and the resulting changes it led to in the school,
was another product of the desire among educational reformers to protect children from the harmful effects of city life and to provide a mechanism for controlling the process of socialization. One major goal of this
movement was to reduce juvenile crime by providing parks and playgrounds. This approach to curing urban social problems began with the
development of small sandlots for children in the 1880s and reached a
high point with the establishment of the Chicago park system in 1904.
Between 1885 and 1895, sandlots were constructed in congested areas of
Boston, Chicago, Philadelphia, and New York City. These play areas
were designed for children under 12 years of age and usually included a
kindergarten program. One student of the movement reports that the
dominant motive for establishing sandlots was "to keep children off the
street and out of mischief and vice."[22]

A major result of the play movement is that the school became responsible for the after-school play of urban children. For instance, in 1895 the
chairman of the Advisory Committee on Small Parks of New York City
asked the police to indicate on a map the areas of high rates of juvenile
crime. After the committee found that all areas with newly founded
parks had a decreasing crime rate, it attempted to speed the development of parks by having the city adopt the following law: "Hereafter no
schoolhouse shall be constructed in the City of New York without an
open-air playground attached to or used in connection with the same."

In addition to protecting children from bad influences in the streets, play was to protect individuals from the nervous strain of urban living. In 1917, Henry S. Curtis, an organizer of the Playground and Recreation Association and former supervisor of the playgrounds of the District of Columbia, summarized the following reasons for the widespread movement to establish playgrounds and parks in the United States. In urban areas, children confined to schools and adults trapped in factories and businesses needed fresh air and the opportunity to exercise their bodies in order to avoid "the rapid increase of insanity and the growing instability of the nervous system." But, according to Curtis, "it has not been these reasons that have weighed most strongly with the people that have promoted the movement." Rather, he stated, the dominant motive and major concern of the leaders of the play movement was the fact that there was "little for the children to do in the cities, and that in this time of idleness the devil has found much for idle hands to do. . . . The home seems to be disappearing, and crime, despite increasingly effective police and probation system, is increasing everywhere."[23]

Like the kindergarten, the playground was to replace the socializing influence of family life supposedly lost in the growth of urban America. In addition to providing recreation and physical activity, the playground was to teach good habits, such as cleanliness, and contribute to the general health of the community. The development of small parks included the construction of elaborate recreational and bathing facilities. For example, in 1898, Boston created a bath department as part of its city administration. This department had control of the city beaches, the floating baths, and the municipal bathhouses. The floating baths were platforms supporting a row of dressing rooms around an open area of water. In 1899, Boston had 14 floating baths, 2 swimming pools, and 7 shower baths. In New York, floating baths were started in 1876, and by 1899, a total of 15 had been built. A campaign was waged in New York in the 1890s to increase the number of shower baths available because they were more usable during the winter than were the floating baths.

It was logical that this aspect of the playground movement would also become a school activity. The first reported school bath was a shower opened in a Boston school in 1889. Cremin reports in *The Transformation of the School* that "the teachers of New York, for example, found themselves giving hundreds of baths each week. The syllabi said nothing about baths, and teachers themselves wondered whether bathing was their charge. But there were the children and there were the lice."[24] The addition of the shower room to the public school symbolized the expansion of the school as a social agency.

Historian Paul Violas argues that the playground movement was more than just an attempt to reduce urban crime and supplement the socializing influence of the family. In *The Training of the Urban Working Class: A History of Twentieth Century American Education,* he contends that the leaders of the movement believed that directed play was necessary for producing the types of adults required by corporate industry. An important concept in this argument is that of directed play as opposed to free play. The early leaders of the play movement did not want to establish playgrounds and parks where adults and children came to play without guidance; rather, they believed that the state should interfere and direct play toward social ends. Play-movement leaders like Joseph Lee and Henry Curtis, according to Violas, wanted organized play to produce future workers who would be cooperative, good citizens. Therefore, playground games and activities were organized to produce a sense of team spirit, habits of cooperation, and a willingness to play by the rules. In other words, play was viewed as another method of social control.[25]

The establishment of summer, or vacation, school was another means of extending the influence of the school over children's lives. Cambridge, Massachusetts, was one of the first reported cities to propose a vacation, or summer, school. In 1872, its school committee reported the need for a vacation school because summer was "a time of idleness, often of crime, with many who are left to roam the streets, with no friendly hand to guide them, save that of the police." The superintendent of the same school district was still asking for a summer school as an inexpensive form of police control when he wrote in his school report in 1897, "The value of these schools consists not so much in what shall be learned during the few weeks they are in session, as in the fact that no boy or girl shall be left with unoccupied time. Idleness is an opportunity for evil-doing. . . . These schools will cost money. Reform schools also cost money."[26]

Summer schools were established in rapid succession in urban areas. Boston established them in 1885; New York, in 1894; Cleveland, in 1897; and Chicago, in 1898. The Chicago vacation schools were considered models. They were opened in the most densely populated parts of the city, and enrollment was limited to a first-come, first-served basis. The principal of the system reported that they were received with such enthusiasm that at "one of the schools it was found necessary to call in the police to remove the parents who crowded the halls of the building, insisting that their children must be accepted." At another school, 50 children were held up on their way to school, and their cards of admission were taken from them.[27]

The school as an expanding social agency also became involved in providing school nurses and lunch programs. Cremin found that much of this work was the result of the settlement house movement, which sought to reform conditions among the poor. Workers in the settlement house movement campaigned for a broader view of the social functions of the school and were responsible in the late nineteenth and early twentieth centuries for the first citywide lunch program in New York schools, the first school physician (in 1897), and the first experiments in providing school nurses in Chicago.[28]

Kindergartens, playgrounds, showers, lunches, and nurses were recognized as giving broader social meaning and uses to the public school. In a book published in 1910, Clarence A. Perry's *Wider Use of the School Plant*, the author begins by noting, "The children who went to school back in the eighties skipped out of the school house door at half past three and scampered down the street shouting with glee. . . . Within a couple of decades all this has changed." He found that in 1910 public school buildings were "open not only days but evenings. . . . Children go to them Saturdays as well as Mondays, and in some places the school rooms are not left unvisited even on Sundays."[29]

Another important factor in the wider use of the school was the concern with loss of community. The use of the school as a social center was viewed as one means of reestablishing within an urban context a sense of community that had been lost with the passing of rural and small-town life. It was believed that the neighborhood school could be a means of organizing urban populations into a corporate body of specialized tasks and life styles cemented together by common allegiances. An example of this attitude is provided by J. K. Paulding, a New York writer who argued in 1898 that democracy could function only with the existence of a spirit of democratic fraternalism resulting from the unification of individual aspirations into a common way of life. He argued that the school, by opening its doors a little wider and becoming a social center, could bring in neighborhood life and create the necessary spirit of democratic fraternalism. An article by H. E. Scudder in the *Atlantic Monthly* in 1896 suggested that the school could attract more people by improving the beauty of its buildings, attaching a public library, organizing a museum and conservatory, and using its walls as a public art gallery. The author states, "The common schoolhouse is in reality the most obvious center of national unity."[30]

During the 1890s, social centers developed rapidly throughout the country. New York organized its after-school recreational activities into social centers in 1897. The University Settlement in New York organized clubs in 21 school buildings for the specific purposes of reducing individual selfishness and promoting a spirit of social cooperation. In Chicago, social centers were established in the fieldhouses of the park system, and neighborhood groups engaged in a variety of activities, including community orchestras and choral clubs. A local women's club in Milwaukee persuaded that city in 1907 to open school buildings for local evening meetings. When the Russell Sage Foundation surveyed the so-

cial center movement in 1913, it found that among 788 school superintendents contacted around the country, 330 reported the use of their
schools as social centers. By 1920, the movement had spread to 667
school districts.[31]

Changes in school architecture reflected the growing commitment to
the concept of the school as social center. One school superintendent
complained to his colleagues in 1897 that it was difficult to open schools
to adults because in most buildings access to assembly rooms was
"gained only by climbing flights of stairs, always with embarrassment
and often with risk of accident from fire or other causes." His suggestion, which was incorporated in later school plans, was to construct
assembly rooms on the ground floor, with easy access from the street.[32]

Classroom furniture also had to be changed to meet the multiple
needs of the school and the adult social center. Demands were made to
replace school desks bolted to the floor with flat-top desks that could be
rearranged for use in club and recreational activities. By 1910, schools
such as the Washington Irving High School in New York were being
designed specifically to function as social centers. The lobby of the
school contained a neighborhood art gallery, and the auditorium provided facilities for neighborhood drama groups. Office space was set
aside in the school to accommodate the staffs of local clubs and associations.

One leader of the social center movement, Edward J. Ward, believed
that schools could be a means of reforming urban politics by reducing
political tensions. Ward advocated the establishment of social centers in
schoolhouses as centers for political discussion. He envisioned the day
when voting districts would be the same as school districts and the
ballot box would be placed in the schoolhouse. When this occurs, he
wrote, "the schoolhouse . . . becomes, for all its possible wider uses,
the real social center; and the way is clear and the means are at hand for
supplying the fundamental and supreme lack in the machinery of democracy." The social center, he believed, was the key to developing
political cooperation.[33]

As the school social center idea spread throughout the United States it
took on a variety of forms. In Chicago, the park fieldhouses served the
function of bringing the community together on a social basis, and
schoolhouses were used to promote political cooperation. In 1914, the
Russell Sage Foundation reported that 142 political meetings had been
held in Chicago school buildings during a municipal election. The civic
clubs of Los Angeles fought to have polling booths and political meetings in school buildings instead of in "livery stables and small, dingy,
out-of-the-way and hard-to-find places." They believed that locating the
polling booth in the school would protect it from tampering by corrupt
political forces.[34]

The social center was also seen as a means of helping the immigrant adjust to urban living. For instance, the Women's Municipal League of Boston worked for the opening of social centers in the local schools as part of its more general civic work to improve the lives of immigrants. The president of the league wrote in 1912 that social centers were opened because "it is our endeavor to make our city a true home for the people, it is not enough that we should merely make it a house. . . . We must also ensure that there shall be within it recreation, enjoyment, and happiness for all."[35]

In one sense, kindergartens, social centers, playgrounds, and the wider use of the school plant were intended to handle the problems created by the new immigrants from southern and eastern Europe and can be considered one aspect of the more general attempt to Americanize immigrants. These new uses of the school were justified as necessary for replacing the declining influence of the family and at the same time were considered necessary as a means of socializing immigrant children to the American way of life.

The term *Americanization* was used to refer to more than just the use of the school as a social agency. It also encompassed classroom instruction designed to teach the immigrant child and adult the English language and American customs. As social institutions, American schools in the late nineteenth and early twentieth centuries were faced with massive pressure from immigrant populations. This created major problems in classroom space and instruction. Tyack reports in *The One Best System* that investigators for the United States Senate Immigration Commission in 1908 found more than 60 nationalities in 37 cities and that 58 percent of all students had foreign-born parents. For particular cities, the percentages of students with foreign-born parents were as follows: New York, 72 percent; Chicago, 67 percent; Boston, 64 percent; Cleveland, 60 percent; and San Francisco, 58 percent.[36]

One response of schools to the immigrant population was to offer adult night-school classes in English, government, and naturalization. By offering this activity, the schools were serving a direct need, not trying to compensate for the supposed failure of another institution. Adult night-school classes further opened the door of the schoolhouse to the community and contributed to the claim that the school was becoming the social center of urban America.

In both the adult courses and the accommodation of immigrant children during regular school hours, a tension existed between the wish to protect immigrant culture and the push for Americanization. There is little doubt that most immigrant groups flocked to the schools, but on their arrival there, they often found a great deal of hostility toward their language and customs. Immigrant children found their names being Anglicized and were frequently told not to speak the language of their parents and to forget their native customs. In these situations, Americanization meant cultural imperialism and the building of a national spirit that was suspicious of foreign countries and ways of living.

One important aspect of Americanization was fear of radical political ideas. Many national leaders argued that ideas about socialism and communism were being brought to this country by immigrant groups. One hundred percent Americanism came to mean opposition to radical economic and political ideologies. For example, Tyack quotes Cleveland's superintendent of schools as recommending in 1917 the firing of "any teacher 'whose sympathies are proved to be with our country's enemies' (it was not necessary, he said, to express disloyalty in words, since teachers influenced pupils merely by the convictions and fundamental desires of the . . . heart)."[37]

Therefore, Americanization gave a new meaning to the citizenship training provided by the public schools. Horace Mann had argued that the school should teach a consensus of political and social values. The concept of Americanization changed the political goals of the school to include teaching against radical ideas, particularly socialism and communism. As the social center of the new urban America, the school became a bastion of Americanism and antiradicalism.

One suspects that when educators talked about the collapse of the family and community, they meant either that the style of family and community life was not to their liking or that they wanted the school to take over the social functions of those institutions. Certainly, many immigrant groups maintained strong family structures and community life in urban America, but for those Americans who believed that immigrants were threatening a traditional American way of life, immigrant families and communities were considered to be deviant and in need of change.

Within the context of the preceding argument, the movement to expand the school as a social agency could have had several meanings. It could have meant that traditional institutions were indeed collapsing, and the social role of the school needed to expand to replace those institutions. Or it could have meant that the immigrant forms of family and community were unacceptable, and the school needed to destroy those forms by taking over their functions. The expanded social role of the school could also have been a result of a desire to exert more rational control over the social order by having government institutions assume greater social functions.

Whatever the reasons, by the early twentieth century the school in fact had expanded its functions into areas not dreamed of in the early part of the previous century. Kindergartens, playgrounds, school showers, nurses, social centers, and Americanization programs turned the school into a central social agency in urban America. The one theme that ran through all these new school programs was the desire to maintain discipline and order in urban life. Within this framework, the school became a major agency for social control.

The Changing Classroom in the New Corporate Order

In studying history, one must be careful that statements about what should be are not confused with reality. Nowhere is this more important than in studying the history of classroom practices. Although there is evidence that new theories of instruction advocated in the late nineteenth and early twentieth centuries by the Herbartians, John Dewey, William James, and Edward Thorndike did have an impact on classroom practices, there is no evidence that this impact occurred in any consistent or organized pattern: After closing their classroom doors, teachers tended to teach using a variety of personal instructional methods.

Keeping the preceding caution in mind, in this section we will examine the evolution of classroom practices by discussing the environment of the classroom and new theories of instruction. The description of actual classroom practices up to the time of World War II is based on Larry Cuban's historical work *How Teachers Taught: Constancy and Change in American Classrooms, 1890–1980*.

An important element in classroom environments was the organization of desks. Some pedagogical theories, particularly those of John Dewey, required a classroom environment that allowed increased student activity, whereas other theories, such as Edward Thorndike's, were not particularly affected by classroom organization. Therefore, actual classroom arrangements could determine the use or neglect of a particular pedagogical theory.

Cuban's historical investigations provide a portrait of public school classrooms. For example, in New York City, school architect C.B.J. Snyder designed what would become the standardized classroom plan in the first half of the twentieth century: rows of desks bolted to the floor and facing the blackboard, with "48 permanent desks for grades 1 through 4; 45 desks for grades 5 and 6; and 40 for grades 7 and 8."[38] Cuban estimates that in the period from 1920 to 1940, 79 percent of the desks in secondary schools also were bolted to the floor. Movable furniture was allowed in special classes and in kindergarten, but fixed desks were maintained in large classes to avoid noise and confusion. In more progressive school systems, such as Denver, Colorado's, only 19 percent of desks in secondary schools were stationary; no figures are available for Denver elementary schools. On the other hand, in 1920 in Washington, D.C., almost two-thirds of elementary school desks were bolted to the floor. By 1929, only 200 desks had been replaced by portable ones, but in 1930, a five-year program was initiated that replaced 7,000 stationary desks. In Washington, D.C., high schools, one-third of desks were bolted to the floor.[39]

Cuban's sample of three cities suggests that the majority of classrooms allowed for little student movement. The number of students in a class was another important factor in determining pedagogical method. Small classes allowed for greater experimentation and flexibility, whereas large classes tended to require an emphasis on order and discipline. In other words, large classes often dictated the use of pedagogical methods that exerted control over students.

In New York City around the time of World War I, elementary school class sizes averaged about 50 students. By 1930, this figure had declined to 38 students, but this number varied from school to school, with at least 17 percent of elementary classes having 45 or more students. Although Cuban does not provide figures on the average size of high school classes, he argues that less individual attention was possible in high school because a teacher with five classes of 30 students each dealt with a total of 150 students a day. In Denver in 1923, 60 percent of all elementary school classes had 30 to 40 students, 13 percent had over 40, and 27 percent had fewer than 30. By 1934, the effects of the Depression had increased class sizes: Only 3 percent had fewer than 30 students, 33 percent had more than 40, and 64 percent had between 30 and 40 students. High school classes averaged between 30 and 40 students. Washington, D.C., had a segregated school system, and class size varied with the racial composition of the school. In 1922, the average elementary school class size for whites was 34.3 students, and for blacks it was 37.3. By 1932, these figures had declined to 30.8 whites and 36.1 blacks per classroom. Hidden in these figures is a great deal of variation. In 1927–1928, 29 percent of both black and white elementary classrooms had over 40 students. Averages are not given for secondary schools.[40]

The statistics provided by Cuban on class size and the organization of classrooms suggest that the majority of classroom teachers would have had difficulty adopting pedagogical techniques requiring a great deal of mobile student activity. On the other hand, some classrooms did exist in which such student activity was possible.

An educational approach known as the Herbartian movement was strongest in the United States in the 1880s and 1890s and owed its origins to the work of German psychologist Johann Herbart (1776–1841). The major contribution of the Herbartian movement was the class lesson plan suitable for any type of class size or organization. Undoubtedly, the lesson plan became a fixed feature of American education because it allowed for bureaucratic control over the teacher. More simply stated, the lesson plan became a means by which the school principal or supervisor could quickly check on teacher activity. Also, the lesson plan as it developed reflected a conceptualization of education that placed an emphasis on order and planning. To a certain extent, it fit the requirements of large classes with fixed environments.

Herbartians, of course, believed in more than just lesson plans, but in the final analysis the public school classroom reduced Herbartian ideas to a concern with detailed planning of classroom practices. Charles De Garmo, a leading American exponent of Herbart, argues in a book published in 1895 that Herbart added an essential ingredient to the pedagogy of Johann Pestalozzi. According to De Garmo, Herbart accepted the Pestalozzian ideas of learning through the senses and with objects, but thought that Pestalozzian pedagogy lacked a clear idea of how knowledge is assimilated into the mind. In the chapter "What Pestalozzi Left for Herbart to Do," De Garmo states that the Pestalozzian method "does not show how mental assimilation can best take place, or how the resulting acquisition can be made most efficiently to influence the emotional and volitional side of our nature. Perception is . . . the first stage in cognition, but its equally important correlative is apperception, or mental assimilation."[41]

In Herbartian thought, the key to mental assimilation and to the organization of the lesson plan is interest. One could argue that the doctrine of interest set the stage for child-centered education. In the simplest terms, the doctrine of interest states that knowledge is best assimilated if it is of interest to the student. Interests can arise from knowledge or from social contacts. Interests related to knowledge include speculative, empirical, and aesthetic interests; interests arising from contact with others include sympathetic, social, and religious interests.

According to the Herbartians, the best method of instruction is to present material that is related to a previous interest of the student. Therefore, it is important to properly coordinate subject matter and organize lessons based on the stages of development of student interests. For instance, Herbart argued that the natural interests of the child dictate the teaching of Greek before the teaching of Latin.

The Herbartian lesson plan follows five steps: (1) preparation, (2) presentation, (3) comparison and abstraction, (4) generalization or definition, and (5) application. Preparation involves reminding the student of previous knowledge and interests that relate to the material being presented. Presentation is organized so that the material is related to previous interests and knowledge. Comparison and abstraction show the relationships between the new material and things already known by the students. Generalization attempts to make up a single definition that expresses the central idea of the lesson. Application applies the generalization to some other experience.

Willard Elsbree states, "Without question, these five simply stated steps exercised more influence on teaching practice in America between 1890 and 1905 than all other psychological discoveries and philosophical creations combined.''[42] Although the Herbartian lesson plan underwent significant change over time, the idea of a formally organized daily lesson became a fixed feature of American education. An educational environment of large classes and bolted-down desks was not antithetical to the lesson plan. Daily lesson plans also suited an environment based on hierarchical control, order, and discipline.

In contrast, John Dewey's pedagogical theories found little acceptance in the standard American classroom. In fact, when Dewey was organizing his famous Laboratory School at the University of Chicago in 1896, one problem he encountered was finding tables suitable for the work of groups of children, in place of individual desks designed to be permanently fixed to the floor. In practice, Dewey's methods emphasized student interests, student activity, group work, and cooperation—methods premised on the idea that the school had to serve a new social function in a world of increasing urban life and large corporations.

When John Dewey (1859–1952) founded the Laboratory School, he wanted to develop methods that would demonstrate to the student the social value of knowledge and the interdependence of society. One method Dewey hoped would achieve these objectives was to develop social imagination in cooperative group activities. Dewey defined *social imagination* as "the habit of mentally constructing some actual scene of human interaction, and of consulting that for instruction as to what to do." One of his early educational experiments took place in the 1890s, in a high school ethics class, where Dewey wanted the students to view ethics in relation to real problems as opposed to abstract principles. Dewey presented the students with an actual case of human misery and asked them to use social imagination to work out the problem of charity. Social imagination is the ability to relate isolated ideas to the actual conditions that have given them their original meaning. Dewey argued that this method aided a student in forming "the habit of realizing for himself and in himself the nature of the practical situations in which he will find himself placed."[43]

This method of teaching ethics is based on another important principle. Dewey believed that ideas, values, and social institutions originate in the material circumstances of human life. He rejected the notion that they are of divine origin or reflect some type of ideal. One problem, he thought, is that a belief in ideal forms caused civilization to become trapped by ideas and institutions that were no longer practical. According to Dewey, ideas, values, and institutions should change as the needs of society change. The term *pragmatism*, which is often associated with this school of philosophy, means in its simplest form that humans should adopt those ideas, values, and institutions that best work in a particular social situation.

One can understand why many religious groups in the twentieth century have reacted negatively to Dewey's ideas. Most religious groups believe that human action should be guided by the word of God and that legitimate values are of divine origin, whereas Dewey's philosophy relies on the ability of individuals to interpret their own experience instead of relying on the word of God.

Dewey believed it was necessary for the student to become aware of the relationship between knowledge and social experience and to be given an opportunity to act on ideas. It was his conviction that the product of social imagination remains as mere information until acted on. When acted on, it becomes judgment. "The child," Dewey stated, "cannot get power of judgment excepting as he is continually exercised in forming and testing judgment." Therefore, as Dewey saw it, the school must avoid the teaching of abstract ideas; rather, it must provide actual conditions out of which ideas grow, and the child must be given an opportunity within the school to test moral and social judgments. In other words, according to Dewey, the school had to become a community of real social relationships.[44]

An often-quoted statement by Dewey is that the school is a community with a real social life. Dewey wanted to utilize this community and make it a part of the learning process. He believed that the learning process should be a part of an active solution to a social problem because this provided the best basis for helping the student to see the social value of knowledge. For instance, counting was introduced at the Laboratory School by having nursery school children set the table for the mid-morning snack. The children quickly learned to count by matching the number of utensils with the number of students.

Dewey, like others of his generation, believed that modern urban industrial life was not providing the social context for teaching children habits of order, industry, and cooperation. He hoped students would learn such habits while working in the school community. In 1899, Dewey explored these issues in "The School and Society," a series of lectures given in response to criticism of the work at the Laboratory School. In the lectures, he stressed that the march of industrialism had destroyed a form of household and community life that had given the child "training in habits of order and of industry, and in the idea of responsibility, of obligation to do something, to produce something, in the world." In the past, he argued, these habits had been learned because most occupations centered around the household. Dewey reminded his audience in industrial Chicago that "those of us who are here today need go back only one, two, or at most three generations to find a time when the household was practically the center . . . [of] all the typical forms of industrial occupation."[45]

It was Dewey's contention that at one time the child experienced and participated in the total industrial process of the community. From these community experiences the child learned moral habits, industry, and social cooperation. "But it is useless to bemoan the departure of the good old days of children's modesty, reverence, and implicit obedience," Dewey stated. The problem was to retain the advantages of the present and at the same time introduce "into the school something representing the other side of life—occupations which exact personal responsibilities and which train the child in relation to the physical realities of life."[46]

The work that went on in the Laboratory School was designed to create social interaction among pupils that would foster efficient learning and good social habits. The activity of the younger members of the school centered around household occupations. Work directed toward a common productive end, Dewey believed, created an atmosphere of community. Children between the ages of four and five were given the responsibility of preparing their own mid-morning meals. They discussed their home life and were led to explore marketing, mail service, and other related occupations. The children played at making a dry-goods store that provided them with the opportunity to develop habits of industry, responsibility, and social cooperation. As a requirement of completing their projects, they also learned to read, write, and do arithmetic.

As the children progressed, they were led to ever-widening circles of activity. At age six, the children were introduced to farm activities. They built a farmhouse and barn of blocks and explored the problems of climate and farm production. At age seven, they began to study the historical development of civilization—a theme that persisted throughout the rest of their stay at the Dewey school. Activity was always associated with their work; for example, the children began their study of history by investigating occupations and engaging in activities like weaving and building smelters.

The study of history at the Laboratory School reflected Dewey's ideas about social imagination and community. Children were to develop social imagination by learning to relate ideas, inventions, and institutions to the social condition that gave birth to them. This process was also supposed to make the pupil aware of interdependence within society: "A society is a number of people held together because they are working along common lines, in a common spirit, and with references to common ends."[47] Dewey felt that a community had existed in America's past because the individual had been aware of the total industrial process, and this awareness joined people into a community through a sense of working together.

Dewey believed that modern urban and industrial society had destroyed this sense of community and common goals and that the school had to actively foster its growth. The function of social imagination, learned in the cooperative work of the school, was to help students relate their work to the total industrial process and to become aware of sharing common social purposes.

Facing his audience of critics in industrial Chicago in 1899, Dewey stated, "How many of the employed are today mere appendages to the machines which they operate! This . . . is certainly due in large part to the fact that the worker has had no opportunity to develop his imagination and his sympathetic insight as to the social and scientific values found in his work."[48] In 1902, Dewey argued before the National Education Association that the school should be the center around which a genuine community life is maintained in urban America: "It must interpret to [the worker] the intellectual and social meaning of the work in which he is engaged: that is, must reveal its relations to the life and work of the world."[49]

As other educators translated Dewey's ideas into classroom practice, many of his concerns about social imagination and the historical roots of occupations were lost. For many, Dewey stood for group activity, learning by doing, relating material to the interests of the child, and doing projects. Statements by Dewey such as "the true center of correlation on the school subjects is . . . the child's own social activities" were used to justify a variety of group and social activities within the school. Often these methods placed an emphasis on group conformity that went beyond anything Dewey intended. For instance, Dewey believed that motives and choices grow out of social situations; he did not believe, as many other educators were to argue, that individual motives and goals should conform to the wishes of the group. Dewey wanted to free individual action, not submerge it in the mediocre standard of group consensus.

In 1906, Colin Scott, one popularizer of group activity in the classroom, organized the Social Education Association. The reason Scott wanted to organize classrooms into working groups is because that is how contemporary society is organized, and thus he considered working groups the most efficient form of social organization. He argued that the traditional classroom atmosphere ran counter to modern social organization and that the classroom should initiate group projects as preparation for entering a society of cooperative groups.

Through the Social Education Association, Scott promoted the use of self-organized group activity in the classroom as a means of preparing students for life in a cooperative society. The association's charter states: "The fundamental purpose of education should be to prepare the child for a useful life of social service as an active and creative member of the social organism." Scott's principle of self-organized group activity was to allow children the opportunity to choose their own goals, organize their own groups, and organize their own work.[50]

One example of this method related by Scott is a class where the students were asked, "If you had time given to you for something that you enjoy doing, and that you think worthwhile, what should you choose to do?" Three boys immediately decided on the idea of printing. They formed a printing group and began publishing material for the class. In other examples given by Scott, history classes divided into the Senate and the House of Representatives, selected students to be government printers, and studied history as a series of legislative bills and debates.[51]

With the spread of Dewey's work and the activities of the Social Education Association, the idea of socialized classroom activity became popular. Articles in educational journals and books on group classroom activities appeared in large numbers. The topics ranged from socializing arithmetic drills to teaching cooking with self-organized groups. Following the lead of education professors like Michael V. O'Shea at the University of Wisconsin and Irving King at the University of Iowa, courses in social education began to be offered in teacher-training programs.

At Teachers College, Columbia University, William Heard Kilpatrick used his classes in educational theory to teach a form of group learning called the *project method*. His article on the method was first printed in 1918 and became so popular and widely used that it had gone through seven printings by 1922. The heart of the project method is what Kilpatrick called the "socially purposeful act"—an activity directed toward a socially useful end. As an example, Kilpatrick cited the situation of a girl making a dress. The act of making a dress could be considered a project if the girl was motivated by a social purpose and if she actually planned and made the dress. According to Kilpatrick, the purposeful act is the basic unit of the worthy life and democracy: "A man who habitually so regulates his life with reference to worthy social aims meets at once the demands for practical efficiency and of moral responsibility. Such a one presents the ideal of democratic citizenship." Within the classroom, children were prepared for a purposeful life by pursuing projects that grew out of social situations.[52]

Kilpatrick's project method also reflects the tendency in many social-education proposals of the 1920s to stress social conformity. He considered development of moral character to be one of the important results of the project method and defined *moral character* as "the disposition to determine one's conduct and attitudes with reference to the welfare of the group." In the classroom, the inculcation of this disposition was a function of group acceptance or rejection:

> There are few satisfactions so gratifying and few annoyances so distressing as the approval and disapproval of our comrades. . . . When the teacher merely coerces and the other pupils side with their comrade . . . conformity may be

but outward. But when all concerned take part in deciding what is just . . . conformity is not merely outward.

According to Kilpatrick, moral character is developed when the individual is conditioned always to respond to the desires of the group.[53] The project method, group activity, socialized learning, child-centered education, and the educating of social imagination were ideas that received a wide audience in the educational community. In many ways, these methods of instruction seemed suitable for preparing students for a world of highly organized living in cities and corporations. Undoubtedly, most teachers trained in the first half of the twentieth century received some exposure to these methods. The actual use of the methods depended on the teacher, the school district, the number of students in a class, and the environment of the classroom.

Although large classes with bolted-down desks might not have been suitable for socializing methods of instruction, they were ideally organized for the pedagogical methods advocated by William James and Edward Thorndike. James (1842–1910), a leading Harvard philosopher and psychologist, condensed his two-volume work published in 1890, *Principles of Psychology*, into a one-volume text for teachers, *Talks to Teachers on Psychology: And to Students on Some of Life's Ideals*, published in 1899. Thorndike (1874–1949) studied under James at Harvard and incorporated many of James's ideas into his own work. Thorndike can be considered the father of educational psychology. His major work, *Educational Psychology*, published in 1913, set the tone for the field for several decades.

Both James and Thorndike were associated with the development of *stimulus-response*, or behavioral, concepts of learning. In James's classic example of learning in the opening section of *Principles of Psychology*, a baby is pictured reaching for a candle flame, a reflex action caused by the stimulation of the fire. The baby's fingers are burned, and it learns not to reach for the flame. James contends that in any future stimulation by the fire of a candle, the baby's nervous system would respond with memories of pain, inhibiting the original grasping reflex and causing the hand to be withdrawn.[54]

For James, this simple learning situation initiates the development of habits in the baby. James considered the building of habits to be the most important function of education because through controlled development of habit, social order could be maintained:

Habit is thus the enormous fly-wheel of society, its most precious conservative agent. It alone is what keeps us all within bounds of ordinance, and saves the children of fortune from the envious uprisings of the poor. It alone prevents the hardest and most repulsive walks of life from being deserted by those brought up to tread therein.[55]

James extended the concept of habit into the thought process. As he envisioned it, the mind contains a steady stream of consciousness, and when confronted with a choice, the individual selects an action out of that stream of thought. Of course, the individual is conditioned to attend to particular ideas in the stream of consciousness in particular situations. That is, James believed that choices are determined by previous stimulus-response learning. This reasoning about human action was problematic for James because it seems to deny free will. If all actions and choices are determined by previous learning, then there is no free will and no individual responsibility for one's actions. This issue has been a central problem in behaviorism since the time of James's original study. James argued his way out of the dilemma by claiming that individuals have the power to make the effort to attend to particular things in the stream of consciousness.

Although James never advocated specific classroom practices, his psychological theories suggest that correct habits can be built through exercise and drill. Edward Thorndike made these two classroom practices part of his pedagogical theory when he translated stimulus-response learning into what he called *connectionism*. Connectionism refers to the connection or relationship between stimulus and response. Thorndike argued that all changes in the human intellect are the result of certain fundamental laws that affect these connections.

What Thorndike called *fundamental laws of change* became his basic methods of instruction. In general, they are mechanical methods that had been traditional classroom practices. In some ways, Thorndike only justified the traditional by making it sound scientific. For instance, his first fundamental law, the Law of Exercise, states that "other things being equal, the oftener or more emphatically a given response is connected with a certain situation, the more likely it is to be made to that situation in the future." He gives as an example a child responding "six" to the question, "How many are four and two?" Supposedly, if the child repeats the answer to the question enough times, it will be permanently connected in the mind. Thorndike states this law more briefly: "Other things being equal, exercise strengthens the bond between situation and response."[56]

Thorndike's second law of learning, the Law of Effect, states: "The greater the satisfyingness of the state of affairs which accompanies or follows a given response to a certain situation, the more likely that response is to be made to that situation in the future." For instance, in the example of the child responding "six" to the question, "How many are four and two?" the correct answer would be strengthened if the child were rewarded with candy or a smile.[57]

Thorndike viewed teaching as a science concerned with the control of human behavior: "Using psychological terms, the art of teaching may be defined as the art of giving and withholding stimuli with the result of producing and preventing certain responses." The power of the teacher was in his or her control of the stimuli. Thorndike divided stimuli into two categories: "under direct control" and "under indirect control." Stimuli under direct control include the use of love and tact by gestures, facial expressions, and speech. Stimuli under indirect control refers to the physical conditions of the school and classroom.[58]

Thorndike's dream was to turn all teaching into a scientific profession in which all educators would be guided by the scientific method and spirit. As scientific professionals, educators would be concerned with controlling the learning of students and with scientific measurement of results. In Thorndike's world, the scientifically constructed test is at the heart of the educational process: "Testing the results of teaching and study is for the teacher what verification of theories is to the scientist. . . . It is the chief means of fitting teaching to the previous experience and individual capacities of pupils.[59]

Like Dewey, Thorndike had a social vision that is directly related to the educational methods he advocated. At the center of his social vision is the concept of tests and measurement. He believed that the ideal social organization is one in which people are scientifically selected for their social roles through testing. According to Thorndike, human classification through tests and measurement would produce a more efficient society by matching individual talent with social needs. This theory made psychologists and schools the major determiners of the distribution of human resources.

Thorndike's social ideals had important implications for the meaning of democracy and equality of opportunity (see Chapter 8). What is important to understand at this point is the central importance of measurement in Thorndike's social philosophy, based on his role in the development of intelligence tests.

Thorndike believed that intelligence is determined by nature and that it can be measured by tests. He defined *intelligence* as the number of connections the mind can make between stimuli and responses: A "person whose intellect is greater or higher or better than that of another person differs from him in the last analysis in having, not a new sort of physiological process, but simply a larger number of connections of the ordinary sort." This definition of intelligence allows for measurement of the number of connections and, consequently, for the quantification of intelligence.[60]

The idea that intelligence is primarily a product of nature, as opposed to environment, had major implications for social policy. Thorndike stood squarely on the nature side of the nature-nurture debate. Regarding measurement of intelligence, he states, "What is essential to the hypothesis is that by original nature, men differ in respect of the number of connections or associations with ideas which they can form, so that despite identical outside environments, some of them would have many more than others."[61] Psychologists who believed that nature is the primary determiner of intelligence also believed that intelligence can be inherited (see Chapter 8), which usually led to the conclusion that racial differences exist regarding intelligence. For instance, a common belief of the period was that northern Europeans had naturally superior intelligence as compared with southern Europeans.

The classroom environment of bolted-down desks and large numbers of students was more conducive to Thorndike's stimulus-response, drill, reward, and measurement methods of instruction than to the types of group activity and socialized forms of instruction advocated by the social educators. One can easily imagine that a teacher trained in both traditions, when faced with a controlled and structured classroom environment, would tend to adopt Thorndike's scientific methods. One also can imagine that, under these conditions, many teachers accepted the doctrines of classroom control as preached by William Bagley in his popular book *Classroom Management*.

Classroom Management became a standard teacher-training text during the first quarter of the century and was reprinted 30 times between 1907 and 1927. Bagley believed that the primary role of the school is to build good industrial habits of the type needed on the assembly line. Bagley's ideal teacher is one who would "rigidly 'hew to the line' in all of those initial stages of habit building," and in his ideal school everything is reduced to rigid routine. Bagley states that the expert observer could immediately gauge the efficiency of the teacher by "the manner in which lines pass to and from the room."[62]

Because Bagley could find no arguments against pupils' keeping step while walking, he advocates the Lancasterian method of lockstep marches. He also insists that students be given drills in packing their desks in a certain order, in going to assigned places at the blackboard, in leaving the room, and in marching through the cloakroom to collect coats. To reduce the problem of children interrupting class activities, he states that "regular habits should be speedily established with regard to the bodily functions." He recommends that lines of children pass through the lavatories at recess time before they are allowed on the playground. Bagley urges teachers to train their students to give physical attention on command: "In general, the command, Attention! should be stimulus for the habitual adjustment of the body in a certain definite posture." He recommends as the idea posture "head erect, eyes turned toward the teacher, hands or arms folded (preferably the former), feet flat on the floor, instant cessation of all . . . school work or activity."[63]

Many teachers faced with large classes and wanting to maintain order probably followed Bagley's recommendations. As the most popular system of classroom management, it complemented Thorndike's instructional methods more than those of the social educators. But what teachers actually did in their classrooms demonstrated a great deal of variation. In his analysis of classroom activity in the New York schools between 1920 and 1940, Larry Cuban found that in elementary schools most (41 percent) group instruction was a mix of teacher- and student-centered instruction. Strictly teacher-centered instruction occurred 27 percent of the time, and student-centered instruction occurred 32 percent of the time. He found similar variation in different proportions for classroom activities and for high school instruction. He found more student-centered instruction during this period in Denver than in New York, whereas patterns in Washington, D.C., were closer to those in New York.

Cuban's general conclusion about teaching during this period is that teachers used a variety of methods depending on the conditions they encountered and their own personal philosophies. The problem was that many of these approaches to instruction contradicted one another. It was difficult to reconcile the doctrines of John Dewey with those of Edward Thorndike, for example, or the demands for efficiency with those for child-centered education. Cuban argues that teachers were beset with contradictory "impulses to be efficient, scientific, child-centered, and authoritative," and the result was that "teachers construct[ed] patchwork compromises to contain these competing, often contradictory, impulses but (and here I can only speculate) at a cost of leaving within many a vague uneasiness over the aims of teaching, classroom discipline, and relations with students that seldom [went] away."[64]

Conclusion

The variety and contradictory nature of classroom practices highlight a major problem in understanding the functioning of the American educational system. At times, there has been little relationship between the expressed goals of education and actual educational practices. In part, this was caused by the variety of social forces acting on the school. Elites and educational leaders might have wanted the school to expand as a social agency to provide order and discipline and training and control of future workers, but these desires were often countered by students and parents who wanted to use the schools as a means of gaining upward mobility and greater political power and by teachers who had other social objectives. Therefore, although the educational system may have been structured to exert social control, that goal may have been modified by other social forces.

Notes

1. Ellwood Cubberley, *Public Education in the United States: A Study and Interpretation of American Educational History* (Boston: Houghton Mifflin, 1934), pp. 485–486.

2. Ibid., pp. 488–489.

3. Ibid., pp. 502–504.

4. Lawrence Cremin, *The Transformation of the School: Progressivism in American Education, 1876–1957* (New York: Random House [Vintage Books], 1961), pp. viii–ix.

5. Merle Curti, *The Social Ideas of American Educators* (Paterson, N.J.: Pageant Books, 1959), pp. 218–222.

6. Ibid., p. 242

7. Clarence Karier, *Shaping the American Educational State, 1900 to Present* (New York: Free Press, 1975), p. xix.

8. Edward A. Ross, *Social Control* (New York: Macmillan, 1906), p. 175.

9. Ibid., p. 168.

10. David Tyack, *The One Best System: A History of American Urban Education* (Cambridge, Mass.: Harvard University Press, 1974), p. 7.

11. David Hogan, "Education and the Making of the Chicago Working Class, 1880–1930," *History of Education Quarterly* (Fall 1978): 227.

12. Ibid., p. 230.

13. Ibid., p. 232.

14. Ibid., p. 244.

15. Julia Wrigley, *Class Politics and Public Schools: Chicago, 1900–1950* (New Brunswick, N.J.: Rutgers University Press, 1982), p. 13.

16. John Dewey, "The School as Social Center," *National Education Association Proceedings* (1902): 373–383.

17. Friedrich Froebel, *Pedagogics of the Kindergarten*, trans. Josephine Jarvis (Englewood Cliffs, N.J.: Prentice-Hall, 1899), pp. 1–15.

18. Quoted in Selwyn K. Troen, *The Public and the Schools: Shaping the St. Louis System, 1838–1920* (Columbia: University of Missouri Press, 1975), p. 101.

19. Ibid., p. 104.

20. Quoted in Marvin Lazerson, *Origins of the Urban School: Public Education in Massachusetts, 1870–1915* (Cambridge, Mass.: Harvard University Press, 1971), p. 50.

21. Ibid., p. 55.

22. Clarence E. Rainwater, *The Play Movement in the United States* (Chicago, 1922), p. 52.

23. Henry S. Curtis, *The Play Movement and Its Significance* (New York, 1917), pp. 1–10.

24. Cremin, *Transformation of the School*, p. 71.

25. Paul C. Violas, *The Training of the Urban Working Class: A History of Twentieth Century American Education* (Skokie, Ill.: Rand McNally, 1978), pp. 67–92.

26. Sadie American, "The Movement for Vacation Schools," *American Journal of Sociology* (November 1898): 310–312.

27. O. J. Milliken, "Chicago Vacation Schools," *American Journal of Sociology* (November 1898): 291–295.

28. Cremin, *Transformation of the School*, p. 64.

29. Clarence Arthur Perry, *Wider Use of the School Plant* (New York, 1910), pp. 3–4.

30. J. K. Paulding, "The Public School as a Centre of Community Life," *Educational Review* (February 1898): 148; H. E. Scudder, "The Schoolhouse as a Centre," *Atlantic Monthly* (January 1896): 103–109.

31. Clarence Arthur Perry, *The Social Centers of 1912–13* and *School Center Gazette, 1919–1920* (Russell Sage Publications).

32. A. Gove, "Public Schoolhouses and Their Uses as Centers of Instruction and Recreation for the Community," *Education* (March 1897): 407–411.

33. Edward J. Ward, *The Social Center* (New York, 1913), p. 18.

34. Clarence Arthur Perry, *The School as a Factor in Neighborhood Development* (Russell Sage Foundation, 1914).

35. T. Bowlker, "Woman's Home-Making Function Applied to the Municipality," *American City* 6 (1912): 863–869.

36. Tyack, *One Best System*, p. 230.

37. Ibid., p. 234.

38. Larry Cuban, *How Teachers Taught: Constancy and Change in American Classrooms, 1890–1980* (White Plains, N.Y.: Longman, 1984), p. 49.

39. Ibid., pp. 49, 71–72, 86–89.

40. Ibid., pp. 50, 71, 87.

41. Charles De Garmo, *Herbart and the Herbartians* (New York: Scribner, 1895), p. 7.

42. Willard Elsbree, *The American Teacher: Evolution of a Profession in a Democracy* (New York: American Book Company, 1939), p. 407.

43. John Dewey, "Teaching Ethics in the High School," *Educational Review* (November 1893): 316.

44. John Dewey, "Ethical Principles Underlying Education," *The Third Yearbook of the National Herbart Society* (Chicago, 1897), p. 31.

45. John Dewey, "The School and Society," in Martin Dworkin, ed., *Dewey on Education: Selections* (New York: Teachers College Press, 1959), p. 36.

46. Ibid., p. 37.

47. Ibid., p. 39.

48. Ibid., p. 46.

49. John Dewey, "School as Social Center," p. 381.

50. "Social Education as Association," leaflet included in bound edition of *Social Education Quarterly* 1.

51. Colin A. Scott, *Social Education* (Boston, 1908), pp. 102–146.

52. William Heard Kilpatrick, *The Project Method* (New York: Teachers College Press, 1918), p. 6.

53. Ibid., p. 14.

54. William James, *Principles of Psychology* (1890; reprint, New York: Dover, 1950), Vol. 1, pp. 24–26.

55. Ibid., p. 121.

56. Edward Thorndike, "Education, A First Book," in Geraldine Joncich, ed., *Psychology and the Science of Education: Selected Writings of Edward L. Thorndike* (New York: Teachers College Press, 1962), p. 79.

57. Ibid.
58. Edward Thorndike, "The Principles of Teaching Based on Psychology," in Joncich, *Psychology*, pp. 60–61.
59. Ibid., pp. 65–66.
60. Edward Thorndike, "The Measurement of Intelligence," in Joncich, *Psychology*, p. 104.
61. Ibid., pp. 105–106.
62. William Chandler Bagley, *Classroom Management* (New York, 1925), pp. 18–40.
63. Ibid.
64. Cuban, *How Teachers Taught*, pp. 103–104.

7

Education and Human Capital

A major argument used by Horace Mann in support of the organization of a common school system was that it would promote economic development. This justification for public schooling became extremely important in the late nineteenth and the twentieth centuries as vocational education and vocational guidance were introduced on a large scale and the high school developed as an institution to serve all youth. In fact, one could argue that schooling as a means of developing human capital has become the most important goal of the educational system in the twentieth century.

The early concepts surrounding the relationship between education and human capital are explored in this chapter by discussing the development of segregated education, vocational education, vocational guidance, and the high school. In considering the history of these aspects of education, three important factors must be taken into account. The first is the use of segregated educational systems as a means of conferring an inferior social status that would justify economic exploitation. The common school, contrary to the rhetoric of educational reformers, never became common to all people. The establishment of segregated schools, particularly in the South, was directly related to maintaining a system of economic exploitation.

Second, the school was used to select individuals for particular occupations. The institution that most clearly embodied this goal was the high school, which developed a differentiated curriculum based on the future occupational destination of the student. Together with vocational guidance, the modern high school was viewed as one of the primary means of sorting individuals to meet the needs of the labor market.

Third, it was argued in the nineteenth and twentieth centuries that education improved the skills of individuals and made them more productive on the job and that, in turn, increased productivity resulting from increased education enhanced economic growth. Within the context of this argument, increased investment in education would increase the economic wealth of society.

The Development of Segregated Schools

Segregated schooling was a means of conferring an inferior status on a minority group and of educating individuals for particular roles in the political and economic structure. Prior to the Civil War, slaves in the South were denied an education by law. Resistance to educating slaves was rooted in fear that education would give them access to ideas that would threaten the institution of slavery. Of course, education can provide training either for obedience or for political and economic power. Many Southerners believed that Sunday schools for slaves could serve as a means of inculcating obedience and maintaining slavery. Consequently, the major effort to educate slaves came from southern religious groups that argued, according to Henry Bullock in *A History of Negro Education in the South,* that despite "the general fear that literacy would expose the slaves to abolition literature . . . literacy was the potential savior of the slave system."[1]

Some slaves were given a limited education as a means of increasing their economic worth. In some cases, this meant training for skilled occupations. For example, Bullock reports stories of owners sending slaves away for training as carpenters and mechanics; many of these educated slaves provided valuable essential services for the operation of plantations. However, this education was narrowly limited to training for particular occupations and did not offer any instruction that might threaten the order of the slave society. Of course, any education has the potential nonetheless of providing the tools that lead to demands for freedom.

Slavery by its very nature conferred a status of inferiority. Outside of the slave system, segregation was often related to a concept of racial inferiority that justified economic exploitation. Employment opportunities for a particular racial group might be limited to particular low-paying jobs. The majority white group could justify this occupational segregation in their own minds by claiming the inferiority of the minority racial group and might demand segregated schooling for that particular racial group as a means of restricting educational opportunity and perpetuating a low social status. In addition, the white majority's belief in racial inferiority created a desire to keep its own children segregated from the children of the minority group.

The state of California provides the best example of the relationship between segregated education and economic exploitation. At one time or another, Japanese, Chinese, Mexican-Americans, Indians, and blacks were forced into segregated schools. In each case, a relationship existed between segregation and some form of economic exploitation. For instance, by the 1880s, 75,000 Chinese were living in California and working on railroads and farms and in factories. According to Charles Wollenberg in *All Deliberate Speed: Segregation and Exclusion in California Schools, 1855–1975*, as California's largest nonwhite minority, the Chinese were "regarded as 'yellow barbarians' and potential economic rivals."[2] Whites were concerned about keeping Chinese workers confined to particular occupations and, at the same time, feared that the Chinese might move into other occupations and take jobs away from them. During the 1870s, a general movement arose in San Francisco, which had the largest concentration of Chinese, to deport all Chinese from the country.

Reflecting the general anti-Chinese sentiment, the San Francisco school system refused to admit Chinese children. In 1884, when a Chinese couple tried to enroll their child in the school system, the San Francisco Board of Supervisors responded with the following statement:

Guard well the doors of our public schools that they [the Chinese] do not enter. For however stern it might sound, it is but the enforcement of the law of self-preservation, the inculcation of the doctrine of true humanity and an integral part of the iron rule of right by which we hope presently to prove that we can justly and practically defend ourselves from this invasion of Mongolian barbarism.[3]

The California courts ruled in favor of admission of the Chinese child, but the San Francisco school district responded to the court decision by asking the California assembly to allow separate facilities for "Mongolians." During the same period, the San Francisco schools rushed to establish a separate school for the Chinese. Sacramento followed San Francisco's example and established a segregated school for Chinese in 1893. According to Wollenberg, the rigid policy of segregation broke down by 1905, when the board of education had to let Chinese youth attend the regular city high school.

The establishment of segregated schools for Japanese children in California caused an international incident. Japanese immigrants did not enter California in large numbers until the early twentieth century. Although California employers saw Japan as a cheap source of Asian labor, antioriental hysteria greeted the Japanese, as it had the Chinese. While native whites worried about job competition and resulting low wages, Japanese entered the country with expectations of becoming permanent citizens and with high educational standards. The Japanese, like the Chinese, were caught between American companies wanting to use cheap oriental labor and American workers who did not want the competition. In either case, arguments of racial inferiority and "yellow menace" were used to justify either exclusion from the United States or economic exploitation.

The resolution that segregated Japanese children in the San Francisco school district stated that segregation was "not only for the purpose of relieving the congestion at present prevailing in our schools, but also for the higher end that our children should not be placed in any position where their youthful impression may be affected by association with pupils of the Mongolian race."[4] In 1906, the San Francisco Board of Education established a separate school for Chinese, Japanese, and Korean children. A majority of the Japanese parents boycotted the school, and the Japanese community then tried to win public opinion in Japan to its side as a means of forcing favorable action from the United States government. Editorials began to appear in Tokyo newspapers claiming that segregation was an insult to the nation, and in October 1906, the American ambassador to Japan warned the United States government of the developing international situation. The result was that President Theodore Roosevelt threatened the San Francisco school system with federal action if segregation did not end. However, the involvement of the federal government did not end segregation for the Japanese in other areas; they continued to face various exclusionary laws and legal actions through World War II.

Like that of the Japanese, the peak immigration of Mexicans to California occurred in the late nineteenth and early twentieth centuries. Again, employers viewed Mexican-Americans as a cheap source of labor, and white workers considered them to be unfair competition. By the 1920s, the increasing number of Mexican-American children, particularly in southern California, resulted in the establishment of segregated schools. Some employers resisted any education of Mexican-Americans because they believed it would lead them to reject work as farm laborers. The problem of segregation of Mexican-Americans was not resolved until the desegregation struggles of the 1960s and 1970s.

The history of education in California provides an example of the varieties of segregation that have occurred in public schools, whereas the history of education in the South offers an example of the most extensive form of school segregation resulting from economic exploitation, racial prejudice, and the desire by majority whites to create a permanent underclass of workers. After the Civil War, former slaves struggled to establish schools, and, in many cases, they were assisted by teachers from the North. In Reconstruction conventions following the Civil War, blacks fought for the establishment of state school systems. In the early 1870s, black children were enrolled in school systems at percentages higher than those for whites, but by the 1800s, this situation began to change as whites exerted greater control over the state political systems and passed discriminatory laws. By the 1890s, as a consequence of sharecropping and other forms of economic exploitation and discriminatory laws, many blacks found themselves living in conditions that were close to slavery.

The real struggle over the future of black education in the South occurred in the 1890s. By this time, some members of the white community in the South had hopes of rapid industrial development. In the minds of these industrialists, blacks represented a potential source of cheap labor who, unlike northern workers, would not form unions. For this reason, these southern industrialists tended to favor some form of education for blacks. However, other whites, including farmers and workers, resisted the education of blacks because they saw blacks as economic competitors and education of blacks as a potential threat to white supremacy.

Within the black community in the 1890s, divisions developed over how to pursue the struggle for education. This division was most often associated with two major black leaders—Booker T. Washington and W.E.B. Du Bois. Washington accepted compromise with white demands and the establishment of segregated industrial education; Du Bois maintained that no compromise with white demands should be made and that black education should be concerned with educating future leaders of the black community. To a certain extent, however, the preceding statements oversimplify the positions of Washington and Du Bois. Their hopes for schooling were interwoven with their hopes for their race, the realities of southern society, and their political strategies. In the history of schooling, Washington is most often associated with the establishment of segregated schools, whereas Du Bois was instrumental in the founding in 1909 of the National Association for the Advancement of Colored People (NAACP), which has led the successful struggle against school segregation in the United States.

The speech that most clearly outlined the southern compromise and the role of blacks in the developing industrial order was given by Washington at the International Exposition in Atlanta in 1895. Prior to that speech, Washington had received recognition throughout the South for his establishment of the Tuskegee Institute. The Tuskegee idea originated in Washington's educational experiences at the Hampton Institute. Washington had been born to slavery and after the Civil War attended Hampton, which had been established by General Samuel Armstrong, whose missionary parents had organized an industrial school for natives in Hawaii. The basic idea of Armstrong's approach to education was to emphasize the teaching of practical subjects, such as personal care, farming, and mechanical skills. For instance, Washington always stressed the importance of education in the use of objects like the toothbrush. The Tuskegee idea was to provide practical education for blacks so that they could find their place in the economic system.

Washington scorned the traditional forms of education brought South by northern teachers. He felt that traditional education was useless and left the student with false promises for a better life. In his autobiography, *Up From Slavery,* he tells the story of mothers who taught their daughters the skill of laundering. "Later," Washington says, "these girls entered the public schools and remained there perhaps six or eight years. When the public-school course was finally finished, they wanted more costly dresses, more costly hats and shoes." Washington summarizes the effects of a traditional public school education: "In a word, while their wants had been increased, their ability to supply their wants had not been increased in the same degree. On the other hand, their six or eight years of book education had weaned them away from the occupation of their mothers." In another situation, Washington criticizes a young man fresh out of high school who "sitting down in a one-room cabin, with grease on his clothing, filth all round him, and weeds in the yard and garden, engaged in studying French grammar."[5]

Washington realized that industrial education alone was not enough to win an economic place for blacks in the new industrial order; it was also necessary for black workers to gain acceptance by the white population. Consequently, Washington opened his speech before the all-white audience in Atlanta in 1895 with a story of a ship lost at sea whose crew was dying of thirst. The ship encountered a friendly vessel, which signaled for the crew to cast down their buckets in the surrounding water. After receiving the signal four times, the captain finally cast down his bucket to find fresh water from the mouth of the Amazon River. This, Washington told his audience, was what the South needed to do to build its industrial might: cast down its buckets and use black workers. Washington continued his speech by outlining the advantages of black workers for the South. Of primary importance was that the South would not need to rely on foreign workers. "To those of the white race," Washington exclaimed, "who look to the incoming of those of foreign birth and strange tongue and habits for the prosperity of the South, were I permitted I would repeat what I say to my own race, 'Cast down your bucket where you are.'"[6] Washington continued by extolling the virtues of black workers and their faithfulness during the years of slavery. He claimed that blacks could show a devotion that no foreign workers would ever display and called for an interlacing of the interests of black and white Southerners.

Then, in one sentence that would become famous in both the South and the North, Washington presented the compromise he saw as necessary for winning white Southerners to his argument: "In all things that are purely social we can be as separate as the fingers, yet one as the hand in all things essential to mutual progress." Here was the great compromise—acceptance by blacks of social segregation for the opportunity to participate in the new industrial order of the South. As Washington explained in the conclusion of his speech, he believed that once the economic value of blacks had been established, social acceptance would follow. "No race," he argued, "that has anything to contribute to the markets of the world is long in any degree ostracized." In Washington's mind, "the opportunity to earn a dollar in a factory just now is worth infinitely more than the opportunity to spend a dollar in an opera-house."[7]

Washington's message was heard throughout the North and South. It was particularly welcomed by those trying to organize the southern school system. The idea of segregated industrial education for blacks in the South not only was supported by the work of Washington and the Hampton Institute but also received support from major educational conferences and private foundations. In Bullock's words:

> *The industrial curriculum to which many Negro children were exposed, supposedly designed to meet their needs, reflected the life that accompanied their status at that time. They had always farmed. The curriculum aimed to make them better farmers. Negro women had a virtual monopoly on laundering, and Negro men had [worked] largely as mechanics. The industrial curriculum was designed to change this only in so far that Negroes were trained to perform these services better.*[8]

The spread of segregated education for blacks was accompanied by an inequality in educational expenditures throughout the South. In his classic study *The Education of the Negro in the American Social Order,* Horace Mann Bond collected information on school expenditures from a variety of southern states. For instance, a table illustrating spending in Alabama shows that in 1875–1876 expenditure per capita was actually higher for blacks than for whites. This relationship existed until the 1880s. By 1900, the situation had so reversed that expenditure per capita for whites was from four to five times higher than spending for blacks. Bond found similar statistics throughout the South.[9]

The effect of the human-capital argument was that blacks were educated for their particular station within a segregated social order. In this case, education for improvement of human capital meant improving blacks' skills for existing occupations and reinforcing, by contributing to a feeling of inferiority, their acceptance of a subservient place in a segregated southern society.

The major resistance to school segregation came from the NAACP, which has struggled for integrated education from its founding in 1909 to the present time. W.E.B. Du Bois, a founder of the NAACP and editor of the magazine *Crisis,* became the leading opponent of Washington's southern compromise. Du Bois was born in Great Barrington, Massachusetts, earned a Ph.D. at Harvard, studied in Europe, and became one of America's leading sociologists. However, like most blacks in the late nineteenth and early twentieth centuries, he had difficulty finding a university teaching position. Some of his most famous studies were done while he taught at Atlanta University; *The Philadelphia Negro: A Social Study* was written with the support of the University of Pennsylvania but without an appointment to its faculty. One of his major public statements attacking the arguments of Booker T. Washington is *The Souls of Black Folk*, published in 1903.

In *The Souls of Black Folk*, Du Bois claims that Washington's compromise resulted in disaster for black people in the South:

> *Mr. Washington distinctly asks that black people give up, at least for the present, three things—First, political power, Second, insistence on civil rights, Third, higher education of Negro youth,—and concentrate all their energies on industrial education, the accumulation of wealth, and the conciliation of the South.*

The result, Du Bois argues, was the "disfranchisement of the Negro," the "legal creation of a distinct status of civil inferiority for the Negro," and the "steady withdrawal of aid from institutions for the higher education of the Negro."[10]

Du Bois envisioned a different type of education for blacks, one that would provide leaders to protect the social and political rights of the black community and make the black population aware of the necessity for constant struggle. He also wanted to develop an Afro-American culture that would blend the African background of former slaves with American culture. In part, this was to be accomplished by the education of black leadership.

What Du Bois hoped to accomplish through education is well described in his story of John. In the story, a southern black community raises money to send John to the North for an education. The community's hope is that he will return to teach in the local black school. After receiving his education in the North, John does return to teach. He goes to the house of the local white judge, and, after making the mistake of knocking at the front door instead of the rear door, he is ushered into the judge's dining room. The judge greets John with his philosophy of education: "In this country the Negro must remain subordinate, and can never expect to be [the] equal of white men." The judge describes two different ways in which blacks might be educated in the South. The first, which the judge favors, is to "teach the darkies to be faithful servants and laborers as your fathers were." The second way, the one supported by Du Bois and most feared by white Southerners, is described by the judge as putting "fool ideas of rising and equality into these folks' heads, and . . . [making] them discontent and unhappy."[11]

What was most important for Du Bois was to educate blacks to be discontented with their social position in the South. Unhappiness—not happiness—was his goal. Du Bois describes John, before his meeting with the judge, standing on a bluff with his younger sister and looking out over an expanse of water:

> *Long they stood together, peering over the gray unresting water.*
> *"John," she said, "does it make everyone—unhappy when they study and learn lots of things?"*
> *He paused and smiled. "I am afraid it does," he said.*
> *"And, John, are you glad you studied?"*
> *"Yes," came the answer, slowly and positively.*
> *She watched the flickering lights upon the sea, and said thoughtfully, "I wish I was unhappy,—and—and," putting both arms about his neck, "I think I am, a little, John."*[12]

Du Bois's ideal of an educated black citizenry struggling against oppression became a reality even within a segregated society and educational system. Certainly, segregated education hindered the social and economic advancement of blacks, but at the same time it provided a basic education that was essential for advancement. It took more than a half-century for the NAACP to win its battle against segregated education in the South. During that period of legal struggle, segregated schooling was a major factor in condemning blacks to an inferior status in society.

Segregated education highlights the major negative aspect of the argument for schooling as development of human capital. On the positive side, it might be argued that schooling should be organized to meet the economic needs of society and to educate people so that they are able to find work. On the other hand, to make such decisions about a person's future could lead to condemning him or her to a particular place in society. Power was one important issue; as long as whites held political power in the South, the human-capital argument was used to support the superior position of whites in the economic and social order.

The High School

In the early part of the twentieth century, a complex set of social, economic, and educational conditions shaped the modern high school for service to a broader range of the population. During the nineteenth century, only a small percentage of youth attended high schools offering a primarily classical academic program. The increasing importance of the human-capital argument in the late nineteenth and early twentieth centuries, the social problem of youth, and the general demand by the public for more education led to an increase in the numbers of youth attending high school and to fundamental changes in its curriculum and goals.

The major argument used in shaping and expanding the role of the high school in modern society was that it was necessary to improve the quality of the American work force through proper education and guidance into the labor market. One of the major differences between nineteenth- and twentieth-century high schools was that the latter offered a differentiated curriculum that allowed students to pursue different studies based on their life goals. The nineteenth-century high school was primarily academic, whereas the twentieth-century high school offered academic, general, and vocational studies. These changes in curriculum reflected the more general attempt to have the schools serve the needs of the economic system.

In addition, the modern high school embodied a greater concern with the social development of youth. In concrete terms, this meant the addition of high school activities such as clubs, student government, assemblies, organized athletics, and other social events. These social activities were also justified by their contribution to the workings of the economic system. It was through these activities that American youth were to learn how to cooperate in an industrial society based on large-scale corporations and unions.

The increasing importance of the high school in the twentieth century is best reflected in the changing patterns of school attendance. In 1890, 202,963 students attended 2,526 public high schools. Ten years later, in 1900, these figures had more than doubled, to 519,251 students in 6,005 public high schools. In 1912, the enrollment level reached 1,105,360 pupils. These dramatic increases continued; by 1920, 28 percent of American youth, or 2,200,389 students, between the ages of 14 and 17 were in high school. It was during the 1920s that the high school truly became an institution serving the masses. By 1930, 47 percent of youth between the ages of 14 and 17, or 4,399,422 students, were in high school, and during the Depression years of the 1930s, the American high school began to serve the majority of youth—enrollments increased to 6,545,991 in 1940, representing two-thirds of the population between the ages of 14 and 17.[13]

Although the preceding figures clearly indicate that the high school as an institution serving the majority of youth was a product of the twentieth century, important stages in its development occurred during the nineteenth century. The first American high school, the Boston English Classical School, established in 1821, was inspired by the academies founded in the eighteenth and early nineteenth centuries. Like the academies, the high school sought to provide a more practical course of studies than those being offered in traditional grammar schools.

The establishment of the Boston English Classical School was a direct result of the concerns of parents in Boston about sending their children out of town to private academies. The committee that recommended the establishment of the school complained that

> *many children are separated from their parents and sent to private academies in this vicinity, to acquire that instruction which cannot be obtained at the public seminaries. Thus, many parents, who contribute largely to the support of these institutions, are subjected to heavy expense for the same object out of town.*

The other "public seminaries" referred to in this complaint were the grammar schools, which according to this committee were not meeting the needs of some parents in Boston. In fact, the committee indirectly compared the type of education provided in the publicly supported grammar school with that provided in the private academy when it stated,

> *A parent who wishes to give a child an education that shall fit him for an active life, and shall serve as a foundation for eminence in his profession, whether Mercantile or Mechanical, is under the necessity of giving him a different education from any which our public schools can now furnish.*

Three years after its opening, the Boston English Classical School changed its name to English High School. It offered a course of studies ranging from navigation and bookkeeping to moral and political philosophy.[14]

In 1827, the Massachusetts legislature passed a law that further stimulated the growth of high schools within the commonwealth. The law did not use the term *high school*, but required every town of over 500 households to have a master to teach American history, bookkeeping, geometry, surveying, and algebra; in addition, every community with over 4,000 people was required to have an instructor in Latin, Greek, history, rhetoric, and logic. Most of the 26 schools established by 1840 as a result of this law were called high schools.

The number of high schools slowly grew during the nineteenth century. State authorization was instituted in Pennsylvania in 1836 and in New York in 1853. The general legal status of high schools was uncertain until the famous *Kalamazoo* decision of 1874, which was interpreted as supporting the general development of the public high school. The case resulted from a Michigan law of 1859 authorizing school districts with more than 100 children to establish high school departments if so mandated by the vote of the people. In the *Kalamazoo* case, *Charles E. Stuart and Others v. School District No. 1 of the Village of Kalamazoo and Others* (1874), the plaintiffs claimed that the high school in their area was illegal because a vote had never been taken and that no authority existed in the state to create free high schools through taxation levied on the people. In his written decision, Justice Thomas M. Cooley of the Supreme Court of Michigan dismissed the issue of the public vote by noting many irregularities in municipal administration and by arguing that the public showed its approval through its support of the institution.

Of course, the major issue was taxation for support of the high school. This complaint by the plaintiffs raised the whole issue of public taxation for support of higher education. Judge Cooley expressed surprise at the questioning of this idea: "We supposed it had always been understood in this state that education, not merely in the rudiments, but in an enlarged sense, was regarded as an important practical advantage to be supplied at their option to rich and poor alike." Cooley went on to argue that the provision in the state constitution for the establishment of free schools inferred the establishment of high schools. He stated that "beginning in 1817 and continuing until after the adoption of the present constitution," state policy had been moving clearly "in the direction of free schools in which education, and at their option the elements of a classical education, might be brought within the reach of all the children of the state." This interpretation meant that the provision in the state constitution for free schools included high schools and gave constitutional legitimacy to their development. Other state courts followed Michigan's lead, with the result that general support grew for the development of public high schools.[15]

According to Edward Krug, the most "significant expression in the decision was the one including 'the elements of a classical education.'"[16] A classical education was still considered a prerequisite for college admission. As Judge Cooley portrayed the system, the high school was made part of an organizational ladder extending from early grades to college. The inclusion of classical education made the high school both an institution providing practical education and an institution preparing students for college.

Although the *Kalamazoo* decision laid the groundwork for the inclusion of high schools in the general interpretation of state constitutional provisions for free schooling, some confusion developed over the purposes of a high school education and the relationship between high schools and colleges. In 1892, at the beginning of the period of rapid expansion of the high school, the National Education Association formed the Committee of Ten on Secondary School Studies under the leadership of Harvard president Charles Eliot. The initial concern of the committee was to create uniform requirements for admission to colleges. Many high school educators found it difficult to organize a course of studies when different colleges had different requirements for admission. Of course, any decision about the organization of studies had to consider the general purposes of a high school education.

The importance of the Committee of Ten's final report was that it established a general framework for discussion of the goals of secondary education. In many ways, the report of the committee reflected the crossroad between an educational system designed to provide everyone with a common education and an educational system organized to provide everyone with a specific education based on a future social destination.

One of the major questions facing the Committee of Ten was whether or not different courses of study should be offered to students ending their education at the secondary level and those planning to go on to college. In other words, should preparation for life differ from preparation for college? This seemingly innocuous question had important implications for the role of education in a democratic society. Because the children of wealthy families tended to go to college more often than those of poor families, a difference in curriculum for the college- and non-college-bound student had the potential to create a class system of education.

The response of the Committee of Ten to this issue was to recommend against any differences in the courses of study for the two groups of students. Debate immediately following the issuance of the report in 1894 gave clear recognition to the social implications of the decision against separate curricula for college- and non-college-bound high school students. For example, at the first official presentation of the report, Francis Parker stated, "One unanimous conclusion of all the conferences [that produced the report], a conclusion without a single dissenting voice, or vote, is worth all the cost and all the pains that were necessary to produce the report. That conclusion is that there should be no such thing as class education." He went on to argue that an attempt was under way to reduce city schools to charity schools and to provide the poor with only a partial education. In the context of rejecting a class-based education, Parker stated, "There is no reason why one child should study Latin and another be limited to the '3 R's.' "[17]

While attempting to avoid class-based education, the Committee of Ten tried to balance individual interests and needs with the educational programs that did not differentiate between college- and non-college-bound students. It was hoped that this balance could be achieved by high schools offering four different courses of study of equal value for college admission. Only one of the proposed courses of study, Classical, required both Latin and Greek. The Latin-Scientific program required only Latin, the Modern Language sequence required neither Latin nor Greek, and the English course of study made Latin an option. The four courses of study proposed by the Committee of Ten marked the beginning of a decline in the importance given to classical studies in college admission requirements.

Ironically, the major criticism of the report of the Committee of Ten was that it was elitist because it did not propose a special course of study for non-college-bound students. This debate highlights one of the complex issues in the relationship between education and a democratic society. For instance, one can argue that providing an education that meets individual needs and interests is democratic because it places the individual at the center of educational decisions. But it can also be claimed that such an education is undemocratic because it results in people receiving an education that locks them into their social class.

Central to all of these discussions were the differences between the rich and the poor. Some argued that the poor needed a practical education that would prepare them for the realities of their future lives—this would constitute the meeting of individual needs and interests. Of course, meeting those needs in this fashion limited the educational opportunities of the poor and provided the rich with a superior education as measured by the social and cultural power it conferred.

The debate over the meaning of education in a democratic society was fundamental to the organization of the American high school. The most influential position taken on this issue was that of educators and civic leaders concerned with social efficiency. In *The Shaping of the American High School*, Edward Krug, the great historian of the American high school, identifies social efficiency as the most predominant school of thought in influencing the development of the high school. As a doctrine, social efficiency was one aspect of the argument for the development of human capital. Educators and civic leaders interested in social efficiency wanted education to produce individuals who were trained for a specific role in society and who were willing to work cooperatively in that role.

Social-efficiency doctrines had broad implications for education. First, the argument suggested that school curricula should be organized to meet the future social needs of the students. Second, it was believed that school activities should be designed to teach cooperation as preparation for future social activities. Third, social-efficiency arguments proposed a differentiated curriculum based on the future social destination of the student.

Krug quotes one leading early-twentieth-century educator, William C. Bagley, as claiming in 1905 that "social efficiency is the standard by which the forces of education must select the experiences that are impressed upon the individual. Every subject of instruction, every item of knowledge, every form of reaction, every detail of habit, must be measured by this yardstick." Although Bagley's statement illustrates the range of application of the idea of social efficiency, an article by Arthur Call in 1909 reveals how educators committed to social efficiency believed they held a revolutionary position in contrast to a traditional position on academic education. Call states that the primary aim of education is "not to promote academic training, [but] to enable the pupils by means of free, fair and genial social intercourse, under the leadership of friendly and large-spirited men and women, to obtain practice in real life, to become socially and serviceably efficient." In this case, "socially and serviceably efficient" means an ability to perform a job well and to get along with others.[18]

The educational doctrines of social efficiency were part of a more general reconceptualization of the American economic system. In the early nineteenth century, most of the population was rural and involved in agriculture, and industrial development was in its early stages. For most Americans, the doctrines of laissez-faire capitalism, with their stress on economic individualism, seemed to best explain the ideal workings of the economic system. Within this social vision, the economic system worked best when individuals were allowed to pursue their own individual interests within a free marketplace. Of course, as represented by the earlier discussion in this book of Whigs and Democrats, differences arose about the degree of government intervention and freedom to be allowed in the marketplace.

Laissez-faire doctrines have continued up to the present in the United States but have been tempered and, in some cases, challenged by a differing view of the economic system, which resulted from the development of urban areas, large corporations, and large unions. This new view of the economic system can roughly be called twentieth-century liberalism; it was this economic vision that produced socially efficient-minded educators and had the major impact on the shaping of the high school in the twentieth century.

Twentieth-century liberalism and socially efficient education accepted the growth of large-scale organizations in a modern corporate society but felt that certain changes needed to occur to ensure efficient operation of the new economic system. Of primary importance was ending traditional ideas about economic individualism and the pursuit of self-interest. It was argued that the new large-scale organizations required cooperation, not competition. What this meant for public schools was that students needed to be taught to work together and that the stress of competition needed to be reduced. During the early part of the twentieth century, these ideas resulted in an emphasis in the schools on group activities, sharing, and working together. Some educators saw the student sitting at an individual desk and working alone as a symbol of economic individualism and competition and sought to replace that scenario with groups of students working together around a table.

Social-efficiency doctrines and the new economic thought stressed the importance of specialization and expertise in the new large-scale organizations. Specialization, it was reasoned, increased efficiency by allowing each person to concentrate on a single individual task. This was the model of the assembly line and modern bureaucracy, where individual tasks were coordinated through the organization. For educators, specialization meant education of the student for a particular occupation. Within the doctrines of social efficiency, the ideal was to socialize the student for cooperation in large-scale organizations where each individual would be performing a specialized task.

A second important aspect of twentieth-century liberalism was the acceptance of the idea of government intervention to ensure the fair operation of the economic system. At one level, this meant the establishment of government regulatory agencies to supervise various industries, such as transportation, and government attempts to break up and regulate monopolies. At another level, this meant the attempt by the school to ensure equality of opportunity in the labor market by objectively selecting students for different educational programs.

All of these aspects of twentieth-century liberalism were important elements in the doctrine of social efficiency. Cooperation, specialization, and equality of opportunity were the key concepts around which the modern high school was organized. Of course, these doctrines of social efficiency ran counter to the traditional academic thrust of the high school.

The battle between the older academic concepts of the high school and the new doctrines of social efficiency was waged in the popular presses in the early part of the twentieth century. For instance, in 1912 the *Saturday Evening Post* published two articles opposing the academic tradition in the high school. One article, by William Mearns, carries the opinionated title "Our Medieval High Schools: Shall We Educate Children for the Twelfth or the Twentieth Century?" The author argues that "culture" had come to dominate the high school, which he stereotyped as an institution wherein "it is clean hands and a pure collar . . . it is knowledge of Hegelian philosophy; it is Greek; it is Latin; it is a five-foot shelf of books; it is twenty thousand a year; it is a sight of truth and a draught of wisdom; it is a frock coat and pearl gloves." In contrast to what he labeled the medieval concept of high schools, he argues that the modern high school should become a democratic institution in which the only studies offered would provide for "efficient service to the community about it."[19]

The other *Saturday Evening Post* article, "The High School and the Boy," by William Lewis, argues that "the high school's largest service is the best possible training for economic efficiency, good citizenship, and full and complete living for all its pupils." The author thought this could best be accomplished by eliminating the dissection of literary masterpieces, providing a wide range of mathematics (but not algebra), and offering foreign languages only as electives. In a later book, *Democracy's*

High School, Lewis calls for an education "in citizenship and in right social thinking."[20]

Related to the concept of social efficiency were attitudes about the social development of adolescents. Within the context of psychological thought in the early twentieth century, adolescence was the most important age for developing the sense of cooperation and social service required by modern society. The most influential psychologist in this area was G. Stanley Hall (1844–1924)—founder of the child study movement in the 1890s and pioneer in the field of adolescent and developmental psychology.

In his classic work *Adolescence*, published in 1904, Hall states, "The whole future of life depends on how the new powers [of adolescence] now given suddenly and in profusion are husbanded." According to Hall's theory of recapitulation, each stage of individual development parallels a stage of social evolution. Childhood, the years between 4 and 8, corresponds to a cultural epoch when hunting and fishing were the main activities of humanity. From 11 to 12, according to Hall, the child recapitulates the life of savagery. During puberty, the new flood of passions develops the social person: "The social instincts undergo sudden unfoldment and the new life of love awakens."[21]

Hall's theories supported other contemporary beliefs that adolescent interests and abilities must be harnessed and directed to some socially useful function. This meant the establishment of institutions such as the high school to capture and channel the sexual-social drives of the adolescent. Hall argues that the utilization of adolescent drives should be the criterion by which institutions are evaluated. He believed that the proper socialization of adolescents is the panacea for most social problems: The "womb, cradle, nursery, home, family, relatives, school, church and state are only a series of larger cradles or placenta, as the soul . . . builds itself larger missions, the only test and virtue of which is their service in bringing the youth to ever fuller maturity."[22]

The image of adolescence projected by Hall's psychology and represented in the popular press of the time was of a romantic stage of life during which the developing sexual-social drives could lead the adolescent to either a life of decadence or a life of social service. The romantic and poetic impulses of youth, it was believed, could be captured and directed toward socially useful projects such as helping the poor, the community, or the nation. Boy Scouts, Girl Scouts, the YWCA, YMCA, and other youth organizations were justified by their ability to channel the sexual-social drives of the teenager for the good of society. On the other hand, when youth of the 1920s adopted the style of the Jazz Age, the popular press warned of the imminent collapse of civilization. In other words, youth represented either a promising future or a collapsing civilization.

The role played by youth in shaping the psyche of the twentieth century had important consequences for the development of the high school, which became the primary social institution for capturing and channeling the sexual-social drives of teenagers. As discussed in more detail later in this section, the students' social life or extracurricular activities became an important aspect of high school culture in America. Given the importance Americans placed on the development of youth for the future of the nation, the high school in the twentieth century came to symbolize the promise of American life.

As the role of youth increased in the public mind and social-efficiency educators continued their attack on academics in the high school, the National Education Association organized a commission in 1913 whose report eventually established the basic framework for the modern high school. This group, the Commission on the Reorganization of Secondary Education, issued its final report in 1918 as the now-famous *Cardinal Principles of Secondary Education*. The report, which reflects the strong influence of social-efficiency rhetoric, attempted to shape the high school to meet the needs of the modern corporate state. Its final recommendation calls for the creation of a comprehensive high school that would include a wide variety of curricula designed to meet the needs of different types of students. The comprehensive high school became the standard for secondary education for more than half a century.[23]

Unlike the report of the Committee of Ten, *Cardinal Principles of Secondary Education* calls for a broad program of various courses of study: "Differentiation should be, in the broad sense of the term, vocational . . . such as agricultural, business, clerical, industrial, fine-arts, and household-arts curriculums." One of the major questions facing the commission was whether or not a differentiated curriculum should require the establishment of separate schools to teach the different curricula; for instance, separate academic and vocational schools.[24]

The commission's answer to this question provided the framework for the organization of the comprehensive high school. The commission argued for comprehensive schools in which all students would come together because this would aid "the pupil through a wide variety of contacts and experiences to obtain a basis for intelligent choice of his educational and vocational career" and would assure the choice of a curriculum best suited to the student's need. According to the commission, specialized schools might introduce distracting influences, such as location, athletic teams, and friendships. These influences, rather than consideration of curriculum, might determine which school the student attended. The comprehensive high school, in the opinion of the commission, would eliminate these factors from consideration—everyone would attend the same school regardless of his or her choice of course of study.[25]

The commission also used the rhetoric of social efficiency to justify the comprehensive high school, which, the commission argued, allowed for what it called the two components of democracy—specialization and unification. The commission's report states: "The purpose of democracy is so to organize society that each member may develop his personality primarily through activities designed for the well-being of his fellow members and of society as a whole." The specialized and differentiated curriculum of the comprehensive high school was to train each student to perform a specific task that would benefit society. Within the context of this argument, democracy was viewed mainly as a means of social organization that would allow each individual to do what she or he is best able to do for the good of the social whole. Education was supposed to fit the individual into a social position that would enable him or her to make a maximum contribution to society. The report stated in bold type that "education in a democracy . . . should develop in each individual the knowledge, interests, ideals, habits, and powers whereby he will find his place and use that place to shape both himself and society toward ever nobler ends."[26]

According to the report, the second component of democracy, or social efficiency, is unification. This democratic ideal shaped the social organization of the modern high school. The report defined *unification* as that part of the ideal of democracy that brought people together and gave them "common ideas, common ideals, and common modes of thought, feeling, and action that made for cooperation, social cohesion, and social solidarity." Although educators in the nineteenth century stressed the importance of schooling in building social cohesion, their primary focus was on the early grades. The *Cardinal Principles*, however, gave the major responsibility for socialization to the high school: "In this process the secondary school must play an important part because the elementary school with its immature pupils cannot alone develop the common knowledge, common ideals, and common interests essential to American democracy."[27]

The major problem in providing social cohesion was the fact that different students pursued different courses of study. To compensate for the separation caused by the differentiated curriculum, the commission proposed three means for creating a sense of unity. The first, which was directed at the immigrant, emphasized the need for teaching the "mother tongue" and social studies. The other two were organizational techniques; one was "social mingling of pupils through the organization and administration of the school," and the other, directly related to this proposal, was "participation of pupils in common activities . . . such as athletic games, social activities, and the government of the school."[28]

Thus, the twentieth-century solution to building unification and cooperation through education was to provide extracurricular activities in the high school. The various elements of school life that were included in the term *extracurricular activities* were in existence long before the issuance of the *Cardinal Principles,* but during the 1920s extracurricular activities developed into an educational cult. Courses in organizing extracurricular activities were offered in teacher-training institutions, and textbooks and books of readings on the topic were published. In 1926, the *Twenty-Fifth Yearbook of the National Society for the Study of Education* was devoted to the topic. As in any educational movement, certain figures emerged as leaders. One in particular was Elbert K. Fretwell of Teachers College, who organized summer courses for school administrators on preparation of extracurricular programs. Between 1923 and 1927, Fretwell flooded the *Teachers College Record* with long bibliographies of material on assemblies, clubs, student government, and homerooms.[29]

The central feature of all extracurricular activities programs was student government. The important place student government assumed in the public schools resulted from activities by urban reform groups in New York City in the 1890s. These groups saw student government as a method of preparing the children of immigrants for participation in democratic government. In 1904, Richard Welling organized the National Self-Government Committee, which campaigned vigorously into the 1940s for student government in public schools and colleges. Before organizing the student government campaign, Welling claimed he realized that education was the key to civic reform. In 1903, he lamented that merely "telling the voters that their taxes were too high did not lead to action at the polls." The best method for encouraging political involvement, he decided, was to give citizens an opportunity to practice the intelligent use of political rights. Having reached this conclusion, he contacted Charles Eliot, then president of the National Education Association, and asked permission to address the organization's annual convention. Before the convention, he made a ringing appeal for student government as a means of curing corrupt government. He told gathered educators, "The New generation must be imbued with a new spirit of civic patriotism . . . you must teach the machinery of government by means of some form of applied civics."[30]

Student governments were instituted by American schools at a phenomenal rate, and by the middle of the twentieth century very few high schools were without some form of student government. Throughout this course of development, no serious suggestion was ever made that students be given real power. The purpose of student government was to provide applied civics, not to run the school. A typical attitude was that taken by William McAndrew, one-time superintendent of the New York City public schools. Writing in 1897 on a proposed student government plan, he stated, "I believe the plan of delegating any of the executive powers of that officer [principal] to those so irresponsible as students would be unwise."[31] There was general agreement, at least among educators during this period, that, as one writer stated, "any plan that gives pupils full control of the government of a school, a school city, or a school democracy, without the advice and aid of teachers will necessarily lead to an ignominious failure."[32]

The other organizations composing extracurricular activities were justified as contributing to the unification of the school and the preparation of students for participation in a cooperative democracy. In most plans, student governments or student associations were to work with the faculty in the administration of additional extracurricular activities, which usually included the student newspaper, clubs, athletics, and assemblies. One principal stated in 1917 that an organized program of this nature would "assist in making the spirit of democracy, 'all for each and each for all' to pervade the school."[33]

The school newspaper was justified as a means of teaching both English and teamwork and of creating a spirit of unity within the school. Publication of a paper, like any school club activity, was considered a means of teaching people to work cooperatively. The school newspaper was to contribute to a feeling of unity by providing each student with news about school events. Some supporters of school newspapers considered the creation of unity or school spirit to be the most important function of this activity. One supporter wrote: "The Press Association . . . meets an important demand. It is a unifying organization, and is therefore a wholesome factor if properly directed. Its purpose is to edit a school paper through which a school spirit may be awakened and nourished."[34] Through reading the paper, the student was to gain a sense of the unity of school life and a feeling of loyalty. To a certain extent, the paper was to be a public-relations method of building a good image of the school in the student's eyes. As one writer put it, "The school paper . . . will create school patriotism and an increased interest in all the activities of the school, educational, athletic, and social."[35]

Clubs in high school programs ranged across a variety of areas. Most high schools and academies in the nineteenth century had some social organizations—usually literary and debating societies—but in the twentieth century a much broader choice of club activities was offered and was justified with claims that the clubs would teach participation in cooperative activities. After the 1918 publication of the *Cardinal Principles*, which suggested that one of the purposes of education was the development of meaningful leisure-time activities, the argument frequently appeared that clubs served to prepare students for worthy use of leisure time. For example, one article in 1921 on club activities stated: "A school's service to the future makers of America does not end with preparing them for working hours which occupy only a third of the day. It must also provide specifically for the worthy use of leisure."[36]

The argument was made that athletics could contribute to training for participation in a democratic community in two ways. First, as part of a general health program, it would ensure individual physical efficiency. In language common to human capital theories, the *Cardinal Principles* stressed good health as a means of assuring the maximum development of human resources. Second, athletics taught the student how to cooperate and work with a team. This orientation was one reason for the rapid growth of football in the public schools. As a team game, football fostered the coordination and cooperation believed to be needed in a corporate organization. A Seattle high school principal told the National Education Association in 1915, "In the boy's mind, the football team is not only an aggregation of individuals organized to play, but a social instrument with common needs, working along common lines, and embodying a common purpose."[37]

The spirit generated by athletic games between schools was considered another means of uniting students and was also considered an important public-relations method. The problem, as seen by one professor of physical education in 1914, was to maintain a balance between the development of the individual and the entertainment of spectators. His confidence that this could be achieved is expressed in his statement that 15 years earlier, high school athletes had been "accustomed to playing a game unrestrained and without cooperation. All sorts of tricks were used to win a contest, such as importing players, choosing biased officials, and resorting to unfair tactics in general. . . . Today our athletes from the high schools represent the best sportsmanship possible."[38] The success of football in uniting the community and generating spirit eventually unbalanced the two purposes. In 1923, a high school teacher complained, "Rivalry between certain schools has become so intense that players meet in a spirit of hatred and revenge, and special policing is necessary to guard against outbreaks of hostility between rival rooters."[39]

According to the *Cardinal Principles*, the activity that was most important in contributing to school unity was the assembly, because it brought together students who were otherwise separated by grades, courses of studies, and ability groups. A statement in 1925 by an associate superintendent of schools in Pittsburgh, Pennsylvania, illustrates this point of view: "Students are divided into classes according to their academic advancement, further divided by their curricula. . . . Blocking the pathway to unity is an almost infinite variety of individual differences. The assembly is the one agency at hand capable of checking these tendencies."[40] Assemblies became one of the great events in American high schools. Books, programs, and articles with suggestions for auditorium exercises flooded the educational market. Band concerts, vocational talks, drama productions, class projects, and patriotic celebrations all became part of the public school paraphernalia. The importance of the assembly as school unifier continued through the 1920s. This is exemplified by the opening words of a book entitled *Assemblies for Junior and Senior High Schools*, published in 1929:

> *Junior and senior high schools daily accept the challenge to prepare students for life in a democracy. . . . Specialized organization and complex activities necessitate unification through athletics, the school newspaper, and the assembly. Because of its frequency and provision for universal participation, the assembly may be considered the foremost integrating factor.*[41]

The desire to create a cooperative and unified spirit was one of the major factors in the organization of the comprehensive high school. The *Fifth Yearbook of the Department of Secondary-School Principals*, published in 1921, states with regard to extracurricular activities, "What we wish the state to be the school must be. The character of our citizens is determined by the character of our pupils and the development of character in this broadest sense must be the goal of education."[42]

The comprehensive high school became a mixture of planned social activities and a variety of curricula, all of which were attempts to prepare a new generation for a society based on large organizations and occupational specialization. In this context, the development of human capital meant selection and training for a specialized task and socialization for a society based on cooperation.

Vocational Education, Vocational Guidance, and the Junior High School

Vocational education, vocational guidance, and the junior high school were important elements in the development of the comprehensive high school and key parts of the attempt to organize the educational system to develop human capital. By emphasizing training for specific occupations in public-supported institutions, vocational education represented a revolution in the role of schooling. Vocational education made the development of human capital through training an important part of the educational system. Vocational guidance became the institutional mechanism for matching students and educational programs with the needs of the labor market. Together, vocational education and vocational guidance assumed the function of promoting industrial efficiency through proper selection and training of labor power. Early junior high schools experimented with ideas about vocational guidance and preparation for the corporate world and thus contributed to the development of the comprehensive high school.

The early development of vocational education has often been associated with the manual-training movement. In 1880, Calvin Woodward founded the Manual Training School at Washington University in St. Louis, Missouri. The idea of manual training was not to teach a trade but to provide the student with manual activities that would complement a liberal education. In most cases, the emphasis in manual training was on metal- and woodworking and drafting.

Woodward described manual training in an address to the National Teachers Association in 1883 as being "for all children as an element in general education." He argued that a truly liberal education prepared the child for all activities, both mental and physical. Although he supported manual training as part of a liberal education, he also claimed that it would provide opportunities for better occupational choices, elevate the quality of work, and solve labor problems. The way it would end labor problems was by giving future workers the skills to adapt to industrial changes. The exposure to manual labor would make the student aware of the variety of occupations requiring educated labor and, in Woodward's words, "bring into the manual occupations a new element, a fairly educated class, which will greatly increase their value, at the same time it gives them new dignity."[43]

Prior to 1900, little support existed for public education that would train students for specific occupations. A major factor in changing attitudes about specific job training was concern about the position of the United States in world markets relative to other industrialized countries, such as Germany. This concern was made explicit in a series of reports in the early twentieth century urging the development of vocational education. The 1905 *Report of the Committee on Industrial Education of the National Association of Manufacturers* states, "Technical and trade education for youth is a national necessity, and the . . . nation must train its youth in the arts of production and distribution." Germany was both feared for its activities in world markets and admired for its educational system, which included vocational and trade schools. For many, copying the German vocational system of education was necessary for improving America's position in international trade. For example, the 1905 report states: "The German technical and trade schools are at once the admiration and fear of all countries. In the world's race for commercial supremacy we must copy and improve upon the German method of education."[44]

In its 1912 report, the Committee on Industrial Education directly related concerns about developing human capital to fears of foreign competition. The report argues that two types of capital exist in the world. One type includes land, machinery, and money, and "the other kind is human capital—the character, brains and muscle of the people . . . . This capital we have not developed; we have overlooked the whole question of its complete and efficient development." The failure to develop this human capital, according to the report, was leading to great industrial waste. The report warns: "We should act at once because of the stress of foreign competition. We are twenty-five years behind most of the nations that we recognize as competitors. We must come nearer to the level of international competition."[45]

Discussions about vocational education included arguments that traditional secondary education was not suited for a majority of students and that academic training for those students needed to be replaced with vocational training. It was this type of argument that the writers of the *Cardinal Principles* feared would result in a class-based education, and they accepted this argument as justifying a differentiated curriculum in a comprehensive high school. For example, the 1912 *Report of the Committee on Industrial Education* crudely divides children into "abstract-minded and imaginative," "concrete, or hand-minded," and "the great intermediate class, comprising all degrees of efficiency." It states that although traditional academic education fulfilled the needs of the abstract-minded, the intermediate class required an academic education with "highly developed, practical and extended courses of prevocational and manual training." The report claims that concrete-minded students were "one half of the youth of the land, that our present educational system has been horrible, unmindful, uninformed and inconsiderate." Using a German model, the report recommends the establishment of continuation schools for children who left school and went to work as a means of improving the quality of this type of worker.[46]

The real development and expansion of vocational education came with the passage by the United States Congress of the Smith-Hughes Act in 1917. The fact that this action took place at the federal level is indicative of the consideration given to vocational education as part of America's economic and foreign policy. This act symbolizes the increasing tendency in the twentieth century to define a national interest in education that would be used to justify federal intervention.

The most important document in the early vocational education movement, the recommendations of which were incorporated into the Smith-Hughes Act, is the 1914 report of the Commission on National Aid to Vocational Education, established by the United States Congress. Historically, the document is important because it outlines all the major arguments for vocational education and resulted in the passage of the Smith-Hughes Act. The report opens with a general plea for vocational education as a means of reducing waste in the use of human resources. It also argues that vocational education is justified from a purely educational point of view because it meets the individual needs of students; provides equal opportunity for all to prepare for their life work; develops a better teaching process—learning by doing; and introduces the idea of utility into education. The report also claims that vocational education would reduce the discontent of workers: "Industrial and social unrest is due in large measure to a lack of a system of practical education fitting workers for their calling."[47]

The report of this congressional commission elaborates on the necessity for vocational education as a means of developing human capital through addressing problems in natural resources and the traditional dependence of American industry on foreign labor. The report argues that as America's natural resources were being depleted, foreign countries were finding new sources of supply. "We can not continue to draw indefinitely on Europe for cheap labor, nor will cheap labor in the immediate future meet the urgent need in American industry for the more intelligent service necessary if we are to satisfy the rising demand for a better product from our domestic as well as our foreign markets." Vocational education was advocated as an important answer to economic problems facing the United States.[48]

Like other reports of this period, that of the Commission on National Aid to Vocational Education claims that vocational education would meet the individual needs of students. In making this claim, the report gives a particular meaning to the term *equality of opportunity*. The report states:

1. Vocational Training Is Needed To Democratize The Education Of The Country:
   (a) By recognizing different tastes and abilities and by giving an equal opportunity to all to prepare for their life work.[49]

During the common school period in the nineteenth century, equality of opportunity meant giving everyone the same education so that they could compete on equal terms in the labor market. In the context of the reasoning of this report, equality of opportunity meant giving students different types of education based on the individual's future occupation. This change in meaning of equality of opportunity had important implications for the general organization of the educational system and was one of the major shifts in educational ideology to take place between the nineteenth and twentieth centuries.

The commission's report resulted in the passage of the Smith-Hughes Act. This legislation contained a very narrow definition of vocational education, which, according to Marvin Lazerson and W. Norton Grubb in their introduction to their *American Education and Vocationalism: A Documentary History, 1870–1970*, resulted in "strengthening and legitimizing the evolving dual system of education." The legislation defined vocational education as dealing with specific occupational skills. The alternative, according to Lazerson and Grubb, was a broad concept of vocational education that would have prepared the individual for a wide variety of occupations and made individuals competent to change their skills to keep up with changes in technology. The Smith-Hughes Act reinforced a dual system of education—a differentiated curriculum—by clearly separating vocational training from academic training and providing federal money to accomplish that task.[50]

The legislation established a federal Board for Vocational Education, whose tasks were to advise local communities and states, administer vocational education funds, and publish research. This act recognized three types of vocational education: vocational schools providing all-day training, part-time schools for young workers, and evening schools for adult workers. The money provided by the legislation was to motivate action by states and communities but was not meant to cover the full cost of vocational programs.[51]

According to Grubb and Lazerson, federal expenditures in 1917 to 1918 represented 27 percent of money spent nationally on vocational education, and in 1925 to 1926, it represented 24 percent. The Smith-Hughes legislation did not result in a rapid growth in the number of students in full-time vocational education courses. In 1912 to 1913, 6.9 percent of high-school students were in vocational programs, and in 1924, the figure was only 6.7 percent.[52]

The campaign for vocational education led to more general consequences for American schooling. Edward Krug argues that this campaign reinforced arguments for elective courses and differentiation of the curriculum. More important, according to Krug, it contributed "to a widespread bias against the so-called academic side of school work, particularly for the alleged 'masses.' This bias flowed from the attempt to promote industrial education by disparaging the work of what were referred to as the 'literary' schools."[53] By distinguishing between the "abstract minded" and the "concrete minded," the vocational education movement opened the door for a class-based education, which assumed that the majority of the children of workers would be best served by vocational programs.

Vocational guidance was the other important aspect of selection and training of students based on the development of human capital. Its purpose was to reduce inefficiency in the distribution of human resources. Vocational guidance developed in a number of cities during the early days of the twentieth century. The movement was inspired by the drive for industrial efficiency and, like other movements in education, contained utopian hopes for the general reform of the social system. For example, Eli Weaver, the pioneer of vocational guidance in New York City, envisioned the establishment of a central government vocational bureau that would function as a commodity-exchange market. He made this proposal after organizing, between 1906 and 1910, committees of teachers in the New York high schools to work with students in planning the students' careers. The function of the central bureau would be to determine the type of training and character needed in available occupations. The bureau would also conduct surveys of the labor market to determine labor shortages and surpluses. This information would be used to encourage or discourage training in particular occupations depending on the needs of the labor market. Within the schools, vocational guidance and educational programs would be based on information supplied by the bureau. Also, the bureau would place high school graduates in appropriate occupations. Weaver claimed that the guidance agency would "facilitate the exchange of labor between the workers and employers as the exchange of other commodities is now assisted through the standardizing operations of other exchanges."[54]

In addition, vocational guidance was conceived of as a means of changing the general pattern of industrial development. One way of doing this was to keep workers out of certain types of industry. J. Adams Puffer, principal of the Lyman School for Boys and director of the Beacon Vocation Bureau in Boston, argues in a book published in 1913 that vocational guidance should channel youth into constructive, not neutral or destructive, occupations. Puffer labels liquor, patent medicines, unwholesome foods, and vicious amusements as destructive occupations. Neutral occupations were harmless but did not contribute to the efficiency of the social order. According to Puffer, "If each teacher in the United States, each year, guided into constructive work one single boy or girl who would otherwise have followed some neutral or destructive occupation, that alone would probably wipe out the whole of both non-constructive groups."[55]

There was a tendency in the early stages of the guidance movement to view the client as raw material for the industrial machine and to assume the responsibility for shaping good industrial character. For instance, as reported in 1913, as part of the guidance program at the De Kalb Township High School in Illinois, the principal would quote business maxims such as, "It is none of my business what you do at night, but if dissipation affects what you do the next day, and you do half as much as I demand, you will last half as long as you hoped." Frank Parsons, founder of the first vocational bureau in Boston in 1908 and often called the "father of vocational guidance," would use an interview and a self-analysis sheet to determine what personality adjustments would be necessary for his clients. During the course of an interview, Parsons would make his own character appraisal by watching the manners and habits of his subject. This appraisal would be followed by a take-home questionnaire. The instructions on the questionnaire told the client: "Look in the glass. Watch yourself. Get your friends to . . . tell you confidentially what they think of your appearance, manners, voice. . . .Get your family and friends to help you recognize your defects." Following these instructions, the individual would answer questions ranging from issues of self-reliance and industriousness to queries such as, "Do you wear your finger-nails in mourning and your linen overtime?"[56]

Although these aspects of general reform were present in the early vocational guidance movement, its main thrust remained that of promoting industrial efficiency. The role of the vocational guidance counselor as it emerged from these more general social goals was part labor specialist, part educator, and part psychologist. As labor specialist, the guidance counselor needed an understanding of the job market and its requirements. At the founding meeting of the Vocational Educational Association in 1913, Frederick G. Bonser of Teachers College demanded that a professional education be developed that would train the vocational counselor to know the "relationship between present and probable supply and demand, the relative wages, and the changes in methods, devices, and organization effecting the workers." Bonser emphasized the importance of studying the physical and mental requirements of occupations.[57]

As psychologist, the early guidance counselor used a variety of tests to determine occupational abilities. The earliest tests were developed by Harvard psychologist Hugo Munsterberg, who pioneered vocational-aptitude testing when he designed tests to determine which Boston streetcar motormen would be least likely to have accidents. In historical terms, Munsterberg believed he was bringing together two major movements in American life: scientific management and vocational guidance. In the same way that scientific management studied industrial organization, Munsterberg wanted to study the job performance and aptitudes of the individual worker. His tests of Boston streetcar motormen were designed to measure powers of sustained attention as a means of determining the likelihood of an accident. Working later with the American Telephone and Telegraph Company, Munsterberg developed tests of memory, attention, and dexterity for job applicants.[58]

Tests of the type developed by Munsterberg were quickly adapted to the purposes of vocational guidance. For instance, Jesse B. Davis, a high school principal in Michigan and early vocational guidance leader, inspired by Hugo Munsterberg's streetcar and telephone tests, worked with the Michigan State Telephone Company in 1912 and 1913 to develop aptitude tests for telephone operators. These tests included measurements of ability to remember numbers, of speed, and of motor accuracy.

In the schools, vocational guidance became educational guidance and evaluation of individual interests and abilities. The Grand Rapids Central High School in Michigan became an early model for vocational guidance. The first meeting of the Vocational Guidance Association, in 1913, was held in Grand Rapids, and the principal of the school, Jesse B. Davis, was elected the first secretary of the association. The following year, he was elected its president. Davis believed that the major function of education was to guide students into their proper place in the corporate structure and socialize them for that structure through the social life of the school. The social life of Central High School was organized into a pyramid of activities; the base of the pyramid included clubs, athletics, and student government and, in ascending order to the top of the pyramid, a Boys and Girls Leadership Club, a student council, an advisory council, and at the top, the principal. Davis believed that this school organization reflected the realities of an organized industrial system. He compared his position as principal to that of a general manager: "The ideals upon which honest living and sound business stand, are the ideals of the public schools."[59]

While these industrial traits were being learned in the social life of the school, classwork was organized to help students to find a job. Topics in English composition were assigned in progressive steps designed to lead to self-understanding and career choice. In the ninth grade, students at the high school analyzed their own character and habits. In the eleventh grade, each student chose a career and investigated the type of preparation he or she would need. In the twelfth grade, students made "a special study of the vocation with respect to its social obligations, its peculiar opportunities for human service, and responsibilities [to] the community." Davis believed that people should enter an occupation with the idea that "it was the best means by which, they, with their ability, might serve their fellow man."[60]

More typical of the developing role of the counselor was the one suggested by Meyer Bloomfield, Frank Parsons's successor as director of the Boston Vocation Bureau. In an article in Charles Johnston's 1914 anthology *The Modern High School,* Bloomfield states that the "vocational-guidance movement has . . . made clear one of the most important and generally neglected services which a school can render, and that is educational guidance."[61] Educational guidance was defined as helping students select educational programs that matched their interests, abilities, and future occupations. Within this framework, the curriculum was to be subservient to the occupational goals of the students. Ideally, the school counselor would match a student to an occupation and then to a course of study that would prepare the student for his or her vocation.

One of the main arguments for the establishment of the first junior high schools was that they would facilitate the vocational guidance of students and the differentiation of the curriculum. As Edward Krug states in *The Shaping of the American High School,* the junior high school "put forward as advantageous features . . . the advancement of practical subjects, the provision for early differentiation, and the fostering of socialized aims." For instance, Krug reports that a survey of New York

City junior high schools conducted between 1911 and 1913 listed as opportunities offered by the junior high "(a) an opportunity to offer different courses of study; (b) an opportunity to adapt the instruction to the two sexes and to the requirements of high schools and vocational schools; (c) an opportunity to classify pupils according to ability."[62]

This survey of New York junior high schools appeared at a time when the New York schools were considering expanding their intermediate schools or junior highs to include the ninth grade as well as the seventh and eighth grades. New York had established its first seventh- and eighth-grade intermediate schools in 1905 and began adding the ninth grade in 1915.

In 1910, differentiation of the curriculum was one of the major features of the first junior high to receive national attention. Superintendent Frank Bunker of the Berkeley, California, school system wrote in support of his nationally publicized three-year intermediate school, "To force all children in the seventh and eighth grades . . . to take the same work is clearly wrong."[63]

Within the new junior high schools, guidance personnel were to have the role of aiding seventh- and eighth-grade students to choose a course of study. A report on the Rochester, New York, junior high schools stated that they provided "vocational counselors, teachers with shortened teaching programs, [who] confer with pupils and visit homes to consult with parents."[64] In other school systems, the principal often functioned as counselor. For instance, the Los Angeles school system opened its first junior high in 1911; in this school, pupils chose, with the aid of the principal, among six courses of study.

Another response to the guidance problem was to institute the advisory, or homeroom, period. This special period was eventually utilized as both a center for social activity in the school and a part of the guidance program. One highly publicized example was the Ben Blewett Junior High School in St. Louis, Missouri. Beginning in the seventh grade, each child at the Ben Blewett School spent 150 to 200 hours a year in advisory periods. In the course of the seventh-grade advisory periods, the student made a choice of a future career. In the eighth grade, students were programmed into three different courses of study depending on their vocational choice. Principal Philip Cox, who organized the school in 1917, stated that a guiding principle was the "responsibility [of the school] to each child as an individual, and to society, whose agent it is for leading the children as individuals and as groups toward the goal of social efficiency."[65]

In the same way that arguments were made for developing unity and cooperation in the comprehensive high school, it was argued that socialization was an important goal of the junior high school. One enthusiastic supporter of the junior high school idea wrote in the May 1919 issue of the *Educational Review* that a new spirit would pervade the junior high school. "This spirit will be the spirit of cooperation, the spirit of service and of sacrifice for the common good." As in the comprehensive high school, the vehicle for the new social spirit was to be extracurricular activities. A survey in 1922 of the nine years of development of New York junior high schools showed 387 clubs and 68 other after-school activities in operation. The clubs ranged from 83 centering around physical training to 31 devoted to history projects.[66]

The focus for socialization in junior high schools was clubs. Because clubs were centered around specific activities, they helped to guide students' developing interests. This, of course, was the justification used for providing vocational guidance at the junior high school level. The organizational center for club activities and guidance in most junior high schools was the homeroom period. Like most educational innovations of the time, the homeroom developed its own supporting rationale. One basic argument given for the homeroom was that the junior high school student tended to be lost and confused by departmental teaching. The homeroom was to provide a "home" where the student could seek direction and advice. The principal of Garfield Junior High in Richmond, Indiana, wrote, "The work of teacher-advisers or home-room teachers, as they are sometimes called—is to unify the school life of the pupil."[67]

The wedding of vocational guidance and socialization in the junior high school provided the complete educational program for the development of human capital. Differentiation would prepare the student for a particular place in society, and socialization would teach the student to cooperate and work for the good of the entire organization. One example of this combination was evident at the Ben Blewett Junior High School. Its principal claimed that teachers could differ with him on anything except "the two fundamental principles for which the school stands." The first principle was a differentiated curriculum, and the second was that "the school cannot be a preparation for adult social life except as it reproduces within itself situations typical of social life."[68]

One of the major debates about the junior high school was the degree of differentiation that should be undertaken with early adolescents. This was one of the issues considered by the Commission on the Reorganization of Secondary Education in *Cardinal Principles*. The commission concluded that the junior high school years should be a period of vocational exploration and prevocational counseling and that differentiation based on vocational choice should be delayed until high school. In general, this became the accepted pattern for junior high education in the 1920s.

In summary, vocational education, vocational guidance, and the junior high school were all justified by appeals to the need for development of human capital. National concerns about international economic competition provided support for educational innovations designed to train and socialize students for the new corporate world. Like those instituted in the comprehensive high school, these innovations directly linked public schools to the needs of the economic system.

Conclusion: The Meaning of Equality of Opportunity

One of the dominant themes in schooling in the twentieth century was equality of opportunity. The differentiated curricula of the junior and senior high schools and vocational guidance were to provide equal opportunity from the perspective of improving human capital. Within this context, equality of opportunity took on special and complex meanings. First, equality of opportunity was considered good for society because it increased industrial efficiency by matching individual talents with specific occupational requirements. Everyone was to be given an equal chance to rise or fall on the social ladder according to individual abilities. This meant that everyone would be given an equal chance to run the social race—*not* that everyone would have equal income or social status. Second, equality of opportunity was considered good for the individual because it allowed a person to find the best place in the economic system in which to develop personal interests and abilities.

A major change occurred between the nineteenth and twentieth centuries in the school's role in providing equality of opportunity. In the early days of the common school movement, education was to provide equality of opportunity by giving everyone a common or equal education, after which the social race would begin, with everyone competing for places in the social and economic structure. In the twentieth century, the provision for equality of opportunity was made a part of the school system through vocational guidance and a differentiated curriculum. No longer did students receive an equal or common education; rather, they received different educations based on individual differences. The race for social positions was no longer to be a function of the marketplace but of the scientific selection process in the school instead.

A major argument for making the provision for equality of opportunity a function of the school instead of the marketplace was that the marketplace was unfair because of the influence exerted by wealth and family background. It was believed that the school would become more objective about selecting people for their economic and social places through the use of scientific instruments of selection.

Therefore, the science of education, particularly measurement, was considered the key to the efficient use of human resources. Scientific measurement of intelligence, abilities, and interests was to serve as an objective means of providing equality of opportunity. This concept of equality of opportunity gave the expert and the school a major role in determining an individual's place in society. In essence, scientific measurement combined with a differentiated curriculum were to develop human capital by objectively controlling the provision of equality of opportunity.

A major problem with this concept of equality of opportunity, as reflected in the history of segregated education, was that the supposed objectivity of scientific measurement and public schools was often a mask for social-class and racial discrimination. Once the schools tried to determine a person's place in the social and economic system, they were open to charges of discriminating against particular social or racial groups. As a result, a major theme in the history of schooling in the twentieth century has been discrimination against minority groups and certain social classes. The use of schooling to increase economic efficiency through the development of human capital opened the door for education to become a central focus of social controversy in the twentieth century. Interwoven with the theme of human capital has been the politics of education. As demonstrated by the history of education in the South, the group or groups that control the schools have a major influence in determining the outcomes of attempts to provide equality of opportunity.

Notes

1. Henry Allen Bullock, *A History of Negro Education in the South: From 1619 to the Present* (New York: Praeger, 1970), p. 11.

2. Charles M. Wollenberg, *All Deliberate Speed: Segregation and Exclusion in California Schools, 1855–1975* (Berkeley: University of California Press, 1976), p. 30.

3. Quoted in ibid., pp. 28–29.

4. Quoted in ibid., p. 53.

5. Booker T. Washington, "Up From Slavery," in John Hope Franklin, ed., *Three Negro Classics* (New York: Avon Books, 1965), pp. 77, 94.

6. Ibid., p. 147.

7. Ibid., p. 149.

8. Bullock, *History of Negro Education*, p. 88.

9. Horace Mann Bond, *The Education of the Negro in the American Social Order* (New York: Octagon Books, 1966), p. 153.

10. W. E. B. Du Bois, "The Souls of Black Folk," in Franklin, *Three Negro Classics*, pp. 246–247.

11. Ibid., p. 373.

12. Ibid., p. 372.

13. Edward Krug, *The Shaping of the American High School: Vol. 1* (New York: Harper & Row, 1964), pp. 169–170, 284; Edward Krug, *The Shaping of the American High School: Vol. 2, 1920–1941* (Madison: University of Wisconsin Press, 1972), pp. 42, 218–219.

14. Edward Krug, *Salient Dates in American Education: 1635–1964* (New York: Harper & Row, 1966), pp. 46–50.

15. Ibid., pp. 91–95.
16. Ibid., p. 93.
17. Quoted in Krug, *Shaping*, Vol. 1, p. 68.
18. Quoted in ibid., pp. 274–275.
19. Quoted in ibid., p. 280.
20. Quoted in ibid., p. 281.
21. G. Stanley Hall, *Adolescence* (Englewood Cliffs, N.J.: Prentice-Hall, 1904), Vol. 1, p. xv; G. Stanley Hall, "Childhood and Adolescence," in Charles Strickland and Charles Burgess, eds., *Health, Growth, and Heredity* (New York: Teachers College Press, 1965), p. 108.
22. Hall, *Adolescence*, Vol. 2, p. 125.
23. Commission on the Reorganization of Secondary Education, National Education Association, *Cardinal Principles of Secondary Education*, Bureau of Education Bulletin (1918). The remainder of the discussion of *Cardinal Principles*, the comprehensive high school, and extracurricular activities is taken from Joel Spring, *Education and the Rise of the Corporate State* (Boston: Beacon Press, 1972), pp. 108–125.
24. Commission on the Reorganization of Secondary Education, *Cardinal Principles*, p. 109.
25. Ibid, pp. 109–110.
26. Ibid, p. 110.
27. Ibid.
28. Ibid, p. 111.
29. For instance, Elbert K. Fretwell, "Extra-Curricular Activities of Secondary Schools," *Teachers College Record* (January 1923; January 1924; May 1926; June 1926; June 1927).
30. Richard Welling, *As the Twig Is Bent* (New York, 1942), p. 91; Richard Welling, *Self Government Miscellanies*.
31. William A. McAndrew, *School Review* (September 1897): 456–460.
32. Walter L. Phillips, "Pupil Co-operation in Self-Government," *Education* (April 1902): 543.
33. Edward Rynearson, "Supervised Student Activities in the School Program," *First Yearbook, National Association of Secondary School Principals* (1917), pp. 47–50.
34. D. E. Cloyd, "Student Organizations in City High Schools," *Education* (September 1910): 17–20.
35. Frank K. Phillips, "The School Paper," *Industrial Arts Magazine* (July 1917): 268–271, reprinted in Joseph Roemer and Charles F. Allen, eds., *Readings in Extra-Curricular Activities* (New York, 1929), pp. 462–467.
36. Mary A. Sheehan, "Clubs—A Regular Social Activity," *High School Journal* (October 1921): 132–135, reprinted in Roemer and Allen, *Readings*, p. 304.
37. V. K. Froula, "Extra-Curricular Activities: Their Relation to the Curricular Work of the School," *National Education Association Proceedings* (1915): 738–739.
38. James Naismith, "High School Athletics and Gymnastics as an Expression of the Corporate Life of the High School," in Charles H. Johnston, ed., *The Modern High School* (New York, 1914), p. 440.
39. C. M. Howe, "The High-School Teacher and Athletics," *School Review* (December 1923): 781–782.

40. Charles R. Foster, *Extra-Curricular Activities in the High School* (Richmond, Va., 1925), pp. 108–109.
41. Eileen H. Galvin and M. Eugenia Walker, *Assemblies for Junior and Senior High Schools* (New York, 1929), p. 1.
42. Francis H. J. Paul, "The Growth of Character Through Participation in Extra-Curricular Activities," *The Fiftieth Yearbook of the Department of Secondary-School Principals* (1921), Vol. 2, pp. 54–60.
43. Calvin Woodward, "The Fruits of Manual Training," in Marvin Lazerson and W. Norton Grubb, eds., *American Education and Vocationalism: A Documentary History, 1870–1970* (New York: Teachers College Press, 1974), pp. 60–66.
44. National Association of Manufacturers, "Reports of the Committee on Industrial Education (1905, 1912)," in Lazerson and Grubb, *American Education*, p. 91.
45. Ibid., pp. 92–96.
46. Ibid., pp. 97–100.
47. U.S. Congress, House, 63d Cong., 2d sess., 1914, "Report: Commission on National Aid to Vocational Education," in Lazerson and Grubb, *American Education*, pp. 116–132.
48. Ibid.
49. Ibid.
50. Lazerson and Grubb, *American Education*, pp. 30–31.
51. Ibid.
52. Ibid.
53. Krug, *Shaping*, Vol. 1, pp. 243–244.
54. Eli W. Weaver, *Wage-Earning Occupations of Boys and Girls* (New York, 1912). The remainder of the discussion of the history of vocational guidance and the junior high school is taken from Spring, *Education and the Rise of the Corporate State*, pp. 91–108.
55. J. Adams Puffer, *Vocational Guidance* (Chicago, 1913), p. 274.
56. Frank Parsons, *Choosing a Vocation* (Boston, 1909), pp. 32–44.
57. Frederick G. Bonser, "Necessity of Professional Training for Vocational Counseling," in *Vocational Guidance: Papers Presented at the Organization Meeting of the Vocational Association, Grand Rapids, Michigan, October 21–24, 1913*, United States Bureau of Education Bulletin no. 14 (1914), p. 38.
58. Hugo Munsterberg, *Psychology and Industrial Efficiency* (Cambridge, Mass., 1913), pp. 36–55.
59. Jesse B. Davis, *Vocational and Moral Guidance* (Boston, 1914), pp. 46–123.
60. Jesse B. Davis, "Vocational and Moral Guidance in the High School," *Religious Education* (February 1913): 646.
61. Meyer Bloomfield, "Vocational Guidance in the High School," in Johnston, *Modern High School*, p. 612.
62. Krug, *Shaping*, Vol. 1, pp. 327–335.
63. Quoted in ibid., p. 328.
64. Quoted in *Report of the Committee to Make a Survey of the Junior High Schools of the City of New York* (1924), p. 236.
65. Philip Cox, "The Ben Blewett Junior High School: An Experiment in Democracy," *School Review* (May 1919): 345–359.

66. Thomas W. Gosling, "Educational Reconstruction in the Junior High School," *Educational Review* (May 1919): 384–385.

67. N. C. Hieronimus, "The Teacher-Adviser in the Junior High School," *Educational Administration and Supervision* (February 1917): 91.

68. Cox, "Ben Blewett Junior High School," p. 346.

8

Meritocracy:
The Experts Take Charge

A new elite emerged in the late nineteenth century composed of public administrators, efficiency experts, professional managers, and social scientists who were captivated by the vision of a scientifically managed society. This vision of social organization placed the expert in charge. Throughout the country, political-reform groups sought to replace the politician in government with a public servant or bureaucrat. The new professional administrators were to bring expert knowledge and skills to the management of organizations. It was claimed that the politician served only special interests, whereas the professional administrator or public servant served the general public. Of course, the creation of government bureaucracies had serious implications for the meaning of democracy.

For the public schools, the vision of scientific management included a professionally trained corps of administrators who would assume greater control of the schools as the governing power of school boards diminished. "Keep the schools out of politics!" became the war cry of the new professional educators. In practice, these changes resulted in small school boards composed of community elites and having limited functions. These school boards relinquished many of their traditional functions to the new professional administrators.

Schools also were given an important role in the vision of a scientifically controlled society because they were considered the central social institution for the selection and training of human capital. In the schools, the measurement expert became the manager of human resources. The psychologists marched into the schools armed with batteries of tests to measure students for their future places in society.

Within the schools, psychologists and professional administrators joined hands to preach a new version of equality of opportunity. No longer were the schools to play a passive role in the provision of equality of opportunity, simply providing an equal education and letting social position be determined by competition in the marketplace. The new breed of scientific managers distrusted the free interaction of the marketplace, because uncontrollable factors such as family wealth or poverty could cause a mismatch between individual abilities and occupational requirements. The free marketplace was considered both unfair and inefficient in the distribution of human resources.

During the earlier part of the nineteenth century, it was thought that the school would provide equality of opportunity by offering an equal education that would allow for equal competition among individuals after they completed their education. The major hope was that the school would make it possible for children of poor families to compete on equal terms with children from rich families. The newer version of equality of opportunity, which emerged in the 1920s and 1930s, combined the hope of providing the opportunity for equal competition between children of the rich and the poor with a desire to create an efficient society in which interests and abilities matched social position.

The new school leaders hoped to replace the alleged unfairness and inefficiency inherent in free-marketplace competition with the supposedly scientific objectivity and fairness of the scientifically managed public school. Instead of leaving social selection to the uncertainties of the marketplace, it was hoped that social selection—the provision of equality of opportunity—would become a function of scientific management and measurement in educational institutions. The new tools for providing equality of opportunity were the junior and comprehensive high schools, with their differentiated curricula, and the new tests being developed within the expanding field of psychology.

Behind the claims of fairness and scientific objectivity lurked important questions about the meaning of democracy in a scientifically managed society. First, there was the problem of reconciling governance by expertise with governance by the will of the majority. Second, there was the problem of values. Claims of fairness and scientific objectivity lose meaning when the role of individual values is considered. Decisions about the management of organizations, the use of tests, the contents of tests, and the abilities and attitudes that should be taught were based on individual values, not scientific principles. Consequently, claims of scientific objectivity often masked personal prejudices and self-interests. For instance, tests often relegated certain racial groups to an inferior position in society and, at the same time, through claims as to the importance of scientific measurement, ensured the social prestige and importance of the new test makers.

The source of the new elite of professional managers and social scientists and the citadel of hope for the scientific understanding and management of society were the new universities. By the end of the nineteenth century, colleges and universities began to change from institutions that simply conferred a liberal education and prepared students for the professions into institutions that were to be centers for the creation of new knowledge through research and training grounds for the scientific management of society. Spurred by the increasing importance of science and the model of the German university, American higher education underwent a major transformation with the creation of graduate education and the new vision of the social role of the college and university.

The attempt to use the school to scientifically manage society and the professionalization of school management are explored in this chapter. First, the professionalization of school administration and the changing political structure of American education are considered. Second, the early history of and the philosophical problems that emerged in the field of tests and measurement are discussed. Last, the new role of higher education and the development of graduate schools of education are described.

Meritocracy and Efficient Management

Meritocracy is a concept of society based on the idea that each individual's social and occupational position is determined by individual merit, not political or economic influence. Scientific management of human capital and scientific management of organizations are central ideas in the meritocratic concept. For the schools, meritocracy was both a social goal and a method of internal organization. To achieve meritocracy as a social goal, the schools were to create a society based on merit by objectively selecting and preparing students for their ideal places in the social order. As a method of internal organization, meritocracy meant the creation of an administrative structure in which the positions held by professionals depended on their training and abilities as opposed to their political influence and power.

The attempt to create a meritocracy in the organization of the schools was concurrent with the establishment of small school boards. In fact, several related changes in the administrative and political structure of American schools occurred at the same time that the concept of meritocracy gained prominence. Of major importance was the establishment of small school boards and the resultant increase in the number of duties and, consequently, the power of school administrators. As this occurred, school administrators adopted techniques of scientific business management for use in the administration of the schools.

Three important sets of ideas were used to justify these political and administrative changes. The first was the concept that the school should be kept out of politics. In most cases, this meant putting the major power and control of the schools in the hands of administrators serving the interests of the children, not in the hands of politicans serving special interests. This argument justified the increasing power of school administrators in relation to boards of education.

The second set of ideas centered on the concept of democratic elitism and was used to justify the creation of small school boards. What is meant here by the term *elitism* is control of the schools by local civic elites composed primarily of people who exercise power over local public policy without, in most cases, holding offices in government. They usually work through informal networks and civic organizations such as a local chamber of commerce or service club. The civic elites involved in school administration in the early twentieth century did not view themselves as conspiratorial groups working behind the scenes for their own self-interest, but as enlightened leaders working for the good of the entire community. One recent study of the occupations of civic elites found that over 50 percent were bankers, industrialists, and heads of local businesses, and the remainder included heads of local utilities, newspaper people, civic-association executives, clergy, university administrators, and professionals (lawyers, doctors, and the like).[1]

In the rhetoric of democratic elitism, only the "best"—the elite—should determine important public matters, because they have proven themselves successful and possess superior knowledge of public affairs. For instance, it was argued that a factory worker would have less ability than a banker to make correct decisions about the public interest regarding schooling. Following this line of reasoning, reformers argued that the schools should be governed only by the "best" members of the community and, therefore, that school board elections should be structured so that only the "best" could be elected.

The third set of ideas dealt with the proper relationship between the school board and the school administration. As the rhetoric of school administration developed in the early twentieth century, it became common to argue that the proper role of the board of education was to establish policy and the proper role of the administrators was to administer that policy *without interference from the board of education*. These distinctions between roles helped to increase and justify the power of school administrators.

These changes in the administration and political control of the schools and their accompanying justifications were caused by a complex and interwoven set of historical changes. No single factor explains all the changes, but all the factors were closely related. The establishment of small school boards sometimes resulted from the fear of local elite groups that their control over the schools would be lost to the political machines gaining ascendancy in urban politics at that time. In this case, local elites sought the restructuring of school board elections to ensure that their own control over the system would continue. In other cases, new elites composed of professionals viewed small school boards as a means of wresting power from the control of traditional elites.

The reduction in size of school boards was one factor that contributed to increasing administrative power. As school boards declined in power and ability to function in the schools, their traditional activities were passed on to the school administration. Also, the very growth in size, particularly of urban school districts, required more administration and coordination. In turn, school administrators welcomed these changes because they increased their power, status, and income. School administrators championed ideas such as keeping the schools out of politics and maintaining clear lines between the functions of the school board and those of the administration. Administrators willingly adopted the principles of scientific management because it gave them comparable status with members of the business community.

The close relationship between local elites and school administrators became an important factor in the politics of education in the twentieth century. This relationship can be traced in the history of early school board reforms. One historical study of these changes is Joseph M. Cronin's *Control of Urban Schools: Perspectives on the Power of Educational Reformers.* Cronin argues that the major concern of reformers in urban schools in the 1890s was to reduce the power of local ward bosses, whose influence encompassed the appointment of teachers and members of the board of education. Within the context of this argument, the influence of ward bosses was a threat to the power of middle- and upper-class reformers.[2]

The way to destroy the influence ward bosses had over urban schools was to centralize control, reduce the size of school boards, and make elections nonpartisan and at-large. Middle- and upper-class reformers also hoped that the social composition of boards of education would change by eliminating the participation of workers and small-business people. In other words, these changes were intended to ensure the power of the groups campaigning for them.

For example, a pamphlet published by the Voter's League of Pittsburgh for the 1911 fall election deplored the fact that school boards contained only a small number of "men prominent throughout the city in business life . . . in professional occupations . . . holding positions as managers, secretaries, auditors, superintendents and foremen." The pamphlet argued that a person's occupation was a strong indication of her or his qualifications for the school board: "Employment as ordinary laborer and in the lowest class of mill work would naturally lead to the conclusion that such men did not have sufficient education or business training to act as school directors." Included on the list of those the reform group thought should not be on school boards were "small shopkeepers, clerks, workmen at any trades, who by lack of educational advantages and business training, could not, no matter how honest, be expected to administer properly the affairs of an educational system."[3]

The city of Cincinnati provides an example of how local elites consolidated their control after changing the procedures for the election to the board of education. In Cincinnati and throughout Ohio, the reform movement was headed by John Withrow, who was associated through marriage with the leaders of finance and business in the Cincinnati community. After the death of his first wife in the 1890s, Withrow, a struggling physician, married the daughter of local utilities magnate General Andrew Hickenlooper. After the marriage, Withrow's financial and social position changed from that of a physician of moderate income living in modest surroundings in the downtown area of Cincinnati to that of a socially prominent physician living in a mansion and financed by his new father-in-law. His fortunate marriage allowed him the leisure to devote considerable time to educational reforms and also gave him the opportunity to meet informally and establish relationships with leading members of the Cincinnati community. He worked with James N. Gamble, a founder of Procter and Gamble, a company that would exert major influence over the schools throughout the twentieth century.[4]

What is important about Withrow's activities is that after he had successfully worked for legislation to implement school board reforms, he created an organization of civic leaders for the purpose of maintaining control of the school system. This model was followed in many cities around the country. Initially, Withrow worked for the passage of a small-school-board bill in 1913 that reduced the size of urban school boards from roughly 30 to 40 members to 7. In addition, elections were made citywide as opposed to election by district, and all school board elections were made nonpartisan.

It is important to understand how these changes in procedure for election of school board members affected the social composition of the board. When elections took place on a citywide basis, the citizen who wanted to get on the school board needed enough money and organizational backing to campaign throughout the city, whereas under the previously used method of election by district, the candidate needed to campaign only within a small geographical area. Election by district had allowed candidates with limited financial resources and organizational backing to compaign door-to-door within a small district and talk to friends and neighbors. After elections were made citywide, as the previously cited quote from the Pittsburgh reform pamphlet indicates, it became more difficult for clerks, workingpeople, or small shopkeepers to be elected.

Making school board elections nonpartisan eliminated political parties from the nomination and campaign process. With the elimination of participation by organized political parties, the business and financial community became the major group with financial resources and organizational skills. Thus, reduction in size of the school board reduced the opportunity for average citizens to be represented in school affairs. The combination of these reforms almost guaranteed that school boards would represent the views and values of the financial, business, and professional communities.[5]

After passage of the small-school-board legislation in 1913, Withrow was concerned with consolidating the power of upper-class reformers over the school boards. What was required was the creation of an organization to fill the vacuum left by the establishment of nonpartisan elections. Shortly after the passage of the legislation, Withrow wrote to his friend Frank Dyer, superintendent of the Boston schools and former superintendent of the Cincinnati schools: "The small school board bill has passed and I am hoping to be set free from further cares and worries in connection with public education. I can't, however, help being anxious about getting the proper board under the new laws." What he wanted from Dyer was advice about establishing an organization that would ensure a "proper board." Withrow continues his letter to Dyer:

Therefore I write you to send me the method of formation of the Boston school council or association, or whatever they call that organization that they have there, as I am told, entirely apart from the legally elected board. I am wanting here to start a federated education council . . . to make nominations for the school board and express opinions on the fitness of all nominations made from any other source.

It is clear from Withrow's letter that he viewed this form of organization as a method for circumventing the nonpartisan sections of the 1913 small-school-board bill. Withrow states in his letter to Dyer: "Now that the new law forbids any political party, by primary or convention, from naming candidates for the board of education, these candidates are to be nominated by petition only. What I want to know is, is there a similar or substantially similar committee or council or federation in Boston?"[6]

No record exists of Dyer's response to Withrow's letter. What Withrow did in Cincinnati in 1913 was to form the Citizen Council on Public Education, composed of representatives of the leading civic organizations in the community. The Citizen Council used a nominating committee to select school board candidates and a campaign committee to ensure their election. In 1921, the nominating and campaign committees were merged, and the original organization was absorbed under the banner of the Citizens School Committee.

The Citizens School Committee informally controlled elections to the school board from the 1920s until the time of the desegregation controversies of the late 1960s. As stated by former acting superintendent of the Cincinnati public schools Robert Curry, whose career in the Cincinnati schools spanned the half-century from 1925 to 1975, "Until the 1960s, the Board members, with few exceptions had been nominated by the Citizens School Committee and had not been opposed by other candidates." During those years, most board members held their positions for long periods of time. Of the 49 Cincinnati school board members elected between 1914 and 1964, 18 were from the business and financial community, 10 were lawyers, 3 were physicians, 3 were religious leaders, and 4 were former educators (including retired superintendent Frank Dyer, who served on the board between 1920 and 1931); the occupations of the remaining 11 members are unknown. Clearly, the social composition of the board of education in Cincinnati in the first half of the twentieth century did not represent the social composition of the community.[7]

Similar patterns of shifting control occurred in other communities. Sol Cohen shows in *Progressives and Urban School Reform* how reform movements in New York City combined destruction of ward control of the schools with anti-Catholic sentiments. In the 1894 New York mayoral election, a reform mayor was elected who fought for centralization of control and removal of schools from the power of the politician. Under the traditional New York ward system, the mayor appointed 21 commissioners of common schools, and they in turn appointed 5 trustees for each ward. The ward trustees appointed all teachers and janitors, nominated principals and vice principals, and furnished school supplies. This system provided opportunity for graft, but it also created a situation wherein the trustee had to be sensitive to local needs and desires. As Cohen states, "The reformers' battle cry, 'Take the schools out of politics,' not only meant take the schools out of the hands of Tammany Hall, it also meant take the schools out of the hands of the Roman Catholic Church."[8]

Some debate has taken place among historians about whether these school board reforms were a product of upper-class desires to assume control of the schools or of the vying for power of one group of community leaders against another. David Plank and Paul Peterson argue in their article "Does Urban Reform Imply Class Conflict? The Case of Atlanta's Schools" that "while the reformers in Atlanta were members of the middle and upper classes . . . the Atlanta school reforms were carried out not over the objections of working-class politicans but rather at the expense of the city's most prestigious civic leaders."[9]

The actual reforms that took place in Atlanta were slightly different from those in other cities. The Atlanta school board traditionally had been elected on a citywide basis, which meant, according to Plank and Peterson, that the city's social elite had always been in control. The actual reforms instituted in the late 1890s involved a reduction in school board membership from 17 to 7 and in the number of board committees from 10 to 2. These reductions meant less participation by board members in the functioning of the schools and, consequently, increased power for the school administrators. This shift in power was evidenced by increased responsibilities for the superintendent and by the hiring of an additional full-time assistant superintendent.

Where Plank and Peterson locate the sources of these reforms suggests an interesting hypothesis about the influence of reformers on the adoption of business-management techniques by school administrators. Plank and Peterson argue that in Atlanta, the reforms were a product primarily of the activities of middle-class professionals who were concerned with modernization. In this context, school board reforms were designed not to wrest power from the working class but to introduce modern administrative techniques while retaining power within one faction of the urban elite.

Whether the goal of school board reforms was to empower one elite group over another or to allow elites to wrest power from politicans representing the working class, the end result was that school boards did come to be dominated by civic elites. In 1916, Scott Nearing, a professor of economics at the University of Pennsylvania, wrote to the superintendents of 131 school systems in cities with populations over 40,000 according to the 1910 census to find information about the social composition of their boards of education.

One important discovery by Nearing was the low representation of women on boards of education. He found that in large cities (with populations over 500,000), 12 percent of board members were women. In cities with populations of 100,000 to 500,000, 8 percent were women, and in cities of under 100,000, 5 percent were women. In general, Nearing found that 75 percent of all board members from reporting cities were business or professional people and that business people composed more than 50 percent of the total number of board members.[10]

In 1927, George Counts published a similar study of 1,654 school boards, half of which were rural. Like Nearing, Counts found women excluded from control; only 10.2 percent of board members were women, and they were mainly on urban school boards. He found that urban school boards were dominated by proprietors, professionals, and business executives and that farmers were the majority on rural school boards. One cause of this situation, Counts noted, was the argument that developed in the twentieth century that it was necessary for professional and business leaders to control school boards.[11]

Accompanying the rise of elite school boards was the introduction of modern business techniques in the management of the schools. The earliest study of this phenomenon, one that is critical of this direction in twentieth-century American education, is Raymond E. Callahan's *Edu-*

cation and the Cult of Efficiency. Callahan portrays the school administrator in the early twentieth century as capitulating to a business-person mentality because of both public pressure and the rewards that could be gained by adopting a status equal to that of members of the business community. He suggests that school administrators had abandoned the scholarly role of educational philosopher and curriculum leader for that of school administrator as business person.[12] Although more recent studies suggest that school administrators had traditionally viewed their role in business terms,[13] all agree that school administration became professionalized around concepts of scientific management borrowed from the business community.

Scientific management, or Taylorism, exploded on the American scene in the early part of the twentieth century under the leadership of time-and-motion-study pioneer Frederick W. Taylor. Taylor believed that the basic problems of American industry stemmed from unsystematic organization and control of work. He argued that scientific study could determine the proper method for doing every job. The problem in the past, he maintained, was that workers in factories and business organizations were allowed to follow their own decisions or rules of thumb for the completion of a task. Scientific management promised to replace the unsystematic actions of workers with a planned and controlled work environment.

One principle of Taylorism with important consequences for the organization of schools is hierarchical organization, with management directing the actions of workers. In Taylor's words, in the past, "almost all of the work and the greater part of the responsibility were thrown upon the men."[14] Under Taylorism, management assumed more duties by reducing workers' responsibilities and need for decision making. An organization was envisioned in which decisions would be made at the top, based on scientific studies, and would flow to the bottom.

Taylorism complemented the social-efficiency thinking of educators because it mandated that workers be scientifically selected and trained for their particular jobs and that cooperation between management and workers occur "so as to insure all of the work being done in accordance with principles of the science which has been developed." The principles of hierarchical management, scientific study and control of the elements in the organization, selection and training of individuals for places within the organization, and cost efficiency became the focus for the professionalization of public school administration. Public school leaders jumped on the scientific-management bandwagon with a vengeance. For instance, well-known efficiency expert Harrington Emerson was asked to speak at the 1911 meeting of the High School Teachers Association of New York City on the topic, "Efficiency in the High Schools through the Application of the Principles of Scientific Management." After telling his audience it needed high ideals, good counsel, discipline, and common sense, he presented the practical side of the administrative efficiency movement. He stated that the most important element in practical methods or principles was standardization: planning, standard records, standard conditions, standardized operations, standard instructions, and standard schedules.[15]

Across the country, school administrators applied themselves to their newly acquired roles by trying to establish uniform procedures and lines of control. *Standardization* became the magic word. Administrators were preoccupied with standardizing student forms, evaluations of teachers and students, attendance records, personnel records, and hiring procedures. Cost efficiency also became an important part of this process as administrators worried about cost effectiveness in the classroom, the ordering of supplies, the purchase of insurance, the maintenance of buildings, and office management. For many superintendents, the dollar became the major educational criterion. For instance, Callahan cites as an example Frank Spaulding, a nationally renowned superintendent of the period who conducted studies of the economic value of different parts of the curriculum. Using a complex and vague formula, Spaulding reported in 1920 on the comparative worth of high school subjects. He argued that educational administrators needed to determine the cost and educational value of the subjects taught so that scientific decisions could be made about the cost efficiency of the curriculum. For example, he determined "that 5.9 pupil-recitations in Greek are of the same value as 23.8 pupil-recitations in French; that 12 pupil-recitations in science are equivalent in value to 19.2 pupil recitations in English." Based on these calculations and a concern with cost efficiency, Spaulding argued that "when the obligations of the present year expire, we ought to purchase no more Greek instruction at the rate of 5.9 pupil recitations for a dollar. The price must go down, or we shall invest in something else."[16]

Business values affected thinking about both administration and the value of education. Between 1900 and 1924, school administration rapidly professionalized around these values of cost efficiency and scientific management. An important factor in professionalization was specialized training, and one measure of this factor was the increase in the number of graduate courses in educational administration. In 1910, when principles of scientific management began to sweep the nation, Columbia University's Teachers College conferred 13 graduate degrees in administration and supervision out of a total of 73. By 1916, the institution granted 316 graduate degrees, of which 95 were in administration and supervision. By 1924, the number of degrees not only had jumped to 939, but 390 of these were in administration and supervision.[17]

More revealing is the actual content of the education of professional administrators. Callahan describes one content analysis of textbooks in educational administration conducted in the early 1930s (which means that the texts analyzed were written in the 1920s or earlier). This content analysis found "over four-fifths of eight thousand pages are devoted to the purely executive, organizational, and legal aspects of administration." These texts lacked critical analysis of educational problems, educational philosophy, or educational issues in a social context. The focus of training for school administrators was not scholarship and learning, but principles of management.[18]

A shared belief developed among the community of educational administrators that their major concern should be management. A survey of professors of administration and superintendents of city schools conducted in the early 1930s found that school finance was considered the most important topic in a school administrator's education, followed in descending order by business administration, organization and administration of supervision, organization and supervision of the curriculum, administration of teaching personnel, public relations and publicity, and organization of schools and the school system. The list continued through issues of school housing, school law, and school records, without any mention of instruction or discussion of broader concerns about the role of education in society, the nature of learning, or issues in educational policy.[19]

A survey of doctoral dissertations written in educational administration between 1910 and 1933 revealed the major topics of research to be the following: 55 dissertations out of 290 were on fiscal administration, followed by business administration (34), pupil personnel (29), personnel management (29), and legal provisions (24). The remainder of the dissertation topics ranged from buildings and equipment to educational organization. Many of them dealt with topics such as "school plumbing, the school janitor, fire insurance and the cafeteria."[20]

The professionalization of educational administration around principles of scientific management, cost efficiency, and a business mentality did not escape criticism. Jesse Newlon, a school administrator and president of the National Education Association, warned his colleagues at the 1925 association meeting of the danger of superintendents' functioning only as business managers. Callahan states that "he told his audience of administrators that they must be 'students of the social sciences, of all that is included in the fields of history, sociology, economics, psychology, political science . . .' The educational leader, [Newlon] said, 'must be a reader and a student.'"[21]

In his history of the professionalization of educational administration, Callahan bemoans the fact that educational administration took the route of business rather than that of scholarship. From another perspective, in *The One Best System*, David Tyack labels this new breed of school executive as the "administrative progressive[s]" who "(1) were a movement with identifiable actors and coalitions; (2) had a common ideology and platform; and (3) gained substantive power over urban education."[22]

Tyack stresses that an interlocking set of interests, values, and purposes existed among civic elites, reform groups, and the new breed of administrative progressives. From Tyack's perspective, the actions of this informal network shaped the modern school system. Therefore, educational reform took place from the top down.

Within Tyack's framework, it is logical that the new forms of school boards dominated by civic elites appointed administrators who reflected their business values and interests. Of course, it cannot be determined whether the administrative progressives adopted these values in response to the civic elites, or, given the spirit of the period, whether they actually had a common culture. Whatever the reason, between 1890 and the Depression years of the 1930s, business dominated in the control of the schools, and business values dominated the management of the schools. Tyack states, "Educational administrators drew elaborate comparisons between the roles of business leaders and superintendents." He gives as an example Professor Franklin Bobbit of the University of Chicago, who in 1916 contrasted a manufacturing company of 1,200 people with a school system of similar size. After comparing citizens to stockholders and superintendents to corporate managers, Bobbit concluded, "When it is asserted that educational management must in its general outlines be different from good business management, it can be shown from such a parallel study that there is absolutely no validity to the contention." Tyack reports that Bobbit's comparison was used verbatim by the United States commissioner of education.[23]

An almost symbiotic relationship developed between the new breed of school administrators and the elite school boards. The smaller school boards required increased administrative assistance and welcomed a sharing of business values. In turn, the administrative progressives depended on elite school boards for their appointments as school superintendents. For instance, in Cincinnati a system of mutual support was established between the Citizens School Committee (the organization of civic leaders that had gained control of school board elections) and the superintendent. In the 1921 school board election, Superintendent Ralph Condon actively campaigned for the candidates of the Citizens School Committee. When a resolution was introduced at the September 26, 1921, board meeting condemning his actions, Condon responded: "I want to repeat . . . that it was my duty . . . to advocate election of candidates who represented the non-partisan control of education, for, to my mind, there is no greater issue involved in the administration of education than this: Keep the schools out of politics; keep politics out of the schools." In this context, keeping the schools out of politics simply meant keeping the schools within the control of the local civic elite.[24]

With the professionalization and increase in duties of educational administrators and the decrease in functions of boards of education, clear definitions of proper roles developed. In the rhetoric of the times, school boards were to establish general education policies, and administrators were to administer those policies without interference from the boards. In part, self-interest and self-protection prompted school administrators to support these clear distinctions in roles. They wanted freedom from the school board and the resultant increase in power.

For example, in a report to the board of education made in 1923, after a trip across the country to inspect other school systems, Superintendent Condon of Cincinnati gave expression to this ideal relationship between school board and administrators. In his report, he identified characteristics he believed made one school system superior to another.

The best schools are likely to be found where there is the clearest recognition of what constitutes executive and administrative responsibility, with the Superintendent and his staff in charge of the administration of educational policies clearly and distinctly responsible to the Board of Education . . . but unhampered in the execution of educational plans and policies which have been approved.

Condon told the board that where he had seen this relationship between the board and superintendent, there was "peace, harmony, good understanding . . . and good results. Where this relationship did not exist there was controversy, misunderstanding and a general level of distrust."[25]

The concerns of the new educational administrators and elite school boards matched the general educational rhetoric about social efficiency and the development of human capital. In one sense, the administrative progressives became the new social engineers, organizing and directing a school system that would produce measured and standardized workers for the labor market, much the same as factories standardized products. The business attitudes and cost consciousness of the school administrators pleased the business people who dominated the boards of education. These professional and business people were happy to relinquish functions to an administration that promised to provide more education at less expense and to graduate students who would meet the occupational requirements of American business. Of course, this was not the entire story—other political forces also played a role in shaping American schools (see Chapter 9).

Measurement and Democracy

"Great will be our good fortune," wrote Robert Yerkes, head of the United States Army psychology team, "if the lesson in human engineering which the war has taught is carried over directly and effectively into our civil institutions and activities." The decisive point in the development of the science of measurement was World War I and the organization of the modern American army. Psychologists involved in constructing intelligence tests for the classification of army personnel, which later became models for tests used in the public schools, considered the army the ideal form of modern social organization because it embodied what was considered the proper classification of labor power. Expressing great hope for the future, Yerkes stated, "Before the war mental engineering was a dream; today it exists and its effective development is amply assured."[26]

The vision of a society in which social organization would be a product of scientific measurement raised basic questions about the meaning of democracy. The fundamental problem for social scientists was to resolve the conflict between a belief that only those of high intelligence should rule and the concept of a democratic society in which people with low intelligence are allowed to vote. In addition, during the post–World War I period, most psychologists believed that intelligence is inherited and can be controlled through selective breeding. For many, this meant that eugenics and the elimination of defective forms of intelligence were the major hopes for the improvement of civilization.

For many psychologists, the concept that intelligence is inherited also meant that intelligence levels vary among different ethnic groups. A major result of the army tests developed during World War I was alleged proof that ethnic groups from southern and eastern Europe had lower levels of intelligence than those from northern Europe. This finding led many psychologists to argue that the new wave of immigration from southern and eastern Europe was reducing the general level of intelligence of the American people. These findings played a major role in the passage of legislation restricting immigration into the United States.

Psychologists saw the schools as playing a major role in achieving a society in which intelligence would rule and students would be scientifically selected and educated for their proper places in the social organism. It was hoped that testing in the schools would enable schools to fulfill the dream of providing fair and objective equality of opportunity through scientific selection. Tests were considered the key to a socially efficient society.

Henry Herbert Goddard captured this vision in a lecture given in 1920: "[It] is not so much a question of the absolute numbers of persons of high and low intelligence as it is whether each grade of intelligence is assigned a part, in the whole organization, that is within its capacity." Goddard went on to suggest that humans could learn from the busy bee how to achieve "the perfect organization of the hive." "Perhaps," he stated, "it would be wiser for us to emulate the bee's social organization more and his supposed industry less."[27]

The most significant analysis of the implications of this testing is made by historian Clarence Karier in *Shaping the American Educational State, 1900 to the Present*. Karier's book is both an analysis of the movement and an anthology of original articles. Karier argues that the use of intelligence testing as a means of establishing a meritocracy became another method of justifying social-class differences and racial discrimination. Now the wealth of the rich was justified on the grounds of innate levels of intelligence. Indeed, psychologists at the time argued that the rich deserved to be rich because they were more intelligent than the poor. In Karier's words: "The hierarchical social class system was effectively maintained then as it is today, not so much by the sheer force of power and violence, but by the ideological beliefs of people within the system." One method of getting people to accept their position in society was to convince them that the particular position they held reflected their individual merit. The measurement of intelligence was one method of convincing a person of his or her particular social worth. Karier states,

> There is, perhaps, no stronger social class stabilizer, if not tranquilizer, within a hierarchically ordered social class system than the belief, on the part of the lower class, that their place in life is really not arbitrarily determined by privilege, status, wealth and power, but is a consequence of merit, fairly derived.[28]

The army intelligence tests were developed by a team of psychologists who met at Henry Herbert Goddard's Vineland Institute in New Jersey. Goddard founded the Vineland Institute in the late 1880s as a training school for the feeble-minded. He later translated and introduced into the United States the writings and intelligence tests of French psychologist Alfred Binet, who, at the request of the French minister of public instruction, developed tests to separate mentally retarded children from normal children. Binet's intelligence test became a model for the development of intelligence tests in the United States.

In the 1890s, Goddard argued that many of the social problems of urban and industrial society would be solved through classification of intelligence and institutionalization of individuals with lower levels of intelligence. He believed that the major problem in modern society was that people of lower intelligence, who were suitable for agricultural and rural societies, had migrated to urban areas, where they were unable to deal with the complexities of living. He contended that this situation was responsible for the increase in urban crime. For Goddard, the social importance of intelligence testing was its ability to identify persons of lower intelligence before they committed crimes and were institutionalized.

As mentioned previously, lurking behind the early discussions of intelligence were assumptions about the relative intelligence of different ethnic groups and social classes. Because the definition of the term *intelligence* often was vague, psychologists tended to build their own personal prejudices into tests. For instance, underlying Binet's test was a definition of intelligence that was both vague and relative. On the one hand, Binet defined native intelligence as "judgment, other wise called good sense, practical sense, initiative, the faculty of adapting one's self to circumstances," and on the other hand, he claimed that intelligence is relative to the individual's social situation. Thus "an attorney's son who is reduced by his intelligence to the condition of a menial employee is a moron . . . likewise a peasant, normal in ordinary surroundings of the fields, may be considered a moron in the city." While admitting that important differences in language ability between social classes might affect test results, he stated that social-class differences added validity to the test:

> That this difference exists one might suspect, because our personal investigations, as well as those of many others, have demonstrated that children of the poorer class are shorter, weigh less, have smaller heads and slighter muscular force, than a child of the upper class; they less often reach the high school; they are more often behind in their studies.[29]

Early test writers never distinguished between native intelligence and character. For example, Goddard argued that the score achieved on intelligence tests indicated how well an individual could control his or her emotions; in other words, level of intelligence indicated type of character—the wise person is also the good person. Edward L. Thorndike went so far as to suggest that ability to do well on tests gives evidence of justice and compassion. He purposely tried to make his intelligence tests difficult and long, so they would demonstrate the "ability to stick to a long and, at the end, somewhat distasteful task." A report from one institution of higher learning using the Thorndike test in the early 1920s states, "Two or three students fainted under the three-hour strain, and the faculty became indignant at this alleged imposition of hardship."[30]

The team of psychologists gathered at Vineland in 1917 had little time to debate the meaning of the word *intelligence*. Working with amazing speed, the group completed its work by June 10 and, after trying out the tests in army camps, sent a copy of the examiner's guide to the printer on July 7. Two forms of the test were developed—the Alpha, for literate soldiers, and the Beta, for illiterate soldiers. By the end of World War I, the tests had been given to 1,726,966 members of the army.

After the 1918 armistice, the government flooded the market with unused test booklets, which educators immediately utilized. Guy M. Whipple, a leading psychologist at that time, reported in 1922 that the army Alpha test was most widely used in colleges both because it was the first test constructed by a team of well-known psychologists to be tried on large numbers of men in the army and because "the test blanks were procurable for several months after the armistice at prices far below what other tests could be produced."[31]

The results of the army tests raised some important questions in the minds of psychologists about immigration and the functioning of democracy. Analysis of the tests yielded the startling conclusion that the average mental age of Americans was 13. This finding caused Goddard to ask, in a book published shortly after World War I bearing the suggestive title *Human Efficiency and Levels of Intelligence*, "What about democracy, can we hope to have a successful democracy where the average mentality is thirteen?" According to Goddard, the ideal would be for the top 4 percent of the population in intelligence to rule the other 96 percent. The problem, however, was the lack of confidence among the masses in those with higher intelligence. In Goddard's words: "Here is the root of our social troubles and here is found the explanation of everything from local labor troubles to Bolshevism. Intelligence has made the fundamental error of assuming that it alone is sufficient to inspire confidence."[32]

According to Goddard, once confidence was established, those with little intelligence would elect those with a great deal of intelligence: "Intelligence can only inspire confidence when it is appreciated. And how can unintelligence comprehend intelligence?" Goddard then argued that although the morons and imbeciles at the Vineland Training School did not elect the superintendent, "they would do so if given a chance because they know that the one purpose of that group of officials is to make the children happy."

Goddard argued that those with intelligence must devote themselves to the welfare of the masses. In his words,

> *Whenever the four million choose to devote their superior intelligence to understanding the lower mental levels and to the problem of the comfort and happiness of the other ninety-six million, they will be elected the rulers of the realm and then will come perfect government—Aristocracy in Democracy.*

This vision of the ideal meritocracy—rulership by an aristocracy of intelligence—was Goddard's solution for reconciling a belief in a meritocracy based on intelligence with the concept of democracy.

Building the confidence of the masses in those with intelligence is an important element in maintaining a meritocratic society of experts. Building this type of confidence also was a self-serving endeavor for psychologists, because it required that people respect the ability of psychologists to manage human resources. Thorndike captures the spirit of this reasoning in a 1920 article in *Harper's* magazine, "The Psychology of the Half-Educated Man." Thorndike portrays the "half-educated" person as one with just enough knowledge to think he or she can act independently of the expert. In Thorndike's words: "Such a man is likely to try (and fail) to understand the specialist instead of obeying him. He does not 'know his place' intellectually."[33]

For Thorndike, the person who tries to act independently of expert opinion is a public danger and at the mercy of clever charlatans. The rural society of the past, Thorndike reasoned, could rely on the common sense of individuals, but modern complex society depends on the rule of experts: "Wherever there is the expert . . . should we not let him be our guide? Should we not, in fact, let him do our thinking for us in that field?"

Out of this discussion of the half-educated person emerged a startling description of the educated person. "The educated man," Thorndike proclaimed, "should know when not to think, and where to buy the thinking he needs." This is another important element in reconciling meritocracy with democracy—the masses must be made confident so they will elect the most intelligent, and they must be educated not to think but to buy the thinking they need. In such a society, the role of the school is to select individuals for their places in the meritocracy and to provide an education that prepares individuals to live in a society ruled by merit and intelligence.

In addition to raising concerns about the functioning of democracy, the army intelligence tests fueled the flames of prejudice against immigrants from southern and eastern Europe. A major study of the test results was published by Carl Brigham in 1923 as *A Study of American Intelligence*. Although he later disavowed the racist conclusions of his study, in the mid-1920s Brigham developed the Scholastic Aptitude Test (SAT), which was destined to dominate the field of college-entrance examinations. Brigham divided the ethnic stock of America into Nordic, Alpine, Mediterranean, and Negro categories: Nordic stock originated in countries such as Sweden, Norway, and England; Alpine stock came from countries such as Romania, Austria, and Hungary; and Mediterranean stock came from areas such as Italy, Greece, and Spain. According to Brigham's analysis of the Alpha and Beta tests, Nordic groups were intellectually superior to Alpine and Mediterranean groups, Alpines were superior to Mediterraneans, and Mediterraneans were superior to Negroes.[34]

Brigham was concerned that the intermixture of these ethnic groups would cause a decline in the general level of American intelligence: "We must now frankly admit the undesirable results which would ensue from a cross between the Nordic in this country with the Alpine Slav, with the degenerate hybrid Mediterranean, or with the negro, or from the promiscuous intermingling of all four types." After examining immigration patterns in the nineteenth and twentieth centuries, he warned, "According to all evidence available, then, American intelligence is declining, and [this decline] will proceed with an accelerating rate as the racial admixture becomes more and more extensive." The only hope for stopping this downward spiral of American intelligence, he maintained, was restrictive and highly selective immigration laws and "the prevention of the continued propagation of defective strains in the present population."

Thus, as the use of tests spread through the schools, serving to separate students into different curriculum groups, the tests also served the purpose of reinforcing ethnic and social-class differences. For educators who adhered to the arguments of the psychologists, it appeared natural to channel children from lower economic and social groups into vocational education and those from upper social groups into college-preparatory courses. In fact, the allegedly scientific nature of the tests gave an air of objectivity to ethnic and social-class bias.

The widespread adoption of intelligence tests in the 1920s created a major debate over whether nature or nurture exerted the greatest influence on level of intelligence. An important defense of nature was given by Lewis M. Terman (1877–1956), an original member of the army team of psychologists who had gained fame for his revision of the original Binet test, which is now known as the Stanford-Binet test. Terman also developed the intelligence quotient (IQ) scale, which assigns normal intelligence a value of 100. Terman accepted the existence of ethnic differences in intelligence, and in an article in *World's Work* in 1922, he claimed that "the immigrants who have recently come to us in such large numbers from Southern and Southeastern Europe are distinctly inferior mentally to the Nordic and Alpine strains we received from Scandinavia, Germany, Great Britain, and France."[35]

The major educational debates about nature versus nurture occurred within the National Society for the Study of Education. In the society's 1928 yearbook, Terman considers the importance of this debate in relation to the future goals of education: "If the differences found are due in the main to controllable factors of environment and training, then theoretically, at least, they can be wiped out by appropriate educational procedures—procedures which it would then become our duty to provide."[36] However, the majority of studies reported in the yearbooks reached the opposite conclusion; they found that the number of days of attendance, amount spent on education, and preschool education were not as important as factors in predicting achievement as was measured native intelligence.

Faced with what he considered to be overwhelming evidence for the dominant role of native intelligence, Terman did not reject the importance of schooling but argued that emphasis should be placed on nonacademic goals. He argued that even though intelligence-test scores were not influenced by schooling, mass education should not be rejected, nor should it be concluded "that we might as well discard our alphabet, nail up our schools, and retreat to the jungle." For Terman, the question was not whether the school should be abandoned, but what form education should take. He thought studies of the relationship among schooling and intelligence and educational achievement suggested that schools placed too much emphasis on mastery of subjects, because mastery depends not on length of schooling, costs, or other factors, but on a factor that is independent of schooling: intelligence. He argued that the school, viewed in this context, should "place more emphasis than we now do upon the ethical and social ends of education, and care more than we now do about making the school a wholesome place to live."[37]

Ironically, at the same time that measurement people were giving the school a central role in the distribution of human resources, they were also promulgating a doctrine of native intelligence that undercut the ameliorative role of the school. What this means is that the early measurement movement reinforced social-class and ethnic differences by claiming they reflected differences in intelligence, but at the same time, it discounted the role of the school in doing anything about these differences. In the eyes of the leaders of the measurement movement, the role of the school was to build correct social attitudes, select individuals for their places in society, and educate them for those places. For Terman, Thorndike, Goddard, and others, improvement in the population could be achieved only through sterilization, restrictive immigration, and selective breeding.

The University and Meritocracy

In the minds of those who envisioned a scientifically managed society, the university was at the pinnacle. The role of graduate schools in the evolving world of public education was to provide the research and to educate the leaders for the scientific management of the system. In the twentieth century, schools of education were expanded to include graduate studies and educational research in addition to teacher-training programs. These new graduate schools of education became centers of professional control.

Although German and English universities were important models for the development of American higher education, the university in America became a unique institution devoted to a concept of service. This concept of social service is part of the general ideology of placing the expert in charge and in service to society. In an article published in 1906, Lyman Abbot, a clergyman and editor of *Outlook* magazine, explores this role of the American university. Abbot argues that the English universities emphasized culture and the education of aristocrats, whereas the German universities focused on scholarship and the education of scholars. American universities emphasized service to society and education for a life of social service.[38]

The idea of the institution of higher education as a center of expert service for society represents a sharp break with traditional goals. As described in Chapter 3, colleges in the nineteenth century focused on liberal education to provide the discipline and furniture of the mind. By the end of the nineteenth century, the role of higher education had shifted dramatically to that of servicing the needs of the corporate state. Several important events occurred as these changes evolved in the goals of higher education. First, the passage of the Morrill Land Grant Act of 1862 was the beginning of federal government involvement supportive of a broad social role for higher education. Second, large numbers of American students went to Germany in the latter half of the nineteenth century and returned with the idea of organizing graduate schools patterned after German universities. Third, modern industry began to depend on research to maintain a competitive edge in the marketplace. Over time, industry and government increasingly used universities as centers for research and development.

This new role for higher education generated a persistent tension in the twentieth century between the earlier concept of providing a liberal education and the emerging concept of servicing industrial and government needs and conducting research. In addition, the concept of academic freedom, which allowed escape from the narrow and restrictive thought of the nineteenth-century college, came into conflict with the new emphasis on service to society.

The 1862 Morrill Act establishing land-grant colleges was the culmination of many years of work by reformers in higher education to achieve a greater service orientation in institutions of higher education. Henry Tappan (1805–1881), foremost among these early reformers as a critic of the *Yale Report* and as president of the University of Michigan between 1852 and 1863, tried to give new direction to higher education. In his 1852 inaugural address at Michigan, he embraced the model of the German university and proclaimed the university as a major center for the creation and expansion of national wealth: "In demanding the highest institutions of learning, . . . [we are] creating not only, important and indispensable commodities in trade, but providing also, the very springs of all industry and trade, of all civilization and human improvement, of all national wealth, power and greatness."[39]

Tappan argued that the university's pursuit of science would lay the groundwork for the future prosperity of business and industry. As he told his audience, "A people aiming at large increases of wealth by agriculture, manufactures, and commerce, of all others should aim to found and foster the noblest institutions of learning. . . . They of all others require men of science." He said a university should encompass all areas of knowledge, including knowledge of the objective world and knowledge about oneself. Following what he called the Prussian model, Tappan proposed the establishment of a scientific course of study that would parallel the classical curriculum. Tappan tried to convince his audience that he was not discrediting classical learning by proposing a scientific course of study, but attempting to provide an education suited to differing individual interests and tastes. He argued that both the classical and the scientific curricula were equally good and equally responsive to someone's needs, and, in an example indicating the direction in which Tappan wanted the university to move, he stated, "A farmer may find Chemistry very closely connected with his calling but what can he do with Latin and Greek and the higher mathematics?"[40]

The Morrill Act was passed against a backdrop of arguments that the role of higher education was to provide an education suited for one's place in life and that science played an important role in industrial and agricultural advancement. The sponsor of the legislation was Representative Justin Morrill of Vermont, who had first tried to get federal aid for higher education in 1859. Along with Tappan, many other national leaders had been calling for more practical forms of higher education similar to that proposed in the Morrill Act. Of particular importance was Jonathan Baldwin Turner's 1851 plan for an industrial university, eventually endorsed by the Illinois state legislature. Turner divided society into two classes and argued that traditional liberal education served the interests of the upper class, but not those of the industrial class. He wanted a university to be established with a dual curriculum to serve both classes. He warned that a system of higher education that served only one class created the possibility "that they should form a ruling caste or class by themselves, and wield their power more or less for their own exclusive interests and the interests of their friends."[41]

The Morrill Act of 1862 specificially dealt with the issue of educating the industrial classes. The legislation stated that the money derived from lands granted under the act would be used "to teach such branches of learning as are related to agriculture and the mechanic arts, in such manner as the legislatures of the States may respectively prescribe, in order to promote the liberal and practical education of the industrial classes in the several pursuits and professions in life." The Morrill Act gave to each state 30,000 acres of public land per each senator and representative the state sent to Congress. Because the Civil War was in progress at the time, the teaching of military tactics was included in the legislation. The major effect of the legislation was to create a rapid expansion after the war of higher education designed to aid the agricultural and industrial sectors.

The emphasis on providing higher education to serve the agricultural and industrial sectors was only one aspect of the changes occurring in higher education. The other major changes resulted from the influence of the German universities and their emphasis on science, research, and academic freedom. The authors of the *Yale Report* of 1828 did not incorporate in their document any goals related to higher education as producer of new knowledge, but the universities in the latter part of the nineteenth century had become centers of research aimed at discovering new knowledge to improve society and the economic system.

In the latter half of the nineteenth century, many outstanding American students made pilgrimages to study at German universities. Before 1850, roughly 200 American students had made the trip, but after the Civil War, the numbers increased rapidly, and during the decade of the 1880s, almost 2,000 made the journey. Many of these students earned their doctorates in Germany and returned to hold important positions in universities.

Students returned from Germany with ideas about the importance of science and research. In Germany, and later in the United States, scholars began to apply scientific methods of research to every field of knowledge, including economics, history, and theology. German research began to take on the characteristics of specialization, objectivity, and the use of heavily documented evidence.

The German concept of science emphasized the pursuit of truth for its own sake, not merely for utilitarian purposes. Although this concept of research did take hold in the United States, it was often in conflict with demands for research to produce useful products. This tension has existed in science and other fields of research up through the twentieth century.

The idea of the university as a center for research in pursuit of truth changed the concept of teaching. In the American college of the nineteenth century, teaching involved students' learning traditional forms of knowledge, often by recitation or through the explication of texts. In the German universities, these methods were replaced with lectures on the results of research. In addition, the research seminar and laboratory were used to train students to conduct research under the supervision of a professor.

The German idea of the university became the model for the American graduate school. Specialized learning, the research seminar, and an emphasis on research became hallmarks of the graduate school concept. These changes in higher education gave new meaning to the role and status of the college professor. No longer did professors simply educate the future generation; now they were experts producing new knowledge and often serving as consultants to business, industry, government, and educational institutions.

With its new sense of social importance, the American professoriate became dissatisfied with traditional methods of college governance, which placed strictures on the actions of faculty in and out of the classroom. Of major importance in justifying increased freedom of and control by the faculties was the German concept of academic freedom. German academics believed that the pursuit of truth required absolute freedom of inquiry, so that any avenue of investigation could be followed. In Germany, academic freedom included the concepts of *Lernfreiheit* and *Lehrfreiheit*.

Lernfreiheit refers to the right of German students to determine their field of studies, follow any sequence of courses, govern their own private lives, and assume primary responsibility for final examinations. This concept of academic freedom for the student found little support in American higher education, except for freedom of choice through an elective system. On the other hand, *Lehrfreiheit* became an important part of academic life in the United States. Based on the idea that the pursuit of truth requires freedom to conduct research, the ideal of *Lehrfreiheit* gave university professors freedom to lecture and report on their research and freedom to conduct any type of research. In Germany, freedom of teaching and inquiry became a distinctive feature of the academic profession, one not shared with other members of society. In fact, a distinction was made between freedom within the university and freedom outside the university. Within the university, the academic profession was expected to make bold statements about society and their field inquiry work.

In the United States, the concept of academic freedom underwent considerable modification, in part because American institutions of higher learning were governed by boards of trustees that often represented important economic and political interests outside the universities. At times, these boards of trustees prevented the independence of the faculty.

What evolved in the United States was a concept of academic freedom in which professors were not expected, as they were in Germany, to attempt to win students to their point of view. In Germany, academic freedom included the idea that faculty members had freedom to teach whatever they wanted and the right to persuade students to accept their personal opinions and interpretations of a field of knowledge. For the

American professoriate, the tradition that developed was one of objectively presenting a variety of points of view on a controversial topic and refraining from commenting on issues outside the professor's area of expertise.

Ideas about academic freedom and the new role of the university were introduced into older American institutions. For instance, in his 1869 inaugural address as president of Harvard University, Charles Eliot, who later headed the Committee of Ten and served as president of the National Education Association, told his audience: "A university must be indigenous; it must be rich; and above all, it must be free. The winnowing breeze of freedom must blow through all its chambers. It takes a hurricane to blow wheat away. An atmosphere of intellectual freedom is the native air of literature and science." While recognizing the importance of freedom in the university, Eliot prescribed faculty actions befitting the particular notion of academic freedom that evolved in the United States. "It is not the function of the teacher," Eliot stated in his inaugural address, "to settle philosophical and political controversies for the pupil, or even to recommend to him any one set of opinions as better than any other. Exposition, not imposition, of opinions is the professor's part."[42]

A factor that restrained academic freedom in the United States was the underwriting of new American universities by industrial barons. During the latter half of the nineteenth century, the model of the German university found its home in these newly established schools. In 1865, Ezra Cornell, having earned a fortune in the telegraph business and public lands, endowed Cornell University, which was to serve the industrial classes and be a model research institution. In 1867, Johns Hopkins, who had gained a considerable fortune through commerce, endowed Johns Hopkins University. The primary purpose of this university was to function as a graduate school. New England industrialist Jonas Clark's endowment of Clark University in 1887 allowed G. Stanley Hall to turn it into a major center for graduate studies. A railroad empire provided the money for Leland Stanford to found Stanford University in 1885, and oil money allowed John D. Rockefeller to establish the University of Chicago in 1890. The Armour Institute was funded by the meat-packing industry, and the Carnegie Institute, by the steel industry.

These are only a few of the major institutions of higher learning that were backed by large-scale corporate wealth and adapted the German model of the university to research in service to industry and government. In the words of David Noble in *America by Design: Science, Technology, and the Rise of Corporate Capitalism*, "The growing need within industries for scientific research, and the drive toward cooperation with educational institutions to secure it, paralleled the development of research with the universities." Noble argues that these new universities, like the public schools, were given the task of educating individuals to meet the needs of the industrial system:

> While the primary mission of the university within the industrial system was the "efficient production of human material" according to "industrial specifications"—which made not only the building of universities, but education itself an industry—the role of universities as centers of research for industry was also a vital one.

Within the context of Noble's argument, the "efficient production of human material" refers to the education of scientists, managers, and engineers and to the training of economists, psychologists, and sociologists to aid in industrial production.[43]

An inevitable tension developed between the interests of corporate wealth that came to dominate American higher education, and the increasing independence and prestige of the American professoriate. In the late nineteenth and early twentieth centuries, many professors were threatened because of their political views. For example, in 1894, Richard Ely, director of the University of Wisconsin School of Economics, Politics and History, was accused by the Board of Regents of believing in strikes and boycotts. Ely was charged with threatening to boycott a local firm in support of an employee strike and with expressing the same prounion sentiments in his writings. The regents eventually exonerated Professor Ely and issued what has been called the Wisconsin Magna Charta, which contains the famous lines, "Whatever may be the limitations which trammel inquiry elsewhere we believe the great State University of Wisconsin should ever encourage that continual and fearless sifting and winnowing by which alone the truth can be found."[44]

At Stanford University, Professor Edward Ross, educated in Ely's seminars at the University of Wisconsin, defended socialist Eugene V. Debs and wrote a pamphlet in favor of free silver that was used by the Democratic Party. Mrs. Leland Stanford was upset by Ross's actions and wrote a letter to the president of Stanford complaining that Ross was playing "into the hands of the lowest and vilest elements of socialism."[45] In May 1900, Ross spoke at a meeting of organized labor to protest immigration of Chinese labor. This action struck home for the Stanfords because Chinese labor had been widely used in their railroad empire. Again, Mrs. Stanford reacted and this time forced Ross's resignation. Ross defended himself in his resignation letter, declaring: "I had no choice but to go straight ahead. The scientist's business is to know some things clear to the bottom, and if he hides what he knows, he loses his virtue."[46] Ross expressed the moral imperative of academic freedom— the constant quest for truth regardless of the difficulties. Of course, this quest was sometimes hindered by self-interested trustees and by faculty members interested in personal security and gain.

Ross's resignation led to an investigation by the American Economic Association. This action established a precedent for the protection of academic freedom that eventually led to the organization of the American Association of University Professors (AAUP) in 1915. As in previous defenses of academic freedom, the AAUP rested its case for academic freedom on the requirements of science. Of course, underlying the argument that freedom is necessary for research was a defense of the new independent status of the American professoriate as leaders of technological, scientific, and social change.

In this atmosphere of research, science, and the new role of universities, graduate schools of education blossomed. Several factors complicated the development of colleges and departments of education in American universities. First, a tradition existed of training elementary school teachers in two-year normal schools. Second, the standards for admission to normal schools were low—in most cases not even a high school diploma was required. Finally, many secondary school teachers who were educated at colleges did not receive any professional training.

In the late 1800s, several factors began to change this nineteenth-century pattern of teacher training. First, the requirements for admission to normal schools were tightened. In 1895, 14 percent of a sample of 51 normal schools required a high school diploma for admission. By 1905, the percentage had increased to 22 percent. The Department of Normal Schools of the National Education Association passed a resolution in 1908 in favor of requiring a high school diploma for admission to normal schools. By the 1930s, most normal schools required a high school diploma.

Second, the four-year teachers college began to replace the normal school. It was argued that the two-year normal school course did not provide the teacher with a broad enough liberal education. This transition occurred rapidly during the 1920s. In 1920, there were 137 state normal schools and 46 teachers colleges in the United States. By 1933, the number of normal schools had decreased to 30, and the number of teachers colleges had increased to 146.

Last, as part of the more general trend toward establishing graduate schools, colleges and universities began to add departments and colleges of education. The first permanent chair of education in the United States was established at the University of Iowa in 1873, and the University of Iowa created the College of Normal Instruction in 1878. The University of Michigan opened the Department of the Science and Art of Teaching in 1879; in 1881, the Department of Pedagogy was opened at the University of Wisconsin; in 1887, Teachers College at Columbia University was founded. By 1899, departments or chairs of education had been established at 244 American universities.

Working in the midst of these changes in the organization of professional training in education and as a professor of education at Stanford University, Ellwood Cubberley viewed the rapidly proliferating graduate schools of education as producers of and leaders in the new scientific study of education. Writing about the first quarter of the twentieth century, he states, "Within this period of time entirely new means of attacking educational problems have been developed through the application of statistical procedures, the use of standardized tests, and the devising of scales for the measurement of the intelligence of school children." He goes on to argue that the development of the scientific study of education allowed for the evaluation of educational results in quantitative terms.[47]

Like their colleagues in other divisions of the university, faculties in graduate schools of education tried to increase their status through conducting research and applying the scientific method to problems in education. As noted earlier, graduate schools of education enhanced the status of practitioners by conferring graduate degrees. In turn, graduate students in education, seeking improved employment by gaining advanced degrees, created an avalanche of often-useless educational research.

Although graduate schools of education became important for conferring status in the world of the public schools, they often struggled for status among other university disciplines. Theodore Sizer and Arthur Powell argue that the low status of the education faculty on university campuses was a result of the type of recruiting that occurred when education faculties rapidly expanded in the early part of the twentieth century. They contend that most of the positions were filled by people who had received their basic training through their work in the field of education. Thus, colleges of education were staffed with former school administrators and teachers who primarily taught and wrote about their personal experiences. In most cases, the study of education was not grounded in theory, but reflected the professors' individual experiences. Sizer and Powell paint an uncomplimentary picture of the professor of education as he or she emerged in the early twentieth century: a "gentle, unintellectual, saccharine, and well-meaning . . . bumbling doctor of undiagnosable ills, harmless if morosely defensive. He is either a mechanic . . . or he is the flatulent promoter of irrelevant trivia."[48]

Even though graduate schools of education struggled for status on university campuses, their power was soon felt in the education world. In *Managers of Virtue: Public School Leadership in America, 1820–1980*, David Tyack and Elisabeth Hansot depict the leading professors in the new graduate schools as important members of what they call the "educational trust." They argue that the alliance of these faculty members with school administrators, elite school boards, and big business produced the major changes in education during the early twentieth century.

A major source of power for some of these faculty members and graduate schools derived from the education and placement of school administrators. On a national level, the most powerful faculties were at Teachers College at Columbia University, the University of Chicago, and Stanford University. Tyack and Hansot describe the leading faculty in school administration at these institutions as the "placement barons." Citing Robert Rose's 1969 dissertation, "Career Sponsorship in the School Superintendency," they report that George Strayer, Paul Mort, and Nicolaus Engelhardt at Teachers College established an "old boy's network"—that is, faculty members were known to board members and other school administrators around the country. They quote one of Rose's informants as saying: "All of them had the knack of conveying the feeling that they were definitely aware of you as a person, had an affinity for you, and were concerned with being helpful to you in your future career. . . . They took pride in talking about 'their boys.'" The power of the "placement barons" at Teachers College is reflected in the 1939 roster of the American Association of School Administrators; Tyack and Hansot report that according to this roster, "287 superintendents held Teachers College M.A.'s and 32 had doctorates, a far greater proportion than that represented by any other university."[49]

Tyack and Hansot also report that at the University of Chicago, Professor William C. Reavis's endorsement of students prompted students to establish a Reavis Club. In California, Ellwood Cubberley, the educational historian whose more traditional historical interpretations have been cited in this text, endorsed and was a mentor to most of the administrators in California in the early twentieth century. Cubberley was often referred to as "Dad Cubberley" and reportedly was admired and emulated throughout the state.

While Teachers College, Stanford, and the University of Chicago were powerful on a national level, many state universities came to dominate local areas. According to Tyack and Hansot, at institutions such as Ohio State University, for instance, professors of administration knew most school superintendents by their first names and exerted influence over boards of education in the region. It was also the case that many of the faculty members at these "local" institutions were trained at "national" institutions—this created an informal national alliance of educational faculties.

In addition to their power to recommend school administrators and influence their opinions, important faculty members earned a great deal of money by consulting with local school districts. The magic words of the new progressive administrators were *research* and *study*, and for university people, this meant extra income. Tyack and Hansot quote a comment made by one graduate of Teachers College: "Once when Strayer and Engelhardt came out to ———— for a meeting . . they expressed disappointment that they were not getting some consulting work in this state. I told them I couldn't see why I shouldn't be making that money as well as they."[50]

Conclusion

Graduate schools of education were one important link in the educational power structure that came to dominate public schools in the early part of the twentieth century. They joined hands in their quest to create a well-ordered and scientifically managed society with the new breed of school administrators using business-management techniques, elite school board members, faculties in graduate schools of education, and experts in measurement. Their common vision of a meritocracy organized around the school was one that promoted their own self-interests. It probably is not inaccurate to assume that when Henry Herbert Goddard divided American society into 4 million that should be leaders and 96 million that should be followers, he considered himself a member of the 4 million. A scientifically managed meritocracy would guarantee most of the members of this alliance positions of power and privilege.

The major flaw in this alliance was the potential for conflicts of interest among its members. As described in Chapter 9, the greatest tension in the alliance was between the business people, who wanted the system to be inexpensive, and the school administrators and professors of education, who wanted to ensure the continued growth of their educational empire. Also, the vision of meritocracy excluded many groups, particularly minority groups, from positions of affluence and power, and this created another level of tension between the educational alliance and those who suffered discrimination and exclusion. Furthermore, any failure of the schools to meet national goals made them vulnerable to criticism.

Eventually, the alliance collapsed under the economic pressures of the Depression of the 1930s, when educators resisted the desire of business elements to reduce financial support to the public schools. In addition, professional educators, who as a group included school administrators and professors of education, came under attack after World War II for supposedly having "weakened" the academic training offered by the schools, thus making it difficult for the United States to compete with the Soviet Union in developing military weapons for the cold war. Finally, the very dream of a meritocracy based on the sorting function of the school came under severe attack by the civil rights movement in the 1950s and 1960s.

The dream of a scientifically managed society collapsed under the tensions created by the self-interests of the movement's leaders, who used the mantle of science to legitimize and protect their economic and social power. However, the educational structures created in their quest for meritocracy have lasted up to the present time, and even though the dream of equality of opportunity through schooling has been seriously questioned, management of human capital is still one of the primary goals of education.

Notes

1. David Kirby, T. Robert Harris, and Robert Crain, *Political Strategies in Northern School Desegregation* (Lexington, Mass.: Lexington Books, 1973), p. 116.

2. Joseph M. Cronin, *The Control of Urban Schools: Perspectives on the Power of Educational Reformers* (New York: Free Press, 1973).

3. Quoted in Samuel P. Hays, "The Politics of Reform in Municipal Government in the Progressive Era," *Pacific Northwest Quarterly* (October 1964): 163.

4. Margaret Withrow Farny, *Sevenmile Harvest: The Life of John Withrow, 1854–1931* (Caldwell, N.J.: Progress Publishing, 1942), pp. 57–172.

5. The conservative effect of nonpartisan elections is analyzed in Willis D. Hawley, *Nonpartisan Elections and the Case for Party Politics* (New York: Wiley, 1973).

6. Quoted in Farny, *Sevenmile Harvest*, p. 174.

7. Robert P. Curry, *Fifty Years in the Cincinnati Public Schools, 1925–1975* (Cincinnati: Cincinnati Historical Society, n.d.); Paul Erwin, *Cincinnatians Promote City Schools, 1913–1963* (Cincinnati: Citizens School Committee, 1964).

8. Sol Cohen, *Progressives and Urban School Reform* (New York: Teachers College Press, 1964), pp. 16–55.

9. David N. Plank and Paul E. Peterson, "Does Urban Reform Imply Class Conflict? The Case of Atlanta's Schools," *History of Education Quarterly* 23 (Summer 1983): 152.

10. Scott Nearing, "Who's Who in Our Boards of Education?" *School and Society* 5 (January 20, 1917): 89–90.

11. George S. Counts, *The Social Composition of Boards of Education: A Study in the Social Control of Public Education* (Chicago: University of Chicago Press, 1927).

12. Raymond E. Callahan, *Education and the Cult of Efficiency* (Chicago: University of Chicago Press, 1962).

13. Barbara Berman, "Business Efficiency, American Schooling and the Public School Superintendency: A Reconsideration of the Callahan Thesis," *History of Education Quarterly* (Fall 1983): 297–319.

14. Quoted in Callahan, *Cult of Efficiency*, p. 27.

15. Ibid., pp. 27, 55–57.

16. Quoted in ibid., p. 73.

17. Ibid., p. 214.

18. Ibid., p. 200.

19. Ibid., p. 201.

20. Ibid., p. 202.

21. Ibid., p. 203.

22. David Tyack, *The One Best System: A History of American Urban Education* (Cambridge, Mass.: Harvard University Press, 1974), p. 128.

23. Ibid., p. 144.

24. *Cincinnati Board of Education Proceedings,* September 26, 1921, pp. 5–7.

25. *Cincinnati Board of Education Proceedings,* January 8, 1923, pp. 16–19.

26. Quoted in Joel Spring, "Psychologists and the War: The Meaning of Intelligence in the Alpha and Beta Tests," *History of Education Quarterly* 12 (Spring 1972): 3.

27. Henry Herbert Goddard, *Human Efficiency and Levels of Intelligence* (Princeton, N.J.: Princeton University Press, 1920), pp. 35, 62.

28. Clarence J. Karier, *Shaping the American Educational State: 1900 to the Present* (New York: Free Press, 1975), p. 138.

29. Alfred Binet and Theodore Simon, *The Development of Intelligence in Children* (Baltimore: Williams and Wilkins, 1916), p. 318.

30. Guy M. Whipple, "Intelligence Tests in Colleges and Universities," *National Society for the Study of Education Yearbook* 21 (1922), p. 260.

31. Ibid., p. 254.

32. Goddard, "Human Efficiency," in Karier, *Shaping the American Educational State,* pp. 165–170.

33. Edward L. Thorndike, "The Psychology of the Half-Educated Man," in Karier, *Shaping the American Educational State,* pp. 238–244.

34. Carl C. Brigham, "A Study of American Intelligence," in Karier, *Shaping the American Educational State,* pp. 207–215.

35. Lewis M. Terman, "Were We Born That Way?" in Karier, *Shaping the American Educational State,* pp. 197–207.

36. Quoted in Edgar Gumbert and Joel Spring, *The Superschool and the Superstate* (New York: Wiley, 1974), p. 101.

37. Ibid., pp. 104–105.

38. Frederick Rudolph, *The American College and University* (New York: Knopf, 1962): 356–357.

39. Henry Philip Tappan, "Inaugural Discourse," in Theodore Rawson Crane, ed., *The Colleges and the Public, 1787–1862* (New York: Teachers College Press, 1963), p. 150.

40. Ibid., p. 165.

41. Jonathan Baldwin Turner, "Plan for an Industrial University for the State of Illinois (1851)," in Crane, *Colleges and the Public,* pp. 172–190.

42. Quoted in Walter Metzger, *Academic Freedom in the Age of the University* (New York: Columbia University Press, 1955), p. 126.

43. David F. Noble, *America by Design: Science, Technology, and the Rise of Corporate Capitalism* (New York: Knopf, 1977), pp. 131, 147.

44. Quoted in Metzger, *Academic Freedom,* p. 153.

45. Ibid., pp. 164–165.

46. Edward Ross, "Statement Regarding Forced Resignation from Stanford University, November 13, 1900," in Karier, *Shaping the American Educational State,* pp. 25–28.

47. Ellwood Cubberley, *Public Education in the United States: A Study and Interpretation of American Educational History* (Boston: Houghton Mifflin, 1934), p. 689.
48. Arthur G. Powell and Theodore Sizer, "Changing Conception of the Professor of Education," in James Cornelius, ed., *To Be a Phoenix: The Education Professoriate* (Bloomington, Ind.: Phi Delta Kappa, 1969), p. 61.
49. David Tyack and Elisabeth Hansot, *Managers of Virtue: Public School Leadership in America, 1820–1980* (New York: Basic Books, 1982), pp. 140–142.
50. Quoted in ibid., p. 143.

9

The Politics of Education

The political structure of American education emerged in the twentieth century as a complex set of alliances, multiple levels of power, and continual struggles among various educational factions and public groups. The politics of education can best be described as the politics of professionalism; professional educators fought for power with one another and with political and other community leaders.

Alliances between school boards and school administrators in the early twentieth century created strong tensions between political leaders and professional administrators. The cry "Keep the schools out of politics" was used by professional school administrators in their attempt to consolidate their power over the educational system. A major result was the creation of lasting tensions between politicans and school officials. By the Depression years of the 1930s, this tension erupted into a full-scale debate over whether the public schools or the federal government should have responsibility for youth programs. In the climate of the cold war following World War II, politicians blamed the professional educators for having "weakened" the public school curriculum and made the schools allegedly inferior to those in the Soviet Union. Extensive federal involvement in education during the 1950s was in part a result of a feeling that political actions were required to save the schools from the anti-intellectual clutches of the professional educators.

In attempting to protect their power from politicans, administrative progressives established alliances with business elites. At one level, this alliance developed smoothly because both groups advocated scientific management and hierarchical control. Business communities were pleased with school administrators who promised efficient, cost-effective school systems.

At another level, an almost inevitable conflict developed between the cost consciousness of the business community and the desire of the administrative progressives to protect and expand their educational empires. The economic pressures of the Depression split the close alliance that had existed between educators and the business community, and by the 1950s, business had joined with politicians to declare that professional educators had made the schools the weakest link in America's defense against communism. Criticism of this type has continued into the 1980s, with schools being blamed for America's difficulties in international competition with Japan and West Germany.

The politics of educational professionalism involved both links between the profession and outside political interests and struggles for power within the profession. The reforms of administrative progressives resulted in teachers occupying the lowest rung of the administrative hierarchy and becoming objects of the new techniques of scientific management. Low pay coupled with resentment of administrative reforms resulted in the creation of militant teachers' organizations.

Some teachers believed their major hope was in organizing unions similar to other unions and joining forces with organized labor. In some cases, this created a situation in which teachers were allied with local trade unionists in a struggle for more pay, better working conditions, and a greater voice in educational policy making. These struggles pitted teachers against administrators interested in protecting their own power and a business community interested in keeping teacher salaries at a low level. Actions such as these led to the establishment of the American Federation of Teachers (AFT), which for many years pioneered the use of union tactics in education.

Teachers also tried to gain control of the National Education Association (NEA) and turn it into an organization with a primary interest in teacher welfare. Teachers lost this battle against school administrators in the early twentieth century but finally captured control in the 1960s and 1970s and turned the NEA into the largest teachers' union. By the 1980s, the NEA and the AFT had become important factors in national politics. Both groups attempted to establish alliances with politicians to gain legislation favorable to their interests.

While these struggles were being waged and alliances were being formed, the federal government began to play an increasing role in education. The role of the federal government in education must be understood in the context of the development of national educational policies. Because education is a power given to the states by the Constitution, there did not exist a political body that could enforce a national educational policy. But even with the absence of national control, a great deal of similarity could be found among public schools throughout the United States. This was mainly due to the existence of national professional groups that shared information and ideas and issued policy statements. In addition, superintendents and other school administrators moved from community to community, instituting similar educational programs. Colleges of education across the country tended to use the same methods for training teachers and administrators. Also, textbooks were published for a national market. Therefore, despite local control of education, American schools became increasingly alike.

Prior to the 1940s, the most important organization for establishing national educational policy was the NEA. Although the organization lacked real political power, it was influential because its membership of professional educators held strategic positions in school systems around the country. Through official policy statements and informal contacts, the NEA exerted a great deal of national influence until the 1940s and 1950s. As the power of the NEA over national educational policy declined, the organization underwent dramatic change, and in the 1960s and 1970s, it emerged as more powerful than the AFT, the other of the two teachers' unions.

Before the Depression, the primary influence of the federal government over national educational policy was through its support of vocational education, as mandated by the 1917 Smith-Hughes Act. The Smith-Hughes Act was a response to concern over the United States's role in international trade (see Chapter 7). In this case, the federal government intervened in educational policy to protect an identified national interest. Federal intervention in education increased during the Depression, when unemployed youth became a national problem. In the 1940s and 1950s, the cold war created a framework for massive federal intervention, and as a result, the federal government replaced the NEA as the major source of national educational policy.

The second major cause for the increased role of the federal government was the civil rights movement of the 1950s and 1960s, which attempted to rectify the discriminatory actions of local school administrators and community elites. Factors contributing to racially segregated education were testing, differentiated curricula, laws in southern states requiring segregation, and school-attendance zones in areas outside the South. The nature of control of local schools forced minority groups to bypass local government and seek redress and protection from the federal government.

In summary, the political world of education in the early twentieth century included alliances between school administrators and local business elites, alliances between some urban teachers and trade unions, an alliance between school administrators and college professors to keep the NEA from serving as a teacher welfare organization, and a growing grass-roots movement to end segregation in the schools. National educational policy was formulated in the hallways of the NEA and was spread through the informal networks of school administrators and college professors.

In this chapter, these political developments are covered up to World War II, when inherent tensions began to break down many of these alliances, organizational changes started to take place, and the federal government emerged as the major source of national educational policy.

The Politics of Professionalism: Teachers versus Administrators

By the late nineteenth century, low wages, lack of retirement funds, and the scientific-management plans of administrative progressives caused some teachers to seek aid through mutual organization. Low salaries and lack of retirement funds had been persistent problems throughout the nineteenth century. In many ways, because of the number of women who entered teaching after the Civil War, these problems were directly related to other feminist issues of the period. Viewed from this perspective, the early attempts to organize teachers can be considered primarily a women's movement.

The scientific-management reforms of administrative progressives contributed to an increased sense of powerlessness among many teachers. Scientific management institutionalized and provided justification for the traditional educational harem of female schoolteachers ruled by male administrators. Within the hierarchical structure of the new corporate model, teachers were at the bottom of the chain of command. Orders flowed from the top of the administrative structure to the bottom. Teachers became objects of scientific management, having no power or organizational means of directly influencing educational policy. Consequently, one reason teachers began to organize was to gain influence on educational policy.

Many of the early struggles of teachers' organizations focused both on wages and working conditions and on administrative reforms. This was particularly true of the Chicago Teachers' Federation. Organized by Margaret Haley and Catherine Goggin in 1897, this organization was the forerunner of the American Federation of Teachers, established in 1916, and struggled for many years against the reforms of administrative progressives.

The issue of merit pay versus seniority as a means of determining pay scales was a major issue for teachers during this period and has continued to be so throughout the twentieth century. Obviously, administrative progressives tended to favor pay scales based on some scientific determination of teacher quality, and merit pay fit neatly into the concept of meritocracy. On the other hand, teachers tended to favor pay scales based on seniority. They believed pay scales based on a supposedly scientific determination of teacher quality only gave administrators more power and control and considered arguments for scientific assessment of teacher quality to be no more than justifications for administrators rewarding favored teachers.

An excellent study of the development of teachers' organizations is Wayne Urban's *Why Teachers Organized*. He argues that teachers organized for two major reasons: to improve wages and working conditions and to secure seniority. In Urban's words, "First, teachers organized to pursue material improvements, salaries, pensions, tenure, and other benefits and policies which helped raise teaching in the cities to the status of a career for women who practiced it." In other words, the struggle for increased economic benefits made it possible for women to consider teaching a lifelong career, not just an interim occupation before marriage. In addition, Urban states, "Through the pursuit of salary scales and other policies, teachers sought to institutionalize experience, or seniority, as the criterion of success in teaching."[1]

Urban uses the history of teachers' organizations in Atlanta, Chicago, and New York to support his interpretation. Although these three cities differ in size and location, Urban argues that the teachers' organizations in each shared similar goals and concerns. One common theme was resistance to administrative reforms. This was particularly true in the Chicago Teachers' Federation and the teachers' associations organized in New York City. These organizations resisted not only scientific management but also centralization of power in small school boards, which they considered elitist and anti-immigrant. Consequently, teachers' organizations in these cities struggled against both administrative progressives and urban elites. The resistance to elite takeover of the schools was an important factor in causing some teachers to associate with organized labor, in what was viewed as a common struggle against corporate managers and control by the rich.

From Urban's perspective, these conflicts resulted in differing interpretations of the meaning of *professionalism:* "Teachers sought to preserve their existing employment conditions and therefore labeled attacks on them 'unprofessional,' while administrative reformers labeled their innovations attempts to 'professionalize' the teaching force."[2] Thus, for some teachers, the word *professional* meant greater teacher control of educational policy, and for administrators, it meant improving the quality of the teaching force through scientific management. Administrators thought teachers were acting in an unprofessional manner if they resisted administrative control.

Urban also points out that most teachers' associations in the early part of the twentieth century, in contrast to those in New York and Chicago, tended to be politically conservative and did not join the organized labor movement. As an example, he describes the development of the Atlanta Public School Teacher's Association (APSTA), which was formed in 1905. This organization, he argues, was more typical of most teachers' associations: "The Atlanta teachers' reluctance to formally affiliate with labor and their hesitancy to link their own salary battles to political reforms like women's suffrage were representative of the caution which characterized teachers' associations in most cities."[3]

The goals adopted by APSTA when it was organized remained consistent throughout its first 15 years of existence: improving salaries and working conditions, general promoting of teachers' rights and interests, and providing a means of social contact for teachers. According to Urban, "From 1905 to 1919, the association devoted itself to pursuing higher salaries."[4]

Clearly unlike the Chicago and New York teachers' associations, APSTA avoided taking positions on educational policy issues and forming alliances with organized labor. The organization even avoided involvement in educational policy issues such as promotion of students and grading policies. On the other hand, the association responded rapidly to issues involving wages. For instance, in 1915, the Atlanta Board of Education adopted a merit system of pay in response to pressure exerted by APSTA.

The fight in Atlanta over merit pay illustrates the conservative nature of many of the reforms resulting from the work of administrative progressives. In this case, merit pay was a means of reducing the payroll by $15,000. The savings would come from the anticipated reduction in the salaries of high-seniority teachers considered undeserving of merit increases. To battle against merit pay, the teachers' association became directly involved in school board elections in 1918 and proposed a slate of school board candidates who opposed the policies of the dominant elite. In 1919, in an attempt to strengthen its general political power, APSTA joined the AFT.

Urban's Atlanta example demonstrates the tensions that had developed among teachers, school board members, and school administrators. In this case, the arguments for scientific management through merit pay clearly worked in the interests of those concerned with keeping down the costs of public education. To conservative interests, merit provided a "scientific" means of justifying reductions in teachers' salaries. For school administrators, merit pay strengthened their positions within the educational system by giving them more control over teachers and expanding their range of activity. This situation led naturally to a sharp division of interests between school administrators and teachers, and between teachers and the local power elite.

The lack of a radical political ideology distinguished APSTA and most other teachers' associations from those in New York and Chicago. Although APSTA recognized the differences between their own economic interests and those of the administrators and power elite, it did not conclude that they reflected a more general difference between the economic interests of capital and labor. Organized labor, on the other hand, did articulate its position that the goals of scientific management would turn the worker into a well-controlled and poorly paid employee. From the perspective of organized labor, the differences between teachers and school boards reflected the more general differences between the interests of the worker and of the capitalist, and the desire of elite school boards and school administrators was to deny children of workers a quality public school education through the device of reducing costs.

Although most teachers' associations did not make this radical ideological analysis, the Chicago Federation of Teachers (CFT) did ally itself with organized labor because it believed that workers and teachers shared a set of interests. The ideological position taken by the CFT is important because the efforts of this group were primarily responsible for the formation of the AFT. Also, the political battles of the CFT clearly illustrate the differing economic interests of those who supported and those who rejected the reforms of administrative progressives.

One of the finest studies of the political struggles of the CFT is Julia Wrigley's *Class Politics and Public Schools: Chicago, 1900–1950*. Wrigley's book protrays a sweeping battle in which organized labor and teachers were on one side and conservative business interests and school administrators were on the other. The struggle she depicts involved issues of educational policy in addition to those of wages and working conditions. According to Wrigley, these differences were linked to the opposed interests of capital and labor.

In part, the more radical position of the CFT is explained by its association in 1902 with the Chicago Federation of Labor (CFL). It is impossible to know whether the CFT would have independently maintained a radical perspective. Certainly, its linkage of educational issues with more general political and economic problems made the CFT the most radical teachers' organization in the United States in the early twentieth century. The motivation for the CFT to join the CFL in 1902 was a letter from the president of the CFL that declared, "The time has come for the workingmen of Chicago to take a stand for their children's sake, and demand justice for the teachers and the children so that both may not be crushed by the power of corporate greed."[5] When the CFT aligned itself with the CFL, it told the many teachers who hesitated to take such a bold step that the children of working-class people were more interested in education than was any other group in Chicago. In political terms, the leadership of the CFT saw workers as representing the largest group of organized voters concerned with schooling.

From this perspective, affiliation with organized labor meant increased political power for teachers. Later, this theme was stressed by the teachers' union as the reason for its superiority over the NEA. Even with fewer members than nonaffiliated organizations, labor-affiliated teachers' associations claimed they were in a better bargaining position because they were backed by the money and large membership of organized labor.

Concerns about gaining political power and winning the allegiance of a large block of organized voters spurred the CFT to link its efforts to the women's suffrage movement. Margaret Haley's description of Catherine Goggin, cofounder with Haley of the CFT, captures the spirit of the relationship between the teachers' unions and the women's suffrage movement.

> *[Goggin] brought home to the teachers in her unique, forceful way the revelation of their disadvantage as nonvoters. I remember the effect it had on the audience of teachers when she said, "Why shouldn't the City Council give our money to the firemen and policemen? Haven't they got votes?" There was no doubt but that this incident converted many a teacher to the cause of woman's suffrage.[6]*

Organized labor took definite positions on educational policies that in turn were reflected in the policies of the CFT. For instance, in 1913, the Chicago Federation of Labor and the Illinois Federation of Labor opposed the Cooley bill, a plan for vocational education that would have established a dual school system. Commercial and business groups supported the plan because they wanted the schools to train students to meet their employee needs.

Wrigley reports that the Commercial Club, an organization for the purpose of long-range business planning, hired Edwin Cooley, for whom the legislation was named, to study European systems of vocational education. One objective of the Commercial Club was complete reorganization of the schools as a means of increasing the supply of skilled workers. Cooley was clearly impressed with the vocational schools in Germany. On his return from Europe in 1906, he gave a speech, "Public School Education in Morals," that, according to Wrigley, linked vocational education with the building of morality. He argued that vocational education was necessary because working-class students were not interested in academic subjects. His arguments took on a racist tone when he stated, "In dealing with the moral, intellectual, and social conditions of the inferior races, the statesman of to-day tries to approach them from a practical point of view and to induce them or to compel them to form habits of industry." He continued, "Slavery was wrong, but whatever else it did or did not do, it compelled the acquisition of habits of industry in the slave and marked a step in advance over the previous condition of savagery."[7]

Cooley believed three major virtues should be taught in the schools: industry, punctuality, and obedience. He suggested that punctuality was more important than spelling and that the insistence by the schools "on this virtue is doing much to suppress a certain kind of selfishness and waste that seems to be inseparable from the man or woman who refuses to conform to time regulations." According to Cooley, obedience might be in disfavor in a democracy, but it is the basis for all civilization.[8]

The specific vocational plan developed by Cooley and the Commercial Club called for regular common schooling for all children up to the age of 14, after which children would choose between going to work or entering an academic program. Under the Cooley bill, vocational continuation schools would be established for children who went to work; the children would be released from work activities to attend these schools. The dualism in this program is clear: It separated children who attended full-time academic programs from those who worked and attended part-time vocational schools.

From the first discussions about the Cooley bill, organized labor charged that the true purpose of the legislation was to produce docile workers. At both the local and the state levels, organized labor maintained that children of workers did not necessarily leave school voluntarily but often were forced to work by economic conditions. Organized labor argued that working-class children were being punished by receiving an inferior form of education and that all children should be guaranteed a general education until the age of 16. Organized labor rejected the model of German education because this type of education helped to maintain a class-oriented society. In general, labor argued that employers wanted children to experience a dreary education as preparation for dreary working conditions.

The position of organized labor and the CFT on the Cooley bill exemplifies the economic and political concerns interjected into debates about educational policy. In the end, the Cooley bill was defeated. This was interpreted as proof of the power of organized labor and as evidence for why teachers should join hands with labor organizations.

Progressive administrative reforms were introduced into the Chicago school system during the superintendency (1900–1909) of Edwin Cooley, the same man who authored the Cooley bill. During his administration, Cooley placed the hiring and firing of teachers at the superintendent's level, increased the power of the superintendent's office, tightened the organizational structure of the schools, tied teachers' salaries to examinations and outside course work, and developed an allegedly scientific method of evaluating teachers for promotion. When the Chicago school system began to adopt these administrative methods of scientific management, the CFT joined with other organized labor groups in denouncing the methods as simply a new system to control workers.

The CFT denounced progressive administrative reforms in general, claiming they reduced democratic control of the schools and turned them into institutions to primarily serve the needs of employers. More specifically, teachers were enraged at the idea of promotion based on an efficiency rating. They argued that the proposed secrecy of the evaluation system led to favoritism and to violation of teachers' democratic rights.

According to Wrigley, CFT activism in opposition to scientific management resulted in the appointment by the Chicago Board of Education of Ella Flagg Young as superintendent of schools in 1909. Young was one of the first women in the United States to hold the position of superintendent in a large city. She believed in democratic control of the schools and had excellent rapport with the CFT. It can be argued that her appointment by a conservative school board was an attempt to decrease militancy among teachers. In fact, however, after her appointment, she established teachers' councils as a method of increasing teacher participation and control of the educational system. Young's first major disagreement with the school board was over the issue of vocational education. She opposed the Cooley bill because, in Wrigley's words, "she did not believe 'in training the young to belong to a lower industrial class.'" Young's comments led a local newspaper to claim that she was stirring up class antagonisms. After her attack on the Cooley bill, she began to lose favor in the eyes of school board members. She also resisted board demands that teacher union members be demoted. In 1913, Young was forced to resign her position.[9]

Young's perspective on the nature of teachers' organizations is historically important. At first, she had worried about the affiliation of teachers with organized labor and the general militancy of the CFT, but she claimed these reservations were removed with the unfolding of teacher militancy. At the 1916 convention of the NEA, president of the Chicago Board of Education Jacob Loeb delivered a speech attacking the CTF to which Young replied, "I was not large enough in the beginning to see, I had not the insight to see, that these women were realizing that they had not the freedom, the power, which people should have who are to train the minds of the children." As for the CFT's affiliation with organized labor, Young said she at first thought it was a mistake but later accepted it because it increased the political power of teachers. She argued before the convention:

> They [the teachers] found that in order to get anything done they must have voting power behind them. And they found that the people, the men, in their own station and rank in life, the college-bred men, were not ready to do anything for them; therefore they were compelled to go in with those who had felt the oppression and the grind of the power of riches.

Young concluded her speech by arguing that the cause of disagreements between the teachers and the board of education was "class antagonism."[10]

Young's speech reflects the atmosphere and the language in use during the first decades of the 1900s. In the latter part of the twentieth century, it became unusual for educational leaders to refer to class antagonisms and the power of the rich. In fact, since the 1970s, teachers' unions have tended to adopt a much more conservative approach to social and political issues.

The American Federation of Teachers was formed in 1916 at a meeting of three Chicago teachers' organizations (the CFT, the Chicago Federation of Men's Teachers, and the Chicago Federation of Women High School Teachers) in Gary, Indiana. The membership quickly expanded to include locals from Indiana, New York, Pennsylvania, and Washington, D.C. The American Federation of Labor (AFL) quickly welcomed the AFT into its membership. At the presentation ceremony accepting the AFT into the AFL, Samuel Gompers, president of the AFL, welcomed the new union with the hope that it "may bring light and hope in the lives of American educators, and give and receive mutual sympathy and support which can be properly exerted for the betterment of all who toil and give service—Aye, for all humanity."[11]

Until the 1970s, the AFT was considered the radical alternative to the National Education Association. Certainly, the CFT exemplified the more radical wing of the teachers' movement. Whether radical, like the CFT, or more conservative, like APSTA, all groups involved in the movement to organize teachers shared certain themes. Wages and working conditions were central to the concerns of teachers. Throughout the nineteenth century, low wages had discouraged long-term employment in teaching. Reforms instituted by progressive administrators and school boards did not include increasing teacher salaries as a central focus of concern. In fact, many school boards wanted to keep down the cost of education and opposed salary increases. Certainly, these economic conditions contributed to a feeling among teachers that they needed to organize for increased wages. In addition, teachers were motivated to oppose the attempts of administrators to gain greater control and administrative use of the principles of scientific management.

The movement to establish teachers' organizations added a new dimension to the politics of education in the twentieth century. It created an organizational forum for the expression of tension generated by the reforms of administrative progressives and the continuing problem of low teacher salaries. These new organizations created a political struggle both within the educational establishment and against conservative groups wanting to maintain low teacher salaries and impose a conservative ideology in the schools. The importance of teachers' unions in the politics of education increased in the 1960s, when the unions accepted the use of strikes, and the NEA became a militant teachers' organization.

The Rise of the National Education Association

The National Education Association was formed in 1857 by 10 state teachers' organizations with the common objective of upgrading the teaching profession. By the 1890s, the NEA had become the major leader in formulating educational policies and the center for development of educational policy. The original name of the group, National Teachers' Association, was changed in 1870 to National Education Association. Although the professed goal of the organization was to improve teaching, teachers had a difficult time gaining power within the organization. Nothing better exemplifies the early attitudes of the NEA than the fact that women were excluded during the first year of the organization's existence.

By the 1870s, the NEA had developed into an umbrella organization with four policy-making divisions named after their particular areas of concern—Normal Schools, Higher Education, Superintendence, and Elementary Education. As the NEA evolved, more divisions were added to encompass most areas in education. From about 1890 to the 1950s, general educational policy was formulated through formal and informal contacts within these divisions. In the 1950s, the federal government began to assume the leadership role in national educational policy.

Particularly within the NEA's Department of Superintendence, powerful cliques formed and became part of what David Tyack calls the "educational trust." Their contacts within the NEA and other organizations allowed administrative progressives to spread their reforms—which, as discussed earlier, were from the top down.

Attempts were made within the organization in the early twentieth century to get the leadership of the NEA to concentrate on teacher welfare issues. Margaret Haley, who had helped to organize the CFT, was a leader in this attempt. As David Tyack and Elisabeth Hansot state in *Managers of Virtue: Public School Leadership in America, 1820–1980*, "Margaret Haley was the main leader among those female militants who challenged the male old guard in the NEA and sought to force them to attend to the concerns of the women teachers who made up the vast majority of the profession." According to Tyack and Hansot, the first signs of Haley's militancy appeared at the 1901 NEA convention, at the conclusion of William T. Harris's remarks on the flourishing condition of public education and the advisability of the rich giving money to the schools. Haley jumped up and attacked the idea of big-business support, arguing that low teacher salaries were the important issue. Harris responded with words reflecting the sexism within the organization and the elitist mentality of its leaders:

> *Pay no attention to what that teacher down there has said, for I take it she is a grade teacher, just out of her school room at the end of the year, worn out,*

tired, and hysterical. . . . It was a mistake to hold NEA meetings at this time of year . . . and if there are any more hysterical outbursts, after this I shall insist that these meetings be held at some other time of the year.[12]

Tyack and Hansot report that Haley envisioned an organization controlled by and operated for the benefit of teachers. She argued that her opponents wanted central control by a small group that was part of a "conspiracy to make a despotism of our entire school system."[13] Greater control by teachers could be achieved only through a reorganization to distribute increased power to the rank-and-file teacher, but the actual reorganization resulted in decreased teacher power. Improvements brought about by teacher activism were the establishment of the Department of Classroom Teachers within the NEA in 1912 and greater attention by the leadership to teacher welfare issues.

By 1917, the NEA had become large enough to warrant hiring its first full-time secretary and moving its headquarters to Washington, D.C. Once located in Washington, the NEA's leaders believed that World War I would offer an excellent opportunity for strengthening relations with the federal government and increasing membership. The decision to work with the federal government was the first step in the forging of close ties between the NEA and educational bureaucrats in the government. As part of the war effort and its desire to work with the federal government, the NEA established the Commission on the National Emergency to publicize its war work in the schools and to develop new ideas about the role of government in education. Several of the commission's ideas became realities several decades later. Federal aid to education is one important and highly debated idea that emerged from the commission. Another proposal called for the creation of a separate department of education in the federal government.

The drive during World War I to increase NEA membership not only was successful, but, ironically, it contributed to the demise of teacher power in the NEA. Between 1917 and 1920, NEA membership increased from 8,000 to 50,000. In the campaign to bring in more members, the NEA leadership organized discussions of a national program for improving teacher salaries and gaining greater support for the schools and called for greater participation by teachers in the administration of the schools. The massive increase in membership led to a reorganization that virtually eliminated teacher power in the NEA for the next five decades.

Prior to its reorganization, NEA conventions were conducted like town meetings, with each member in attendance allowed one vote. Thus, teachers in the city in which the NEA held its convention could attend en masse and cast more votes than the sum of those cast by delegates from other cities. For instance, at the 1918 and 1919 NEA conventions, attendance by local teachers was large enough to defeat plans for reorganization.

The leadership of the NEA proposed a representative form of governance under which each state association would elect delegates to the convention. The plan was to limit voting rights to these elected delegates. Although the leadership argued that more orderly meetings would result, activist teachers did not accept this argument because they felt the reorganization was a threat to teacher power within the NEA. This threat was a reality. In *Why Teachers Organized,* Wayne Urban demonstrates the effect of reorganization on teacher power. He cites as an example the 167 voting delegates from Illinois in the 1920s; of these, 135 were "county and city superintendents, college presidents and professors, or elementary- and high-school principals." Of the remaining delegates, only 14 were elementary school teachers.[14]

Until the 1920 convention, activist teachers were able to defeat reorganization plans by packing the convention with local teachers. These efforts were defeated in 1920, when the convention was held in Salt Lake City, Utah. In a conservative state like Utah, teachers listened to their administrators and bowed to authority. At the convention, teachers voted in town-meeting style to eliminate that voting format in favor of voting by delegates. In addition, state superintendents and NEA state officers were made ex officio delegates. Consequently, the NEA became an organization dominated by administrators, with little power given to teachers.

Urban argues that the takeover of the NEA by administrators was part of the general increase in school administrators' power during the 1920s. He concludes, "The defeat of teachers' power in the NEA was one case among many where teachers lost to the new educational executives. The consequence of reorganization was a large-membership, administrator-dominated NEA which retained that character until the early 1970s."[15]

The NEA continued as a powerful force in the development of educational policy until the rise of federal government power in the 1950s. In the 1950s, when the public schools came under attack and professional educators were blamed for the anti-intellectual state of the schools, the NEA was considered a major source of the problem. And, of course, the 1920 reorganization only increased the tension existing between teachers and administrators. This tension was not eased until the 1960s and 1970s, when the NEA was reorganized into a militant teachers' union.

The Political Changes of the Depression Years

The economic depression of the 1930s caused several major political shifts in the educational world. First, the economic crisis began to split the alliances among local school administrators, school boards, and local elites. Many school administrators and school boards wanted to maintain educational programs in the face of demands by other local leaders to reduce educational spending. Second, the economic pressures of the Depression led some leading educators to advocate use of the schools to bring about a radical transformation of society. This created the image that radicals were taking over the schools, which contributed to right-wing arguments in the 1940s and 1950s that public schools had come under the influence of communism. Last, the federal government introduced new programs to solve the problem of youth unemployment. This expanded the role of the federal government in education and set the stage for later intervention in the 1940s and 1950s. In addition, it created tension between professional educators and the federal government as to each group's role in control of youth.

Jeffrey Mirel's prize-winning essay "The Politics of Educational Retrenchment in Detroit, 1929–1935" is an excellent study of educational politics during the Depression. According to Mirel's study, the Detroit school board resisted demands by the conservative business and financial community to reduce educational spending. Obviously, school administrators supported the position of the school board. What is interesting about this situation is that school board membership was drawn from the same elite group that was demanding reductions in spending.

Mirel points out that the Depression hit the Detroit public schools after a decade of growth and reform. The city's educational program had been expanded to include junior high schools, vocational education, and manual training. Reforms in the administration of the schools paralleled those in other school systems around the country. In addition, the Detroit school system became heavily indebted for construction of new school buildings to accommodate an increasing student population. Between 1920 and 1930, the student population of the school system increased from 122,690 to 250,994, and the number of administrators and teachers increased from 3,750 to 7,525. In 1916, the school board had been reorganized to reduce its membership from 21 members elected by ward to 7 members elected at-large. In Mirel's words, "Where the old Board had had a sizable number of clerks and tradesmen, the new Board was composed entirely of important businessmen, professionals, and, in the case of Laura Osborn, the wife of a prominent attorney."[16]

When the Depression hit Detroit, school revenue plummeted from $17,885,000 in 1930 to 1931 to $12,875,000 in 1932 to 1933. Furthermore, the student population increased, and debts continued from the school-building boom of the 1920s. Faced with these conditions, members of the business and financial community began to call for reductions in teacher salaries and educational programs. The school board accepted the idea of salary reductions but resisted cutbacks in educational programs.

A major demand by the business community was to eliminate "fads and frills" in the schools. In particular, vocational education and kindergarten were singled out as areas that could be eliminated. The board's resistance to these cuts indicates a dedication by board members to the use of the schools to improve the workings of the economic system. In Mirel's words: "Recent scholarship has specifically identified kindergartens, manual training, home economics and athletics as programs designed to shape proper roles and attitudes for future workers and managers. The Detroit school board's [action] to save programs and cut salaries is consistent with that model."[17] The split between school board members and the business community indicates an emerging division at the time between those wanting to solve the problems of the Depression by reducing government spending and those wanting to use the government to protect the economic system.

Other factors complicated these political divisions. On issues other than those involving money, the school board and the business community remained in agreement. For instance, the school board joined with the business community to resist demands by Communist groups to hold weekend rallies in the schools. On the other hand, labor groups and socialists supported the school board's resistance to program cuts. This did not mean that the school board and the socialists had a common ideology, but that both groups were interested, for different reasons, in protecting social institutions.

David Tyack, Robert Lowe, and Elisabeth Hansot stress the tensions that arose between school people and the business community during the Depression in *Public Schools in Hard Times: The Great Depression and Recent Years*. They argue that as the Depression worsened and the public became more critical of business interests, "school leaders attacked their former allies. In part, their new-found hostility stemmed from a common belief that industrial and commercial leaders were spearheading a campaign to cut school taxes." The educational retrenchment proposals of the United States Chamber of Commerce exemplify the growing tension between the business community and public educators. In 1932, all members of the United States Chamber of Commerce received letters from the manager of the organization's finance committee asking for consideration of a range of possible educational cutbacks in their communities. According to Tyack, Lowe, and Hansot, this letter proposed retrenchment through "the elimination of evening classes and kindergartens, the shortening of the school day, an increase in the size of classes, and the imposition of tuition for high school attendance."[18]

Responding to calls for retrenchment by the United States Chamber of Commerce and other business organizations, in 1933 the NEA established the Joint Commission on the Emergency in Education (JCEE). The JCEE and many school administrators believed public relations was the key to fighting retrenchment. The JCEE used the public-relations model as a two-pronged attempt to unite all educators to resist attempts at retrenchment and to provide publicity to persuade the public to support the schools. Tyack, Lowe, and Hansot quote the comments of the superintendent of the Pasadena, California, public schools about the onset of the Depression:

> *The immediate response of the friends of public education was to turn to the public relations agent, the professional public opinion builder, the fashion setter in a desperate and dramatic appeal to rebuild the faith of the American people in public education and to restore the support of public education.*[19]

In their quest for better public relations, the JCEE and Phi Delta Kappa, the honorary education fraternity, analyzed public criticisms of the schools as reported in the popular press. They found the top five criticisms to be as follows: "soft pedagogy, lack of contact with life, overemphasis on vocations, severe discipline and overwork, and neglect of character."[20] These findings were distributed as a mimeographed booklet, "Evaluating the School Program," for the purpose of responding to proposals for cutbacks made by the United States Chamber of Commerce.

The arguments between the JCEE and the United States Chamber of Commerce illustrate the tensions occurring at the national level between professional educators and the business community. As relations grew more strained, some members of the education community began to issue radical critiques of the economic system and to propose using the school as a means of social reconstruction. Although the average local school administrator was not very influenced by these more radical arguments, the business community did express concern that radical educators were taking over the schools. The emerging educational philosophy of social reconstructionism contributed to the collapse of relations between professional educators and the business community.

Social reconstructionism was born in a speech, "Dare Progressive Education Be Progressive?" given by George Counts at the 1932 annual meeting of the Progressive Education Association. A version of the speech was later distributed under the title *Dare the Schools Build a New Social Order?* In his speech, Counts attacked the organization of capitalism as being "cruel and inhuman" and "wasteful and inefficient." He argued that concepts of competition and rugged individualism had become outmoded with the development of science and technology and called for a new economic system that would free people from poverty.[21]

During the 1920s, Counts had criticized business control of boards of education. According to Counts, a major requirement of using the schools to build a new social order was to find a group of leaders whose interests focused on the needs of society and its children. He proposed that teachers assume leadership of the reconstruction of society because their primary allegiance was to children, not to private economic interests. In Counts's vision, teachers would lead children down the path of social reconstruction by openly admitting that all teaching was indoctrination. Once this was out in the open, the teacher could rationally select which principles would be indoctrinated into the child.

Counts recognized that teachers would need to choose between indoctrinating children into a conservative or a progressive economic philosophy and that doing so would require teachers to "combine education with political statesmanship." In *The Progressive Educator and the Depression: The Radical Years*, C. A. Bowers quotes Counts's statement, "I am not over sanguine, but a society lacking leadership as ours does, might even accept the guidance of teachers." Counts went on to exhort teachers to reach for power: "If democracy is to survive, it must seek a new economic foundation . . . natural resources and all important forms of capital will have to be collectively owned."[22]

Members of the NEA quickly picked up the challenge of using the schools to build a new social order. At the 1932 convention in Atlantic City, New Jersey, the NEA Committee on Social-Economic Goals for America issued a report in which direct reference is made to the importance of Counts's *Dare the School Build a New Social Order?* The report, which urges the NEA to assume leadership in constructing the new social order, states, "The NEA is saying, and I hope saying more or less militantly, that a social order can be built in which a social collapse such as the present one will be impossible."[23] The committee's resolution was accepted without major debate by the convention. Although the NEA never assumed militant and radical leadership during the 1930s, the very act of approving the report indicated growing militancy among educators and the association's split from the business community.

A journal called *Social Frontier*, founded in 1934, eventually became the focal point of social reconstructionist writings. According to Bowers, three major themes emerged from the journal's editorial writing: (1) capitalism has failed to fully use science and technology for the benefit of humanity; (2) in the capitalistic system, the profit motive has a negative effect on individual morality; and (3) the current economic order in the United States creates economic insecurity for large groups of people.[24]

It would be difficult to measure the impact of the social reconstructionist movement on American education. The actual number of subscribers to *Social Frontier* was only 3,751, and, in fact, during the Depression years, the public schools never did assume a leadership role in the rebuilding of society. Nonetheless, the social reconstructionist movement did contribute to the image that educational leaders were among the more liberal elements in society. This image only helped to widen the gap between the community of professional educators and the business community.

Federal government involvement in education created another arena of political struggle. One important factor in this struggle was President Franklin D. Roosevelt's dislike and distrust of professional educators. The antagonism between the federal government and professional educators continued through the 1950s. Adding to the conflict was the NEA's demand for federal money without federal control. One important consequence of this political friction was that, except for its funding of a few programs, the federal government gave little aid to the public schools. The majority of federal attention was directed to the problem of youth and youth unemployment. Two of the most important programs to emerge from this concern were the National Youth Administration (NYA) and the Civilian Conservation Corps (CCC).

Both these programs were products of general anxiety about the effect on youth of the Depression. This anxiety can be understood by examining the romantic concept of youth that developed in the twentieth century. Early in the twentieth century, thinking about youth concentrated on the relationship between sexual drives and socialization. Many educators during this period argued that institutions such as the high school needed to direct the sexual-social drives of youth to social service (see Chapter 8).

During the 1920s, youth increasingly were displaced from the labor market and attended school in greater numbers. This, plus all the previously mentioned factors, contributed to the development of a unique cultural style that came to be known as the Jazz Age, or Flapper Era. New forms of dress, music, dance, codes of conduct, and technology emerged. The flapper, jazz, modern dance, a new morality, and the automobile all became part of youth culture. Youth fads of the 1920s centered on the consumption of new products of technology. The automobile provided a form of mobility that had never before existed.

Those concerned with the youth problem often traced the supposed decline of morality, as well as youth's free spirit and rebellion against authority, to the automobile. Lengthy articles and discussions on the automobile and morality appeared in popular magazines. In 1926, the headmaster of the Lawrence School lamented the maelstrom his students would be entering. When he was 18, he said, life had been less difficult because there had been no "prohibition," "ubiquitous automobile," "cheap theater," "absence of parental control," and "emancipation of womanhood."[25]

Many Americans agreed during the 1920s that youth was being led down the path to hell—a place or condition of hedonistic pleasure and liberated sexuality. In 1926, *Forum* magazine published two articles by

members of the younger generation under the title "Has Youth Deterio-
rated?" The affirmative response to this question in one article reflects
concern that unrepressed sexuality led to chaotic and uncivilized disorder. Young people, one of the youthful authors states, "rush in an
impetuous, juvenile stampede, not knowing what lies ahead. They have
hurled aside all conventions; accepted standards are 'nil'. . . .'Liberate
the Libido' has become, through them our national motto." To the author of the negative response, it is important that "beauty and idealism,
the two eternal heritages of Youth, are still alive. It is a generation which
is constituting the leaven in the rapid development of a new and saner
morality." Both articles refer to youth as "us" and stress that the central
concern of youth appears to be sexual standards. As one of the young
writers states,

> *This tremendous interest in the younger generation is nothing more or less
> than a preoccupation with the nature of that generation's sex life. What people
> really want to know about us, if they are honest enough to admit it is whether
> or not we are perverted, whether we are loose, whether we are what they call
> immoral; and their curiosity has never been completely satisfied.*[26]

When the *Literary Digest* conducted a national survey on the younger
generation in 1922, it found an overriding concern with the decline of
sexual morality. The survey questioned high school principals, college
presidents and deans, editors of college newspapers, and editors of
religious weeklies across the country. The editor of the *Moody Bible Institute Monthly* responded to the survey with a declaration that in both
manners and morals, society "is undergoing not a revolution, but a
devolution. That is to say, I am not so impressed by its suddenness or
totalness as by its steady, uninterrupted degeneration." From a college
newspaper editor at the University of Pennsylvania came the opinion
that "the modern dance has done much to break down standards of
morals." Describing life on his campus, the editor complains, "To the
girl of to-day petting parties, cigaret-smoking, and in many cases drink-
ing, are accepted as ordinary parts of existence. . . . She dresses in the
lightest and most flimsy of fabrics. Her dancing is often of the most
passionate nature." A respondent from the Phi Kappa Psi House at
Northwestern University in Evanston, Illinois, sums up the general
mood of the survey: "One outstanding reflection on the young set today is the reckless pursuit of pleasure."[27]

To those who believed that social order depends on properly directing
social-sexual instincts, the new morality of the 1920s represented a direct
threat to the foundations of civilization. However, the frivolous style of
life associated with youth in the 1920s came to an abrupt end when the
Depression struck. Unemployed youth now became a central issue. Like

the other marginal groups—such as blacks—youth were the last hired and first fired. Lacking the seasoned skills of older workers, young people found it increasingly difficult to obtain jobs during a time of high unemployment. According to the 1940 Census, by the end of the Depression, 35 percent of the unemployed were under age 25, whereas only 22 percent of the total employable population fell within that age range.

In 1935, in response to the crises of the Depression, the American Council on Education established the American Youth Commission to investigate the problems of youth in America. In 1937, the chairman of the council offered the following picture: Defining *youth* as individuals between the ages of 16 and 24, he describes a mythical town of Youngsville, which has a population of 200 youths. Within this town, 76 youths have regular jobs, 40 go to school or college, 5 go to school part-time, 28 are married women, and 51 are out of work and out of school. Half of those out of work receive federal aid. Youngsville is also experiencing a major decline in personal health. According to the statistics of the Youth Commission, 1 out of 4 young people in America at the time had syphilis or gonorrhea, and 5 percent were, would be, or had been in an asylum. Added to these problems was the highest crime rate in the country.[28]

One striking characteristic of youth during the Depression was their reported lack of idealism and rebelliousness. Unlike in the past, marginality in the 1930s was not accompanied by affluence but by a desire for economic security. When Howard Bell of the American Youth Commission surveyed the young people of Maryland in the 1930s as a representative sample of all American youth, he found that 57.7 percent of the youth surveyed named lack of economic security as the major problem for young people in America. Concerns about economic security were accompanied by a realization that youth was a special group in society. Bell found "that only one-fourth of the youth believed that there was no youth problem."[29]

A second important condition affecting youth during the Depression was the cultural and social climate of the period. *McCall's Magazine* assigned Maxine Davis to travel around the country and report on the state of youth. Traveling for four months and covering 10,000 miles through the cities and back roads of America, she produced not only articles but also a book in which she labeled the youth of the Depression as the "lost generation." Among the "lost generation," she reports, "we never found revolt. We found nothing but a meek acceptance of the fate meted out to them, and a belief in a benign future based on nothing but wishful thinking." The major problem among the lost generation was lack of economic security. The collective nature of the lost generation, Davis argued, was a product of the psychopathic period in which these young people grew up.

Boys and girls who came of voting age in 1935 were born in 1914. Their earliest memories are of mob murder and war hysteria. Their next, the cynical reaction to war's sentimentality and war's futility. Their adolescence was divided between the crass materialism of the jazz 1920's and the shock of economic collapse. In effect, they went to high school in limousines and washed dishes in college.[30]

In the context of these attitudes about youth, the federal government launched the National Youth Administration (NYA) and the Civilian Conservation Corps (CCC). Of the two programs, the CCC was the more important in terms of future developments because it became a model for youth-corps-type programs. The major goal of the NYA, which was started in 1935, was to relieve youth unemployment by providing economic incentives for returning to school. In a very crass way, the schools were considered to be custodial institutions that could take the pressure off unemployment rates. During the first year of its existence, the program provided $6 a month for high school students, $15 a month for college students whose parents were on relief, and other financial aids to older youth out of school. In addition, institutions were asked to develop special work projects for students receiving NYA aid. Many institutions organized beautification and landscaping projects.

The first CCC camp opened in 1933 amid great hopes that outdoor group living would solve problems of unemployment and implant a spirit of democratic cooperation among the participants, who lived a semimilitary life with reveilles, inspections, and physical training. Some of the leaders of the CCC came from the army and the Forest Service. These leaders believed that a productive adult could be created through hard work, clean living, and discipline. Educators in the camps played a subordinate role to both the camp administrators and the camp's organizational goals.

Participants in the CCC would usually rise at 6:00 A.M. After breakfast and perhaps physical exercise, they would work at planting trees, building bridges, clearing trails, fighting fires, and other types of forestry activities. At the end of the day, members of the CCC could take classes. Attendance at the courses was voluntary, and the subject matter was determined by the choices of the participants. In general, the courses were devoted to either remedial training, vocational education, or general instruction.

In *The Shaping of the American High School: 1920–1941*, Edward Krug argues that the CCC set the stage for a battle between professional educators and members of the federal government over who should control American youth. Although there was no winner of this battle, the consequence was increased strain between the federal government and the educational community. According to Krug, the cause of the problem was that since World War I, educators had placed hopes in the development of a total youth program. The CCC had the potential to be such a program, but it was under the control of the federal government, not the educational establishment. In Krug's words: "It seemed to educators at this point that the country was ready for the total youth program envisioned since the end of the War. Now, with victory in their grasp, the ideologues of social efficiency faced the loss of all this to the extraschool agencies of the New Deal."[31]

The war of educators against the NYA and the CCC was highlighted by the publication of *The Civilian Conservation Corps, The National Youth Administration and the Public Schools* by the Educational Policies Commission in 1941, after the beginning of World War II. The Educational Policies Commission had been organized in 1932 by the Department of Superintendence of the NEA and the Commission on the Social Studies in the Schools. The book recommends that during periods of unemployment, the federal government provide money for public works but not for the purpose of training, and also that federal funds be used under state and local control. The report argues that the CCC and the NYA should be abolished as soon as emergency defense work has been completed and all their functions have been transferred to state and local governments. The book criticizes the federal programs for high costs per enrollee in comparison with the cost of educating a public school student.

Although this book represented a declaration of total war against the New Deal programs, World War II was responsible for their actual demise. Congress, in a desire to eliminate nonwar spending, eliminated appropriations for the CCC in 1942 and the NYA in 1943. In one sense, the war solved the problem of unemployed youth, but the CCC model would remain for years in legislators' minds. Even during the war, government officials searched for some form of total youth program similar to the CCC (see Chapter 10).

Conclusion

As World War II arrived on the scene, the political factions within the world of education were in disarray. Teachers had been organizing for almost half a century for the purpose of improving salaries and working conditions and increasing their power in the educational bureaucracies that had been established by administrative progressives. The strain between teachers and educational administrators would smolder until the 1960s and 1970s, when teachers' associations stepped up their militant activities for better wages and increased teacher power.

The split between local elites and school administrators and between professional educators and the federal government was a major factor in educational politics through the 1950s. During the 1940s and 1950s, professional educators were continually criticized for making the public schools academically weak in comparison with those in the Soviet Union. After World War II, anticommunism and the cold war became issues in the debates between local groups and professional educators and between professional educators and the federal government. The displacement of the NEA's national-policy role by the power of the federal government took on increasing importance. The CCC and the NYA symbolized the growing presence of the federal government in education and the rift between federal policy makers and professional educators. The Depression set the stage for the next round of political battles in education, which were fought at the conclusion of World War II.

Notes

1. Wayne Urban, *Why Teachers Organized* (Detroit: Wayne State University Press, 1982), p. 22.
2. Ibid., p. 41.
3. Ibid., p. 45.
4. Ibid., p. 53.
5. Quoted in Julia Wrigley, *Class Politics and Public Schools: Chicago, 1900–1950* (New Brunswick, N.J.: Rutgers University Press, 1982), p. 34.
6. Quoted in ibid., pp. 34–35.
7. Quoted in ibid., p. 67.
8. Ibid.
9. Ibid., p. 124.
10. Quoted in ibid., p. 127.
11. Quoted in William Edward Eaton, *The American Federation of Teachers, 1916–1961* (Carbondale: Southern Illinois University Press, 1975), p. 17.
12. Quoted in David Tyack and Elisabeth Hansot, *Managers of Virtue: Public School Leadership in America, 1820–1980* (New York: Basic Books, 1982), pp. 186–187.
13. Quoted in ibid., p. 186.
14. Urban, *Why Teachers Organized*, p. 127.
15. Ibid., p. 133.
16. Jeffrey Mirel, "The Politics of Educational Retrenchment in Detroit, 1929–1935," *History of Education Quarterly* 24 (Fall 1984): 325.
17. Ibid., p. 350.
18. David Tyack, Robert Lowe, and Elisabeth Hansot, *Public Schools in Hard Times: The Great Depression and Recent Years* (Cambridge, Mass.: Harvard University Press, 1984), pp. 22, 58.
19. Quoted in ibid., p. 74.
20. Quoted in ibid., p. 75.
21. C. A. Bowers, *The Progressive Educator and the Depression: The Radical Years* (New York: Random House, 1969), p. 15.
22. Quoted in ibid., p. 19.

23. Quoted in ibid., p. 23.

24. Ibid., p. 24.

25. Quoted in Mather A. Abbott, "The New Generation," *The Nation*, 8 December 1926, p. 587.

26. Anne Temple, "Reaping the Whirlwind," *Forum*, no. 74 (July 1926): 21–26; Regina Malone, "The Fabulous Monster," *Forum*, no. 74 (July 1926): 26–30.

27. "The Case against the Younger Generation," *Literary Digest*, 17 June 1922, pp. 40–51.

28. "Outlook for Youth in America: Report on Panel Discussion," *Progressive Education*, no. 14 (December 1937): 595.

29. Howard Bell, *Youth Tell Their Story* (Washington, D.C.: American Council on Education, 1938).

30. Maxine Davis, *The Lost Generation* (New York: Macmillan, 1936), p. 4.

31. Edward A. Krug, *The Shaping of the American High School: Vol. 2, 1920–1941* (Madison: University of Wisconsin Press, 1972), p. 325.

10

Education and National Policy

After World War II, American schools increasingly were linked to the policy needs of the federal government. The cold war between the United States and the Soviet Union spawned demands for more academic courses in the schools and a greater emphasis on science and mathematics as a means of winning the weapons race with the Soviet Union. This emphasis on science and mathematics was considered essential to producing enough scientists and engineers to keep the United States technologically ahead of the Soviet Union. The federal government's concern with the school's role in the cold war was behind its decisions to continue selective service into peacetime as a means of controlling human resources, to establish the National Science Foundation (NSF), and to pass the National Defense Education Act (NDEA). These actions affected the curriculum of the schools and the educational choices made by students.

During the 1960s, when civil rights and poverty were national concerns, the federal government made education part of a national campaign against poverty. Like common school reforms of the nineteenth century, the federal government's War on Poverty of the 1960s attempted to eliminate poverty through special educational programs. In addition, civil rights legislation gave the federal government the responsibility to ensure that schools were not committing discriminatory actions against minority groups.

The expansion of the role of the federal government in education took place in a climate of strong public reaction against the schools. This negative reaction came from several sources. Immediately following World War II, members of the radical right charged that the schools had been infiltrated by Communists. Right-wing groups demanded the removal of anti-American literature from the schools and the dismissal of left-leaning teachers. At the same time, those committed to victory for the United States in its technological race with the Soviet Union accused the public schools of being anti-intellectual and charged that professional educators had led the schools to ruin.

In addition, the civil rights movement of the 1950s was a grass-roots protest against school segregation and discriminatory educational policies. In 1954, the United States Supreme Court ruled that segregated education was unconstitutional, but the lack of quick enforcement of this ruling by federal officials and the courts convinced minority-group leaders that direct action was required to achieve integrated quality education. Also, civil rights leaders wanted to end all forms of segregation and discrimination. These factors led to the emergence of a political and social protest movement that eventually forced the passage of federal civil rights legislation and special educational legislation. In a political context, by seeking redress against the discriminatory actions of local elites, the civil rights movement was forced to seek aid from the federal government. A major consequence was increased involvement and power of the federal government over local school systems.

Two major historical interpretations of these post–World War II events have been offered. One is presented in Joel Spring's *Sorting Machine: National Educational Policy since 1945*, and the other is put forth by Diane Ravitch in *The Troubled Crusade: American Education, 1945–1980*. The interpretation given in *The Sorting Machine* stresses the expanded role of the corporate liberal state in the management of human resources. Within the framework of this interpretation, selective service, the NSF, the NDEA, and the War on Poverty are considered part of the general trend in the twentieth century to use the schools as a means of cultivating human resources for the benefit of industrial and corporate leaders. This interpretation recognizes the problems and failures of the schools in achieving these goals and the evolving complexity of political relationships in the educational community. Spring's major criticism of educational events is that schools increasingly were used to serve national economic and foreign policies and, as a result, failed to prepare students to protect their political, social, and economic rights.[1]

Ravitch, in contrast, provides a neoconservative interpretation of educational events after World War II. She argues that a major concern after the war was to provide equality of opportunity. "At every level of formal education, from nursery school to graduate school, equal opportunity became the overriding goal of postwar educational reformers." Ravitch does not link the evolution of educational policy with the needs of corporate and industrial leaders. Her major criticisms of events during this period are of the tendency, from her perspective, for the schools to dilute the curriculum and for the civil rights movement to expand its demands for equal treatment for minority groups to include a demand for special treatment to overcome previous discriminatory actions. She is highly critical of affirmative action programs for admission of minority groups to higher education and to employment opportunities. In general, Ravitch agrees with the critics in the 1950s who claimed that the schools had been made anti-intellectual by the control of professional educators.[2]

Spring's and Ravitch's major differences in interpretation are over the relationship between educational events and larger social and economic problems, and the criticism of programs designed to provide special advantages to social groups subjected to discriminatory actions. These differing frameworks lead to differing conclusions. Spring concludes that the major problem for the future is to separate educational policy from other national-policy goals and to develop a philosophy of schooling based on concepts of liberty. *The Sorting Machine* ends with the hope that the book "will aid in an understanding of this issue [that education can be used for liberation or social enslavement] and that we might begin to formulate a national educational philosophy based on individual liberty, not on service to the state or corporate interests."[3] Ravitch concludes her book on an optimistic note, expressing confidence in the steady expansion of educational opportunities:

> *To believe in education is to believe in the future, to believe in what may be accomplished through the disciplined use of intelligence, allied with cooperation and good will. If it seems naively American to put so much stock in schools, colleges, universities, and the endless prospect of self-improvement and social improvement, it is an admirable, and perhaps even a noble, flaw.*[4]

A discussion of the effect of the cold war on education, the civil rights movement, and the War on Poverty follows.

The Cold War and National Educational Policy

Interrelated social and political problems and public criticism of the schools shaped national educational policy after World War II. First was the persistent youth problem. World War II had ended the Depression problem of youth unemployment, but government policymakers feared that the end of the war and the return of members of the armed forces to the labor market would create new mass unemployment. Second, the split between professional educators and the business community that occurred during the Depression widened. The conflict further intensified when the academic community and federal officials criticized control of the schools by professional educators, claiming control by this group had made the schools anti-intellectual and turned them into the weakest link in America's defense against the Soviet Union. Third, public criticism of the schools increased when the radical right charged that American education had been infiltrated by Communists. Finally, the cold war arms race generated demands by government and industry that the schools educate more scientists and engineers. All these factors became interwoven to form educational policy in the 1940s and 1950s.

During World War II, President Franklin D. Roosevelt wanted to solve the youth problem and maintain world peace by requiring universal military training for all males. This concept of a year of service had existed since World War I and had been one reason for the formation of the CCC during the Depression. In June 1945, the congressional Select Committee on Postwar Military Policy proposed a training plan that would "be universal and democratic, applicable to rich and poor alike, and with a minimum of exceptions." After Roosevelt's death in 1945, President Harry S Truman quickly seized the banner of universal military training and proposed one year of training for all American youth. Truman believed that universal training would be a panacea for many of America's problems. He told a joint session of Congress that a plan of this type would provide for national security and "raise the physical standard of the Nation's manpower . . . lower its illiteracy rate, and . . . develop in our young men the ideals of responsible American citizenship."[5]

When Truman urged the establishment of a plan for universal training, Congress expressed little enthusiasm for such legislation. Congress was hoping to solve any unemployment problems by providing funds for returning members of the military to attend school. Like NYA and CCC programs during the Depression, this approach to unemployment relied on reducing the available labor force by having large numbers of the population attend school rather than enter the labor market. Congress passed the Servicemen's Readjustment Act of 1944 (commonly known as the GI Bill of Rights) with provisions for educational benefits. Under the terms of the legislation, veterans would receive support for tuition, books, and living expenses. The legislation had a major impact on college enrollments. In 1945, 1,013,000 veterans attended college, doubling the existing college population. In the seven years in which benefits were provided, 7.8 million veterans received some form of post-secondary education.

Although the GI Bill solved part of the problem of youth unemployment, calls for universal service continued until the early 1950s, when the Korean War provided a final impetus for serious consideration of universal training. The drama that led to passage of the Universal Military Training and Service Act of 1951—legislation that directly affected the lives of young American men for the next two decades—began on the morning of January 10, 1951. On that day, Senator Lyndon B. Johnson, chairman of the Preparedness Subcommittee of the Committee on Armed Services, opened hearings on universal military service. The committee was in session for over three weeks. The major problem it considered was how to balance security needs for more engineers and scientists with military needs. The agenda included debate of the concept that universal military service could be used to channel and control the distribution of human resources in American society.

The major witnesses testifying before the committee were officials of the Department of Defense and representatives of the academic and scientific establishments, all of whom agreed on compulsory military duty but differed on how deferments should be used for channeling human resources. The university community, of course, was concerned that a sudden introduction of universal training would greatly reduce college enrollments during the first years of operation, causing serious disruption and economic strain on universities. The Department of Defense feared it would be required to handle "all" American youth and wanted assurance that only individuals qualified to serve in the armed forces would be drafted.

Also, opposition to drafting all men came from the scientific establishment, which wanted potential scientists and engineers deferred from service. The scientific establishment included the growing number of scientists who, during and after World War II, began to move freely among centers of power in government, industry, and the military. These scientists began to exert a growing influence on national policies, and in discussions about human resource development and education, their point of view was received with a great deal of sympathy. Charles A. Thomas, chairman of the Scientific Manpower Advisory Committee of the National Security Resources Board and executive vice president of Monsanto Corporation, appeared before Lyndon Johnson's Preparedness Subcommittee in January 1951. The Scientific Manpower Advisory Committee, established to advise the president of the United States, included leaders from the military, industry, and the academic community. The group proposed the deferment each year of 75,000 men, who would receive education as scientists and engineers, and additional deferments for those attending graduate school.

Vannevar Bush and James B. Conant, two other important representatives of the scientific establishment, also supported universal training. Bush and Conant had worked together on scientific research for the federal government during World War II and had been architects of the government's scientific policies during and after the war. Both had also worked for the establishment of the National Science Foundation (NSF). In 1944, President Roosevelt asked Bush to prepare a plan for continued government involvement in research after the war. Bush responded with an enthusiasm reflecting his own belief that science was the panacea for the world's problems.

Bush had unlimited faith in the power of science and technology to improve society. Even in his autobiography, written during the turmoil and student rebellions of the 1960s, he expressed faith that science and technology would end poverty, save the environment, and serve as the foundation stone of a better world. In 1945, Bush issued his reply to the president in a report with the glowing and hopeful title *Science—The Endless Frontier*.[6] Bush argued that continuation of basic scientific research was essential for maintaining full employment, world leadership, national security, and national health. The keys to increasing scientific capital were, first, to ensure that large numbers of men and women received scientific training, and, second, to support basic scientific research in colleges, universities, and research institutes. This could be accomplished, Bush felt, through the establishment of a National Science Foundation that would become a focal point for planning and supporting a scientific work force.

Two important functions of the NSF in addition to supporting basic research, as envisioned by Bush, were to improve science education in the public schools and to establish a system of undergraduate and graduate fellowships for training and scientific research. Bush believed that the improvement of science teaching in high schools was imperative if latent scientific talent were to be properly developed. He viewed the prospect of high school science teachers' failing to awaken interest or provide adequate instruction as a great danger. The NSF had an important effect on public education in later years, when the foundation began to support studies of science curricula and helped to introduce many new programs into the public schools.

Bush appeared before the Senate Preparedness Subcommittee in 1951, shortly after the passage of the National Science Foundation Act of 1950. The primary conflict in the battle to establish the foundation focused on the issue of executive versus independent control. The first act to establish a National Science Foundation was passed by Congress in 1947 but was vetoed by President Truman because he felt the board of the foundation was given too much independent power and he wanted the director to be appointed by the president. When the 1950 bill passed, Bush claimed that he was able to convince Truman not to veto it by arguing that an independent board with the power to select its own director would have an easier time working with the university community. The establishment of the NSF did not dissuade Bush from seeking additional measures to increase the number of scientists.

Bush's testimony before the Senate subcommittee was given in the name of a group called the Committee on the Present Danger. This group believed the first key step in the free world's defense was military manpower legislation that would act "both as a deterrent to a major aggression and as a defense if war should come."[7] The membership of this group included 33 important leaders from the military, industry, and universities.

James B. Conant, then president of Harvard University and the first chairman of the board of the NSF, also testified for the Committee on the Present Danger in support of universal military training and the channeling of human resources into science and engineering. Conant, like Bush, represented the new breed of scientists who were gaining influential positions and exerting power over national policy. Conant was an important figure in discussions on the channeling of human resources because of his leadership role in science and his later study of the American high school. His support of universal military training and the channeling of manpower provided the basic framework for his discussions about the American high school.

Conant's ideas on the channeling of human resources were given before a congressional hearing in 1947, when he was asked to testify in favor of legislation supporting the establishment of the NSF. Conant told the committee that his primary concern was to secure provisions for granting scholarships and fellowships: "It is men that count. And today we do not have the scientific manpower requisite for the job that lies ahead."[8]

For Conant, it was most important to tap the latent talent of many high school students who either did not enter a scientific career or were unable to pursue a college education because they lacked financial resources to do so. A system of scholarships would ensure that superior high school students who needed financial aid could continue their education. During the discussion, one member of Congress asked Conant if he thought the public schools could accomplish more toward channeling scientific human resources if they set apart superior students and gave them special training. Conant replied that this was already being done to a certain extent in the public schools but required a greater emphasis. To emphasize the importance of this idea, Conant submitted an abstract of a speech he had given two days earlier to the American Association of School Administrators titled "The Dilemma of American Education."

The dilemma, as described by Conant, was similar to the dilemma facing those considering universal military training: How do you make treatment equal but at the same time make provisions for channeling superior human resources into needed occupations? Conant never resolved the dilemma, but he did suggest that "we pay a price for the fundamental democracy of our undifferentiated system of public schools . . . if we are wise the price need not be as high as it is at the present moment." For Conant, reducing the price of providing democratic schools meant increasing their role as social sorting institutions; this would be accomplished by placing greater emphasis on the guidance and counseling of superior students and by setting a greater intellectual pace for these students, who would be required to take four years of mathematics and three years of a foreign language and to gain a mastery of the English language. These superior students would be the pool from which scholars would be selected to receive federal subsidies for higher education. Conant made it clear to the congressional committee that he did not advocate a federal subsidy to enable *all* students to attend college—only to allow superior students to enter professions considered necessary to national interests.

Out of the hearings held by Lyndon B. Johnson came a plan for universal training that satisfied the concerns of both the scientific establishment and the academic world. The legislative compromise involved amending selective service legislation from World War II instead of passing entirely new legislation. The amendments of 1951 provided for the control and channeling of human resources by authorizing the president to defer individuals whose academic training was necessary to the national health, safety, or security interests. College students could be deferred by receiving a certain score on the national Selective Service College Qualification Test or by maintaining a certain class rank. Ultimate power over the system was placed in the hands of local draft boards, and restriction of presidential power was ensured by specifically exempting draft boards from the obligation to defer students solely on the basis of federally established criteria.

The 1951 amendments to the Selective Service Act established the major form of government youth policy in effect in the 1950s and 1960s. Young males could chose either to remain in school or to serve in the armed forces. Complaints about the inequalities inherent in the system began within a year after the passage of the amendments. Obviously, the system favored those who were able to attend universities and colleges, which often meant that the poor went into the military, while the middle class and the rich attended college.

Administrators of colleges and universities were pleased with the selective service amendments because they guaranteed an increasing student population. In fact, by the late 1960s, when the selective service system was abandoned, the number of college graduates had increased to a point of flooding the labor market. The result was educational inflation—that is, a decline in the economic value of a college degree in the labor market. As a system of controlling human resources, selective service failed because it was based on the erroneous assumption that channeling talent into higher education would result in increased economic growth.

Both Conant and Bush were satisfied with the selective service legislation because it promised to channel more youth into science and engineering, but they also feared that public schools were not academically advanced enough to meet the challenge of the cold war. In part, the NSF was designed to provide some impetus for public schools to emphasize science and mathematics, but it did not answer all concerns about the academic quality of American schools. Consequently, Conant and Bush joined the chorus of voices raising doubts about the academic quality of American schools. Two major groups led public criticism of the school system. One group, the radical right, linked the alleged decline of academic standards to Communist infiltration of American education. The other group, primarily from the academic community, claimed that professional educators were anti-intellectual and that scholars should have the major influence over the public school curriculum.

The fears caused by the cold war made the public receptive to the radical right's criticisms. In 1951, the executive secretary of the NEA's National Commission for the Defense of Democracy through Education reported in a slightly hysterical tone that the number of "attacks" on public schooling had increased rapidly since the closing days of World War II. According to the commission's survey, the pace of "attack" was so swift that more than twice as many attacks had occurred in the three-year period since 1948 as in the three-year period before 1948. The phraseology and reaction of educators often made them appear as warriors doing battle with an enemy that was storming the walls of the public schools. Words like *attack, counterattack,* and *siege* were hurled around in describing the plight of the professional educator. The executive secretary of the National Commission for the Defense of Democracy through Education, in reporting the increasing criticism of the schools, exemplified the battle mentality. He stressed that the "attacking groups are not as dangerous as they seem. . . . But we all need to be alarmed as were the Minute Men by Paul Revere in 1775." He went on to call the educational troops together with this plea: "If, like the Minute Men, we are ready to carry out individual responsibilities of intelligent group planning, professional unity, organized action, and friendly contact with our allies, we will be as successful in defending our cause as were the gallant men at Concord."[9]

The incident that put right-wing attacks on the schools into the national press and probably left other school administrators in a state of apprehension was the forced resignation in 1950 of Superintendent Willard Goslin of Pasadena, California. Goslin was a national figure in professional education circles, having served in 1948 as president of the American Association of School Administrators. In 1949, when Goslin proposed a tax increase, members of the local community mounted an attack charging that the schools had fallen under the control of communism. This charge, plus the publicity it aroused, forced Goslin's resignation.

The anti-Communist campaign directed at Superintendent Goslin was based on pamphlets distributed by the National Council for American Education, headed by Allen Zoll—one of many national organizations focusing attention on subversion in the schools. Other organizations of this type included the American Coalition of Patriotic Societies, the American Council of Christian Laymen, the Anti-Communist League of America, the California Anti-Communist League, the Christian Nationalist Crusade, Defenders of American Education, the Daughters of the American Revolution, and the Sons of the American Revolution.

Zoll organized the National Council for American Education in 1948. He reportedly began his crusade with the "Michigan statement": "We form hell-raising groups to find out what is being taught in the schools, and then we raise hell about it." Pasadena, of course, was not the only community influenced by Zoll's pamphlets. In 1951, the *Saturday Review of Literature* devoted a large section of its education issue to school controversies around the country. In Denver, Colorado, Zoll's pamphlets, including one titled *The Commies Are after Your Kids*, supposedly provided a good deal of ammunition for local citizen groups. In Englewood, New Jersey, and in Port Washington, New York, Zoll's writings reportedly exerted a significant influence. In Pasadena, the Zoll pamphlet that attracted attention was *Progressive Education Increases Juvenile Delinquency*, which stated that "so-called progressive education, shot through as it is with the blight of Pragmatism, has had a very deleterious effect upon the original character of American education."[10]

The textbook industry was also being charged with Communist infiltration. In 1949, Lucille Cardin Crain began issuing a quarterly newsletter, the *Educational Reviewer*, which had as its goal the weeding out of subversive material from public school textbooks. Her first target was a popular high school text, *American Government* by Frank Abbott Magruder. She claimed that Magruder's view of democracy led "straight from Rousseau, through Marx, to totalitarianism" and that the book gave a very favorable view of the workings of the government of the Soviet Union. Convinced that the text was designed to undermine the free-enterprise system, she gave wide circulation to her critique of the book. Her arguments eventually reached the ears of national radio commentator Fulton Lewis, Jr., who used portions of Crain's analysis on a coast-to-coast broadcast and added a scare statement: "That's the book that has been in use in high schools all over the nation, possibly by your youngster."[11]

Other groups joined in the work of the *Educational Reviewer*, including Allen Zoll's National Council for American Education, the Daughters of the American Revolution, the Sons of the American Revolution, and the Guardians of American Education. These groups published their own lists of subversive books and texts. Throughout the country during the 1950s and 1960s, community members armed with one of these lists would demand that certain subversive books be removed from library shelves and from the curriculum of the school. Suggestions were even made that textbook writers be required to take a loyalty oath. These actions alarmed the textbook industry, and in 1953, an official statement of the American Textbook Publishers Institute warned against a loyalty oath for authors because it would lower the quality of textbook authorship and material. The institute claimed that the highly individualistic and competitive system in the textbook industry provided adequate safeguards against "the deliberate introduction of harmful or subversive material." To curb local attacks, it recommended that states establish public agencies to monitor complaints about textbooks.

The academics' attack against the public schools was led by historian Arthur Bestor. In 1952, he delivered a paper at the annual meeting of the American Historical Association titled "Anti-Intellectualism in the Schools: A Challenge to Scholars." As part of his presentation, Bestor submitted a series of proposals based on a detailed resolution he had drafted and started to circulate among scholarly friends for their approval and signatures. By the time of the meeting, he had collected 695 signatures. Of the signatories, 199 were historians; 93 were in English; 86, in biological sciences; 77, in mathematics; and the others, in a variety of academic fields. The preamble of the resolution expressed alarm at the "serious danger to American intellectual life arising from anti-intellectual tendencies" and the "anti-intellectualist conceptions of education among important groups of school administrators and educational theorists." The actual resolutions proposed a close working relationship between the scholarly community and professional educators.

What prompted Bestor to prepare his resolution was the life-adjustment education movement that was launched in 1945 at a conference sponsored by the Vocational Education Division of the United States Office of Education. At this meeting, a well-known leader of vocational education, Dr. Charles Prosser, introduced the following resolution: "The vocational school of a community will be able better to prepare 20 percent of the youth of secondary school age for entrance upon desirable skilled occupations; and . . . the high school will continue to prepare another 20 percent for entrance to college." The question in Prosser's mind was what to do with the other 60 percent. He gave the following answer in his resolution: "We do not believe that the remaining 60 percent of our youth of secondary school age will receive the life-adjustment education they need . . . unless . . . the administrators of public education with the assistance of vocational education leaders formulate a similar program for this group."[12]

Bestor's anger was sparked by copies of the life-adjustment education materials distributed by the Illinois Secondary School Curriculum Program. He quickly recognized and criticized the methods used by educators to sell life-adjustment curricula to the public. In his criticisms of the public schools, Bestor quoted from the Illinois materials: "Given the American tradition of the local lay-control of public education, it is both necessary and desirable that a community (patrons, pupils, teachers) consensus be engineered in understanding support of the necessary changes before they are made."[13] Bestor responded, "We approach here the real meaning of what educationists euphemistically describe as 'democracy in education.' It is the democracy of the 'engineered consensus.' " He concluded that control of the educational system was not in public hands, but in the hands of professional educators or, as he referred to them, "educationists."[14]

Life-adjustment education also convinced Bestor that professional educators were responsible for the anti-intellectual quality of American schools. He notes, for example, that in one of the Illinois documents, "Problems of High School Youth," an overwhelming proportion of problems cited deal with what he calls trivia and that no mention is made of mathematics, science, history, or foreign languages. In the list of 55 "Problems of High School Youth," he cites as trivia such items as "the problem of improving one's personal appearance"; "the problem of selecting a family dentist"; "the problem of developing one or more 'making things,' 'making it go,' or 'tinkering' hobbies"; and "the problem of developing and maintaining wholesome boy-girl relationships."[15]

Bestor wanted the public schools to reject the traditional emphasis on socialization and the social-sorting function of schooling. From his perspective, curricula should be organized around traditional subject-matter disciplines. In the schools, he argues, "the important books must be read. . . . Fundamental problems must be studied, not merely talked about."[16] This would occur in a climate where the basic scientific and scholarly disciplines were presented as systematic ways of thinking, with each discipline organized around a structure and methodology of its own. The disciplines to be studied would include mathematics, science, history, English, and foreign languages.

Bestor rejected the notion of a differentiated course of study based on the future social destination of the individual. He accepted the existence of differences in intellectual ability among students, but argued, in reference to students of lower mental ability, "Most of them, I believe, can be brought at a slower pace along the same route."[17] Elimination of the emphasis on socialization and the sorting of human resources in the schools, Bestor felt, could curb the tide of anti-intellectualism in society by creating a new respect in the student and in the home for knowledge and cultural achievement.

In 1952, the American Historical Association was unable to reach a consensus on Bestor's proposal. In its place was substituted a weakly worded resolution supporting Bestor's basic concerns and calling for further study of the possibility of working with other learned societies. Undetered by the setback, Bestor searched for another means of implementing his ideas. In 1956, he helped to organize the Council for Basic

Education and became its first president. Shortly after the founding of this group, Mortimer Smith became its executive director and the major dynamic force behind the operations of the organization.

Within a short time after Bestor's initial criticism, a chorus of other voices joined in condemning the schools and their control by professional educators. Alan Lynd's *Quackery in the Public Schools*, published in 1953, criticized the anti-intellectual quality of college and university courses in teacher education. He blamed this situation on control of higher education by professional educators.

Smith made his views known nationally in two publications: *And Madly Teach: A Layman Looks at Public School Education* (1949) and *The Diminished Mind: A Study of Planned Mediocrity in Our Public Schools* (1954). Smith, like his colleagues, charged the schools with anti-intellectualism and domination by the professional educator, but he gave greater emphasis to the idea that the schools were undemocratic. Bestor had complained that a differentiated curriculum was undemocratic because it did not allow the schools to prepare students equally for participation in the world. For Smith, a differentiated curriculum worked against the functioning of a democratic society because it resulted in inequality of individual educational development.

The most widely heard of the critics in the 1950s was Vice Admiral Hyman G. Rickover, often called the "father of America's nuclear navy." He carried his message of the dismal failure of American schools to such meetings as the one held by the Society of Business Magazine Editors in 1956, the Westinghouse Science Talent Search Award Ceremony in 1957, the Engineering Society of Detroit in 1957, and the Harvard Club of New York in 1958, and finally into a best-selling book, *Education and Freedom*. Admiral Rickover's basic message asserted that the United States was losing the technological and military race with the Soviet Union because America's public schools were failing to identify and adequately educate talented youth as future scientists and engineers. In an interview conducted by news commentator Edward R. Murrow, Rickover stated that education "is even more important than atomic power in the navy, for if our people are not properly educated in accordance with the terrific requirements of this rapidly spiraling scientific and industrial civilization, we are bound to go down. The Russians apparently have recognized this." Like other critics of the time, Rickover blamed professional educators for creating an anti-intellectual atmosphere in the schools and claimed that the schools were the weakest link in America's overall defense strategy.[18]

These attacks on the public schools provided the background for the most significant educational legislation of the 1950s. Throughout the late 1940s and 1950s, educators had been seeking some form of federal legislation to help build schools and pay teacher salaries. Local schools were seriously pressed for space and for money to educate the increasing number of children born in the baby-boom period after World War II. National political leaders failed to respond to these requests by neither passing nor approving legislation for federal aid to local school districts.

Resistance to federal aid to education rapidly disappeared on October 4, 1957, when the Soviet Union launched *Sputnik I*. That the Soviet Union was the first in space indicated to many Americans that America was losing the technological and military race. Of course, the public schools were blamed for the lag in technological development, and voices were lifted to demand a greater stress on mathematics and science.

In 1958, responding to *Sputnik I* and public outcries about conditions in the schools, Congress passed the National Defense Education Act (NDEA). The very name of the legislation defined its intended goals. Before the legislation was passed and immediately after the launching of *Sputnik I*, President Dwight D. Eisenhower had outlined the relationship between education and cold war strategy and set the stage for passage of the legislation.

In Oklahoma City on November 13, 1957, Eisenhower gave a speech pointing out that the Soviet Union had converted itself in only 40 years from a nation of peasants to an industrial nation that had accomplished major technological achievements and established a rigorous educational system. He went on to warn, "When such competence in things material is at the service of leaders who have so little regard for things human, and who command the power of an empire, there is danger ahead for free men everywhere." Eisenhower argued that the United States must meet the Soviet threat on its own terms by outmatching the Soviet Union in military power, technological advancement, and specialized research and education. Essential to a program of national defense was increased military research, which would be directed toward the production of intercontinental ballistic missles. Eisenhower tried to assure the nation that it was well on the way to developing adequate missle power. "Young people now in college," he emphasized, "must be equipped to live in the age of intercontinental ballistic missiles." Specifically, Eisenhower called for a system of nationwide testing of high school students and a system of incentives to persuade students with high ability to pursue scientific or professional studies. He urged a program to stimulate quality teaching in mathematics and science and fellowships to increase the number of teachers.[19]

On January 27, 1958, Eisenhower delivered a special message to Congress outlining his program of education for national defense. The first item on his list of recommendations was a fivefold increase in appropriations for the educational activities of the NSF. Second, he called for reducing the waste of national talent by providing grants to states for improved testing programs and guidance and counseling services. This recommendation eventually became Title V of the 1958 NDEA. Title V appropriated $15 million for each of four succeeding fiscal years for guidance, counseling, testing, and identification of able students. All these programs were considered essential for controlling and developing human resources for the cold war.

Third, Eisenhower recommended federal funds to improve the teaching of science and mathematics through the hiring of additional science teachers and for the purchase of equipment and materials. This became Title III of the NDEA, and it appropriated $70 million for each of the next four fiscal years to be used for equipment and materials and for the expansion and improvement of supervisory services in the public schools in science, mathematics, and modern foreign languages. Eisenhower's fourth recommendation was for a graduate fellowship program to prepare more students for college-teaching careers. This became Title IV of the NDEA and resulted in the National Defense Fellowship program.

The issue of foreign languages and their relationship to national security was the subject of Eisenhower's fifth recommendation. Eisenhower argued: "Knowledge of foreign languages is particularly important today in the light of America's responsibilities of leadership in the free world. And yet the American people generally are deficient in foreign languages, particularly those of the emerging nations in Asia, Africa, and the Near East."[20] The foreign-language sections of the NDEA were clearly seen as provisions to strengthen America's competition with the Soviet Union for influence over the developing nations of the world.

The categorical nature of aid given under the NDEA reflected the government's negative feelings toward professional educators and its decision to take responsibility for establishing educational policies that would serve other national policies, such as defense. At the hearings on the NDEA, the head of the NEA defended the schools and requested that money be appropriated for general use by local schools. On the other hand, there was strong testimony from scientists and other officials not to give general aid to the public schools, given the fact that professional educators had the power to determine the use of the funds. These critics of the schools and educators wanted the federal government to specify the categories under which the money could be used; this was written into the NDEA.

As a consequence, the NDEA became a means by which the federal government could control local educational policy simply by offering money for the establishment of specified educational programs. Local educators did not have to accept the federal money, but few refused because financial conditions in most school districts made them eager for the funds.

Cold war concerns also got the federal government involved in developing new curricula, particularly in the areas of mathematics and science. Money flowing from the NSF was used to develop curriculum materials and to train teachers. The most dramatic development in this area was the "new mathematics," as it was called in the early 1960s. The new mathematics was based on the idea of teaching students basic mathematical concepts such as set theory and functions. When it swept the nation, many parents found themselves unable to understand and to help their children with the material.

In summary, a major effect of the cold war on educational policies was to link the youth issue to selective service and to push the federal government into a leadership role in educational policies. Mounting criticism of the schools, which had begun during the Depression years, created a major split between professional educators and the public. This split widened in the 1960s when the schools were accused of being racist. Another major consequence of the cold war was to emphasize the idea that schooling is the key to the development of human resources and to the distribution of human resources in the labor market. This has continued to be an important theme through the 1980s.

The Civil Rights Movement and School Desegregation

The desegregation of American schools was the result of over a half-century of struggle by the black community. As discussed previously, the NAACP had struggled since its founding in the early part of the twentieth century to end discriminatory practices against minority groups. The school desegregation issue was finally decided by the United States Supreme Court in 1954 in *Brown v. Board of Education of Topeka*. The decision did not bring immediate results because resistance to court-ordered desegregation arose. The frustration caused by the slow pace of school integration and the continuation of other forms of discrimination contributed to the growth of a massive civil rights movement in the late 1950s and early 1960s. The response of national political leaders to the civil rights movement was the enactment of strong civil rights legislation and an effort to eliminate poverty in the United States.

It is important to remember that school desegregation and civil rights legislation were not the products of a benign government but were the result of tremendous struggle and public demonstrations. Politically, minority groups were forced by their lack of power at local and state levels to seek redress for their grievances from the federal government. National leaders tried to avoid dealing with civil rights issues but were finally forced by public demonstrations to take action. With regard to schooling, federal actions resulted in greater federal control of local schools and a feeling among school board members that local control of education was rapidly disappearing.

The key legal issue in the struggle for desegregation was the interpretation of the Fourteenth Amendment to the Constitution. This constitutional amendment had been ratified in 1868, shortly after the close of the Civil War. One of its purposes was to extend the basic guarantees of the Bill of Rights into the areas under state and local government control. The most important and controversial section of the Fourteenth Amendment states: "No State shall make or enforce any law which shall abridge the privileges or immunities of citizens . . . nor . . . deprive any person of life, liberty, or property, without due process of law; nor deny to any person within its jurisdiction the equal protection of the laws."

A major test of the meaning of the Fourteenth Amendment with regard to segregation occurred in 1895 in a Supreme Court case involving Homer Plessy, who was one-eighth black and seven-eighths white and had been arrested for refusing to ride in the "colored" coach of a train, as required by Louisiana law. The Supreme Court ruled that segregation did not create a badge of inferiority if segregated facilities were equal and the law was reasonable. In establishing the "separate but equal doctrine," the Supreme Court failed to clearly define what constitutes equal facilities and what is reasonable.

The overturning of the separate but equal doctrine and a broader application of the Fourteenth Amendment came in 1954 in the historic and controversial Supreme Court decision *Brown v. Board of Education of Topeka*. In 1953, *Brown* was one of five school segregation suits to reach the Supreme Court. It became the first case simply because the five cases were heard in alphabetical order. The *Brown* case began in 1951, when Oliver Brown and 12 other parents represented by NAACP lawyers brought suit to void a Kansas law that permitted but did not require local segregation of the schools. In this particular case, Oliver Brown's daughter was denied the right to attend a white elementary school within 5 blocks of her home and forced to cross railroad tracks and travel 21 blocks to attend an all-black school. The federal district court in Kansas ruled against Oliver Brown, using the argument that the segregated schools named in the suit were substantially equal and thus fell within the separate but equal doctrine.

In preparing its brief for the Supreme Court, the NAACP defined two important objectives: to show that the climate of the times required an end to segregation laws and to show that the separate but equal doctrine contained a contradiction in terms—that is, that separate facilities were inherently unequal. Evidence from recent findings in the social sciences presented by the NAACP to prove that separate facilities were inherently unequal provided the basis for overturning the separate but equal doctrine. It also caused a storm of protest alleging that the Supreme

Court was basing decisions on nonlegal arguments. Throughout the South, it was widely believed that the Court was being persuaded by Communist-oriented social scientists. Billboards appeared on highways demanding the impeachment of Chief Justice Earl Warren for his role in subverting the Constitution.

The Supreme Court argued in the *Brown* decision, "In the field of public education the doctrine of 'separate but equal' has no place. Separate educational facilities are inherently unequal." To support this argument, the Supreme Court wrote one of the most controversial single sentences ever to appear in a Court decision: "Whatever may have been the extent of psychological knowledge at the time of *Plessy v. Ferguson* this finding is amply supported by modern authority."[21]

Two social scientists, Kenneth Clark and Gunnar Myrdal, had a major influence on the Court's decision. Clark, a social psychologist at the College of the City of New York, acted as general social-science consultant to the NAACP. His central argument, and the one given in the NAACP brief to the Court, was that officially sanctioned segregation by a state or local government organization caused personality damage to the children of both minority and majority groups. Minority-group children became aware of their inferior status and often reacted with feelings of inferiority and a sense of personal humiliation. This created internal conflict between a need for a sense of personal worth and the lack of respect provided by the majority group. As a means of coping with this conflict, Clark argued, certain patterns of behavior develop that are related to the socioeconomic class of the minority child. "Some children," the argument states, "usually of the lower socio-economic classes, may react by overt aggressions and hostility directed toward their own group or members of the dominant group. Antisocial and delinquent behavior may often be interpreted as reactions to these racial frustrations."[22]

Clark and the NAACP claimed before the Supreme Court that segregation caused behavioral patterns that led to crime and violence among lower-class blacks. For middle- and upper-class minority children, they claimed, racial segregation was likely to result either in withdrawal and submissive behavior or in rigid conformity to middle-class values and standards. Racial segregation was believed to cause a lowering of morale and depression in the level of educational aspirations for all minority-group children. For majority-group children, they stated, "confusion, conflict, moral cynicism, and disrespect for authority may arise . . . as a consequence of being taught the moral, religious and democratic principles of the brotherhood of man . . . by the same persons and institutions who, in their support of racial segregation . . . seem to be acting in a prejudiced and discriminatory manner."[23]

Another major influence on the Court's decision was Gunnar Myrdal's book *An American Dilemma*. Myrdal, a Swedish social scientist, had been invited in 1937 by the Carnegie Corporation of New York to do a study of the social conditions of blacks in the United States. The major thesis of the resulting book is that Americans faced a major moral dilemma between the ideals of American democracy and the actions regarding race relations. He defines the "American Dilemma" as the conflict between "the valuations preserved on the general plane . . . of the 'American Creed'" and "the valuation on specific planes of individual and group living." This dilemma, Myrdal argues, has a direct effect on behavioral patterns. People who act in conflict with their belief in the American Creed need to find a means of defending their behavior to themselves and others. This is accomplished by twisting and mutilating social reality and by producing emotionally loaded rationalizations for particular behavior. As a result of this distortion of social reality, firmly entrenched popular beliefs developed concerning blacks, which the study states are "bluntly false and which can only be understood when we remember the opportunistic ad hoc purposes they serve."[24] The purpose of the study was to undercut these false belief systems and help to end the American Dilemma by providing a true picture of social reality and a careful depiction of the actual conditions of American black people.

In 1955, the Supreme Court issued its Enforcement Decree for the desegregation of schools. One problem facing the Court was the lack of machinery for supervising and ensuring the desegregation of vast numbers of segregated school districts. The Court resolved this problem by relying on federal district courts as the determiners of equitable principles for desegregation. Federal judges were often part of the social fabric of their local communities and resisted attempts at speedy desegregation. Consequently, integration occurred at a slow pace until additional civil rights legislation was passed in the 1960s and the mounting frustrations in the black community fed the flames of a militant civil rights movement.

The evolution of mass media in the 1950s was an important factor in the civil rights movement because it became possible to turn local problems into national issues. Thus, even though presidents had traditionally shown a great deal of deference to the important white southern political structure, the emergence of the mass media as a powerful force allowed both the federal government and civil rights groups to put unprecedented pressure on southern political leaders, forcing them to comply with national civil rights legislation. In fact, enforcement of the Supreme Court school desegregation ruling depended in large part on civil rights groups making effective use of television. In one sense, the struggle that took place was a struggle between public images. Concern over America's international image grew as pictures of racial injustice flashed around the world, and the president's public image was often threatened when examples of racial injustice were shown to millions of television viewers and the question was asked, What is our president doing about this situation?

The most dramatic technique used by civil rights groups was nonviolent confrontation. The massive nonviolent response of black people in the South confronted with an array of cattle prods, clubs, and fire hoses wielded by cursing southern law-enforcement units provided dramatic and shocking television viewing for the nation. The Congress on Racial Equality (CORE), the Student Nonviolent Coordinating Committee (SNCC), and the Southern Christian Leadership Conference (SCLC), led by the Reverend Martin Luther King, Jr., provided the national drama and the final push for national civil rights legislation.

The introduction of nonviolent confrontation into the civil rights movement came from the Christian student movement of the 1930s, which, under the leadership of the Fellowship for Reconciliation, was committed to use of the Gandhian technique of *satyagraha* (nonviolent direct action) in solving racial and industrial problems in the United States.

CORE, a major organization in the civil rights movement, was organized at the University of Chicago in 1942. The two basic doctrines of the early CORE movement were commitment to racial integration and the use of Christian nonviolent techniques.

CORE did not rise to national prominence until the late 1950s, when another Christian leader, Dr. Martin Luther King, Jr., made nonviolent confrontation the central drama of the civil rights movement. King was born in 1929 in Atlanta, Georgia, into a family of Baptist ministers. His maternal grandfather had founded the Ebenezer Baptist Church, and his father had made it one of the largest and most prestigious Baptist churches in Atlanta. King entered Morehouse College in Atlanta in 1944, where he claimed to have been influenced by his reading of Henry David Thoreau's *Essay on Civil Disobedience*. He later wrote about the essay, "Fascinated by the idea of refusing to cooperate with an evil system, I was so deeply moved that I reread the work several times. This was my first intellectual contact with the theory of non-violent resistance."[25]

In 1948, King entered the Crozier Theological Seminary in Chester, Pennsylvania, where for the first time he became acquainted with pacifism in a lecture by A. J. Muste. King wrote that at the time he considered Muste's pacifist doctrine impractical in a world confronted by the armies of totalitarian nations. Of more importance to King's intellectual development was his exposure to the social-gospel philosophy of Walter Rauschenbusch, which actively involved the church in social reform as a means of creating a kingdom of God on earth. Although he rejected the optimistic elements in the social gospel, King argued that any concern with the souls of humans required a concern with social and economic conditions.

King also studied the lectures and works of Mohandas K. Gandhi. The Indian leader's work convinced King that the Christian doctrine of love could be a force for social change. King wrote, "Gandhi was probably the first person in history to lift the love ethic of Jesus above mere interaction between individuals to a powerful and effective social force on a large scale." Like the early members of CORE, King became convinced that nonviolent resistance "was the only morally and practically sound method open to oppressed people in their struggle for freedom."[26]

The incident that launched Martin Luther King's civil rights activities and provided scope for his Gandhian form of the social gospel occurred on December 1, 1955. On that date, Rosa Parks, who had worked a regular day as a seamstress in one of the leading department stores in Montgomery, Alabama, boarded a bus and took the first seat behind the section reserved for whites. Later during the journey home, several white passengers boarded the bus. The driver ordered Rosa Parks and three other black passengers to stand so that the white passengers could have seats. Rosa Parks refused and was arrested. The black ministers in the community quickly organized in response to this incident, and on December 5, the Montgomery bus boycott began.

The bus boycott lasted for over a year and finally ended on December 21, 1956, when, after a Supreme Court decision against segregation on buses, the transit system of Montgomery was officially integrated. King emerged from the struggle a national hero among minority groups. In 1957, he organized the Southern Christian Leadership Conference, which became the central organization in the civil rights struggle.

After SCLC was formed, boycotts and nonviolent demonstrations began to occur throughout the South. On May 17, 1957, Martin Luther King gave his first national address in Washington, D.C. He told his audience, "Give us the ballot and we will quietly, lawfully, and nonviolently, without rancor or bitterness, implement the May 17, 1954, decision of the Supreme Court." For King, meaningful school desegregation depended on the power of the black voter.

As civil rights demonstrations increased in intensity, national leaders began to work for federal legislation. In 1957 and 1960, two ineffective forms of civil rights legislation were passed by Congress. The most important civil rights legislation was not enacted until 1964, when violence in Birmingham, Alabama, and a mass march on Washington forced a response from the federal government. The civil rights movement made Birmingham and its director of safety, Eugene "Bull" Connor, symbols of the oppression of black people in the United States. President John F. Kennedy was quoted as saying: "Our judgment of Bull

Connor should not be too harsh. After all, in his way, he has done a good deal for civil rights legislation this year."[27] The March on Washington symbolized to Congress and the American people the growing strength of the civil rights movement and provided the stage for television coverage of speeches by civil rights leaders.

The result of these activities was the Civil Rights Act of 1964. Under 11 different titles, the power of federal regulations was extended in the areas of voting rights, public accommodations, education, and employment. Title IV and Title VI of the legislation were intended to end school segregation and provide authority for implementing the *Brown* decision.

Title VI, the most important section, established the precedent for using disbursal of government money as a means of controlling educational policies. Originally, President Kennedy had merely proposed a requirement that institutions receiving federal funds must end discriminatory practices. In its final form, Title VI required mandatory withholding of federal funds to institutions that did not comply with its mandates. It states that no person, on the basis of race, color, or national origin, can be excluded from or denied the benefits of any program receiving federal financial assistance and requires all federal agencies to establish guidelines to implement this policy. Refusal by institutions or projects to follow these guidelines will result in the "termination of or refusal to grant or to continue assistance under such program or activity."

The power of Title VI rests in its ability to withhold federal money from financially pressed school systems. This became a more crucial issue after the passage in 1965 of the Elementary and Secondary Education Act. The rate of desegregation was more rapid after the 1964 Civil Rights Act than before, but abundant evidence by the end of the 1960s showed that segregated education continued in the South. One political scientist argued that school desegregation in the South by 1968 looked massive compared with the level in the early 1960s, but compared with an ideal of total integration, the actual results could be labeled as token. By defining a segregated school as one where blacks attended and more than 20 percent of the school population was white, a sample of 894 counties in the South found that 5 percent or less of the black pupils

were attending integrated schools in 25 percent of the counties, 10 percent or less in 40 percent of the counties. At a level approaching genuine integration, 90 percent or more of the Black pupils were reported to be attending integrated schools in 20 percent of the counties. For all Southern counties, the median attending integrated school was 15.6 percent.[28]

School desegregation moved at even a slower pace in the North. Originally, it was believed that the *Brown* decision affected only those states whose laws required segregated education. However, by the late 1960s, the courts began to rule that the *Brown* decision applied to all schools in the country, if it could be proved that segregation was the result of intentional actions by school boards or school administrators. In addition, forced integration by busing was ruled by the United States Supreme Court in *Swann v. Charlotte-Mecklenburg Board of Education* (1971) as a legal means of desegregating a school district. In many communities, busing sparked violent demonstrations, and alternative, or magnet, schools became a popular, more conservative, means of integrating school districts (see Chapter 11).

The civil rights movement and the struggle to implement the *Brown* decision constitute the most massive protest against educational policies in the history of the United States. The central plea of the movement was for equal educational opportunity. But as the civil rights movement began to take on the character of a poor people's campaign, national leaders began to search for a means of providing equality of economic opportunity for all people, and, of course, the school was seen as a solution to the problem of poverty in the United States. The civil rights movement provided the impetus for the federal government to launch a war on poverty.

The War on Poverty

The federal government's War on Poverty during the 1960s was reminiscent of the beliefs of nineteenth-century common school reformers that education could reduce social-class divisions and eliminate poverty. In some ways, President Lyndon Johnson can be considered a twentieth-century version of Horace Mann. But the difference between nineteenth-century reformers and twentieth-century leaders is the latter's belief that the schools should develop and sort human resources. By the 1960s, it was commonly believed that discrimination and poverty were the two basic problems preventing the use of the schools as a means of discovering and classifying talent for service to the national economy and national defense. Within this framework, school integration and the elimination of poverty were necessary to ensure unbiased development and selection of human talent.

Congress's response to the issue of poverty was passage of the Economic Opportunity Act of 1964 (EOA) and the Elementary and Secondary Education Act of 1965 (ESEA). Two of the most important programs of EOA were the Job Corps and Head Start. Head Start was established to provide an opportunity for children of the poor to enter the social-sorting process of education on equal terms with children from more affluent backgrounds. The ESEA contained major provisions for improving educational programs for children from low-income families.

The War on Poverty encompassed three major areas of concern: unemployed and delinquent youth; disadvantaged students for whom education did not provide equality of opportunity; and the cycle, or circle, of poverty.

The concept of a circle of poverty gained popularity with the publication of Myrdal's *American Dilemma*. This 1940 study describes poverty among poor blacks as a set of interdependent causal factors. For instance, a poor education restricts employment opportunities, which causes a low standard of living and, consequently, leads to poor medical care, diet, housing, and education for the next generation. This model of poverty suggests that one can begin at any point in the set of causal relationships and move around the circle of poverty.

This model captured the imagination of the Kennedy administration in the early 1960s. A story was told that the idea for launching a massive federal program against unemployment and poverty came directly from President Kennedy in 1962, when he told Walter Heller, chairman of the Council of Economic Advisers, to gather all the statistics on poverty. At the time, Kennedy requested copies of Michael Harrington's recently published *The Other America: Poverty in the United States*. By 1963, President Kennedy had decided to launch a War on Poverty that would attack the very social structure that caused poverty.

Michael Harrington's book influenced the final report on poverty written by the Council of Economic Advisers and presented to Congress as the basic program for the EOA. Harrington believed that insulation of the poor from the rest of America is dividing the nation into two cultures. Within the circle of poverty, the poor get sick more often because of unhealthy living conditions in slums and inadequate nutrition. Inadequate medical care causes their illnesses to last longer, resulting in lost wages and work. Because of lost wages, the poor cannot afford adequate housing, education, and medical care. Harrington argues that there is a much richer way of describing this circle—as a *culture*. The vicious circle of poverty has created its own cultural patterns. Its family structure is different from that of the rest of society—it has more homes without fathers, early pregnancy, different attitudes toward sex, and less marriage. Millions of children of the poor, Harrington claims, do not know affection or stability. The culture of poverty is also defined by the actions of other institutions in society. For instance, there is a marked difference between how the police treat the poor and how they treat the middle class.

Of significance for modern times, Harrington argues, is the fact that the culture of poverty is beginning to perpetuate itself under the pressures of modern technology. As technology increases, so do educational requirements for occupations. As technological progress sweeps through the rest of society, the poor are increasingly left behind, and it becomes more difficult for them to move up in the social structure. Poverty is passed on from generation to generation because of the increasing difficulty for children of the poor to receive adequate education and job training. The price of more-complex technology is the growing existence of a culture that cannot participate in its benefits.

An attack on the culture of poverty became a central focus of the Kennedy administration. In October 1963, Walter Heller began to draw together various plans for an invasion of the culture of poverty. Heller sent government agencies a memorandum requesting plans that would help people to avoid entrapment in the culture of poverty and would provide a means of escape. In November 1963, while responses to the memorandum were being reviewed, President Kennedy was assassinated. Almost immediately, President Johnson announced his intention of supporting the program and directed Heller to complete his task. In January 1964, Heller's report was included in *The Annual Report of the Council of Economic Advisers* as "The Problem of Poverty in America."

The report strongly emphasized the role of education in uprooting the culture of poverty. Certainly, social scientists like Myrdal and Harrington considered education to be a link in the circle of poverty, but the Heller report placed education in the central role in the battle strategy: "Equality of opportunity is the American dream, and universal education our noblest pledge to realize it. But, for the children of the poor, education is a handicap race; many are too ill motivated at home to learn at school." The report goes on to claim that poverty is directly linked to education: "The chief reason for low rates of pay is low productivity, which in turn can reflect lack of education or training, physical and mental disability, or poor motivation." This argument places the responsibility for low incomes directly on the shoulders of wage earners, not on the economic system. "The importance of education," the report continues, "as a factor in poverty is suggested by the fact that families headed by persons with no more than 8 years of education have an incidence rate of 37 percent."[29]

The Heller report underlines the importance of education in the War on Poverty when it claims: "The severely handicapping influence of lack of education is clear. The incidence of poverty drops as educational attainments rise for nonwhites as well as white families at all ages." One section of the report, labeled "The Vicious Circle," begins with the straightforward statement, "Poverty breeds poverty." The report defines the role of education in this circle: "It is difficult for children to find and follow avenues leading out of poverty in environments where education is deprecated and hope is smothered."

The major strategy the report advocates is the use of education to end poverty. It flatly states, "Universal education has been perhaps the greatest single force, contributing both to social mobility and to general economic growth." In addition, the report argues, if the children of poor families were given skills and motivation, they would not grow up to be poor adults. The current problem, the report maintains, is that many young people are condemned to inadequate schools and instruction, and many school systems concentrate their efforts on children from higher income groups. Effective education for children at the bottom of the economic ladder requires special methods and greater expenses: "The school must play a larger role in the development of poor youngsters if they are to have, in fact, 'equal opportunity.' " In language pointing toward the eventual plans for Head Start, the report continues, "This often means that schooling must start on a pre-school basis and include a broad range of more intensive services." In addition, the report urges the development of a Youth Conservation Corps, adult-education programs, day-care centers for working mothers, improved health programs, and increased assistance to the aged. In sum, the Heller report outlined a total package designed to uproot and destroy the environment and culture of poverty.

President Johnson accepted the argument that the problem of poverty in the 1960s was different from that of the Depression. He wrote about his meeting with Heller, "The most significant aspects of this new poverty, once the spotlight of attention was thrown on it, were the dismaying nature of its stubborn entrenchment and total entrapment of its victims from one generation to the next." Johnson announced plans for the War on Poverty in his State of the Union Message to Congress on January 8, 1964. He told Congress it was its responsibility to replace despair with opportunity and declared "this administration today, here and now, declares unconditional war on poverty in America." he also told Congress and the American people that the chief weapons of the battle would be better schools, better health, better homes, and better training and job opportunities. This would be a battle to help Americans escape squalor, misery, and unemployment.[30]

The War on Poverty began with the signing of the EOA on August 20, 1964. Part A of Title I of the EOA established the Job Corps—a unique combination of approaches to the youth problem. First, it attacked unemployment among youth by providing urban and rural residential training centers. This program was modeled on the CCC of the 1930s, with residents devoting their time to conserving and managing natural resources. Parts B and C of Title I provided programs for Work-Training and Work-Study. In both programs, youth were to learn skills while working on a government project.

Head Start was developed under Title II of the legislation, which provided for community-action programs. It was the first and probably the most popular of the national community-action programs. The Economic Opportunity Act of 1964 made no specific mention of the education of younger children as a component of the War on Poverty. One reason for this is that the highly explosive issues of race and church-state relationships had in the past hindered the passage of federal education bills. A congressional amendment to establish a preschool program had been attached to the original EOA but was withdrawn when assurances were given that the Office of Economic Opportunity would support the program. In January 1965, President Johnson announced the decision to fund a preschool program named Head Start under the antipoverty program. In February, Sargent Shriver, head of the Office of Economic Opportunity, announced that the program would be launched during the summer of 1965. The response to the announcement was immediate and enthusiastic, and during the first summer, 560,000 children entered the Head Start program.

The ESEA was signed by President Johnson on April 11, 1965, in a one-room schoolhouse near Stonewall, Texas, where his own education had begun. For the occasion, his first schoolteacher was flown in from retirement in California, to stand at his side. The most important section of the ESEA was Title I, which provided funds for improved educational programs for children designated as educationally deprived. Title I specifically states: "The Congress hereby declares it to be the policy of the United States to provide financial assistance . . . to expand and improve . . . educational programs by various means . . . which contribute particularly to meeting the special educational needs of educationally deprived children."[31]

In essence, Title I was the major educational component of the War on Poverty. At the opening congressional hearings on the bill, Health, Education and Welfare Secretary Anthony J. Celebreeze and Commissioner of Education Francis Keppel provided the president's justification and rationale for special educational assistance to the educationally deprived. In his opening statement to the committee, Celebreeze quoted President Johnson's statement, "Just as ignorance breeds poverty, poverty all too often breeds ignorance in the next generation." Celebreeze went on to claim, "The President's program . . . is designed to break this cycle which has been running on from generation to generation in this most affluent period of our history." He stated that a clear link exists between high educational and high economic attainment.[32]

Commissioner Keppel's statement also drew on the rhetoric and arguments that had come to characterize the government's approach to the problem of poverty. But in this case, as in the report of the Council of Economic Advisers, education was viewed as the major element to be attacked in the cycle of poverty. Keppel told the committee: "Archimedes . . . told us many centuries ago: 'Give me a lever long enough and a fulcrum strong enough and I can move the world.' Today, at last, we have a prospect of a lever long enough and supported strongly enough to do something for our children of poverty." The lever, of course, was education, and the fulcrum was federal financial assistance.[33]

Other sections of the legislation covered a variety of special purposes, which in many cases were included to ensure passage of Title I. Title II provided financial assistance for school library resources, textbooks, and other instructional materials. A primary reason for including Title II was to win support from private school interests, because they would be eligible for the aid. Furthermore, Keppel supported Title II during congressional hearings with statistics showing that the quality of the school library was strongly associated with student performance.

Title III provided funds for the establishment of supplementary educational centers to promote local educational innovations. Educators who helped President Johnson draft the legislation hoped this could be one method for stimulating creativity in local school systems. Title IV provided money for educational research and for the establishment of research and development centers. Title IV was included because the drafters of the legislation believed it would receive minimal legislative support if it were submitted as a separate bill. In a sense, the concept of research and development in education rode in on the coattails of Title I.

Funds for strengthening state departments of education were designated under Title V. The purpose of providing these funds was to allay fears about federal control of education. One of the interesting results of federal support of education under ESEA was the increased power it gave to state departments of education in relation to local school districts.

In general, ESEA followed in the tradition of federal involvement in education that had been evolving since World War II. The basic thread was planning for the use of human resources in the national economy. In the 1950s, under pressure from the technological and scientific race with the Soviet Union, emphasis had been placed on channeling talented youth into higher education. In the early 1960s, the emphasis shifted to providing equality of opportunity as a means of utilizing the poor as human resources. President Johnson, who had chaired the Senate hearings on selective service in the early 1950s, clearly reiterated this in his message to Congress that accompanied the proposals for ESEA: "Nothing matters more to the future of our country; not our military preparedness, for armed might is worthless if we lack the brainpower to build a world of peace; not our productive economy, for we cannot sustain growth without trained manpower."[34]

However, unlike the human-resource policies of the 1950s, the approach of the 1960s was essentially to wage war on a culture. Within the theoretical framework of the War on Poverty, the social and economic system that had created poverty and allowed it to continue was not considered the problem; the problem was the culture of the poor. Indeed, the overall strategy was to integrate the poor into the existing social and economic system. Very simply, this can be called *blaming the victim*—placing the full responsibility for poverty on the shoulders of the poor. They—not the economic system that had produced poverty— were expected to change.

ESEA can be considered a conservative approach to the problem of poverty because it did not propose any dramatic changes in the economic system. The same conservatism was evident in the issue of social-class differences. The approach of the War on Poverty was that no basic conflict exists among the interests of the different social classes. Within the context of the War on Poverty, the economic interest of the poor was to enter the middle class, not to change the economic and social system, and the interest of the middle class was not to repress the poor, but to solve such problems as crime, delinquency, and unemployment by bringing the poor into the mainstream of society. Education plays a major role in this particular analysis of social-class differences because it supposedly would provide the bridge for the poor to enter the opportunity structure of society. In the rhetoric of the War on Poverty, education was considered the hope of the poor and the method of the middle class.

Conclusion

The expanded role of the federal government in education during the 1950s and 1960s ensured that educational policy would be directly related to other national policies. Within the span of only two decades, educational policy had shifted from winning the scientific and technological war with the Soviet Union to winning the War on Poverty. One result of increased federal involvement was that education became an important factor in national politics. After the 1960s, presidential candidates began to address educational issues and define an educational constituency.

Federal protection of the rights of minority groups placed the federal government in the position of policing educational institutions. This was a necessary correction to the past discriminatory actions of local elites, school boards, and school administrators, but it increased the complexity of the distribution of power over the schools. The political structure of education that emerged in the 1980s pitted against one another special-interest groups, politicians, business organizations, teachers' unions, and school administrators. As in the nineteenth century, each pressure group viewed public schooling as the answer to social, political, and economic problems.

Notes

1. Joel Spring, *The Sorting Machine: National Educational Policy since 1945* (New York: McKay, 1976).

2. Diane Ravitch, *The Troubled Crusade: American Education, 1945–1980* (New York: Basic Books, 1983).

3. Spring, *Sorting Machine,* p. 266.

4. Ravitch, *Troubled Crusade,* p. 330.

5. President's Advisory Commission on Universal Training, "Staff Study: Universal Military Training in the United States: A Brief Historical Summary," in *A Program for National Security: Report of the President's Advisory Commission on Universal Training* (Washington, D.C.: Government Printing Office, 1947), pp. 401–406.

6. Vannevar Bush, *Science—The Endless Frontier: A Report to the President* (Washington, D.C.: Government Printing Office, 1945).

7. U.S. Congress, Senate Committee on Armed Services, *Universal Military Training and Service Act of 1951—Hearings before the Preparedness Subcommittee of the Committee on Armed Services,* 82d Cong., 1st sess., 10 January–2 February 1951 (Washington, D.C.: Government Printing Office, 1951), pp. 1082–1083.

8. U.S. Congress, Committee on Interstate and Foreign Commerce, *Hearings before the Committee on Interstate and Foreign Commerce,* 80th Cong., 1st sess., 6 and 7 March 1947 (Washington, D.C.: Government Printing Office, 1947), p. 147.

9. Richard Barnes Kennan, "No Ivory Tower for You," *NEA Journal* 40 (May 1951): 317–318.

10. Quoted in David Hulburd, *This Happened in Pasadena* (New York: Macmillan, 1951), pp. 90–91.

11. Quoted in Jack Nelson and Gene Roberts, Jr., *The Censors and the Schools* (Boston: Little, Brown, 1963), pp. 40–53.

12. Quoted in Franklin R. Zeran, "Life Adjustment in Action, 1944–1952," in Franklin R. Zeran, ed., *Life Adjustment Education in Action* (New York: Chartwell House, 1953), p. 86.

13. Arthur Bestor, *Educational Wastelands* (Urbana: University of Illinois Press, 1953), p. 86.

14. Ibid., pp. 36–38.

15. Ibid.

16. Ibid.

17. Ibid.

18. Quoted by Edward R. Murrow in the Foreword to Hyman G. Rickover, *Education and Freedom* (New York: Dutton, 1959), pp. 5–7.

19. Dwight D. Eisenhower, "Our Future Security," in U.S. Congress, Senate Committee on Labor and Public Welfare, *Science and Education for National Defense: Hearings before the Committee on Labor and Public Welfare,* 85th Cong., 2d sess., 1958 (Washington, D.C.: Government Printing Office, 1958), pp. 1357–1359.

20. Dwight D. Eisenhower, "Message from the President of the United States Transmitting Recommendations Relative to Our Educational System," in Senate

Committee on Labor and Public Welfare, *Science and Education for National Defense*, pp. 239–262.

21. *Brown et al. v. Board of Education of Topeka et al.* (1954), reprinted in Albert P. Blaustein and Clarence C. Ferguson, Jr., *Desegregation and the Law* (New Brunswick, N.J.: Rutgers University Press, 1957), pp. 273–282.

22. "The Effects of Segregation and the Consequences of Desegregation: A Social Science Statement," appendix to Appellants' Brief filed in the *School Segregation Cases*, in the Supreme Court of the United States, October term, 1952, in John Bracey, August Meier, and Elliott Rudwick, eds., *The Afro-Americans: Selected Documents* (Boston: Allyn & Bacon, 1972), pp. 661–671.

23. Ibid.

24. Gunnar Myrdal, *An American Dilemma: The Negro Problem and Modern Democracy* (New York: Harper & Row, 1944), pp. lxxii–lxxiii.

25. Martin Luther King, Jr., *Stride toward Freedom: The Montgomery Story* (New York: Harper & Row, 1958), p. 91.

26. Ibid., pp. 94–97.

27. Quoted in David Lewis, *King: A Critical Biography* (New York: Praeger, 1970), p. 171.

28. James W. Prothro, "Stateways versus Folkways Revisited: An Error in Prediction," *Journal of Politics* 34 (May 1972): 356–357.

29. "The Problem of Poverty in America," in *The Annual Report of the Council of Economic Advisors* (Washington, D.C.: Government Printing Office, 1964).

30. Lyndon B. Johnson, "The State of the Union Message to Congress, 8 January 1964," in *A Time for Action: A Selection from the Speeches and Writings of Lyndon B. Johnson* (New York: Atheneum, 1964), pp. 164–179.

31. "Elementary and Secondary Education Act of 1965, Public Law 89-10," reprinted in Stephen Bailey and Edith Mosher, *ESEA: The Office of Education Administers a Law* (Syracuse, N.Y.: Syracuse University Press, 1968), pp. 235–266.

32. U.S. Congress, House Committee on Education and Labor, *Aid to Elementary and Secondary Education: Hearings before the General Subcommittee on Education of the Committee on Education and Labor*, 89th Cong., 1st sess., 1965 (Washington, D.C.: Government Printing Office, 1965), pp. 63–82.

33. Ibid., pp. 82–113.

34. Ibid., p. 63.

11

The Conservative Reaction and the Politics of Education

The conservative political and educational patterns of the 1970s emerged in reaction to the student protest and civil rights demonstrations of the 1960s and the policies of the War on Poverty. Ironically, the result of the continuing struggles of women, the handicapped, and minority groups for increased equality of educational opportunity was that these groups made most of their gains during the 1970s and 1980s, against a background of conservative political reaction.

Conservative educational policies were set in motion by student demonstrations that erupted on college and high school campuses in the late 1960s. The demonstrations were triggered mainly in reaction to the Vietnam War because the selective service system threatened most young men eligible for the draft. As the demonstrations escalated, they began to call into question many of the institutions and values of American life. Demands were made for greater freedom of expression and more equality in the distribution of wealth. Universities and public schools were attacked as institutions of oppression and racism. Alternative schools began to appear in both the private and the public educational systems.

The irony of the demonstrations is that the participants were mainly college students who were part of the large concentration of youth attending college on deferments from the selective service system. For national leaders, the demonstrations indicated a failure in the use of the selective service system to control human resources and of the idea that simply sending youth to college would improve the national economy.

In 1968, Richard Nixon was elected president on a ticket promising to solve the problem of the Vietnam War and restore law and order to American campuses. Nixon's policies ran counter to the more liberal policies of the Kennedy and Johnson administrations. His administration questioned the value of the War on Poverty educational legislation in providing equality of opportunity for the poor; the use of selective service to control human resources; and the use of busing for desegregation. Nixon favored educational programs designed to prepare students for specific careers, a return to basic education, replacement of selective service with a volunteer armed forces, and an expansion of vocational education.

Within the educational establishment, a period of conservative reaction began. The role and power of professional educators had been strongly criticized during the 1950s and in the demonstrations of the late 1950s and early 1960s, and now demands were made for greater public control of the educational system. One reaction by professional educators was to call for their own accountability to the public through the reporting of test scores. The accountability movement gave more power to professional educators.

Within the schools, educators began to rely heavily on teaching by specific behavior objectives and on using standardized methods of instruction. In other words, the tradition of behaviorism initiated in the early twentieth century by Edward Thorndike came to dominate the schools of the 1970s and 1980s. The tradition of behaviorism fit neatly into the accountability movement.

The conservative reaction to desegregation resulted in one of those ironic twists that occur in history. In the 1970s, alternative schools, which in the late 1960s had been considered part of the radical reaction to the educational establishment, became a method for avoiding forced busing for integration. The existence of alternative, or magnet, schools allowed school systems to use voluntary methods of desegregation. Local conservative groups preferred voluntary desegregation to forced busing. A major outcome of the reliance on alternative schools as a method of desegregation was the use of differentiated curricula for students within a school district. Thus, the dream of nineteenth-century common school reformers—an educational system providing the same education for all students—gave way to a system of highly specific curricula.

As the conservative reaction took place in the schools, a new style of educational politics emerged. As a result of the increased role of the federal government in education, education was given greater emphasis in national politics. One important cause of this change was the transformation of the NEA in the 1960s into a union primarily concerned with the wages and working conditions of teachers. In the late 1970s, the NEA began to play a major role in national politics and, along with its rival the AFT, began to influence national elections.

In the 1980s, a new wave of criticism accused the schools of causing an imbalance in international trade because of their low academic standards. As in the movement for vocational education in the early twentieth century, a new cry was raised for high educational standards as a means of graduating students capable of improving American technology and thus winning the international trade war with West Germany and Japan. In addition, these critics felt that a closer relationship should exist between schooling and the needs of the labor market. This movement continued the dominant pattern in twentieth-century education—using the schools to channel and improve human resources.

The Nixon Administration and the Conservative Reaction

The years of the Nixon administration were a time of conservative reaction to student demonstrations and the demands of the civil rights movement. This conservative reaction included a retreat from the programs of the War on Poverty, the development of career education, a renewed emphasis on the power of the educational expert, the spread of the concept of accountability in education, and increased emphasis on testing and the use of behavioral psychology in the classroom. President Richard Nixon was elected in 1968 in the middle of national turmoil caused by the demonstrations against the war in Vietnam and widespread urban riots. Promises of maintaining law and order were an important part of Nixon's presidential campaigns in 1968 and 1972.

Student demonstrations, the civil rights movement, and urban riots convinced many Americans in the 1960s that the United States was on the verge of radical social change. Given this point of view, it was logical for national leaders to seek some means of restoring a sense of authority in society and in the educational system.

The first major student demonstration took place at the University of California at Berkeley in 1964, when the chancellor announced that students would not be able to use an area in front of the entrance to the university for political activities. The students formed the Free Speech Movement and conducted a sit-in at one of the campus buildings.

The target of many students in the Free Speech Movement was university president Clark Kerr, who in articulating the modern role of higher education had likened universities to service stations providing help to business, government, and other private organizations. Many students objected to the role of universities in giving aid to the military and in implementating American foreign policy. In addition, modern universities had grown to tremendous proportions compared with those in the earlier part of the century. As a result, Kerr and other administrators in higher education became targets of student demonstrators. The administrators were charged with using the university to aid in the war effort and with impersonal treatment of students.

Student demonstrations quickly spread from Berkeley to other campuses. In 1965, the first teach-in against the war was held at the University of Michigan. At other campuses, protestors blocked employment recruiting by Dow Chemical Corporation, a major producer of military chemicals for the government. In 1968, the assassination of Martin Luther King, Jr., added more fuel to campus protests and sparked major urban riots. Campus protests continued after President Nixon's election and reached a high point in 1970 when Ohio National Guardsmen killed four students at Kent State University.

In the midst of these student demonstrations and urban riots, Nixon launched his campaign to restore law and order in American society. Part of Nixon's educational policy centered around the development of career education. In 1971 and 1972, Sidney Marland, Jr., Nixon's commissioner of education, began to earmark discretionary funds provided by Congress to the Office of Education for the development of career-education projects. Marland's method of using discretionary funds turned career education into a reform movement originating at the top of the political structure of education. By 1972 to 1973, Marland was able to announce that in the first year of this program, 750,000 young people participated.

Marland believed that career education was the answer to student rebellion, delinquency, and unemployment. In his first annual report to Congress, in 1971, he argued that disenchantment among youth existed because education did not lead to career opportunities. For Marland, the villian was general education programs that lacked specific goals and were not linked to the job market. Marland argued that education should be meaningful; by *meaningful*, he meant "related to a career objective." He stated, "When we use the word 'meaningful,' we imply a strong obligation that our young people complete the first 12 grades in such a fashion that they are ready either to enter into some form of higher education or to proceed immediately into satisfying and appropriate employment." This, of course, was a restatement of the traditional goal of the comprehensive high school. Marland claimed allegiance to the concept of the comprehensive high school, but he considered its primary weakness to be its general education programs not directly related to entry into either the job market or higher education. "The emergence of the comprehensive high school, properly defined and implemented, carries the ultimate solution."[1]

Therefore, Marland believed, students and schools were in a state of turmoil because the school had never completely achieved the goal of sorting students for the labor market. In his first report to Congress, he stated, "We must eliminate anything in our curriculum that is unresponsive to either of these goals [higher education and employment], particularly the high school anachronism called 'the general curriculum,' a false compromise between college preparatory curriculum and realistic career development."[2] For Marland, all elements of school life needed to be justified by their contribution of career development. In the words of

Marland's associate commissioner, "The fundamental conception of career education is that all educational experiences, curriculum, instruction, and counseling should be geared to preparing each individual for a life of economic independence, personal fulfillment, and an appreciation for the dignity of work."[3] This meant a complete alignment between the job market and the public schools. Marland believed career education offered one solution "to some of our more serious social and economic problems, including high unemployment and the attendant problems of disaffection and drug excess among the young."[4]

Career education was unique in its attempt to make vocational guidance a part of the academic program of the school and to begin the program in the early grades. During the elementary and junior high school years, career education was to acquaint students with the world of work and the varieties of occupations by relating them to the subject matter of the curriculum. After study and preparation in these early grades for an occupational choice, the high school student was to begin preparing for entry into either an occupation or higher education. Advocates of career education also believed that higher education should be organized around this model. The real hope for higher education, Marland believed, was the community college. He argued that the community college should not be viewed as merely a "large anteroom for the four-year institutions"[5] but as a unique institution of higher learning whose developing philosophy was based on the concept of career education. Close ties with local businesses made it possible for the community college to gear its programs to the needs of the labor market.

At the same time that career education was becoming a major program of the Nixon administration, between 1970 and 1973, Nixon vetoed three of six appropriation bills for the Department of Health, Education and Welfare and pocket-vetoed the 1973 appropriation bill. Nixon justified the vetoes as necessary to reduce the federal budget and on the grounds of lack of evidence that federal money for compensatory-education programs resulted in any significant social change.

The individual in the Nixon administration responsible for formulating the argument that money spent on schooling had little effect on social change was White House counselor and Nixon confidant Daniel Patrick Moynihan. Moynihan believed that social change for the poor could be accomplished only through a national policy of economic support for the family. This idea was incorporated into a Nixon plan to provide guaranteed family incomes that supposedly would break the cycle of poverty by stabilizing the family unit.

Moynihan was strongly influenced by the *Coleman Report*'s findings on the social impact of education. This report was written to fulfill the requirements of Title IV of the 1964 Civil Rights Act, which gave the commissioner of education the responsibility for surveying the availability of equality of educational opportunity in the United States. The commissioner had selected James Coleman of Johns Hopkins University to assume major responsibility for the design, administration, and analysis of a simple survey of equality of educational opportunity. Coleman and his staff decided to expand the scope of the survey beyond the intent of Congress after they tried to define the concept of equality of educational opportunity. They outlined five major approaches to the problem. One approach defined the concept as the degree of racial segregation in school systems. The second approach involved determining the inequality of resource inputs from the school system, such as books, school facilities, and student-teacher ratios. The third method was to measure inequality of intangible resources, such as teacher morale. These three definitions clearly fell within the intent of Congress, but the fourth and fifth definitions went beyond this intention. The fourth approach measured inequality of inputs and their effect on educational achievement. The fifth considered inequality of output as evidence of inequality of opportunity. The survey, later called the *Coleman Report*, attempted to measure all five of these approaches to the problem of inequality of educational opportunity.

In this author's opinion, Coleman and his staff attempted to do too much in too little time. The national survey was conducted with blinding speed and was submitted to Congress in 1966. The report should have accomplished well the very minimal task of carefully measuring the resources in schools attended by blacks and those attended by whites and the degree of discrimination. Coleman's response to this criticism was that if his staff had concentrated on the question of equality of school resources, the report would simply have reinforced that definition of equality of educational opportunity. The major virtue in the final report, he felt, was that it shifted policy attention from traditional concerns to the effectiveness of school resources on student achievement.

Regarding the basic issue of school segregation, the *Coleman Report* found that almost "80 percent of all white pupils in the 1st grade and 12th grade" attended schools that were from "90 to 100 percent white." Sixty-five percent of black students in the first grade attended schools with student populations that were between 90 to 100 percent black. This meant that the majority of children in the United States attended segregated schools and that white children were the most segregated.[6]

The *Coleman Report* correlates differences in resources with student achievement. For purposes of the report, student achievement was determined by achievement tests. The report assumes that achievement tests measure "the skills which are among the most important in our society for getting a good job and moving up to a better one, and for full participation in an increasingly technical world." It found that, except for Oriental-Americans, all other minority groups scored significantly lower than whites and that the differences increased from the first through the twelfth grades: "For most minority groups . . . schools provide little opportunity for them to overcome . . . initial deficiency; in fact they fall farther behind the white majority in the development of several skills which are critical to making a living and participating fully in modern society."[7]

When these differences in achievement were correlated with school resources, it was found that "differences between schools account for only a small fraction of differences in achievement." Differences were found in the effect on white and minority students of school resources. The achievement of white students seemed to be less affected by the strengths or weaknesses of curricula and school facilities, whereas these did seem to have some effect on the achievement of minority students. Student achievement was strongly related "to the educational backgrounds and aspirations of the other students in school." The *Coleman Report* concludes that if a white pupil from a family strongly supportive of education was put in a school with pupils who did not come from that type of background, the pupil's achievement would "be little different than if he were in a school composed of others like himself." On the other hand, if "a minority pupil from a home without much educational strength is put with schoolmates with strong educational backgrounds, his achievement is likely to increase." This conclusion provided support for integration.

In general, except for its findings on integration, the *Coleman Report* provides a pessimistic outlook on the ability of the schools to overcome poverty and solve social problems. In 1966, Moynihan and Fredrick Mosteller conducted a faculty seminar at Harvard University on the findings of the *Coleman Report*. One aspect of the report that impressed Moynihan was its contradiction of what he called "conventional wisdom." The report seemed to show that things people assumed were important in improving achievement in the schools in fact had little relationship to achievement. This supposed contradiction of conventional wisdom provided Moynihan with the ammunition to attack social scientists as a group and federal education programs.[8]

In 1967, in a paper titled "On the Education of the Urban Poor," Moynihan accused social scientists of attempting to shape public opinion according to personal rather than objective findings. He argued that social scientists were committed to social change and tended to be at odds with people having wealth and political power. Social scientists, according to Moynihan, tended to be liberal or radical, which resulted in an assumption by poor and minority groups in America that social scientists would always be on their side.[9]

In 1970, Moynihan called for increased spending for educational research but not for educational programs. Part of his argument was that government educational policies needed to be validated by research before being implemented. Writing in the *New York Times* in 1972, he gave support for recent legislation for a National Institute of Education (NIE). The NIE was designed to conduct basic research in education. Moynihan believed that the research findings of the NIE would provide the basic facts for the future development of educational legislation. According to Moynihan, past educational programs had failed because basic research had not been conducted before their implementation. The NIE had been proposed to Congress in 1970 by President Nixon with the objective, as stated by Moynihan, "to bring 'big' science to bear on education, especially the problem of low achievement among students from low-income families."[10]

Moynihan provided the rationalization for the educational retreat of the Nixon administration. "I for one would be willing to bet that the more we learn about formal schooling the less we will come to value it." He even suggested that research findings would show the need for a greater stress on the placement of the school graduate in the job market.

Rather than spending more money on early education, for example, we are likely to conclude that the transition we manage least well in our society is that of the young person leaving the world of school for the world of work, and that accordingly much more resources have to be applied to this period in individual development rather than the much earlier one.[11]

One significant aspect of Moynihan's statement is that it represented an abandonment of the attempt to make the system of social selection in the schools operate fairly by providing equality of opportunity. Moynihan's attitude was essentially that educational research proved that nothing could be done in the schools to increase achievement among the lower class and, therefore, that such efforts were not worth the spending of federal dollars.

The reduction of spending for federal educational programs and the establishment of the NIE represented an important shift in the relationship between the educational establishment and the federal government. More money for research and less money for the schools resulted in the funding of college professors and research units in local school systems rather than teachers and administrators of specific educational programs. The real shift that occurred was away from providing financial support of education for the poor to providing financial support for white-collar research workers. Thus, the consequence of the great retreat of the Nixon administration was that, in the tradition of administrative progressives, funding was given to educational experts, and direct concern with the lives of the poor was diminished.

As government funding shifted from the clients to the experts, the rise of the accountability movement attempted to restore power to the professional educator. In part, the accountability movement was a reaction to attempts to achieve community control of the schools. Community control received its first public attention when instituted in 1966 at Intermediate School 201 in Harlem and in 1968 in the Ocean Hill-Brownsville section of Brooklyn, both in New York City.

The concept of community control emerged from attempts to end racism and discrimination in the schools. In many ways, it was an attempt to capture the nineteenth-century ideal of democratic localism, according to which the schools were to reflect the values and desires of their users. Minority groups felt that racism existed in the schools because the community served by the schools had little power over the hiring of teachers, the spending of money, and the organization of the curriculum. Those in the community control movement believed that these decisions were made by a combination of elite school boards, educational administrators, and teachers' unions. Leaders of the movement felt that decisions made by these groups resulted in racists teaching in schools serving minority communities and in the use of a curriculum that reflected discriminatory attitudes.

The community control movement simply wanted to restore complete control of the schools to members of the local community. Of course, this proposal threatened the power of professional educators, school boards, and teachers' unions. In fact, the first major reaction to community control came from the teachers' union, when the local community in Ocean Hill-Brownsville dismissed a number of teachers for racist attitudes. The resulting reaction from the teachers' union, which viewed the actions of the community as a direct threat to the power of the union, ended the community control movement in New York City.

The accountability movement was an attempt to restore power to professional educators, who had been threatened by the community control movement and the public criticism of schools in the 1950s. Like the administrative progressives in the early twentieth century who argued for control by experts, the proponents of accountability considered education an arena for professional decision making.

Control by experts is an important theme of the book that sparked the accountability movement. Leon Lessinger's *Every Kid a Winner* considers the community control movement a threat to the quality of education.[12] Lessinger uses the model of the hospital to attack the concept of democratic control. He argues that in a hospital, patients and the community in general do not and should not participate directly in decisions regarding medical treatment or surgery because these are areas of decision making that require expert knowledge and training. For Lessinger, the idea of democratic control in surgery is ludicrous and dangerous to the patient. In his opinion, users of medical services have the right to complain, but decisions about how to deal with the complaints should remain in the hands of medical experts.

Lessinger feels that the same model is applicable to education. Modern schooling, he maintains, is based on professional knowledge gained through research and study. The average member of the community does not have the training necessary to make correct educational decisions. Like the hospital clientele, the community has the right to complain but does not have the right or the knowledge to make decisions regarding the resolution of complaints. Only the educational expert should be entrusted with decision-making power.

Lessinger, even with his reliance on the expert, recognizes that in a democratic society, the schools must be responsive to the public. He felt this responsiveness can be achieved by the schools reporting their accomplishments and failures to the public. This public accounting of the results of schooling was the heart of the accountability movement. Lessinger envisions the creation of a national educational accounting firm operated by educational engineers who will measure educational results by the use of achievement tests and report the results to the public. He assumes that these results will provide the public with expert data that can be used to express pleasure with or criticism of the accomplishments of the school system.

As the accountability movement spread in the early 1970s, states and local communities began to require schools to annually publish achievement-test scores. The use of test scores to measure the schools' success kept the power in the hands of the educational expert. In the schools, students found themselves taking an increasing number of achievement tests in order to satisfy the requirements of accountability. One result was that testing, or measurement, was restored to a central place in the educational process. Accompanying this rebirth of interest in standardized testing was an increasing emphasis on behaviorism and on teaching by specific behavioral objectives.

In the early twentieth century, behaviorism received support from the theories of educational psychology advocated by William James and Edward Thorndike. The behaviorist model is extremely mechanistic—a concept of teaching based on the use of measurement (testing) to determine deficiencies and accomplishments and the use of reinforcement to teach specific objectives. This concept of teaching fit nicely into the technocratic world view held by the administrative progressives in the early part of the century.

Beginning in the 1940s, the behaviorist trend in education received an added boost from the work of psychologist B. F. Skinner. Skinner tried to apply behaviorism to the work of the school by developing programmed learning machines and writing about the relationship of behaviorism to the structure and functioning of society. The best introduction to Skinner's philosophy is his utopian novel written in the 1940s with the controversial title *Walden Two*.[13] The title was controversial because many readers could find little resemblance between the society described by Skinner and the Walden described in the original work by Henry David Thoreau. In Skinner's novel, Walden Two is a scientifically managed society organized around the principles of behavioral engineering. Skinner considered democratic control of his utopian society self-defeating, because behavioral engineering requires control by expert managers. The managers were to pay attention to community desires by measuring the degree of happiness and determining what things needed to be changed or improved to increase the happiness of the residents. In one sense, this novel depicts a society in which democracy is replaced by a public survey like the Gallup Poll.

Control by experts and the behavioral engineering of a society do not contradict Skinner's concept of freedom. He believed that if a science of behavior could exist and the laws of behavior be discovered, then traditional ideas regarding freedom would need to be changed. If laws of behavior that can predict human action exist, then free will does not exist, and without free will, individual actions become the product of past actions and the influence of the environment. Within this framework, behavior is determined by reinforcements received from other individuals or social conditions, and this means that individual behavior can be scientifically controlled and the individual does not have the ability to break out of that control.

Skinner changed the meaning of freedom to fit his concept of behavioral control. For Skinner, freedom exists when individuals are not restricted from doing those things they have been conditioned to do. Thus, freedom is a feeling achieved when one is able to act out behavior that has been determined by previous reinforcement. As a concept of society and the individual, behaviorism places the expert in charge of a society that is scientifically engineered. In this engineered society, behavioral control is exerted over citizens who exist in a state of planned happiness.

In the 1950s, Skinner joined the chorus of criticism of the public schools. From his perspective, a major problem with schools was that teachers did not use the scientific findings of behavioral psychology. His answer to this situation was the teaching machine or program. Based on the principles of behaviorism, teaching machines were to instruct by presenting students with small units of knowledge and providing constant reinforcement. By the late 1970s and 1980s, the original principles underlying the teaching machine were incorporated in many educational software programs for the microcomputer.

In the 1970s, the principles of behavioral psychology fit nicely into the use of increased measurement of students that was a result of the accountability movement. Philosophically, behaviorism was compatible with the conservative trends of the Nixon years. Like accountability, behaviorism rejects concepts of democratic control; like career education, with its emphasis on control, behaviorism was considered an antidote to the type of freedom expressed in student demonstrations. Behaviorism combined with accountability supported the competency-based education movement of the 1970s. Competency-based education simply means teaching the student specific competencies and measuring the achievement of that learning before proceeding to new competencies. Like other forms of behaviorism, competency-based education uses a mechanistic model of learning and attempts to exert direct control over student behaviors.

Career education, accountability, behaviorism, and competency-based education were elements of a conservative reaction during the Nixon years to the freedom demanded by student demonstrators, the demands of the civil rights movement for quality schools, and the attempts of minorities and community groups to achieve greater public control of the schools. They were reactionary movements in the true sense of the word because they harkened back to a model of education according to which the expert is in charge, students and teachers are scientifically managed, and the major goal of education is the management of human resources for the labor market. This model of education became dominant in the 1970s and 1980s.

Busing and Magnet Schools

The United States Supreme Court ruled in *Swann v. Charlotte-Mecklenburg Board of Education* (1971) that involuntary busing was a legitimate means of achieving school integration. The Court warned in the decision that "schools all or predominantly of one race in a district of mixed population will require close scrutiny to determine that school assignments are not part of state enforced segregation."[14] The implications of this decision were that de facto segregation in northern urban school districts would come under close scrutiny of the courts and that busing would be considered a legitimate tool for implementing desegregation plans. Traditional arguments about the value of neighborhood schools could no longer be used to avoid integration; now, school districts would be viewed as unitary systems, and wherever possible, racial integration within those districts would be achieved.

Involuntary busing was never popular with large numbers of the white population or with those who were politically conservative. President Nixon promised in his national campaigns to curb the extent of involuntary busing. In March 1972, he sent a special message to Congress requesting a moratorium on student busing. Nixon's arguments were couched in the rhetoric of equality of opportunity: "Conscience and the Constitution both require that no child should be denied equal educational opportunity." He went on to argue that the purpose of the *Brown* decision was to eliminate the dual school system in the South. This purpose, he maintained, had been achieved. Nixon claimed that the major remaining problem was the maze of differing court orders that had developed to end segregation. Many of these plans, including busing, had resulted in violence and community disruption and had imposed hardships on children. Nixon argued that both wrong and right reasons could be given for opposing busing. The wrong reasons were those based on racial prejudice. The right reasons were a dislike of "wrenching of children away from their families, and from the schools their families may have moved to be near, and sending them arbitrarily to others far distant."[15]

Nixon went on to argue that the result of the substantial dismantling of the dual school system was a greater balance of "emphasis on improving schools, on convenience, on the chance for parental involvement." For Nixon, this meant the argument for equality of educational opportunity should concentrate "much more specifically on education: on assuring that the opportunity is not only equal, but adequate."[16] He stated that the legitimate concerns in the busing issue were quality of education, transportation of children to distant schools, and equality of educational resources.

Nixon's attempt to stem the tide of busing was defeated, and busing continued to be a major national issue. In 1974, major community violence occurred as Boston began to use busing as a tool for racial integration of the schools. The violence in Boston screamed across newspaper headlines and seemed to provide a good case for conservatives that busing should be ended. The conservative argument received further reinforcement in 1975, when James Coleman issued a report detailing the negative consequences of involuntary school integration. The 1966 *Coleman Report* had hailed the beneficial aspect of school integration. The 1975 report argued that involuntary school integration was causing "white flight" from the affected school districts. In turn, white flight was heightening the degree of segregation by contributing to the concentration of minority populations in particular communities.[17]

As mentioned earlier, it was ironic that conservative groups in local communities in the middle of the 1970s began to advocate alternative, or magnet, schools as a means of voluntary desegregation. Because of their effect on the curriculum, alternative schools caused a radical change in the traditional structure of American education. The irony in conservative support of magnet schools was that the concept of magnet schools was a product of radical reaction to the school system in the late 1960s and early 1970s.

Alternative schools had a long tradition in American history. In one sense, the Catholic school system of the nineteenth century was an alternative to the Protestant-dominated public school system. In the early twentieth century, alternative schools were established in reaction to what was believed to be the authoritarian and oppressive atmosphere of the public schools. Some of these alternative schools were a product of reaction to the public school's political and economic doctrines. One school of this type was the Modern School, established by anarchists in Stelton, New Jersey. This school existed from the beginning of World War I until the 1950s. Its instructional methods were based on the idea that nothing should be imposed on the child and that learning should be a product of the child's interests. It was hoped that this form of education would create personalities that would not accept authoritarian institutions. The Manumit School for workers' children, another alternative school, was formed in the 1920s as an alternative to anti-union teachings in the public schools. The school operated on the principles of industrial democracy: The children were organized into trade unions, and some students actually organized labor strikes in protest over the conditions at the school.[18]

Summerhill, a more famous and influential alternative school, was started by A. S. Neill in England in the 1920s. In the 1950s, a Summerhill society was organized in the United States, and during the student rebellions of the 1960s, the Summerhill school was often cited as a model of alternative education. Neill organized Summerhill to create non-authoritarian personalities, which he believed would result in a utopian society. Using a simplistic interpretation of the work of Sigmund Freud, Neill argued that children who commit crimes and violent acts are primarily the product of repressed conditions. Given a state of true freedom, children would grow to be loving and happy adults. At Summerhill, children were given complete freedom to attend or not attend classes and were allowed to participate in the operation of the school.

In the 1940s, Neill developed a more sophisticated rationale based on the psychology of Wilhelm Reich. According to this theory, repression of the child leads to a fear of pleasure. As the child develops, the fear or anxiety about pleasure causes him or her to seek the security of authoritarian institutions; for this reason, adults seek situations that are secure but provide little personal pleasure. Neill asked, for example, how could an individual accept a job in a factory or bureaucratic institution that is monotonous and does not provide for individual pleasure? Or, why would an individual support an authoritarian government like that of Nazi Germany? His answer in both cases was that children are repressed within the institution of the modern nuclear family and grow up willing to give up individual pleasure for the security of authority.

The problem with the nuclear family, Neill believed, is the repression of the wife by the husband. This repression in turn causes the wife to repress her children. Neill proposed two solutions to this situation: either the husband and wife must achieve true equality in their relationship or the child must leave the family structure. For Neill, Summerhill was a haven of liberation from the repression of the nuclear family.

When students protested in the 1960s against the repression in public schools and universities, the free school movement blossomed. Not all the alternative schools established in the 1960s and early 1970s followed the Summerhill model; some were more political, and some tried other educational methods. Most of the schools lived for only a short time and often were forced to close because adequate financial support was lacking.

For political conservatives, the free school movement was a threat to existing institutions and to the stability of society. Some liberal communities in the early 1970s, Minneapolis, for example, introduced alternative schools as part of their public school system. Initially, many of these alternative public schools were organized around the Summerhill philosophy, but as the movement spread, alternative schools began to offer a variety of curricula and teaching methods.

The exact time when "alternative" schools became "magnet" schools is not altogether clear, but beginning in the early 1970s, alternative schools began to be incorporated into desegregation plans. The term *magnet* came to describe the function of these schools in desegregation efforts. The idea was that a school would offer a specialized curriculum or teaching method that would be attractive to a broad spectrum of a community. Parents and students would be allowed to choose that alternative school in place of their regular school. In other words, the school would act as a magnet to attract children from throughout the school district. A major consideration in admitting students to magnet schools was maintaining racial balance.

Magnet schools offered an attractive alternative to people opposed to involuntary busing because they were based on free choice and voluntary efforts at desegregation. They also appealed to many community members because they promised an elite, specialized education. For instance, the first magnet schools established in most communities were schools for creative and performing arts and schools for academic enrichment. Offering elite schools of this type, it was argued would reduce the white flight from desegregated school districts.

The use of magnet schools to solve problems of segregation reinforced the twentieth-century trend toward a more differentiated curriculum. By the early 1980s, the variety of choices available to students in some school systems would have astounded educators in the early part of the century. For instance, the Houston school system offered alternative schools for engineering, criminal justice, the petrochemical industry, health sciences, advanced academic work, and creative and performing arts. Philadelphia offered the same range of alternatives along with special programs in foreign affairs. The Cincinnati school system offered alternative schools for computer sciences, athletics, advanced academic work, science and mathematics, creative and performing arts, and languages.

The increased differentiation caused by magnet schools improved the ability of the schools to match curricula with the needs of the labor market. In Houston, for example, most of the alternative schools were geared to preparation for specific segments of the labor market. Although the original vision of alternative schools was that they would aid in the creation of a free society, those that appeared as part of desegregation plans were more often concerned with creating a fully employed society.

During the Reagan administration years in the 1980s, magnet schools became the primary method used to continue desegregation of American education. In 1984, the administration, after many years of inaction on school integration, supported a court-ordered desegregation settlement in Bakersfield, California, that relied mainly on the use of magnet schools. That same year, the Cincinnati schools settled out of court with the NAACP on a desegregation plan that relied solely on magnet schools.

The development of a highly specialized and differentiated curriculum as a result of desegregation was a major break with Horace Mann's nineteenth-century vision of a common school providing a common education for all. It was also a major break with the idea of a comprehensive high school as presented in the *Cardinal Principles of Education* report in the early twentieth century—the goal that schooling should provide for social cohesion through a common curriculum and common schools was no longer a concern. The irony in ending desegregation is that it resulted in the demise of the common school tradition.

The Politics of Education

Conflict is the best word to describe the politics of education in the 1980s. The educational establishment was divided into differing groups. Teachers' unions were more militant and actively engaged in national politics. Many college professors of education and members of large central-city educational bureaucracies lobbied for more federal funds for research. Other segments of the educational establishment wanted a greater emphasis on funding for compensatory-education programs. School administrators started to unionize and could often be found bargaining with representatives from teachers' unions. A variety of public-interest groups organized to put pressure on the school establishment and to seek aid from the courts and other parts of government. Court decisions increasingly were affecting the operation of schooling and were considered an important component of the political structure of education. Business elites continued to try to use the schools to further their own self-interests by working with state governments.

Certainly, the most important changes in the politics of education after World War II were the transformation of the NEA from an organization dominated by school administrators into a militant teachers' union, and the use of the strike and collective bargaining by both the NEA and the AFT. The change in the NEA took place in 1962, when the organization launched a program for collective negotiations. This meant that local affiliates were to try to establish collective-bargaining agreements with local school systems. The result was a dramatic shift in the role of local NEA affiliates and a rewriting of local constitutions. Up to this time, many NEA locals, known in the organization as education associations, had been controlled by local administrators. Collective bargaining reversed this situation and turned the local affiliates into organizations that told boards and administrators what teachers themselves wanted.

A major factor in the growing militancy of the NEA was the success of the AFT in conducting strikes and gaining collective-bargaining agreements. Originally, neither organization supported the idea of teachers striking. In 1944, when the AFT local in Cicero, Illinois, signed the first collective-bargaining agreement between a school board and a teachers' organization, the national AFT maintained a no-strike policy. The national organization maintained the same policy in 1947 when the Buffalo teachers' union went on strike against the local school system. Other local unions joined in the support of this strike, which became a model for teachers around the country.

The major break in the no-strike policy came in 1960 when the New York affiliate of the AFT, the United Federation of Teachers (UFT), voted to strike over the issues of a dues check-off plan, the conducting of a collective-bargaining election, sick pay for substitutes, 50-minute lunch periods for teachers, and changes in salary schedules. On November 7, 1960, the UFT officially struck against the New York City school system. The union declared the strike effective when 15,000 of the city's 39,000 teachers did not report to school, and 7,500 teachers joined picket lines around the schools. In the spring of 1961, the UFT won a collective-bargaining agreement with the school system and became one of the largest and most influential locals within the AFT.

The hero of the UFT strike was Albert Shanker, who became a symbol of the power of the teachers' union. The New York City strike acted as a catalyst for more teachers to join the union and to increase the level of militancy. In 1966, the membership of the AFT was 125,421; by 1981, it had more than quadrupled, to 580,000. This increased membership plus the increased militancy of the NEA heralded a new era in the relationship between teachers' organizations and the managers of American education.

As teacher militancy increased during the 1970s, a major movement developed in the ranks of teachers for more power over educational policy. In part, this was a response to the troubled financial state of many school districts in the 1970s, which made it difficult for teachers to demand salary increases. The teacher power movement, as it came to be known, sought to have collective bargaining decide issues concerning classroom size, the counseling of new teachers, the establishment of teacher-controlled committees to approve policies of boards of education, and the formation of building committees to curb and challenge the power of principals.

The teacher power movement of the 1970s was reminiscent of the concerns of teachers in the early twentieth century when reforms introduced by administrative progressives had left teachers feeling they were just pawns in the educational plans of school administrators. The rebellions of teachers in the early part of the century were not successful against this threat to their power and status. Almost 70 years passed before teachers were able to successfully challenge these earlier school reforms.

The next major step for teachers' organizations was active involvement in politics—a step that represents another aspect of the teacher power movement. The most significant political step taken by the NEA was to give its support to the 1976 presidential campaign of Jimmy Carter. This step began a process of political involvement whereby teachers' organizations supported political candidates who, in turn, promised political favors. In 1976, Carter promised the NEA, in exchange for its support, to establish a Department of Education having a secretary of education who would represent educational interests at presidential cabinet meetings. After his election, Carter fulfilled his promise to the NEA, thus launching a new era in federal involvement in education. The establishment of the Department of Education ensured the role of the federal government in establishing national educational policy.

The involvement of teachers' organizations in national politics caused a major change in the role played by education in national elections. Both the NEA and the AFT tended to favor the policies of the Democratic Party. This left the Republican Party without any clearly defined educational constituency. President Reagan tried to correct this situation for the Republican Party in the 1980 and 1984 presidential elections by appealing to groups that were opposed to the teachers' unions and highly critical of the public school establishment. Part of his appeal went to private school groups that were hoping for some form of federal support through vouchers or tuition tax credits. Another part of his appeal went to groups that felt the schools had lost their role in shaping student character to conform to traditional Christian values. Individuals concerned with the teaching of moral values were organized into a number of groups, including the Moral Majority and groups supporting school prayer. Reagan hoped to win political support from these groups by promising tuition tax credits and a restoration of school prayer.

The fact that Reagan could appeal to groups outside the usual educational establishment that were interested in educational issues highlights one of the major changes in educational politics in the 1970s and 1980s. Beginning with the civil rights movement in the 1950s, an increasing number of organizations had appeared on the national scene to promote specific educational interests; civil rights organizations represented one type of special-interest group. Also, after the 1954 *Brown* decision, courts continued to make controversial rulings that led to the creation of other special-interest groups. The most visible of these court-created special-interest groups were those opposed to the Supreme Court's decision in *Engel v. Vitale* (1962) prohibiting prayer in the public schools.

The Supreme Court's school-prayer decision was greeted with as much controversy as the *Brown* desegregation decision. *Engel* denied the right of a public school system to conduct prayer services within school buildings during regular school hours. The case began in the state of New York when a local school system was granted the right by the New York Board of Regents to have a brief prayer said in each class at the beginning of the school day. The prayer, considered to be denominationally neutral, read, "Almighty God, we acknowledge our dependence upon Thee, and we beg Thy blessings upon us, our parents, our teachers and our country." The New York courts granted the right of local school systems to use this prayer.

When the United States Supreme Court ruled on the case, one of its major objections to school prayer was the fact that a government official had written the prayer. This seemed to violate the First Amendment, that is, to put the government directly in the business of establishing religion. The Court reviewed the early history of the United States and the struggle for religious freedom and the ending of government support of churches. The writing of a school prayer, the Court argued, ran counter to the long tradition of separation of church and state.

The immediate reaction from one sector of the public to the school-prayer decision was to claim that the Supreme Court had removed God from the schools. Historically, given the heavy religious content in nineteenth-century schools, this charge was to a certain extent correct. The only hopes for those groups in favor of school prayer were in the organization of a separate religious school system or the passage of a constitutional amendment allowing prayer in public schools. It was to this sector of the population that President Reagan appealed in the 1980 and 1984 elections by promising the passage of a school-prayer amendment.

At the same time that school-prayer advocates organized to protest changes in the traditions of schooling, groups supporting better education for the handicapped struggled against traditional discriminatory practices. Numerous organizations were formed to promote better education for the handicapped—the largest of these being the National Association for Retarded Citizens and the Council for Exceptional Children.

These organizations fought hard throughout the 1960s to gain special federal funding for educational programs for the handicapped and for protection of the civil rights of handicapped children. The first major breakthrough came in 1971, when a court in Pennsylvania ruled that state schools had to provide a suitable free public education for all retarded and handicapped children. This decision was followed in 1972 by a federal court ruling that the District of Columbia had to provide a suitable free education regardless of the emotional, mental, or physical condition of the child.

A major victory for these groups came in 1973 with the passage of the Rehabilitation Act of 1973. Section 504 of this legislation was equivalent to Title VI of the 1964 Civil Rights Act in that it required the withholding of federal funds from schools that discriminated against the handicapped. This legislation was followed in 1975 by Public Law 94-142, the Education for All Handicapped Children Act, which prescribed that each handicapped child receive an individualized educational program. The most controversial part of the legislation was the detailed requirements to be followed in the writing of each individualized program.

Public Law 94-142 was important because it demonstrated the power of special-interest groups and the growing extent of federal involvement in education. For each handicapped child, the legislation required a written statement about the child's level of performance, a statement of annual goals, a statement of services to be provided, a date for initiation of services, and objective criteria for evaluation. In other words, the legislation actually outlined a specific method for treating each handicapped child that local school officials were required to follow.

The legislation provided new justification for the cries that began to be heard from local school people about the burden of federal regulations. But given the long history of discrimination against minority groups and handicapped children, federal involvement was required to change local educational policies. This fact did not lessen the extreme level of protests heard from local school officials and from conservative groups opposed to any federal interference in local school practices.

In the 1980 and 1984 elections, President Reagan directed his campaign toward those who were upset with federal interference in local schools. In these two national political campaigns, Reagan defined his educational constituency as those opposed to federal interference in the schools, those in favor of school prayer, private school interests, and those concerned with the values taught in the schools. To those opposed to federal interference in the schools, Reagan promised deregulation and the abolition of the Department of Education. The total educational package offered by the Republicans in 1980 and 1984 included a constitutional amendment for deregulation, abolition of the Department of Education, sanction of school prayer, and provision of tuition tax credits. Two aspects of the 1980 and 1984 presidential elections are important in this context. These were the first national elections in which each political party defined a clear educational constituency. The Democrats appealed to the two major teachers' unions and to members of the public who favored increased federal aid to local schools, whereas the Republicans appealed to the constituency described above. Second, these clear differences between the two parties meant that education was viewed as a national issue represented by various national constituencies.

An important consequence of making education part of national politics is that this ensured the linking of education to national issues. Of course, this process had begun during the 1950s when the cold war and educational policies were linked, and in the 1960s when education became an important part of the War on Poverty. Though President Reagan ran on a platform promising less federal interference in schooling, the actual consequence of making education a national political issue was to guarantee a continued dialogue about national educational policies.

Therefore, it is understandable that the administration that had promised less federal involvement in education issued a report in 1983, *A Nation at Risk*, that blamed the schools for America's difficulties in competing in world markets with Japan and West Germany. The allegedly poor academic quality of American public schools was seen as the cause of lower rates of productivity than those of Japan and West Germany, and of the declining lead of the United States in technological development: The report states, "If only to keep and improve on the slim competitive edge we still retain in world markets, we must rededicate ourselves to the reform of the educational system for the benefit of all."[19]

A similar argument was used in the early twentieth century to justify federal aid to vocational education. At that time, the major international competitor was Germany, and the American school system was compared unfavorably with the German school system. The difference between the earlier plea for vocational education and the reform proposals in *A Nation at Risk* is that the latter does not call for increased federal aid. *A Nation at Risk* exhorts states and local communities to increase academic standards, improve the quality of teachers, and reform the curriculum.

A Nation at Risk put the Reagan administration in an interesting political situation. On the one hand, blaming the public schools for international economic problems appealed to those members of the Republican constituency highly critical of the workings of the schools. On the other hand, the report could not call for federal intervention to aid the schools because of Republican promises to decrease federal involvement in education. And finally, the Reagan administration did place the issue of schooling on a national political agenda by linking it to national trade problems. In other words, the net effect of Republican actions was to ensure that education would remain a national issue.

A major strategy of the Republican administration was to increase the role of states in education as the federal role declined. The role of state governments in education had increased with federal legislation in the 1960s. Most federal monies were channeled through state departments of education, and funds were provided to increase the administrative staff at the state level. Thus, the actions of the Reagan administration reinforced existing trends in the distribution of political power. As power over education shifted back and forth between state and federal agencies, the power of local school boards over education declined.

Indicative of the increase of state power over education was state governors' increasing use of education as a political issue. In the 1980s, state governors jumped on the bandwagon with others who blamed the schools for the problems in foreign trade. In addition, governors promised voters that reforms in the educational system would lead to economic prosperity for the state. The increased involvement of governors in education resulted in dramatic changes.

One of the most important changes made was to establish career ladders for teachers. This educational reform was pioneered by Republican governor Lamar Alexander of Tennessee and was quickly copied in differing forms by other states. The basic idea of career ladders is to provide some means by which the teacher can see his or her work leading to future advancement. Traditionally, teaching was "careerless," because the only hope for advancement was to leave teaching for educational administration. Career ladders were designed to allow competent teachers to advance in rank and responsibilities while remaining in the classroom.

Governor Alexander proposed a career ladder to the Tennessee state legislature in 1983. The bill ran into heavy opposition from teachers' organizations, which were concerned with methods of evaluation and the consequences for teachers already covered by the state's existing certification program. In February 1984, the Tennessee legislature passed the legislation after a compromise had been reached with the state teachers' organization. At the time of its passage, it was hailed as the most ambitious program of its type ever put into law.

The career-ladder idea received national recognition among governors in *Action for Excellence*, the 1983 report of the Task Force on Education for Economic Growth. The task force was composed primarily of state governors and heads of American corporations. The report complains: "In every state . . . teachers are paid according to rigid salary schedules based primarily on training and years of experience. No state, to our knowledge, has a system for rewarding exceptional teachers for their superior performance." To solve this problem, the report recommends that "states should create 'career ladders' for teachers."[20]

An important aspect of the Task Force on Education for Economic Growth was the cooperation it stimulated between big business and governors over educational policy. What this meant is that business influence shifted from the local level to the state level. This shift reflected the increasing political role of state government in education. The task force consisted in part of 12 governors, 3 state legislators, 1 representative of organized labor, 6 educators, and 4 organizational leaders. The most impressive component of the membership was 14 business leaders. The co-chairs of the task force were Frank Cary, chairman of the executive committee of the IBM Corporation, and Pierre S. Du Pont IV, governor of Delaware and an heir to the Du Pont chemical fortune. Other members from the business community included the chief executive officers of Texas Instruments, RCA, Ford Motors, Xerox, Dow Chemicals, Control Data, Johnson Publishing, Time Inc., and SFN; the vice chairman of the board of directors of AT&T; and the chairman of the National Association of Manufacturers.

In addition to supporting the idea of career ladders, the report of the task force calls for closer relationships between American business and the schools. The introduction to the report states, "We believe especially that businesses, in their role as employers, should be much more deeply involved in the process of setting goals for education in America and in helping our schools to reach those goals." One of the "action recommendations" called for in the report states, "Business leaders should establish partnerships with schools." And in bold type in the section titled "Education and Growth," the report proclaims: "If the business community gets more involved in both the design and the delivery of education, we are going to become more competitive as an economy." The call for greater participation of the business community in establishing the goals of the public schools was couched in the traditional language of the promise of American schooling. Like the proclamations of school reformers and public leaders in the nineteenth century, the report proclaims education as a panacea for society's ills: "It is the thesis of this report that our future success as a nation—our national defense, our social stability and well-being and our national prosperity—will depend on our ability to improve education and training for millions of individual citizens."[21]

Within the framework of the traditional promise of American education to solve economic and social problems, business and state leaders banded together in the early 1980s to reform education. Although this strong coalition was formed at the state level, local schools also felt pressure from local business leaders. Many schools were adopted by business through an "adopt-a-school" program, and in communities with wide-ranging magnet, or alternative, schools, businesses often helped to plan educational goals according to the needs of the labor market.

In some communities, a formal relationship was established between business and the schools. In the early 1980s, business leaders and the Boston schools signed a formal compact stating that the schools would improve the quality of graduates to meet employer needs, and, in exchange, local business would give preference to graduates of Boston schools. A similar alliance was established in Atlanta. Michael Timpane, in his 1981 study *Corporations and Public Education*, written for the Carnegie Corporation, details the extent of the new cooperative ties between business and the schools and argues that the basic reason for this alliance was the growing shortage of entry-level workers. "For the first time in a generation there will probably be, in several urban locations, an absolute shortage of labor supply for entry level positions. Urban employers already report great difficulty in locating qualified employees for entry level positions."[22]

It is important to place business involvement in the schools in the 1980s in the perspective of the wide range of political pressures on education. Business was only one of the groups attempting to shape education to serve their particular interests. The political pressures came from within and without the educational establishment. Within the establishment, teachers' unions sought greater teacher power, while administrators fought to hold on to their control. Outside the educational establishment, special-interest groups, such as those concerned with school prayer or the handicapped, tried to get the schools to serve their particular interests. Political leaders at the federal and state levels tried to use the schools as a scapegoat for current social and economic problems and, at the same time, tried to advance their own political fortunes by calling for educational reform to solve the problems the schools had supposedly created. The politics of education in the 1980s represents a new web of entangling political pressures that are pushing and pulling American schools in a multitude of directions.

Conclusion

In the nineteenth century, common school reformers placed their hope for a better tomorrow on the growth of the common school. The rhetoric of the nineteenth-century reformer was full of promises to end poverty, save democracy, solve social problems, end crime, increase national prosperity, and provide equality of opportunity. The problem with the promises offered by common school reformers was that they created in the minds of different people differing reasons for supporting education.

As different groups selected their reasons for supporting education, schooling was kept in a constant turmoil over goals and curriculum. Curriculum content was kept in constant flux, as schools were asked to win the cold war in the 1950s, end poverty in the 1960s, and solve problems of unemployment in the 1970s. In addition, special-interest groups made specific demands on the curriculum. At the heart of all this turmoil was the student. One can imagine the confusion of students in the 1950s who started school learning a life-adjustment education and completed their schooling by being prepared to defend America against the Soviet Union. By promising all things to all people, common school reformers left a legacy that almost ensured a continual political battle over the goals and purposes of American education.

By promising to help all people and by generating internal and external political controversy, the American school became a central social institution. Different social groups fixed their hopes on the American school to provide equality of opportunity, improved social conditions, and a democratic political system. Professionals within the school establishment did not discourage the promise of education as society's panacea but promoted the social role of the school as a means of enhancing their social and economic position. Politicans latched onto the school as an expedient means of promising economic and political improvement. Business people hoped that the school would provide them with trained and properly socialized workers. For those concerned with maintaining social order, the school promised the inculcation of moral and political values. For those interested in maintaining freedom, the school promised the knowledge and intellectual skills necessary for individual liberty.

As the American school expanded, it penetrated more and more aspects of life. The school became interested in the whole child and the child's family, and these concerns resulted in school involvement in the child's and the family's personal life, health problems, and social life. If the social role of the school continues to expand at the same rate as it did during the previous two centuries, one can predict that by the end of the twenty-first century, the school will be responsible for engineering the total personality and social life of all citizens and controlling entrance into the labor market. This future role would include responsibility for an individual's work, play, love life, physical and mental health, and political life.

This projected future role raises the questions that have historically plagued the American school. What knowledge is of most worth? Who should determine what knowledge is of most worth? Imagine you are in a position in which others have power to decide your behavior, personality, and knowledge. The quest for this type of power has been implicit in most educational reforms. The question readers must answer for themselves is this: If you were in that position, who would you choose to determine the content of your mind and the nature of your personality and behavior? Should it be teachers, college professors, educational administrators, politicans, business people, or the individual? If the American school continues to expand its concerns and methods, this might be the most important question for the future of education.

Notes

1. "Quoting Marland," *American Education* 7 (January–February 1971): 4.
2. Sidney P. Marland, Jr., "The Condition of Education in the Nation," *American Education* 7 (April 1971): p. 4.
3. Quoted in Robert M. Worthington, "A Home-Community Based Career Education Model," *Educational Leadership* 30 (December 1972): 213.
4. Sidney P. Marland, Jr., "The School's Role in Career Development," *Educational Leadership* 30 (December 1972): 203–205.
5. Sidney P. Marland, Jr., "Career Education and the Two-Year Colleges," *American Education* 8 (March 1972): 11.
6. James S. Coleman et al., *Equality of Educational Opportunity* (Washington, D.C.: Government Printing Office, 1966), pp. 3–20, 35–217.
7. Ibid., p. 21.
8. Fredrick Mosteller and Daniel P. Moynihan, eds., *On Equality of Educational Opportunity* (New York: Random House, 1972).
9. Daniel P. Moynihan, "On the Education of the Urban Poor," in Daniel P. Moynihan, ed., *Coping: Essays on the Practice of Government* (New York: Random House, 1973), pp. 167–194.
10. Daniel P. Moynihan, "Can Courts and Money Do It?" *New York Times,* 10 January 1972, reprinted in Miriam Wasserman, *Demystifying School* (New York: Praeger, 1974), pp. 226–230.
11. Ibid., p. 229.
12. Leon Lessinger, *Every Kid a Winner: Accountability in Education* (New York: Simon & Schuster, 1970).

13. B. F. Skinner, *Walden Two Revisited* (New York: Macmillan, 1976).

14. For a discussion of this case, see Charles Tesconi and Emanual Hurwitz, eds., *Education for Whom?* (New York: Dodd, Mead, 1974), pp. 34–66, 174–188.

15. Richard M. Nixon, "Message to Congress," 17 March 1972, in Dwight W. Allen and Jeffrey C. Hecht, eds., *Controversies in Education* (Philadelphia: Saunders, 1974), pp. 530–534.

16. Ibid.

17. James S. Coleman et al., *Trends in School Segregation, 1968–1973* (Washington, D.C.: Urban Institute, 1975).

18. For a discussion of these schools, see Joel Spring, *Education and the Rise of the Corporate State* (Boston: Beacon Press, 1972).

19. National Commission on Excellence in Education, *A Nation at Risk* (Washington, D.C.: Government Printing Office, 1983).

20. Task Force on Education for Economic Growth, *Action for Excellence* (Denver: Education Commission of the States, 1983).

21. Ibid., pp. 3, 6–7, 18.

22. Michael Timpane, *Corporations and Public Education* (Report written for the Carnegie Corporation and distributed by Teachers College, Columbia University, 1981).

Index